Sadlier

We·Believe™

God Loves Us

WITH PROJECT DISCIPLE
Pray
Learn
Celebrate
Share
Choose
Live

Catholic Identity

For guidance and resources regarding the *We Believe, Catholic Identity Edition* pages in the Student Edition, please see the *Retreat Leader's Guide*, and/or visit **religion.sadlierconnect.com**

School Edition Teacher Guide
Grade One

Sadlier

Nihil Obstat
Monsignor Michael F. Hull, S.T.D.
Censor Librorum

Imprimatur
✠ Most Reverend Dennis J. Sullivan, D.D.
Vicar General of the Archdiocese of New York
January 27, 2010

The *Nihil Obstat* and *Imprimatur* are official declaration that these books are free of doctrinal or moral error. No implications contained therein that those who have granted the *Nihil Obstat* and *Imprimatur* agree with the content, opinion or statements expressed.

The Subcommittee on the Catechism, United States Conference of Catholic Bishops, has found the doctrinal content of this manual, copyright 2011, to be in conformity with the *Catechism of the Catholic Church*.

William H. Sadlier, Inc.
9 Pine Street
New York, NY 10005-4700

ISBN: 978-0-8215-6371-7
4 5 6 7 8 9 10 WEBC 19 18 17 16 15

Sadlier

WE BELIEVE Drawn from the wisdom of the community, this program was developed by nationally recognized experts in catechesis, curriculum, and child development. These teachers of the faith and practitioners helped to frame these age-appropriate and appealing lessons. In addition, a team including respected catechetical, liturgical, pastoral, and theological experts shared their insights and inspired the development of the program.

Catechetical and Liturgical Consultants

Dr. Gerard F. Baumbach
Director, Center for Catechetical Initiatives
Concurrent Professor of Theology
University of Notre Dame
Notre Dame, Indiana

Carole M. Eipers, D.Min.
Vice President, Executive Director of Catechetics
William H. Sadlier, Inc.

Patricia Andrews
Director of Religious Education
Our Lady of Lourdes Church
Slidell, LA

Reverend Monsignor John F. Barry, P.A.
Pastor, American Martyrs Parish
Manhattan Beach, CA

Sister Maureen Shaughnessy, SC
Sisters of Charity of Saint Elizabeth
Convent Station, NJ

Mary Jo Tully
Chancellor, Archdiocese of Portland

Reverend Monsignor John M. Unger
Deputy Superintendent for Catechesis and Evangelization
Archdiocese of St. Louis

Curriculum and Child Development Consultants

Brother Robert R. Bimonte, FSC
Executive Director
NCEA Department of Elementary Schools

Sr. Carol Cimino, SSJ, Ed.D.
National Consultant
William H. Sadlier, Inc.

Gini Shimabukuro, Ed.D.
Associate Professor
Catholic Educational Leadership Program
School of Education, University of San Francisco

Catholic Social Teaching Consultants

John Carr
Executive Director
Director of Justice, Peace, and Human Development
United States Conference of Catholic Bishops
Washington, D.C.

Joan Rosenhauer
Associate Director
Department of Justice, Peace, and Human Development
United States Conference of Catholic Bishops
Washington, D.C.

Mariology Consultant

Sister M. Jean Frisk, ISSM, S.T.L.
International Marian Research Institute
Dayton, OH

Inculturation Consultants

Allan Figueroa Deck, S.J., Ph.D., S.T.D.
Executive Director
Secretariat of Cultural Diversity in the Church
United States Conference of Catholic Bishops
Washington, D.C.

Kirk P. Gaddy, Ed.D.
Educational Consultant
Baltimore, MD

Reverend Nguyễn Việt Hưng
Vietnamese Catechetical Committee

Scriptural Consultant

Reverend Donald Senior, CP, Ph.D., S.T.D.
Member, Pontifical Biblical Commission
President, The Catholic Theological Union
Chicago, IL

Theological Consultants

Most Reverend Edward K. Braxton, Ph.D., S.T.D.
Official Theological Consultant
Bishop of Belleville

Norman F. Josaitis, S.T.D.
Theological Consultant

Reverend Joseph A. Komonchak, Ph.D.
Professor, School of Theology and Religious Studies
The Catholic University of America

Most Reverend Richard J. Malone, Th.D.
Bishop of Portland, ME

Sister Maureen Sullivan, OP, Ph.D.
Associate Professor
St. Anselm College, Manchester, NH

Media/Technology Consultants

Sister Judith Dieterle, SSL
Past President, National Association of
Catechetical Media Professionals

Sister Jane Keegan, RDC
Technology Consultant

Educational Advisors

Grade K Noelle Deinken, Thousand Oaks, CA
Bernadette Miller, Wantagh, NY

Grade 1 Gerry Mayes, Vero Beach, FL
Nancy McGuirk, Staten Island, NY

Grade 2 Joan Fraher, Altamonte Springs, FL
Dr. Jeannette Holmes, Stockton, CA

Grade 3 Robin Keough, Boston, MA
Mary Olson, Buffalo Grove, IL

Grade 4 Michaele Durant, San Diego, CA
Sarah Pollard, Covington, KY

Grade 5 Rose Heinrichs, Grosse Pointe, MI
Anne Kreitsch, Howard Beach, NY

Grade 6 Barbara Connors, Seekonk, MA
Sue MacPherson, Ballwin, MO

Contents

Scope and Sequence, Grade 1 . . . . .T8
Welcome to *We Believe with Project Disciple*. T10
Frequently Asked Questions T12
Profile of a First Grade Disciple T13
Program Overview T14
This Year Go Green! T22
Introductory Chapter 10

UNIT 1 — Jesus Teaches Us About God's Love 17

1 God Is Our Father

Plan and Prepare 19A
Family Reproducible Master. 19E
Scripture Reproducible Master 19F
Chapter Reproducible Master 19G
Lesson Plan 19
• God created the world. • God created all people. • God gives us special gifts. • God promises to love us always.

Genesis 1:1–31; 2—3

As Catholics . . . . Angels

PROJECT DISCIPLE *featuring* Saint Francis of Assisi

Take Home Appreciating God's gifts in the world

Chapter Test

2 We Believe in the Blessed Trinity

Plan and Prepare 31A
Family Reproducible Master. 31E
Scripture Reproducible Master. 31F
Chapter Reproducible Master 31G
Lesson Plan 31
• God sent his own Son, Jesus, to us. • Jesus is God's greatest gift. • There are Three Persons in One God. • The Sign of the Cross is a prayer to the Blessed Trinity.

John 15:9; Mark 10:13–14

As Catholics . . . . Saint Patrick

PROJECT DISCIPLE *featuring* The Sign of the Cross at Mass

Take Home Praying as a family

Chapter Test

3 Jesus Grew Up in a Family

Plan and Prepare 43A
Family Reproducible Master. 43E
Scripture Reproducible Master. 43F
Chapter Reproducible Master 43G
Lesson Plan 43
• God chose Mary to be the Mother of his Son. • Jesus was born in Bethlehem. • Jesus lived in Nazareth with Mary and Joseph. • The Holy Family obeyed God the Father and prayed to him.

Luke 1:26–35, 38; 2:1–7

As Catholics . . . . Las Posadas

PROJECT DISCIPLE *featuring* The Holy Family

Take Home Making a family activity collage

Chapter Test

4 Jesus Works Among the People

Plan and Prepare 55A
Family Reproducible Master. 55E
Scripture Reproducible Master 55F
Chapter Reproducible Master. 55G
Lesson Plan 55
• John the Baptist helped people to get ready for Jesus. • Jesus shared God's love with all people. • Jesus teaches that God watches over us and cares for us. • Jesus helped all those in need.

Luke 12:22–24; 19:1–5; Matthew 20:29–33

As Catholics . . . . Quiet Times for Prayer

PROJECT DISCIPLE *featuring* Sharing God's Love

Take Home Helping people who are sick

Chapter Test

5 Jesus Teaches Us About Love

Plan and Prepare 67A
Family Reproducible Master. 67E
Scripture Reproducible Master. 67F
Chapter Reproducible Master 67G
Lesson Plan 67
• Many people wanted to follow Jesus. • Jesus taught the Great Commandment. • Jesus taught us to love God, ourselves, and others. • Jesus taught us that all people are our neighbors.

Matthew 22:37, 39; Luke 10:30–35

As Catholics . . . . Morning Offerings

PROJECT DISCIPLE *featuring* Good Neighbors

Take Home Learning about people of different cultures

Chapter Test

SEASONAL CHAPTERS

6 The Church Year

Plan and Prepare 79A
Lesson Plan 79
• The Church praises Jesus all year long.

Chapter Reproducible Master 84A
Family Reproducible Master. 84B

7 Ordinary Time

Plan and Prepare 85A
Lesson Plan 85
• The Church celebrates the life and teachings of Jesus.

Matthew 5:9

Chapter Reproducible Master 90A
Family Reproducible Master. 90B

Unit 1 Test 91

UNIT 2 — We Are Followers of Jesus 93

8 Jesus Had Many Followers
Plan and Prepare 95A
Family Reproducible Master................. 95E
Scripture Reproducible Master.............. 95F
Chapter Reproducible Master 95G
Lesson Plan **95**
• Jesus invited people to be his followers. • Jesus' followers believed that he was the Son of God. • Jesus showed his followers how to pray. • We pray the Lord's Prayer.
  Matthew 4:18–20; Luke 8:22–25; 11:1–2
  As Catholics ....The Title Lord

PROJECT DISCIPLE *featuring* Our Daily Bread
  Take Home Praying the Lord's Prayer together
Chapter Test

9 Jesus Died and Rose to New Life
Plan and Prepare 107A
Family Reproducible Master................. 107E
Scripture Reproducible Master.............. 107F
Chapter Reproducible Master 107G
Lesson Plan **107**
• Jesus told his followers that he loved and cared for them. • Many people gathered to welcome and praise Jesus. • Jesus taught in the Temple in Jerusalem. • Jesus died and rose.
  John 10:2, 14; 12:12–13, 19:18, 25, 30, 42; Luke 21:37–38; Matthew 28:1–7
  As Catholics ....We Pray Hosanna

PROJECT DISCIPLE *featuring* Respect for Workers
  Take Home Praising God
Chapter Test

10 Jesus Sends the Holy Spirit
Plan and Prepare 119A
Family Reproducible Master................. 119E
Scripture Reproducible Master.............. 119F
Chapter Reproducible Master 119G
Lesson Plan **119**
• The risen Jesus visited his followers. • Jesus Christ promised that the Holy Spirit would come to his followers. • The Holy Spirit was sent to Jesus' followers. • The Holy Spirit is the Third Person of the Blessed Trinity.
  Luke 24:36, 49; John 21:2–12; Acts of the Apostles 2:1–4
  As Catholics ....Symbol of the Holy Spirit

PROJECT DISCIPLE *featuring* Pentecost
  Take Home Joining the parish for breakfast
Chapter Test

11 The Holy Spirit Helps the Church to Grow
Plan and Prepare 131A
Family Reproducible Master................. 131E
Scripture Reproducible Master.............. 131F
Chapter Reproducible Master 131G
Lesson Plan **131**
• The Church began on Pentecost. • The first members of the Church did many things together. • The Holy Spirit helped the Church to grow. • The Holy Spirit helps the Church today.
  Acts of the Apostles 2:36–38, 41
  As Catholics ....Saints Peter and Paul

PROJECT DISCIPLE *featuring* Saying Thank You
  Take Home Making a Holy Spirit poster
Chapter Test

12 The Church Serves
Plan and Prepare 143A
Family Reproducible Master................. 143E
Scripture Reproducible Master.............. 143F
Chapter Reproducible Master 143G
Lesson Plan **143**
• The Apostles led and cared for the Church. • The bishops lead and care for the Church. • The pope leads and cares for the whole Church. • The Church serves others.
  Matthew 16:18; John 13:15
  As Catholics .... The Vatican

PROJECT DISCIPLE *featuring* A Catholic Missionary
  Take Home Pledging to serve others
Chapter Test

SEASONAL CHAPTERS

13 Advent
Plan and Prepare 155A
Lesson Plan **155**
• The Church has a special time of waiting.
  John 8:12
Chapter Reproducible Master 160A
Family Reproducible Master................. 160B

14 Christmas
Plan and Prepare 161A
Lesson Plan **161**
• At Christmas the Church celebrates the birth of Jesus.
  Isaiah 9:1–2, 5
Chapter Reproducible Master 166A
Family Reproducible Master................. 166B

Unit 2 Test 167

UNIT 3 — We Belong to the Church ... 169

15 We Belong to a Parish
Plan and Prepare ... 171A
Family Reproducible Master ... 171E
Scripture Reproducible Master ... 171F
Chapter Reproducible Master ... 171G
Lesson Plan ... 171
• Our parish is like a family. • We gather together to worship. • We work together as a parish. • Our parish helps many people.
Luke 11:1
As Catholics ... Catechists

PROJECT DISCIPLE *featuring* People in the Parish
Take Home Helping people who are hungry
Chapter Test

16 We Celebrate the Sacraments
Plan and Prepare ... 183A
Family Reproducible Master ... 183E
Scripture Reproducible Master ... 183F
Chapter Reproducible Master ... 183G
Lesson Plan ... 183
• Jesus celebrated God's love. • We celebrate God's love. • Jesus gave us the sacraments. • The Church celebrates Seven Sacraments.
Psalm 100:1–2
As Catholics ... Gifts of Creation

PROJECT DISCIPLE *featuring* Celebrating God's Love at Mass
Take Home Singing songs of praise and thanks
Chapter Test

17 The Church Welcomes New Members
Plan and Prepare ... 195A
Family Reproducible Master ... 195E
Scripture Reproducible Master ... 195F
Chapter Reproducible Master ... 195G
Lesson Plan ... 195
• The Church welcomes new members at Baptism. • At Baptism we receive God's life. • We say and do special things to celebrate Baptism. • In Baptism we are joined to Jesus and one another.
Rite of Baptism
As Catholics ... When We Celebrate Baptism

PROJECT DISCIPLE *featuring* Welcome Banner
Take Home Finding holy water in your parish church
Chapter Test

18 We Are Followers of Jesus
Plan and Prepare ... 207A
Family Reproducible Master ... 207E
Scripture Reproducible Master ... 207F
Chapter Reproducible Master ... 207G
Lesson Plan ... 207
• Jesus is the Light of the World. • We receive the light of Christ. • Jesus asks us to share his peace. • We can make choices as children of God.
Matthew 5:1, 9; John 8:12
As Catholics ... Pope Pius X

PROJECT DISCIPLE *featuring* Peacemakers
Take Home Praying to Jesus, the Light of the World
Chapter Test

19 We Celebrate God's Forgiveness
Plan and Prepare ... 219A
Family Reproducible Master ... 219E
Scripture Reproducible Master ... 219F
Chapter Reproducible Master ... 219G
Lesson Plan ... 219
• Jesus told us about God's forgiveness. • God is always ready to forgive us. • We celebrate God's forgiveness. • Jesus asks us to forgive others.
Luke 15:11–23
As Catholics ... The Reconciliation Room

PROJECT DISCIPLE *featuring* A Forgiveness Story
Take Home Forgiving others in the family
Chapter Test

SEASONAL CHAPTERS
20 Lent
Plan and Prepare ... 231A
Lesson Plan ... 231
• The Church gets ready to celebrate Jesus' Death and Resurrection.
Ephesians 5:10
Chapter Reproducible Master ... 236A
Family Reproducible Master ... 236B

21 The Three Days
Plan and Prepare ... 237A
Lesson Plan ... 237
• The Church celebrates that Jesus died and rose to new life.
Galatians 3:26–28
Chapter Reproducible Master ... 242A
Family Reproducible Master ... 242B

Unit 3 Test ... 243

UNIT 4   We Celebrate and Live Our Faith 245

22 Jesus Gives Us the Eucharist

Plan and Prepare 247A
Family Reproducible Master. 247E
Scripture Reproducible Master. 247F
Chapter Reproducible Master 247G
Lesson Plan **247**
• Jesus shared a special meal with his followers. • We celebrate what Jesus said and did at the Last Supper. • We celebrate the Sacrament of the Eucharist. • We join with our parish for the celebration of Mass.

   Matthew 26:26–28
   As Catholics . . . . Our Sunday Celebration

PROJECT DISCIPLE *featuring* The Last Supper
   Take Home   Listing people who help us worship at Mass
Chapter Test

23 We Celebrate the Mass

Plan and Prepare 259A
Family Reproducible Master. 259E
Scripture Reproducible Master. 259F
Chapter Reproducible Master 259G
Lesson Plan **259**
• We gather to worship God. • We listen to God's Word. • Our gifts of bread and wine become the Body and Blood of Christ. • We grow closer to Jesus and one another.

   The Roman Missal
   As Catholics . . . . The Good News of Jesus

PROJECT DISCIPLE *featuring* Prayers from Mass
   Take Home   Praying for parishioners who are sick
Chapter Test

24 We Share God's Love

Plan and Prepare 271A
Family Reproducible Master. 271E
Scripture Reproducible Master. 271F
Chapter Reproducible Master 271G
Lesson Plan **271**
• Jesus shows us how to love and serve. • When we pray, we show God that we love him. • We share God's love with our families. • We share God's love with others.

   John 13:34; 20:19, 21
   As Catholics . . . . Forms of Prayer

PROJECT DISCIPLE *featuring* Parish Priests
   Take Home   Sharing God's love as a family
Chapter Test

25 We Honor Mary and the Saints

Plan and Prepare 283A
Family Reproducible Master. 283E
Scripture Reproducible Master. 283F
Chapter Reproducible Master 283G
Lesson Plan **283**
• Mary is the mother of Jesus. • The Church honors Mary. • The saints are close to God. • We honor all the saints of the Church.

   Luke 1:26–28, 35
   As Catholics . . . . Honoring Mary

PROJECT DISCIPLE *featuring* Saint Joseph
   Take Home   Making a family tree
Chapter Test

26 We Care for the Gifts of God's Creation

Plan and Prepare 295A
Family Reproducible Master. 295E
Scripture Reproducible Master. 295F
Chapter Reproducible Master 295G
Lesson Plan **295**
• The world is God's gift to us. • Animals are part of God's creation. • We are all important to God. • We care for and respect all people.

   Genesis 1:24–25; Matthew 7:12
   As Catholics . . . . Life: A Gift from God

PROJECT DISCIPLE *featuring* Student Reflection
   Take Home   Caring for God's creation
Chapter Test

SEASONAL CHAPTER

27 Easter

Plan and Prepare 307A
Lesson Plan **307**
• The Church celebrates that Jesus rose to new life.

   Psalm 118:24; Matthew 28:1–10
Chapter Reproducible Master 312A
Family Reproducible Master. 312B

Unit 4 Test 313

PROJECT DISCIPLE RESOURCES 315A

Family Survey. 315B
Grade 1 Log. 315
End-of-Year Prayer Service 317
My Parish Church 318
Grade 2 Sneak Peek 320
Reproducible Prayer Posters. 320A
My Mass Book 321
My Prayer Book. 325
Sacraments/Ten Commandments. 329
Glossary/Index 330

For guidance and resources regarding the *We Believe, Catholic Identity Edition* pages in the Student Edition, please see the *Retreat Leader's Guide*, and/or visit **religion.sadlierconnect.com**

GRADE 1
Scope & Sequence

	Unit 1 Jesus Teaches Us About God's Love	Unit 2 We Are Followers of Jesus
FAITH STATEMENTS FOR EACH CHAPTER	**1** God created the world. • God created all people. • God gives us special gifts. • God promises to love us always. **2** God sent his own Son, Jesus, to us. • Jesus is God's greatest gift. • There are Three Persons in One God. • The Sign of the Cross is a prayer to the Blessed Trinity. **3** God chose Mary to be the Mother of his Son. • Jesus was born in Bethlehem. • Jesus lived in Nazareth with Mary and Joseph. • The Holy Family obeyed God the Father and prayed to him. **4** John the Baptist helped people to get ready for Jesus. • Jesus shared God's love with all people. • Jesus teaches that God watches over us and cares for us. • Jesus helped all those in need. **5** Many people wanted to follow Jesus. • Jesus taught the Great Commandment. • Jesus taught us to love God, ourselves, and others. • Jesus taught us that all people are our neighbors. **6** The Church praises Jesus all year long. **7** The Church celebrates the life and teachings of Jesus.	**8** Jesus invited people to be his followers. • Jesus' followers believed that he was the Son of God. • Jesus showed his followers how to pray. • We pray the Lord's Prayer. **9** Jesus told his followers that he loved and cared for them. • Many people gathered to welcome and praise Jesus. • Jesus taught in the Temple in Jerusalem. • Jesus died and rose. **10** The risen Jesus visited his followers. • Jesus Christ promised that the Holy Spirit would come to his followers. • The Holy Spirit was sent to Jesus' followers. • The Holy Spirit is the Third Person of the Blessed Trinity. **11** The Church began on Pentecost. • The first members of the Church did many things together. • The Holy Spirit helped the Church to grow. • The Holy Spirit helps the Church today. **12** The Apostles led and cared for the Church. • The bishops lead and care for the Church. • The pope leads and cares for the whole Church. • The Church serves others. **13** The Church has a special time of waiting. **14** At Christmas the Church celebrates the birth of Jesus.
CATECHISM OF THE CATHOLIC CHURCH	Paragraphs: 290, 355, 356–357, 410, 422, 423, 234, 232, 484, 525, 532, 531, 535, 542, 305, 544, 544–546, 2055, 1931, 1168, 1163	Paragraphs: 543, 548, 2759, 2776, 754, 559, 584, 638, 641, 729, 730, 732, 767, 2624, 768, 798, 858, 862, 881, 1942, 524, 463
SCRIPTURE AND THE RITES OF THE CHURCH	Genesis 1:1–31; 2—3 John 15:9 Mark 10:13–14 Luke 1:26–35,37; 2:1–7; 19:1–5; 12:22–24; 10:30–35 Matthew 20:29–33; 22:37,39; 5:9	Matthew 4:18–20; 28:1–7; 16:18 Luke 8:22–25; 11:1–2; 21:37–38; 24:36,49 John 10:2, 14; 12:12–13; 19:18,25,30,42; 21:2–12; 13:15; 8:12 Acts of the Apostles 2:1–4; 2:36–38,41 Isaiah 9:1–2,5
SAINTS AND CATHOLIC PROFILES; FEASTS AND DEVOTIONS	Saint Francis of Assisi Saint Patrick Saint John the Baptist Feast of All Saints Feast of the Holy Family The Sign of the Cross Las Posadas The Church Year Ordinary Time	Saint Peter Saint Paul Blessed Teresa of Calcutta The Lord's Prayer Easter The Feast of Pentecost Sign of the Cross Glory Be to the Father Advent The Advent Wreath Christmas

15 Our parish is like a family. • We gather together to worship. • We work together as a parish. • Our parish helps many people.

16 Jesus celebrated God's love. • We celebrate God's love. • Jesus gave us the sacraments. • The Church celebrates Seven Sacraments.

17 The Church welcomes new members at Baptism. • At Baptism we receive God's life. • We say and do special things to celebrate Baptism. • In Baptism we are joined to Jesus and one another.

18 Jesus is the Light of the World. • We receive the light of Christ. • Jesus asks us to share his peace. • We can make choices as children of God.

19 Jesus told us about God's forgiveness. • God is always ready to forgive us. • We celebrate God's forgiveness. • Jesus asks us to forgive others.

20 The Church gets ready to celebrate Jesus' Death and Resurrection.

21 The Church celebrates that Jesus died and rose to new life.

22 Jesus shared a special meal with his followers. • We celebrate what Jesus said and did at the Last Supper. • We celebrate the Sacrament of the Eucharist. • We join with our parish for the celebration of Mass.

23 We gather to worship God. • We listen to God's Word. • Our gifts of bread and wine become the Body and Blood of Christ. • We grow closer to Jesus and one another.

24 Jesus shows us how to love and serve. • When we pray, we show God that we love him. • We share God's love with our families. • We share God's love with others.

25 Mary is the mother of Jesus. • The Church honors Mary. • The saints are close to God. • We honor all the saints of the Church.

26 The world is God's gift to us. • Animals are part of God's creation. • We are all important to God. • We care for and respect all people.

27 The Church celebrates that Jesus rose to new life.

Paragraphs: 2179, 2182, 2444, 583, 1083, 1084, 1113, 1267, 1265, 1234, 1271, 748, 1216, 2304, 1730, 1421, 1431, 1440, 2840, 617, 540

Paragraphs: 1339, 1341, 1346, 2178, 1348, 1349, 1353, 1396, 2196, 2558, 2217, 1825, 964, 963, 954, 956, 2415, 2416, 356, 1825, 641

Luke 11:1; 15:11–23
Matthew 5:1,9
John 8:12
Psalm 100:1–2
Ephesians 5:10
Rite of Baptism
Galatians 3:26–28

Matthew 26:26–28; 7:12; 28:1–10
Luke 22:19; 1:26–28,35
John 13:34; 20:19,21
The Roman Missal
Genesis 1:24–25
Psalms 118:24

Pope Pius X

Holy Water
Gifts of creation used
   in the sacraments
Candlelight Prayer
Lent
The Three Days

Saint Joseph
Saint Katharine Drexel
Saint Andrew Kim Taegon
Saint Francis Xavier
Saint Teresa of Avila
Saint John Vianney
Saint Anne

Celebration of the Mass
Feast of All Saints
Honoring Mary
Processions
Forms of prayer
Easter

Go to **www.webelieveweb.com** for the Scope and Sequence of the *We Believe with Project Disciple* Program, K–6.

Sadlier We Believe **Scope and Sequence**

Welcome to...

Sadlier
We Believe

with PROJECT DISCIPLE

This Program is...

* Rooted in Scripture
* Faithful to the Tradition of the Catholic Church
* Spirited by the General and National Directories for Catechesis
* **Christocentric,** centering on the Person of Jesus Christ
* **Trinitarian,** inviting relationship with God the Father, God the Son, and God the Holy Spirit
* **Ecclesial,** supporting faith that is lived in the domestic church and the universal Church.

New to the program is **PROJECT DISCIPLE,** an exciting and integral feature of every chapter. Built on the Six Tasks of Catechesis, **PROJECT DISCIPLE** pages contain **hundreds and hundreds** of new activities, so disciples at every grade level:

1. **LEARN** about their faith
2. **CELEBRATE** the Mass and sacraments
3. **CHOOSE** to show love and respect
4. **PRAY** every day
5. **SHARE** faith with others
6. **LIVE** out their faith

Six Tasks of Catechesis

"These six tasks of catechesis constitute a unified whole by which catechesis seeks to achieve its objective: the formation of disciples of Jesus Christ."

(National Directory for Catechesis, #20, p.63)

	Tasks of Catechesis	Disciples . . .	In Grade 1 . . .
Learn	Catechesis promotes knowledge of the faith.	**learn** about Jesus Christ and their Catholic faith through Scripture and Tradition.	Children will learn what Jesus taught us about the love God has for us.
Celebrate	Catechesis promotes a knowledge of the meaning of the liturgy and the sacraments.	**celebrate** their faith by learning about and participating in the liturgy and the sacraments.	Children will focus on how we gather in church to worship God and celebrate the sacraments.
Choose	Catechesis promotes moral formation in Jesus Christ.	**choose** to follow Jesus' example and his teachings, to live the commandments and the spirit of the Beatitudes.	Children will understand that Jesus taught us to show love for God, ourselves, and others.
Pray	Catechesis teaches the Christian how to pray with Christ.	**pray** to God—Father, Son, and Holy Spirit—every day and in many different ways.	Children will pray in different ways alone and with others and will pray the Lord's Prayer as Jesus taught us to do.
Share	Catechesis prepares the Christian to live in community and to participate actively in the life and mission of the Church.	**share** in the lives of their families, parish, and school, and participate in the mission of the Church to share the Good News of Jesus Christ.	Children will learn to share God's love in their families and parishes.
Live	Catechesis promotes a missionary spirit that prepares the faithful to be present as Christians in society.	**live** their faith by giving witness to the life and teachings of Jesus Christ through their words and deeds.	Children will spread the Good News of Jesus Christ through simple acts of love and caring.

FaQ's

I try to highlight any Scripture content that appears in a chapter. Are you offering even more Scripture content?

Yes! Our program is based on Scripture. Check out the Scope & Sequence. But we've added even more! Look for *What's the Word?* activities in **Project Disciple** as well as many *Pray Today* activities. In addition, your guide contains a new Scripture reproducible master for every chapter!

What do you have for family?

Lots! The popular *Sharing Faith with My Family* page is now a reproducible master. An informative Parent's page starts each unit and is filled with exciting doable family activities. And don't forget the **Project Disciple** *Take Home* activity offered in each chapter. Plus, you can always go to **www.webelieveweb.com**.

I love your website. Are you updating it?

Always! **www.webelieveweb.com** is a tremendous success. Keep visiting to see new resources for you, the children, and their families that are interactive and downloadable.

Our class is "going green." Are you?

Definitely! Look at pages T22–T23 in this guide to find exciting ways that *We Believe with Project Disciple* can help your class go green. And congratulations!

Is assessment an important part of the program?

Absolutely! Each core chapter ends with a full page chapter test, and we provide unit tests as well. Plus, we offer both standard and alternative forms of assessment to meet your teaching needs. Lots of users supplement all this with the *We Believe Assessment* books and/or *Test Generators*—which feature online testing and reporting!

What exactly will Project Disciple do for me as a catechist?

Evaluate! Grounded in the Six Tasks of Catechesis, the hundreds of new **Project Disciple** activities, while informative and fun, will serve the serious goal of ascertaining whether the children are truly growing in and living out their faith. So **Project Disciple** enables you to monitor the faith formation of your children.

Your primary downloads in *Lives of the Saints* are great! Each saint really comes alive for my group. Please keep them coming!

Thanks! We receive loads of e-mails praising our saint bios/downloads at **www.webelieveweb.com**. We'll keep them coming! And we've added more saints to each text in **Project Disciple** (*see Saint Stories*).

I really like the way you reference each chapter's content to paragraphs from the Catechism. Are there other references to correlations?

Many! Chapter correlations to the Six Tasks of Catechesis, to Catholic Social Teaching, and to Catechetical Formation in Chaste Living are all available on **www.webelieveweb.com**.

Wow. It sounds like there's a lot of great new material in *We Believe with Project Disciple*. I've used *We Believe* for 5 years now. Please keep the "good stuff." We've been very successful.

Terrific! Don't worry. What has made you successful will continue to do so. The music, the prayers, the sound catechetical formation built on Scripture and the doctrine of the Church—it's all still there. But now with all the added advantages of **Project Disciple**! So have another great year!

See **www.webelieveweb.com** for study guides, games and activities and more...

The Profile of a First Grade DISCIPLE

Knowing the characteristics of first graders
will help you to implement
Grade 1 *We Believe* with PROJECT DISCIPLE.

Characteristics of First Graders	Guiding Their Growth as Disciples of Jesus Christ
First graders are open, curious, spontaneous, and full of energy. They move easily between the worlds of reality and imagination. This gives them a natural foundation for a lifelong response to the joys and mysteries of God.	Provide opportunities for the children to express themselves creatively through the use of the fine arts. Draw pictures, make up stories, sing songs, and act out simple plays in order to bring the lessons of faith alive with young children.
First graders are developing concrete thinking skills. They learn quickly by active involvement with concrete things and experiences.	Engage children in tactile experiences that deepen understanding and make catechetical lessons more memorable. For example, teach about gathering to worship through experiences such as *seeing* an altar, *blessing* themselves with holy water, and *smelling* incense and candles.
First graders are growing in their ability to work cooperatively with others.	When engaging children in group or partnering activities, stress the importance of love and mutual respect in the community of faith and beyond.*
First graders are highly imaginative but have limited attention spans.	Vary activities by moving from quiet work to physical movement, such as marching or singing. Be sure to include brief periods of time for silence and prayer.

* *Catechetical Formation in Chaste Living*, United States Catholic Conference of Bishops, #1

The Child's Pages

Each chapter follows a proven **3-step** catechetical process: *We Gather, We Believe, We Respond.*

1 WE GATHER

Children gather in prayer at the beginning of every chapter. They gather to pray and focus on their life as they begin each day's lesson. They respond to God's call and his grace through prayer and reflection on their experience. They pray, sing, and explore the ways the faith speaks to their lives.

2 WE BELIEVE

Each chapter presents the truths of the Catholic faith found in Sacred Scripture and Tradition, and in accordance with the Magisterium of the Church. One of the four main faith statements of the chapter is highlighted on each of days 1 through 4. The content of faith is presented in ways that are age-appropriate, culturally sensitive, and varied.

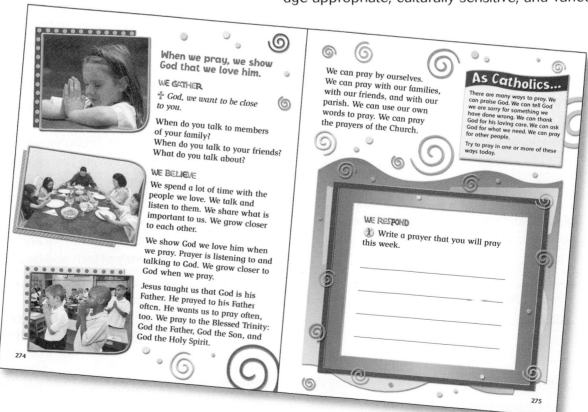

When we pray, we show God that we love him.

WE GATHER

✝ God, we want to be close to you.

When do you talk to members of your family?
When do you talk to your friends?
What do you talk about?

WE BELIEVE

We spend a lot of time with the people we love. We talk and listen to them. We share what is important to us. We grow closer to each other.

We show God we love him when we pray. Prayer is listening to and talking to God. We grow closer to God when we pray.

Jesus taught us that God is his Father. He prayed to his Father often. He wants us to pray often, too. We pray to the Blessed Trinity: God the Father, God the Son, and God the Holy Spirit.

We can pray by ourselves. We can pray with our families, with our friends, and with our parish. We can use our own words to pray. We can pray the prayers of the Church.

As Catholics...

There are many ways to pray. We can praise God. We can tell God we are sorry for something we have done wrong. We can thank God for his loving care. We can ask God for what we need. We can pray for other people.

Try to pray in one or more of these ways today.

WE RESPOND

✍ Write a prayer that you will pray this week.

_____

_____

_____

_____

274

275

3 WE RESPOND

Throughout each chapter children are encouraged to respond in prayer, faith, and life. Each day they are invited to respond to the message of the lesson. Through prayer, song, and actions that express their beliefs, children are called to live out their discipleship among their peers, their families, and their school and parish communities.

People can help us to do these things. People are gifts from God, too. People help us to grow in God's love.

WE RESPOND

Who are the people who help you to grow in God's love?

Write the first letters of their names on the flower. Thank God for these helpers.

As Catholics...

We believe that God created angels. Angels are God's helpers. But they do not have bodies like people do. Angels give people messages from God. They protect and guide us. They never stop praising God.
How can you praise God, too?

Plus **PROJECT DISCIPLE** activities sharpen discipleship skills. Children learn, celebrate, choose, pray, share, and live out their faith.

PROJECT DISCIPLE

Pray · Learn · Celebrate · Share · Choose · Live

 **Show What you Know**

Match the Key Words to the pictures.

● Bible

● creation

Saint Stories

Saint Francis of Assisi loved God. He loved all of God's creation. He took care of God's world. He was kind and gentle to animals. Color this picture of Saint Francis and the animals.

Make it Happen

Think about God's gifts of people, plants, and animals. Which of these are you most thankful that God created? Circle your choices.

People   **Plants**   **Animals**

Reality Check

Check ways you can take care of God's world.

❑ Recycle
❑ Love my family
❑ Try not to be wasteful
❑ Take care of myself

Take Home

Take a walk with your family. Talk about the things you see that God made.

Together say a prayer to thank God for his creation.

Assessment

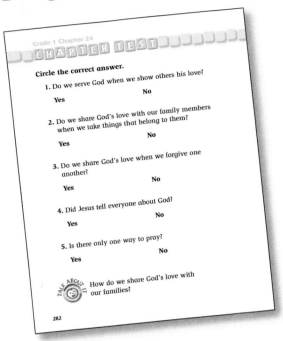

Grade 1 Chapter 24

CHAPTER TEST

Circle the correct answer.

1. Do we serve God when we show others his love?

Yes   No

2. Do we share God's love with our family members when we take things that belong to them?

Yes   No

3. Do we share God's love when we forgive one another?

Yes   No

4. Did Jesus tell everyone about God?

Yes   No

5. Is there only one way to pray?

Yes   No

TALK ABOUT IT How do we share God's love with our families?

282

In the *We Believe* **with Project Disciple** program:

For each chapter a chapter test is provided. A suggestion for an alternative-assessment activity is provided in the guide.

For each unit standard assessment is provided in the text and alternative assessment in the guide.

Assessment Resources
Assessment Book of **Reproducible Masters**, with chapter, unit, semester, and final tests

CD-ROM *Test Generator and Resource* (for MAC or WIN) You can:

- assign/score/report tests online
- customize tests, edit/add questions
- print tests from a question bank
- allow children to take tests on their Local Area Network (LAN)
- plan schedules in calendar format
- access and print chapter resources

Seasonal Chapters

Come, Lord Jesus! Be with us.

This chapter prepares us to celebrate the season of Advent.

155

Give thanks to the Lord, his love is everlasting.

This chapter helps us to understand the season of Ordinary Time.

85

"This is the day the LORD has made; let us rejoice in it and be glad."
Psalm 118:24

This chapter celebrates the entire Easter season.

307

The *We Believe* program integrates liturgy and catechesis through culturally-rich and diverse prayer experiences and ritual celebrations. It also provides special seasonal chapters that help children to understand and celebrate the different seasons and feasts of the Church.

For the Family

In each unit a *Dear Family* page in the child's text is designed specifically for the family. It provides content overview, additional activities, faith formation for parents, and applications for family life.

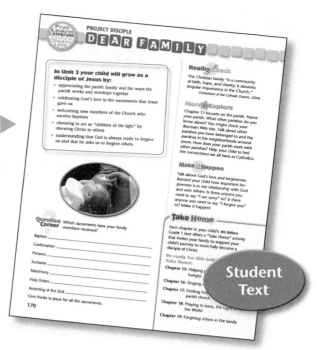

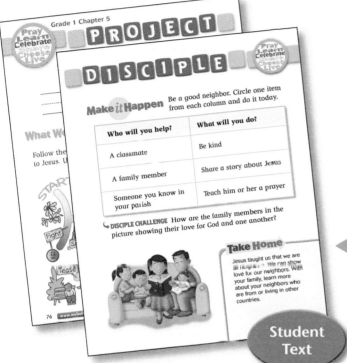

In each chapter a *Take Home* activity in the child's text provides another opportunity to share faith at home. Ways are suggested for all family members to live as disciples.

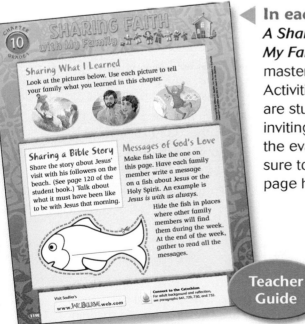

In each chapter *A Sharing Faith with My Family* reproducible master is provided. Activities and discussions are student-initiated, inviting the child to be the evangelizer. Be sure to send this page home.

On the Web Families can visit **www.webelieveweb.com** for study guides, games, safe activities for their children, and great information and enrichment for themselves.

The Catechist's pages

Your guide provides you with everything you need!

Overview and Lesson Planning Guide

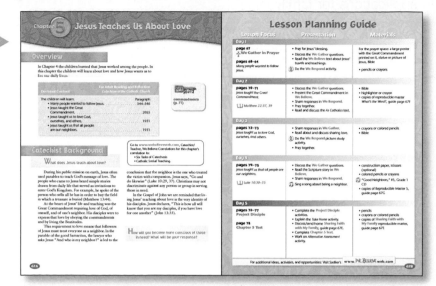

- Goal of the chapter
- References to the *Catechism of the Catholic Church*
- *Key Words*
- References for correlations to The Six Tasks of Catechesis, Catholic Social Teaching, and Catechetical Formation in Chaste Living
- Background for catechists

- All the day-by-day plans you need for a successful lesson
- Resources and materials for clear presentation

Enrichment and Additional Resources

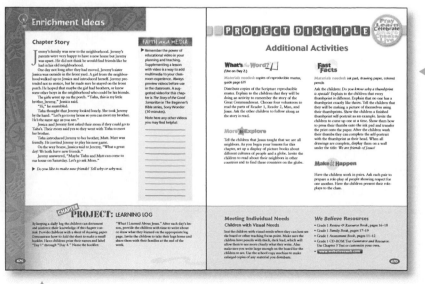

- Directions for using the chapter's *What's the Word?* reproducible master
- Even more activities directly related to the six tasks of catechesis
- Strategies for meeting the individual needs of the children
- Program resources for the chapter

- A *Chapter Story* for use in your lesson presentation
- *Faith and Media* that provides creative ways to connect lesson content to the electronic world

- A *Chapter Project* that gives you the opportunity to further involve the children and extend the chapter

Reproducible Masters

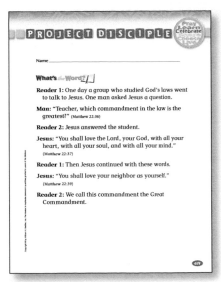

Family

- The children become the evangelizers as they share what they have learned in the chapter.
- The children share activities and prayer with their families.

Scripture

- A Scripture activity gives you the opportunity to deepen the children's understanding of God's Word.
- Skits, interactive activities, and more...

Chapter Content

- Additional fun activities reinforce and enrich the material taught in the chapter.
- Options for alternative assessment or family use

Lesson Plan Pages

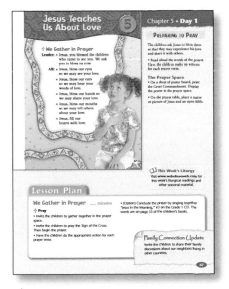

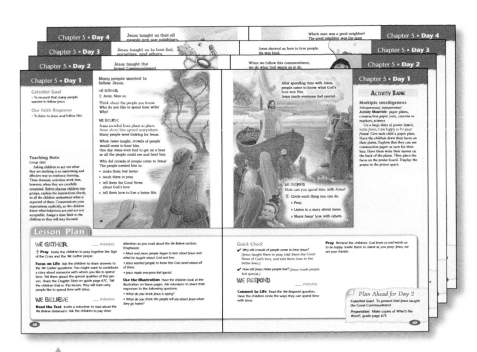

- Ideas on how to enhance the Prayer Space from week to week
- An online link to the week's liturgy
- A *Family Connection Update* that invites volunteers to share the outcome of the *Take Home* activity from the previous lesson

- Clear goals for the lesson
- Key vocabulary words
- Helpful *Teaching Tips*
- A "recipe" for clear presentation of the lesson
- An *Activity Bank* with additional and varied activities
- *Plan Ahead* suggestions for the next lesson

Lesson Plan Pages continued

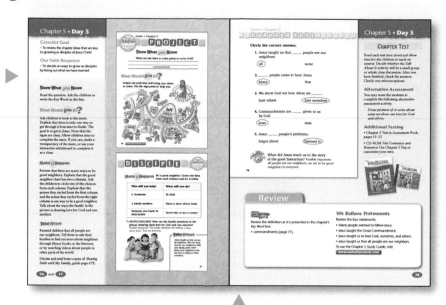

- Clear, concise directions for the activities from the child's pages that relate to the six tasks of catechesis
- Suggestions to encourage children to use the *Take Home* activity with their family

- End–of–chapter test with annotations
- Opportunities for alternative assessment
- Review of key words and faith content statements
- Reference to the chapter online study guide and to ancillary *Assessment Books* and CD-ROM *Test Generators*

Just look at the variety of PROJECT DISCIPLE activities!

Show What you Know . . . Check what's been learned

picture This . . . . See and show disciple skills

Reality Check . . . . "Check-off" ideas and choices

Make it Happen . . . . Live out what's been learned

What's the Word? . . . . . . All about Scripture

Question Corner . . . . Take a quiz or answer a question

Fast Facts . . . . Learn even more

What Would you do? . . . Make the right choices

Pray Today . . . . Talk and listen to God

Celebrate! . . . . All about worshiping God

Saint Stories . . . . Find great role models

More to Explore . . . . Get information from the Internet and library

Take Home . . . . Share faith at home

Now, pass it on! . . . . Evangelize!

DISCIPLE CHALLENGE . . . . . Go a step further!

Sadlier also offers these *We Believe* resources:

- ***Review & Resource Book***
  Even more engaging activities

- ***Family Book***
  Home Lesson Plans for teaching and/or reviewing

- **Music CD and Program Songbook**
  Program songs and lyrics and arrangements

www.webelieveweb.com

your 24/7 Teaching Assistant

* In Your Classroom Study Guides for every grade; Vocations—Letters from Africa; downloadable and whiteboard activities; Project Disciple; Online games—and much more!

* In Your Office This week's liturgy with reflection/discussion and activities based on Sunday readings; catechist development; teaching tips and resources —always relevant to your needs!

* In Your Students' Homes Study Guides; Catechetical Development for families; Project Disciple; Sharing Faith as a Family; From My Home to Yours—always being updated!

"We are with you when you need us!"

This Year
Go Green!

Focus On

The ocean is one of the most awesome aspects of God's creation. More plants and animals live in the ocean than on land. The world's oceans support over 13,000 species of fish. Some animals, such as whales and porpoises, live their entire lives in the ocean. Others, such as seals and sea turtles, spend their lives partly in the water and partly on land. Even though the expanse of the ocean is vast—covering more than 70 percent of the earth's surface—its ecosystem is increasingly threatened by human pollutants, over-fishing, and careless disposal of garbage. Nurturing delight in the wonders of the sea is one way to develop a preliminary understanding of the need to protect and preserve marine life and habitats.

Take Action

Place a small aquarium or fish bowl in the classroom, and involve the children in its maintenance. Use it as an example of the care that must be taken in protecting marine life.

Create an ocean scrapbook. Collect photos of different kinds of fish, mammals, reptiles, and plants found in the ocean, along with pictures and children's drawings of beaches and seashores.

Class Action

Plan a field trip to an aquarium. Invite the children to look for different forms of life that are sustained in the water.

Reflect and Pray

Invite children to offer spontaneous prayers for the gifts of the ocean. These can be prayers of thanksgiving for the abundance of sea life, or prayers of petition for the preservation of endangered species.

Make a simple Japanese sand garden for the class prayer space. Use a small box and add sand, stones, and other decorative elements. Show the children how to use a small rake or comb to create patterns in the sand. Emphasize it as a quiet, relaxing, and meditative activity.

Visit **www.webelieveweb.com** to find a Green Event for your parish or school.

Grade 1
Greenprint!

Focus on
Here is a picture of God's creatures in the ocean.

Take Action
Here I am caring for marine life in our classroom.

Class Action
We visited an aquarium and saw aquatic life. I saw…

1. _____   2. _____

Reflect and Pray
Thank you, God, for _____

_____ _____

Signed   Date

The *We Believe* program will help us to

learn

celebrate

share

and live our Catholic faith.

Throughout the year we will hear about many saints and holy people.

Saint Andrew Kim Taegon	Saint Katharine Drexel
Saint Anne	Saint Patrick
Saint Francis of Assisi	Saints Peter and Paul
Saint Francis Xavier	Pope Pius X
Saint John Vianney	Saint Teresa of Avila
Saint Joseph	Blessed Teresa of Calcutta

Together, let us grow as a community of faith.

Welcome!

✝ We Gather in Prayer

Leader: Welcome everyone to Grade 1 *We Believe*.

As we begin each chapter, we gather in prayer. We pray to God together.

Let us sing the *We Believe* song!

♫ We Believe in God

We believe in God;

We believe, we believe
in Jesus;

We believe in the Spirit
who gives us life.

We believe, we believe
in God.

When we see **We Gather** we come together as a class.

Each day we learn more about God.

WE GATHER

We begin by taking a moment to pray.

✝ *Thank you, God, for our classmates.*

Then we

think about

talk about

write about

draw about

act out

Life

at home

in our neighborhood

at school

in our parish

in our world

Talk about your life right now.

WE BELIEVE

We learn about

- God the Father, God the Son, and God the Holy Spirit
- Jesus, the Son of God, who became one of us
- the Church and its teachings.

We find out about the different ways Catholics live their faith and celebrate God's love.

When we see **We Believe** we learn more about our Catholic faith.

is an open Bible. When we see it, or something like this (John 13:34), we hear the Word of God.

Each of these signs points out something special that we are going to do.

means that we will make the Sign of the Cross and pray as we begin our lesson.

Key Words means it is time to review the important words we have learned in the day's lesson.

means we have an activity. We might

talk   write   act
draw   sing
work together   imagine

There are all kinds of activities!

means it's time to sing! We sing songs we know, make up our own songs, and sing along with those in our *We Believe* music program.

As Catholics...

Here we discover something special about our faith. Don't forget to read it!

WE RESPOND

We can respond by

- thinking about ways our faith affects the things we say and do
- sharing our thoughts and feelings
- praying to God.

Then in our homes, neighborhood, school, parish, and world, we can say and do the things that show love for God and others.

When we see **We Respond** we think about and act on what we have learned about God and our Catholic faith.

In this space, draw yourself as a *We Believe* first grader.

We are so happy you are with us!

Show What you Know

We "show what we know" about each chapter's content. A disciple is always learning more about his or her faith.

We sharpen our disciple skills with each chapter's Project Disciple pages!

Picture This
Pictures are a way for us to see and show our disciple skills.

PROJECT

Grade 1 Chapter 9

Pray
Learn
Celebrate
Share
Choose
Live

Show What you Know

Match the sentence parts.

The Temple •

Easter Sunday •

• is the special day we celebrate that Jesus Christ rose to new life.

• was the holy place in Jerusalem where the Jewish People prayed.

Celebrate!

Circle the ways you can celebrate that Jesus died and rose for us.

Pray

Praise

Sing

116   www.webeli...

DISCIPLE

Pray
Learn
Celebrate
Share
Choose
Live

Picture This
What does this stained glass window show?

Jesus is our

_____

- - - - - - - - - - - - - - -

Reality Check

The Church teaches us to respect all workers. People work in our neighborhood to protect and care for us. Who helps to protect and care for you?

☐ Police officers

☐ Firefighters

☐ People who keep my neighborhood clean

☐ People in my parish and school

Take Home

What are the two words of praise you learned in this chapter?

_____

_____

Say these words as a family.

117

Celebrate!
As disciples, we worship God.

Reality Check
Here we get to "check-off" our ideas and choices.

Take Home
We always get the chance to share our faith "at home."

There are **LOADS of ACTIVITIES** that make us better disciples! Just look at this additional list.

What's the Word?—all about Scripture

Question Corner—take a quiz

Fast Facts—learn even more about our faith

Make It Happen—living out what we have learned

What Would You Do?—making the right choices

Pray Today—talking and listening to God

Saint Stories—finding great role models

More to Explore—getting information from the Internet and library

Now, Pass It On!—invites us to witness to our faith

Don't forget to look for the **Disciple Challenge**—count how many you can do this year!

And every chapter ends with a Chapter Test!

PROJECT DISCIPLE

You are on a journey this year to become a disciple of Jesus Christ.

Have a great year!

This year you will:

- **learn** the ways God has shown his love for us.

- **pray** at home and with the Church community.

- **celebrate** your faith at Sunday Mass and by honoring the saints.

- **choose** to live as a child of God every day.

- **share** God's gifts with family and others.

- **live out** the Catholic faith by caring for God's creation, especially people.

WE BELIEVE
GRADE 1 DISCIPLE CONTRACT

As a disciple of Jesus, this year I promise to

_____

Name

_____

Date

And remember, you can always visit

www.webelieveweb.com

for all kinds of activities, games, study guides, and resources.

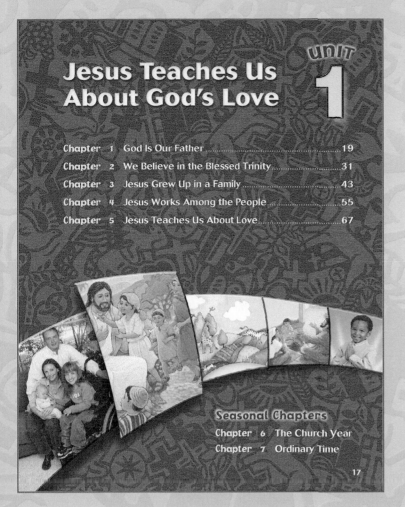

Jesus Teaches Us About God's Love

UNIT 1

Chapter 1   God Is Our Father 19

Chapter 2   We Believe in the Blessed Trinity 31

Chapter 3   Jesus Grew Up in a Family 43

Chapter 4   Jesus Works Among the People 55

Chapter 5   Jesus Teaches Us About Love 67

Seasonal Chapters

Chapter 6   The Church Year

Chapter 7   Ordinary Time

17

PROJECT DISCIPLE
DEAR FAMILY

In Unit 1 your child will grow as a disciple of Jesus by:

• learning about God the Father's love for all people

• praying to the Blessed Trinity: God the Father, God the Son, and God the Holy Spirit

• meeting Jesus, the Son of God, and the Holy Family

• understanding what Jesus taught us about loving God, ourselves, and others

• living the Great Commandment that Jesus taught.

What Would you do?

God wants us to care for all creation. As a family, decide on one way you can do each of the following:

Save water _____

Recycle _____

Add to the beauty of creation _____

Care for animals _____

 Pray Today This week, make the Sign of the Cross your special family prayer. You may also want to bless each other at bedtime by tracing a cross on each other's forehead.

Reality Check

"Education in the faith by the parents should begin in the child's earliest years."
(Catechism of the Catholic Church, 2226)

Picture This

Together look at the artwork on pages 48, 49, and 51 of the text. Talk about the Holy Family. What are Jesus, Mary, and Joseph doing in the pictures? How did they help each other and show their love for each other? Then talk about the ways your family members help and show love to one another.

What's the Word?

Read the Gospel passage from Luke on page 60 in the text. Talk together about the ways God shows he cares for your family. Ask each member to share one way he or she knows God cares. Then offer a prayer of thanks for God's love!

Take Home

Each chapter in your child's *We Believe* Grade 1 text offers a "Take Home" activity that invites your family to support your child's journey to more fully become a disciple of Christ.

Be ready for this unit's Take Home:

Chapter 1: Appreciating God's gifts in the world

Chapter 2: Praying as a family

Chapter 3: Making a family activity collage

Chapter 4: Helping people who are sick

Chapter 5: Learning about people of different cultures

18

CLASS CONNECTION

Read aloud the unit title and the chapter titles. Ask the children: *What do you think you will be learning in this unit?* Invite a few volunteers to respond. Then explain to the children that they will be learning about God the Father, God the Son, and God the Holy Spirit.

HOME CONNECTION

Project Disciple
Dear Family

Sadlier *We Believe* calls on families to become involved in:

• learning the faith

• prayer and worship

• living their faith.

Highlighting of these unit family pages and the opportunities they offer will strengthen the partnership of the Church and the home.

For additional information and activities, encourage families to visit Sadlier's

www.WeBelieveweb.com

Overview

In this chapter the children will learn that God created the world and all people.

Doctrinal Content	For Adult Reading and Reflection *Catechism of the Catholic Church*
The children will learn:	Paragraph
• God created the world.	290
• God created all people.	355
• God gives us special gifts.	356–357
• God promises to love us always.	410

creation (p. 21)
Bible (p. 21)

Catechist Background

What makes this world such an exciting place in which to live?

Go to **www.webelieveweb.com**, Catechist/Teacher, We Believe Correlations for this chapter's correlation to:
- Six Tasks of Catechesis
- Catholic Social Teaching
- *Catechetical Formation in Chaste Living.*

One of the most intriguing titles in classical music is Franz Schubert's eighth symphony. It is known as the "Unfinished." Whether the title was the brainchild of some music critic or not, it does make any listener pause to think about its implications.

We believe that God created our world and everything in it. It certainly is his masterpiece, and we are his special creation. God has gifted us with wonderful gifts and promised to love us always. (See CCC 239.) But just for a moment, entertain the thought of creation as God's "unfinished" symphony. What would be the impact if we took seriously our role as "co-creators" and as stewards or caretakers of God's creation?

When we focus on the mystery of the Incarnation, God the Son becoming one of us, we come to realize the wonder of it all. Jesus' life, Death, and Resurrection are the foundation of the new creation. As Saint Paul proclaims,

"He is the image of the invisible God, the firstborn of all creation" (Colossians 1:15).

Through the Sacrament of Baptism each person becomes a new creation in Christ but remains an unfinished masterpiece. We are fashioned and re-fashioned into God's image and likeness throughout our lives. We need to value all life, especially the human dignity of every person, including ourselves.

The noted educator Maria Montessori saw in each child the incarnation of human love in its most divine dimension. She and other visionary leaders tapped into the child's gift of wonder during every lesson. Chapter 1 would be an ideal place to begin to tap into that gift of wonder.

How can you reverence each child as God's creation in your service as a catechist?

Lesson Planning Guide

Lesson Focus	Presentation	Materials
Day 1		
page 19 ✠ **We Gather in Prayer** **pages 20–21** *God created the world.*  *Genesis 1:1–31*	♪ Thank God in song. • Respond to the **We Gather** question. • Read and discuss the **We Believe** text. • Share responses to the **We Respond** question. 🕴 Do the drawing activity.	For the prayer space: pictures of people taking care of God's gifts; containers of sand, water, soil ♪ "Thank You, God," #2, Grade 1 CD • Bible • crayons or colored pencils
Day 2		
pages 22–23 *God created all people.*	• Follow the **We Gather** directive and respond to the question. • Present the **We Believe** text and discuss the pictures. • Reflect and respond to the **We Respond** question. 🕴 Complete the prayer by drawing.	• copies of Reproducible Master 1, guide page 19G • crayons or colored pencils
Day 3		
pages 24–25 *God gives us special gifts.*	• Discuss the **We Gather** questions. • Read and discuss the **We Believe** text about our God-given gifts. • Share responses to the **We Respond** question. 🕴 Do the activity. • Read and discuss the *As Catholics* text.	• pencils • copies of reproducible master *What's the Word?*, guide page 19F • crayons or colored pencils
Day 4		
pages 26–27 *God promises to love us always.*	🕴 Find a hidden word in the **We Gather** activity. • Present the **We Believe** text about God's never-ending love. • Discuss the **We Respond** question. • Reflect and pray.	• crayons or colored pencils
Day 5		
pages 28–29 **Project Disciple** **page 30** **Chapter 1 Test**	• Complete the **Project Disciple** activities. • Explain the *Take Home* activity. • Discuss/send home **Sharing Faith with My Family**, guide page 19E. • Complete **Chapter 1 Test**. • Work on *Alternative Assessment* activity.	• pencils • crayons or colored pencils • copies of **Sharing Faith with My Family** reproducible master, guide page 19E

For additional ideas, activities, and opportunities: Visit Sadlier's 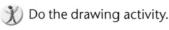 www.WeBelieveweb.com

Enrichment Ideas

Chapter Story

My name is Lisa Marella. Luke is my twin brother. During the past summer, Grandma Marella watched us while our parents were at work.

At the beginning of the summer, Grandma said, "I promise you, you won't get bored. I've planned a lot of adventures for us."

Well, Grandma kept her promise. A few days we went to the beach. We went swimming, looked for seashells, and played in the sand. One day we saw jellyfish on the beach near the water. We didn't want to go swimming that day.

One day we went to a peach orchard. The workers helped Luke and me climb the trees. We picked a lot of peaches and handed them to Grandma. When we got home, we watched Grandma slice the peaches. Then we helped her make peach pies and peach jam.

My favorite adventure was visiting Grandma's sister, Great Aunt Maria. She lives far away from us so we had to stay overnight. Aunt Maria's grandson, Tony, was visiting her. Tony is eleven years old. He had a tent. Tony, Luke, and I slept in the tent overnight. Before we went to sleep, we looked at the night sky through Aunt Maria's telescope. The moon and the stars looked very close to us. I decided that night that when I am older, I want to be a space explorer.

I hope Grandma watches us next summer. She's probably planning new adventures for us right now.

▶ *Have you ever had adventures like the twins did? What was your favorite?*

FAITH and MEDIA

▶ Take advantage of any technology offerings for this chapter's and all lessons in *We Believe*. Classroom or school computer labs, the Internet, interactive white boards, digital video and still cameras, and student responders are just some examples of technology that can enhance your *We Believe* lessons. In Chapter 1, consider scanning student work or asking students to complete activities on a computer's word processing or painting program and saving them in an ongoing interactive student portfolio. Video and audio are also powerful measures of student work and progress.

CHAPTER PROJECT: TREASURE HUNT

Explain that God's gifts of creation are treasures. Each day this week hide a gift of creation in the room. Suggested items include: a pinecone, a shell, a stone, a fruit or vegetable, a colorful leaf, a container of sand or soil, a picture of a wild animal, a picture of the ocean, forest, city park. Give the children clues as to what the gift is. Then after they have guessed the name of the gift, provide the clues as to where in the room you have hidden the gift. After each gift is found, display it in the prayer space.

PROJECT DISCIPLE

Pray
Learn
Celebrate
Share
Choose
Live

Additional Activities

Picture This

Materials needed: small sheets of wrapping paper (with white back), gift bows, markers

Give each child a sheet of wrapping paper. Prompt the children to fold the sheet in half with the wrapping paper on the outside and the blank side on the inside. Encourage children to draw one of their favorite gifts that God created on the inside of the "gift." Have children attach a small bow to the outside of the "gift." Invite the children to exchange gifts with others.

What's the Word?

(Use on Day 3.)

Materials needed: copies of reproducible master, guide page 19F, crayons or colored pencils

Distribute copies of the Scripture reproducible master. Explain to the children that they will be completing each sentence about God's gifts with a picture. Read aloud each sentence, allowing the children time to sketch a simple drawing in each box. Finish by reading the Scripture quote that ends the page. Allow children to go back and add detail to their drawings as they think about all of God's gifts.

More to Explore

Invite the children to share some of God's special gifts to them during a week-long "show and tell" activity. Assign each child a day of the week in which he or she can bring in a favorite object. If a particular person or animal is a special gift he or she would like to share, encourage the child to bring a photo or drawing. Allow the children a minute to present their gifts at the beginning or end of the lesson. If possible, allow time for the children to ask the presenting child a question or two. Consider taking a photo of each child with his or her gift for a classroom bulletin board, poster, or photo slideshow.

Pray Today

Introduce the children to the custom of praying from the psalms. Print the following verse on a sheet of poster board. Ask each child to illustrate a small part of it during the week when time allows.

> Lord, you have made so many things!
> The earth is filled with your creatures.
>
> (based on Psalm 104:24)

Meeting Individual Needs
Children with Special Needs

Throughout the year find ways to showcase the talents of children with special needs. Something as simple as the praising of a child's artwork or a child's shared response can signal your confidence in the unique abilities of each child.

We Believe Resources

- Grade 1 *Review & Resource Book*, pages 4–6
- Grade 1 *Family Book*, pages 5–7
- Grade 1 *Assessment Book*, pages 3–4
- Grade 1 CD-ROM *Test Generator and Resource*: Use Chapter 1 Test or customize your own.
- **www.webelieveweb.com**

Sharing What I Learned

Look at the pictures below. Use each picture to tell your family what you learned in this chapter.

We Are Gifted

Choose a relative or friend of the family.
Together make a card to send to the person.
Have each member of your family write one
thing that they like about that person.
Then have everyone sign the card.
Send the card to your relative or friend.

You are a gift from God.
We are glad
that God created you.

Visit Sadlier's

www.WeBelieve.web.com

Connect to the Catechism
For adult background and reflection,
see paragraphs 344 and 337.

PROJECT DISCIPLE

Pray
Learn
Celebrate
Share
Choose
Live

Name _____

What's *the* Word?

God created the [ ] to shine in the day.

God created [ ] for us to eat.

God created [ ] for [ ] to swim in.

And God created [ ] to share his love.

"God looked at everything he had made, and he found it very good." (Genesis 1:31)

19F

Name _____

Draw pictures to show some of your favorite things.

My Favorite Things

My favorite color is

My favorite animal is

My favorite outdoor place is

My favorite food is

19G Reproducible Master 1

God Is Our Father ①

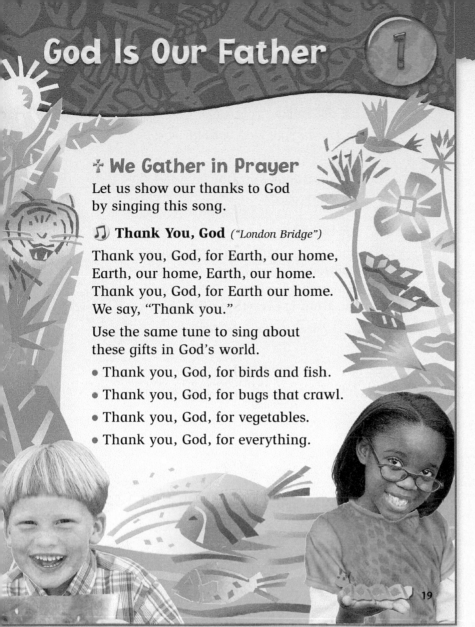

☩ We Gather in Prayer

Let us show our thanks to God by singing this song.

🎵 **Thank You, God** (*"London Bridge"*)

Thank you, God, for Earth, our home,
Earth, our home, Earth, our home.
Thank you, God, for Earth our home.
We say, "Thank you."

Use the same tune to sing about these gifts in God's world.

- Thank you, God, for birds and fish.
- Thank you, God, for bugs that crawl.
- Thank you, God, for vegetables.
- Thank you, God, for everything.

19

PREPARING TO PRAY

The children offer a song of thanks for God's created gifts.

- Play "Thank You, God," #2 on the Grade 1 CD. Have the children practice singing. Invite volunteers to make up actions.

🎵 For words and music to all the songs on the Grade 1 CD, see Sadlier's *We Believe* Program Songbook.

The Prayer Space

- Display pictures of people enjoying and taking care of God's gifts of creation.

- Display gifts of God's creation: a container of water, sand, potting soil, pinecones, rocks, seashells, flowers, and a plant.

📖 **This Week's Liturgy**
Visit **www.webelieveweb.com** for this week's liturgical readings and other seasonal material.

Lesson Plan

We Gather in Prayer ___ minutes

☩ Pray

- Invite the children to gather in the prayer space. Then sing together the verses of "Thank You, God." As they sing, have the children do the actions that they have made up for the different verses.

- Invite the children to make up their own verses and actions for the song "Thank You, God." You may want to sing one or two of the verses for the beginning or ending prayer of each day's lesson this week.

Family Connection Update

Invite the children to recount a story about an adventure that they shared with their families this summer.

Catechist Goal

• To present that God created the world

Our Faith Response

• To identify wonderful things God created

 **creation**
Bible

Lesson Materials

• Bible
• crayons or colored pencils

Teaching Note

Read Along

When you see **Read Along** either read the material to the children or ask a proficient reader to do so. The **Read Along** feature is used to make the children feel comfortable with the material. It is also used since many children enjoy having information read to them.

God created the world.

WE GATHER

✝ *Thank you, God, for our world.*

Look at the picture.
Which things are your favorite?
Tell why.

WE BELIEVE

The word *create* means "to make."
God made everything.
God created our wonderful world.
Creation is everything God made.

Genesis 1:1–31

Read Along
God created light and water. God created fruits and vegetables. God created all kinds of animals.

God created people. Then "God looked at everything he had made, and he found it very good." (Genesis 1:31)

20

Lesson Plan

WE GATHER ___ minutes

✝ **Pray** Read aloud the *We Gather* prayer at the top of page 20.

Focus on Life Call attention to the collage on page 20. Ask the children to name their two favorite things and to tell why they are their favorites. Share the *Chapter Story* on guide page 19C. Have the children raise their hands when they hear the name of one of God's gifts. Tell the children that in this lesson they will learn that God created the world.

WE BELIEVE ___ minutes

Learn About Creation Read aloud the *We Believe* statement at the top of page 20. Then hold up the Bible. Tell the children: *In the Bible we can read about God creating the world. The Bible is the book of God's Word.*

Read Scripture Ask the children to stand as you read aloud the Scripture passage from Genesis. Stress: *Creation is everything God made.* Have the children point to each of God's gifts shown on page 20. For each gift have the children say the name of the gift and *God created this gift.*

We read about God's creation
in the Bible.
The Bible is a special book
about God.
The **Bible** is the book of God's Word.

We believe that God is our Father.
We believe that everything he
created is good.

WE RESPOND

God created our
wonderful world.
What makes the world
so wonderful for you?

Key Words

creation everything
God made

Bible the book of
God's Word

🧍 Draw something beautiful
you saw today.

Now pray together.
God, thank you for everything
you made. God, you are wonderful.

21

ACTIVITY BANK

Multiple Intelligences
Spatial
Activity Materials: modeling clay or
dough, construction paper
Have the children use clay or
dough to shape their favorite animals.
Have them write their names on
construction paper and place their
animals on their papers. Display the
animals in your prayer space.

The Bible
Place of Honor
Activity Materials: foil wrapping paper,
a box to use as a stand, a small table
Ask volunteers to help you to
cover a box with foil wrapping paper.
Place the box on a small table in your
prayer space. Explain to the children
that the box is a stand for the Bible.
Ask the children to gather in the
prayer space. Place the opened Bible
on the stand. Invite the children to
sing to the tune of "London Bridge."

*Thank you, God, for the Bible,
the Bible, the Bible.
Thank you, God, for the Bible
the book of your Word.*

Quick Check

✔ *What is the word for everything God made?* (Creation
is everything God made.)

✔ *What do we believe about everything God created?*
(We believe that everything God created is good.)

WE RESPOND   ___ minutes

Connect to Life Give the children a minute of
quiet to think about what makes the world wonderful
for them. Then ask them to draw something beautiful
they saw today. When they are finished, have them
share their pictures with the children sitting near them.

Pray Read the following prayer and ask the children
to repeat the words: *God, thank you for everything you
made. God, you are wonderful.*

Plan Ahead for Day 2

Catechist Goal: To highlight that God created
all people

Preparation: Make copies of Reproducible
Master 1, guide page 19G.

Catechist Goal

• To highlight that God created all people

Our Faith Response

• To name ways to take care of all God's creation

Lesson Materials

• copies of Reproducible Master 1
• crayons or colored pencils

Teaching Tip

The We Believe **Statement**

Point out the sentence in special blue type at the top of page 20. Explain: *This is the* We Believe *sentence for our lesson. It tells us what our lesson is about.* There is a *We Believe* statement at the beginning of each lesson for Days 1 through 4.

God created all people.

WE GATHER

✝ *God, thank you for the gift of creation.*

Name some of your family members. What makes each one special to you?

WE BELIEVE

God wanted to share his love.
So he created people.
We were created to know, love, and serve God.

We are God's special creation.
God did not create everyone to be exactly alike.
Every person is special to God.

22

Lesson Plan

WE GATHER _____ minutes

✝ **Pray** Read aloud the *We Gather* prayer and ask the children to repeat the words.

Focus on Life Ask volunteers to share responses to the *We Gather* question. Be sensitive to children's family situations. Share a story of a family member who is special to you and the reasons why. Tell the children that in this lesson they will learn that God created all people.

WE BELIEVE _____ minutes

Talk About Differences Read aloud the first two *We Believe* paragraphs. Have volunteers explain some of the differences in looks among people. Also explain that people like to do different things; they like to eat different food; they live in and travel to different places. Stress: *It does not matter to God what a person looks like, where a person lives, or what foods a person eats. Each person is special to God.*

Do the Activity Distribute copies of Reproducible Master 1. Read each category and have the children draw or print their response. Have the children show their papers to each other, noting the different things that they have drawn. Point out: *All the things that you have drawn are gifts from God.*

God wants people to take care of his gift of creation. He wants us to take care of his world.

How are the people in the pictures taking care of God's world?

WE RESPOND

What are some ways you can take care of God's world?

🎨 Draw a picture to finish this prayer.

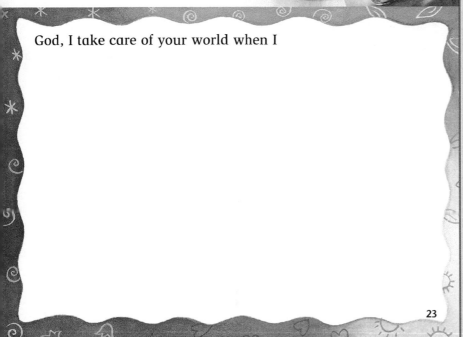

God, I take care of your world when I

ACTIVITY BANK

Multiple Intelligences
Bodily-Kinesthetic
Activity Materials: index cards
Prepare a set of index cards. On each card draw a picture of one of God's gifts of creation (a bird, the sun, a fish, and a tree). Have a volunteer go to the front of the room, choose a card, and then do a pantomime for the picture on the card. Explain that the actor cannot speak. Invite the other children to guess what gift of God the child is pantomiming.

Multicultural Connection
People of the World
Activity Materials: world globe or map
Show the children a globe or world map. Have them take turns randomly pointing out a place in the world. Say the name of the country to which each child's finger points and the name of the people who live there. (*Turkey, Turkish people; Egypt, Egyptians*) Have the children repeat the name of the people and say that they are special to God. (*Turkish people are special to God.*)

Take Care of Creation Point out that God gives all people a special job. Read the third *We Believe* paragraph. Direct attention to the photos on these two pages. Have volunteers tell how the people are taking care of God's world.

Quick Check

✔ *Why did God create all people?* (God created all people because he wanted to share his love.)

✔ *What does God want us to do with his gift of creation?* (God wants us to care for his creation.)

WE RESPOND ___ minutes

Connect to Life Ask the children to name ways they can take care of God's world. Share with them

some of the following ways: not throw papers or cans on the lawn or street, turn off the water faucet and not let water run, learn about animals and plants. Then ask the children to draw a picture to finish the prayer.

Pray Invite the children to hold up their books as you pray aloud: *God, help us to take care of this world.*

Plan Ahead for Day 3

Catechist Goal: To examine the special gifts that God gives us

Preparation: Make copies of *What's the Word?*, guide page 19F.

23

Catechist Goal

- To examine the special gifts that God gives us

Our Faith Response

- To express our gratitude to God for his gifts

Lesson Materials

- copies of reproducible master *What's the Word?*, guide page 19F
- crayons or colored pencils

As Catholics...

Angels

After you have presented the lesson, read the text about angels. Explain: *We call the angels who watch over us our guardian angels.* You may want to share the Angel of God prayer, found on page 14 in the childrens' *My Prayer Book.*

God gives us special gifts.

WE GATHER

✝ *God our Father, we love you.*

What do plants and animals do each day?
What do we do?

WE BELIEVE

We can do many things that animals and plants cannot do.

We can:

- think and learn.
- care for God's world.
- share love with our families and friends.
- listen to and talk to God.

These things are gifts from God. God gives us these gifts so we can know and love him.

24

Lesson Plan

WE GATHER _____ minutes

✝ **Pray** Read aloud the prayer at the top of page 24 and invite the children to pray it after you.

Focus on Life Assign the children to one of two groups. Have the children in one group act out what plants do each day (face the sun, soak up water, grow). Have the second group act out what dogs and cats do (eat, drink water or milk, grow, bark or meow). Then have the children act out what they do each day (eat, drink, clean, study, talk, watch TV). Ask: *What can you do that plants and animals can not do?*

WE BELIEVE _____ minutes

Read About Special Gifts Read aloud the first three *We Believe* paragraphs. Then reread the list of what we can do and have the children repeat each action listed. Stress: *Doing these things can help us to know and love God.*

People Help Us Have the children look at the picture of the family on these pages. Ask: *What are the people doing?* Then read aloud the last *We Believe* paragraph. If time permits, point to each child, say the child's name, and *you are a gift from God.*

People can help us to do these things.
People are gifts from God, too.
People help us to grow in God's love.

WE RESPOND

Who are the people who help you to grow in God's love?

Write the first letters of their names on the flower.
Thank God for these helpers.

As Catholics...

We believe that God created angels. Angels are God's helpers. But they do not have bodies like people do. Angels give people messages from God. They protect and guide us. They never stop praising God.

How can you praise God, too?

25

ACTIVITY BANK

Community

Growing in God's Love
Activity Materials: paint, roll of paper, crayons

On a roll of paper, draw the outline of a flower for each child in your group. Have each child dip his or her right thumb in paint and then put a thumbprint in the center of one of the flowers. Have a container of water and cloths available for the children to remove the paint from their thumbs. Write the child's initials on the leaves of the flower. Then have a group of children, one group at a time, color their flowers. When all the flowers are colored, point out that all the flowers are different, but together they make one beautiful garden. Print on the paper: *We help each other grow in God's love.* Display the garden paper in the prayer space.

Scripture

Linguistic, Spatial

For a Scripture activity, see *What's the Word?*, guide page 19F.

Quick Check

✔ *What special gifts did God give people?* (We can think, learn, speak, care for God's world, share love, and listen and talk to God.)

✔ *Why did God give us special gifts?* (God gave us special gifts so that we can know and love God.)

WE RESPOND   ___ minutes

Connect to Life Read the *We Respond* question. Have volunteers share their responses. Encourage the children to conclude that family members, godparents, and teachers are all people who help us to grow in God's love. Ask the children to write the first letters of people's names on the flower. Some children may need your help.

Pray Ask the children to stand and hold up their books as you pray aloud: *Thank you, God, for the people who help us to grow in your love.*

Plan Ahead for Day 4

Catechist Goal: To teach that God promises to love us always

Preparation: Think of ways to help the children understand the meaning of *always*.

Catechist Goal

- To teach that God promises to love us always

Our Faith Response

- To trust in God's promises

Teaching Note

The Story of Adam and Eve

Present the story of the first people as simply as it is presented in the text. Do not elaborate by providing details given in Genesis. The most important thing for the children to remember is that God promises to love us always.

God promises to love us always.

WE GATHER

✝ *God, we want to grow in your love forever.*

What does the word *forever* mean?

☽ Find another word for *forever*. Color the letters in the flowers.

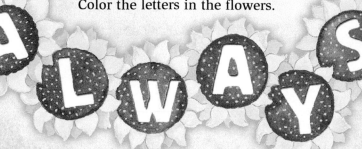

WE BELIEVE

God our Father loves us very much. He wants us to love him. In the Bible, there is a story about Adam and Eve.

📖 Genesis 2—3

Read Along

Adam and Eve lived in the most beautiful garden in the world. Everything was perfect there. God gave them everything they needed to live.

God wanted them to be happy with him forever.

One day Adam and Eve did something God had told them not to do. Then they had to live in a world that was not perfect any more.

26

Lesson Plan

WE GATHER ___ minutes

✝ **Pray** Ask the children to suggest an action which shows something growing. Then ask the children to do the action as they pray the *We Gather* prayer.

Focus on Life Invite volunteers to offer their definitions of the word *forever*. Ask the children to complete the *We Gather* activity. Then write the word *always* on the board.

WE BELIEVE ___ minutes

Preview Ask volunteers to tell how long they think the following items will last: *bike, ice cream cone, shoes, snowman, ice cube, a house.* Explain: *God's love is not*

like everyday things because his love for us will last forever.

Read the Text On the board write the *We Believe* statement, underlining the word *always*. Then read the *We Believe* paragraphs aloud to the children. Stress:

- *God loved the first people very much. God showed his love by giving them everything they needed to live happy lives.*

- *When the first humans disobeyed God, God never stopped loving them.*

- *God promises to be with us and to love us always.*

God never stopped loving Adam and Eve.
He promised that he would be with them always.
He promised to send someone to help them and their children.

God our Father promises to be with us and love us always, too.
He promises again and again to save all people.

WE RESPOND

It is important for us to remember God's promises.
What did God promise?

Put your right hand over your heart.
Pray these words or use your own words.
Thank you, God, for loving me always.
I promise to love you in return.

27

ACTIVITY BANK

Prayer
Thanking God
Activity Materials: colored pencils or crayons, sentence strips

Invite the children to compose simple sentences to make thank-you notes to God. Write these sentences on the board. Examples are:

- *Thank you, God, for animals.*
- *God, thank you for making us.*

When this is completed, read aloud all the suggested sentences. Have each child choose a favorite sentence and then copy the sentence on a sentence strip and decorate it. Ask the children to place their thank-you notes near the Bible on the prayer table. Invite the children to gather in the prayer space. Read the prayers on the papers.

Quick Check

✔ *What did God the Father promise Adam and Eve?* (He would be with them always; he would send someone to help them and their children.)

✔ *What does God the Father promise us?* (He promises to be with us and love us always.)

WE RESPOND ___ minutes

Connect to Life Invite the children to answer the question in the *We Respond* section. Then ask: *How important is it for a person to keep a promise?* Explain: *When a person keeps a promise, we know we can trust* that person. We can trust that God will always keep his promise to love us always.

Pray Invite the children to gather in the prayer space. Remind them: *A promise is something we should make only if we really mean to keep it.* Show them the suggested prayer gesture. Explain: *This is a sign for making a promise.* Read aloud the prayer in the text and then invite the children to repeat the words.

Plan Ahead for Day 5

Catechist Goal: To review chapter ideas and their relationship to our faith life

Preparation: Make copies of *Sharing Faith with My Family*, guide page 19E.

Catechist Goal

• To review the chapter ideas that are key to growing as disciples of Jesus Christ

Our Faith Response

• To decide on ways to grow as disciples by living out what we have learned

Show What *you* Know

Read aloud the activity instruction and the first *Key Word*: *Bible.* Allow time for the children to match the picture to the *Key Word.* Repeat this procedure for *creation.*

Saint Stories

Read aloud the story of Saint Francis. Invite the children to color the picture of Saint Francis and the animals as they discuss ways they can care for God's world with those sitting nearest to them.

Make *it* Happen

Read aloud the paragraph and invite the children to use a pencil to circle their choices. They may circle one, two, or all three pictures. Ask the children to share their choices. As an extension you may chart class favorites and determine the most popular choice.

Reality Check

Explain to the children that this activity is a check list. Model making a check on the board. Read aloud the instruction line. Invite the children to check one, some, or all of the ways. Encourage them to remember these ways during the week.

Take Home

Encourage the children to take a family walk to see and discuss what God has made and to thank God as a family.

Discuss and send home copies of *Sharing Faith with My Family,* guide page 19E.

Grade 1 Chapter 1

PROJECT

Pray Learn Celebrate Share Choose Live

Show What *you* Know

Match the Key Words to the pictures.

Bible

creation

Saint Stories

Saint Francis of Assisi loved God. He loved all of God's creation. He took care of God's world. He was kind and gentle to animals. Color this picture of Saint Francis and the animals.

28 www.webelieveweb.com

DISCIPLE

Pray Learn Celebrate Share Choose Live

Make *it* Happen

Think about God's gifts of people, plants, and animals. Which of these are you most thankful that God created? Circle your choices.

People   **Plants**   **Animals**

Reality Check

Check ways you can take care of God's world.

☑ Recycle

☑ Love my family

☑ Try not to be wasteful

☑ Take care of myself

Take Home

Take a walk with your family. Talk about the things you see that God made.

Together say a prayer to thank God for his creation.

29

CHAPTER TEST

Circle the correct answer.

1. All things made by God are _____.

   little   (good)

2. God created all _____ to know and love him.

   (people)   animals

3. The Bible is a special _____ about God.

   (book)   picture

4. God _____ create everyone to be exactly alike.

   did   (did not)

5. God promises to love us _____.

   only at special times   (always)

How can people care for all God's creation? Possible responses: try not to be wasteful; recycle; take care of people, plants, and animals

30

CHAPTER TEST

Read each test item aloud and allow time for the children to mark an answer. Decide whether the *Talk About It* activity will be a small group or whole class discussion. After you have finished, check the answers. Clarify any misconceptions.

Alternative Assessment

You may want the students to complete the following alternative-assessment activity.

> *Make a sign to show some of God's gifts of creation. You might want to draw or use pictures from magazines.*

Additional Testing

• Chapter 1 Test in *Assessment Book*, pages 3–4

• CD-ROM *Test Generator and Resource*: Use Chapter 1 Test or customize your own.

Review

Review the definitions as they are presented in the chapter's *Key Word* boxes:

• creation (page 21)

• Bible (page 21).

We Believe Statements

Review the four statements.

• God created the world.

• God created all people.

• God gives us special gifts.

• God promises to love us always.

To use the Chapter 1 Study Guide, visit

www.webelieveweb.com

Overview

In Chapter 1 the children learned that God created the world and all people. In this chapter the children will learn that God sent Jesus, his own Son, to us.

Doctrinal Content	For Adult Reading and Reflection *Catechism of the Catholic Church*
The children will learn:	Paragraph
• God sent his own Son, Jesus, to us.	422
• Jesus is God's greatest gift.	423
• There are Three Persons in One God.	234
• The Sign of the Cross is a prayer to the Blessed Trinity.	232

Key Words

Blessed Trinity (p. 36)
prayer (p. 39)
Sign of the Cross (p. 39)

Catechist Background

Go to **www.webelieveweb.com**, Catechist/ Teacher, We Believe Correlations for this chapter's correlation to:
• Six Tasks of Catechesis
• *Catechetical Formation in Chaste Living.*

What do you think about as you make the sign of the cross?

Our faith in the Blessed Trinity is central to our identity as Christians. Although we cannot fully understand this mystery, we believe that "it is the Father who generates, the Son who is begotten, and the Holy Spirit who proceeds" (Lateran Council IV (1215):DS 804). The three divine Persons are inseparable and coeternal.

God the Father's promise to send a savior shows an aspect of the divine toward us—compassion. When the Son of God was sent to us as the gift of the Father, he showed us yet another facet of the Blessed Trinity—infinite love. The life, Death, and Resurrection of Jesus accomplish the redemption of all humankind. Before the risen Christ ascends to the Father, the promise and the Gift of the Holy Spirit is revealed. The Third Person of the Blessed Trinity leads us back to the Father through the Son. The gradual revelation of the Trinity has come full circle.

As you gather with your first graders to pray the Sign of the Cross, be mindful of God's compassion and infinite love. Help your children to become aware of God's love and generosity.

How will you share God's love and compassion this week?

Lesson Planning Guide

Lesson Focus	Presentation	Materials

Day 1

page 31
 **We Gather in Prayer**

pages 32–33
God sent his own Son, Jesus, to us.

- Celebrate in prayer and action.
- Discuss the We Gather questions.
- Read the We Believe text about God sending Jesus to us.
- Do the We Respond message activity.

For the prayer space: Bible and a large heart outline drawn on poster board or chart paper

- copies of Reproducible Master 2, guide page 31G
- crayons or colored pencils
- scissors, glue, and sentence strips

Day 2

pages 34–35
Jesus is God's greatest gift.

 Mark 10:13–14

- Discuss the We Gather directive.
- Present the We Believe text about Jesus.
- Do the We Respond drawing activity.
- Share responses to the question.

- Bible
- crayons or colored pencils
- highlighter or crayon

Day 3

pages 36–37
There are Three Persons in One God

- Respond to the We Gather questions.
- Read and discuss the We Believe text about the Blessed Trinity.
- Color a symbol of the Trinity.
- Discuss the We Respond question.
- Pray together.
- Read and discuss the *As Catholics* text.

- crayons or colored pencils
- three large name cards: God the Father, God the Son, and God the Holy Spirit

Day 4

pages 38–39
The Sign of the Cross is a prayer to the Blessed Trinity.

- Respond to the We Gather questions.
- Present the We Believe text.
- Examine the gestures and words for praying the Sign of the Cross.
- For We Respond pray the Sign of the Cross.

- highlighters or crayons
- three large speech balloons
- copies of reproducible master *What's the Word?*, guide page 31F

Day 5

pages 40–41
Project Disciple

page 42
Chapter 2 Test

- Complete the Project Disciple activities.
- Explain the *Take Home* activity.
- Discuss/send home Sharing Faith with My Family, guide page 31E.
- Complete Chapter 2 Test.
- Work on *Alternative Assessment* activity.

- pencils
- crayons or colored pencils
- copies of Sharing Faith with My Family reproducible master, guide page 31E

For additional ideas, activities, and opportunities: Visit Sadlier's **www.WeBelieveweb.com**

31B

Enrichment Ideas

Chapter Story

Tomás was excited. On Saturday he was going to have a birthday party. He had been looking forward to the party for a long time. This year instead of giving Tomás a big gift, his mom had promised that he could invite his school and neighborhood friends. Eight friends were going to be there.

On Wednesday night Tomás asked his mother, "How many more days until my party?" His mom answered, "Two more days." That seemed like forever to Tomás.

Finally it was Saturday. The time of the party arrived. Tomás answered the door and welcomed each one of his guests. The friends played a few games together.

After the games Tomás and his guests enjoyed cake and ice cream. Then Tomás's mom said, "It's time to open your presents."

Tomás sat on the floor and unwrapped each gift. He received an action figure, some sports cards, and books. Tomás thanked everyone for the gifts.

When the party was over and everyone had left, Tomás's mom asked, "Well, Tomás, did you have a good time?"

"I had a great time! I really liked having all my friends here to play. The party was the best gift of all. Thanks, Mom, for keeping your promise," Tomás said.

▶ *Why do you think Tomás thought that having a party was the best gift?*

FAITH and MEDIA

▶ On Day 3, after reading the *As Catholics* text, you might remind the children that they can learn more about Saint Patrick and the shamrock in other media such as books, videos, and the Internet.

▶ If you decide to use the *What's the Word?* activity (guide page 31F), consider making a video of each group's prayer actions. By taking a digital video, you can create a DVD for each child with this and other material from the year. Or you can embed the video into a presentation to begin a later lesson with a familiar prayer. The children will feel pride and excitement about being featured in a video!

CHAPTER PROJECT: LOVE COLLAGE

Have the children work in small groups to make collages. Provide each group with magazines from which to cut pictures of people demonstrating love or of things that the children associate with love. If the children have ideas that they cannot find in magazines, they may want to draw some of their own pictures to include. Have each group paste the pictures onto a sheet of poster board. Ask the children to talk about a few of the pictures that they selected. Work on this project throughout the week, with the presentations on Day 5.

PROJECT DISCIPLE

Pray
Learn
Celebrate
Share
Choose
Live

Additional Activities

What's *the* Word?

(Use on Day 3.)

Materials needed: copies of reproducible master, guide page 31F

Distribute copies of the Scripture reproducible master. Ask the children to recall that prayer is listening to and talking to God. Explain to the children that we can thank God for all he has done for us with words from the Bible. Divide the children into three groups. Assign each group one of the psalms on the reproducible master. Work individually with each group to read the prayer, commit it to memory, and make up actions. Allow other children to work quietly on another activity. Invite each group to teach the class their psalm and actions.

 Pray Today

Reserve some wall space in your classroom. Distribute a sentence strip to each child. Read aloud the following prompt: *God, you always love me. Your love makes me feel . . . .* Instruct each child to write a descriptive word to complete the sentence. Display the prompt on the wall along with the children's responses. You may want to include your own response.

Celebrate!

Materials needed: heart pattern, craft foam, permanent marker, scissors, hole puncher, yarn

Have children trace a small heart pattern on craft foam three times and cut out the forms. Write *Father* on one heart, *Son* on another heart, and *Holy Spirit* on the last heart. Punch a hole in the top of each heart. Give the children a long piece of yarn and have them string the hearts on it. Tie the ends together to form a necklace. Encourage the children to wear their Blessed Trinity necklaces as a celebration of God's love for us.

Picture This

Materials needed: large cross shape cut from poster board or card board, spray adhesive or glue, glitter, confetti, beads

Point out to the children that when they pray the Sign of the Cross, they are making a cross on themselves. Invite the children to decorate a portion of the cross using glitter, confetti, and/or beads. Prepare the cross in advance by covering it with spray adhesive or glue. Invite several children at a time to decorate a portion of the cross. When finished, display it in the classroom.

Meeting Individual Needs
Children with Attention Deficit Disorder

Help children who have attention deficit disorder (ADD) by varying activities frequently and asking for feedback often throughout the lessons. In order to keep the children's attention directed on the readings, have them underline or highlight certain words or sentences.

We Believe Resources

- Grade 1 *Review & Resource Book*, pages 7–9
- Grade 1 *Family Book*, pages 8–10
- Grade 1 *Assessment Book*, pages 5–6
- Grade 1 CD-ROM *Test Generator and Resource*: Use Chapter 2 Test or customize your own.
- **www.webelieveweb.com**

SHARING FAITH
with My Family

Sharing What I Learned

Look at the pictures below. Use each picture to tell your family what you learned in this chapter.

For All to See and Pray

Pray the Sign of the Cross often with your family.

1 In the name of the Father,

2 and of the Son,

3 and of the Holy

4 Spirit.

5 Amen.

Visit Sadlier's

www.WeBelieveweb.com

 Connect to the Catechism
For adult background and reflection, see paragraphs 422, 423, 234, and 232.

PROJECT DISCIPLE

Name _____

What's *the* Word?

We can thank God for all he has done for us.
We can use words in the Bible.

"All you peoples, clap your hands;
     shout to God with joyful cries."

(Psalm 47:2)

"We thank you, God, we give thanks;
     We call upon your name. . . ."

(Psalm 75:2)

"Know that the LORD is God,
     our maker to whom we belong. . . .
Give thanks to God, bless his name."

(Psalm 100:3, 4)

Name _____

Decorate the letters of the name of Jesus.

We Believe in the Blessed Trinity

✝ We Gather in Prayer

Let us stand to celebrate God's love.
For each action pray together,
"We thank you, God.
We celebrate your love."

Prayer Actions

- Raise your arms in the air.
- Clap your hands.
- Put your hands over your hearts.
- Close your eyes and bow your heads.

PREPARING TO PRAY

The children will pray in word and action to celebrate God's love.

- Practice with the children the words they will pray.

- Show the children each prayer gesture they will use and have the children practice these gestures.

- Draw a heart outline on a sheet of poster board.

- From scrap construction paper, cut confetti-sized pieces. Cut enough pieces to give each child a handful.

The Prayer Space
- Display the heart in the prayer space.

- Place a small table in your prayer space. Cover the table with a cloth. On the table have the Bible opened to the beginning of the Gospel of Luke.

📖 **This Week's Liturgy**
Visit **www.webelieveweb.com** for this week's liturgical readings and other seasonal material.

Lesson Plan

We Gather in Prayer ___ minutes

✝ Pray

- Invite the children to gather in the prayer space. Give each child a handful of confetti.

- Explain: *Today we are going to celebrate God's love.* Then invite the children to throw the confetti in the air.

- Have the children form a circle. Lead them in praying in word and action.

Family Connection Update

Invite the children to share their family discussions about God's creation.

Catechist Goal

• To explain that God sent his own Son, Jesus, to us

Our Faith Response

• To be thankful to God for sending his Son

Lesson Materials

• copies of Reproducible Master 2
• sentence strips
• scissors and glue

Teaching Tip

An Exercise Break

If the children are getting fidgety, have them take an exercise break. Ask the children to stand and stretch out their arms in front of them. Then have them hold their arms at their sides and shake them a few times.

God sent his own Son, Jesus, to us.

WE GATHER

✝ *God, we celebrate your love for us.*

Have you ever waited for something good to happen?
How did you feel while you were waiting?

WE BELIEVE

People waited for God to keep his promise to help us.
God the Father had a plan for keeping his promise.
At a special time he sent his own Son to us.

God sent Jesus to live with us on earth.
God sent an angel to ask Mary to be the Mother of his own Son, Jesus.
Jesus showed us

• how much God loves us
• how to love God
• how to love ourselves
• how to love one another.

32

Lesson Plan

WE GATHER ___ minutes

✝ **Pray** Invite the children to listen carefully as you read aloud the *We Gather* prayer at the top of page 32.

Focus on Life Read aloud the first *We Gather* question. Have the children think quietly about their answers. Then read the second question. Help the children to conclude that we often become excited when we know that something good is about to happen. Share a happy childhood memory about a time in which you were looking forward to something good happening. Share the *Chapter Story* on guide page 31C. Tell the children that in this lesson, they will learn how God showed his love for us and all people.

WE BELIEVE ___ minutes

Learn About Jesus Explain to the children that God had promised people long before Jesus was born to send someone to help them and their children. Invite the children to look at the illustration on pages 32 and 33 as you read aloud the first two We Believe paragraphs.

Think About Promises Ask the children to think about what a promise is. Have volunteers give some examples. Discuss how it is sometimes hard to keep a promise. Stress: *Jesus made a promise to us that he will always keep.* Then read the *We Believe* paragraph at the top of page 33.

Jesus promised to help us, too! He promised to send the Holy Spirit. Jesus promised that the Holy Spirit would always be our Helper.

WE RESPOND

Read each message. Color in the face that shows how each message makes you feel.

- God loves you very much.

- God sent Jesus to us.

- Some people do keep promises.

- Some people do not keep promises.

What messages make you feel happy?

Pray:

God our Father, you kept your promise.
You sent your Son to help us.
Help us to keep the promises we make.

33

ACTIVITY BANK

Catholic Social Teaching
Call to Family, Community, and Participation
Activity Materials: sentence strips, stickers

Tell the children that we can make promises, too. Ask the children to think of things that they can do to help others. Write the suggestions on the board. Examples of these promises are: *I promise to say my prayers each day. I promise not to fight. I promise to be friendly. I promise to do my homework.*

Then give each child a sentence strip on which to write a promise that he or she can make to family and friends. Remind the children to try hard to keep their promises during the week.

During the week, as the children keep their promises, encourage them to tell you about the way that they kept their promise. Then give them a sticker to put on their promise strips.

Quick Check

✔ *What did Jesus teach us?* (how much God loves us and how to love God, ourselves, and one another)

✔ *What promise did Jesus make?* (to send the Holy Spirit to be our Helper)

WE RESPOND ___ minutes

Connect to Life Read the directions for the *We Respond* activity. Help the children read the messages to be sure they understand them. Then have the children complete the activity. Ask: *Which messages make you feel happy? Why?* Have a few volunteers respond.

Distribute copies of Reproducible Master 2 and sentence strips. Explain that they should decorate or color the letters in Jesus' name, cut them out, and glue them in the correct order on sentence strips.

Pray Conclude the lesson by having the children recite the prayer on the bottom of page 33 together.

Plan Ahead for Day 2

Catechist Goal: To emphasize that Jesus is God's greatest gift

Preparation: Have crayons or colored pencils available.

Catechist Goal

- To emphasize that Jesus is God's greatest gift

Our Faith Response

- To affirm that Jesus is God's greatest gift

Teaching Tip

Discussion Time

Sometimes during discussions allow the children to sit in a circle on the floor. Keep most discussion time periods limited to five minutes.

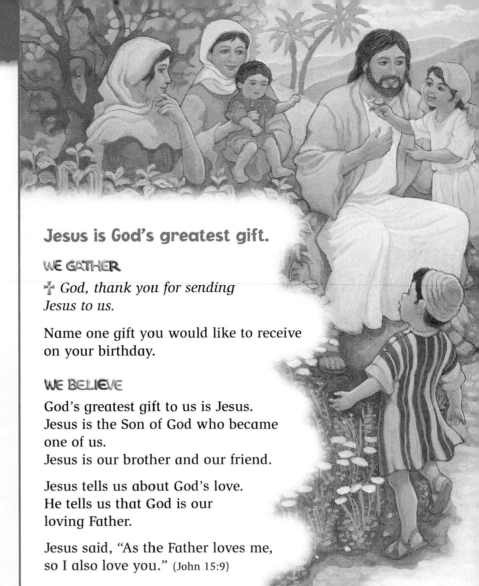

Jesus is God's greatest gift.

WE GATHER

✝ *God, thank you for sending Jesus to us.*

Name one gift you would like to receive on your birthday.

WE BELIEVE

God's greatest gift to us is Jesus. Jesus is the Son of God who became one of us. Jesus is our brother and our friend.

Jesus tells us about God's love. He tells us that God is our loving Father.

Jesus said, "As the Father loves me, so I also love you." (John 15:9)

34

Lesson Plan

WE GATHER ___ minutes

✝ **Pray** Invite the children to stand. Pray aloud the *We Gather* prayer and ask the children to repeat the words.

Focus on Life Ask the children to think of one gift that they would like to receive on their birthday. Provide one minute of quiet time in which the children can think about their responses. Invite volunteers to come to the front of the room, name the gifts, and tell why they would like to receive them. Tell the children that in this lesson, they will learn that God's greatest gift to us is his Son, Jesus.

WE BELIEVE ___ minutes

Read the Text Point to the *We Believe* statement. Read the statement aloud; then have the children repeat it. Read aloud the first two *We Believe* paragraphs. Stress and have the children highlight or underline:

- *Jesus is the Son of God who became one of us.*
- *Jesus is our brother and our friend.*

Then read together Jesus' words at the bottom of page 34.

We always have the gift of Jesus' love. Here is a story about his special love.

📖 Mark 10:13–14

Read Along
One day families came to Jesus with their children. They wanted Jesus to bless the children. Friends of Jesus told these people to go away. But Jesus said, "Let the children come to me." (Mark 10:14)

WE RESPOND

🧍 Why is Jesus God's greatest gift? Add yourself to the picture.

35

ACTIVITY BANK

Multiple Intelligences
Musical
Teach the children to sing the following verses to the tune of "London Bridge."

Jesus is God's greatest gift,
greatest gift, greatest gift.
Jesus is God's greatest gift.
We say, "Thank you."

Jesus shows us God's great love,
God's great love, God's great love.
Jesus shows us God's great love.
We say, "Thank you."

Jesus tells us, "Come to me,"
"come to me, come to me."
Jesus tells us, "Come to me."
We say, "Thank you."

Share a Scripture Story Invite the children to look at the picture of Jesus and the children as you read aloud the Scripture story on page 35. After reading the story, ask: *How do you think the families felt when Jesus wanted the children to come to him?*

Quick Check

✔ *Who is God's greatest gift to us?* (Jesus is God's greatest gift to us.)

✔ *What does Jesus tell us about God?* (God is our loving Father.)

WE RESPOND ____ minutes

Connect to Life Read aloud the *We Respond* ques-

tion. Ask volunteers to share their responses. Help the children to conclude that Jesus is God's greatest gift because he is the Son of God.

Draw and Think Have the children draw themselves walking on the path toward Jesus.

Pray Invite the children to pray the following words: *Jesus, thank you for the gift of your love.*

Plan Ahead for Day 3

Catechist Goal: To introduce that there are Three Persons in One God

Preparation: Make large name cards: *God the Father, God the Son, God the Holy Spirit.*

Catechist Goal

• To introduce that there are Three Persons in One God

Our Faith Response

• To name the Three Persons in One God

 Blessed Trinity

Lesson Materials

• colored pencils or crayons

• three large name cards: God the Father, God the Son, God the Holy Spirit

As Catholics...

Saint Patrick

After you have presented the lesson about the Blessed Trinity, read aloud the *As Catholics* text about Saint Patrick. Draw a shamrock on the board. Point out: *A shamrock is one plant that has three leaves.*

There are Three Persons in One God.

WE GATHER

✝ *Jesus, thank you for showing us God's love.*

Join hands to make a circle. Where is the end of the circle? How can a circle remind us about God's love?

WE BELIEVE

Jesus, the Son of God, taught us about God the Father and God the Holy Spirit.

Jesus taught us that
God the Father is God.
God the Son is God.
God the Holy Spirit is God.
The **Blessed Trinity** is One God in Three Persons.

• God the Father is the First Person of the Blessed Trinity.

• God the Son is the Second Person of the Blessed Trinity.

• God the Holy Spirit is the Third Person of the Blessed Trinity.

God the Father, God the Son, and God the Holy Spirit are joined in love.

Blessed Trinity One God in Three Persons: God the Father, God the Son, and God the Holy Spirit

Lesson Plan

WE GATHER ___ minutes

✝ **Pray** Pray aloud the *We Gather* prayer and ask the children to repeat the words.

Focus on Life Invite the children to join hands to make a circle. Ask the children to look closely at the circle they have formed. Then ask the children the *We Gather* questions on page 36. Help the children to conclude that a circle has no end. Explain: *A circle reminds us of God's love that never ends.*

WE BELIEVE ___ minutes

Learn About the Blessed Trinity Read the first *We Believe* paragraph. Then give a name card to each of three volunteers. Have the child on the left hold up the God the Father card; middle child, God the Son; the child on the right, God the Holy Spirit.

Explain: *These are the names of the Three Persons in One God. We call the Three Persons in One God the Blessed Trinity.* Then read the remaining *We Believe* paragraphs. Have the children use the same colored pencil to underline the names of the Three Persons.

WE RESPOND

Sometimes pictures can help us to understand what we believe about the Blessed Trinity.

✗ Look at the picture of the three circles joined together. Use one crayon to color the circles.

What can this picture help you to remember about the Blessed Trinity?

Pray:

God the Father, God the Son,
God the Holy Spirit,
we believe you are joined in love.

As Catholics...

We honor Saint Patrick. Saint Patrick went to Ireland to teach the people about God. He showed them a shamrock to help them learn about the Blessed Trinity. A shamrock is a plant that has three leaves. It can remind us about the Three Persons in One God. Pray to the Blessed Trinity often.

37

ACTIVITY BANK

Curriculum Connection
Math

Explain to the children that sometimes people use a picture of a triangle to help people understand what we believe about the Blessed Trinity. Draw an equilateral triangle on the board. Point to the shape and explain: *Each side is the same length. There is one triangle that has three equal sides.* Then label each side as shown. Have the children read the names of the Three Persons of the Blessed Trinity.

Quick Check

✔ *Who are the Three Persons of the Blessed Trinity?* (God the Father, God the Son, and God the Holy Spirit)

✔ *How are the Three Persons joined together?* (The Three Persons are joined in love.)

WE RESPOND ___ minutes

Connect to Life Ask the children to name times when it was easier to understand something using pictures instead of words. Use an example of a map or a photograph. Read the *We Respond* section and ask the children to look at the three circles joined together. Have the children color the circles with a crayon or colored pencil.

Read the *We Respond* question. Explain: *The three circles joined together can help us remember that the Three Persons of the Blessed Trinity are joined in love.*

Pray Invite the children to gather in the prayer space. Pray the *We Respond* prayer and have the children repeat the words.

Plan Ahead for Day 4

Catechist Goal: To teach the Sign of the Cross

Preparation: Make copies of *What's the Word?*, guide page 31F.

Catechist Goal

• To teach the Sign of the Cross

Our Faith Response

• To recognize the Sign of the Cross as a prayer to the Blessed Trinity

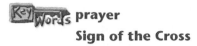 **prayer**

Sign of the Cross

Lesson Materials

• three large speech balloons

• copies of reproducible master *What's the Word?*, guide page 31F

Teaching Tip

Praying Together Respectfully

Remind the children that we show our love for God when we pray. Explain: *When we pray together, we should be respectful. We think about what we are saying. We do not rush through the words and actions.*

The Sign of the Cross is a prayer to the Blessed Trinity.

WE GATHER

✝ *God the Father, God the Son, and God the Holy Spirit, we praise you.*

What are these children doing? What do you think they are thinking or saying?

WE BELIEVE

When we pray, we show our love for God.
Prayer is listening to and talking to God.

Sometimes when we pray, we use special words from the Bible. Sometimes we use our own words. Sometimes we say prayers written by other people.

For some prayers we use actions as we pray.
The **Sign of the Cross** is a prayer to the Blessed Trinity:

In the name of the Father,
and of the Son,
and of the Holy Spirit.
Amen.

38

Lesson Plan

WE GATHER ___ minutes

✝ **Pray** Pray together the *We Gather* prayer.

Focus on Life Read the *We Gather* questions. Display the three speech balloons you have made or draw three balloons on the board. Ask everyone to look at the photos on page 38. Have volunteers tell you what they think each child is saying. Write the words in one of the speech balloons. Help the children to conclude that each child is praying.

WE BELIEVE ___ minutes

Read About Prayer Read aloud the first two *We Believe* paragraphs. Stress: *We can pray*

• *in word and action*

• *by using our own words*

• *by using words written by other people.*

We begin our prayers by praying these words.

1. In the name of the Father,

2. and of the Son,

Key Words

prayer listening to and talking to God

Sign of the Cross a prayer to the Blessed Trinity

3. and of the Holy

4. Spirit.

5. Amen.

WE RESPOND

Let us stand now and pray the Sign of the Cross.
The Sign of the Cross always reminds us that we believe in the Blessed Trinity.

39

ACTIVITY BANK

Family and Community
Teaching Younger Children

When the children have learned to pray the Sign of the Cross, have them pretend they are teaching the words and gestures to younger children. Encourage them to teach the prayer to a younger brother or sister (or family friend). Explain that although they are still learning new things about God and their Catholic faith, they can begin to share with others what they already know.

Multiple Intelligences
Spatial
Activity Materials: drawing paper, crayons or colored pencils

Have the children draw pictures to answer the following two questions.

• *What is your favorite time to pray: in the day or at night?*

• *Where is your favorite place to pray?*

Scripture
Linguistic, Bodily-Kinesthetic

For a Scripture activity, see *What's the Word?*, guide page 31F.

Learn the Prayer Ask the children to look at the five photographs of the child praying the Sign of the Cross. As they study each one, read the prayer words. Remind the children: *We always use our right hand when we pray the Sign of the Cross.* Then have the children stand and practice praying the Sign of the Cross.

Quick Check

✔ *What do we call listening to and talking to God?* (Prayer is listening to and talking to God.)

✔ *What is the name of the prayer to the Blessed Trinity with which we begin our prayers?* (The Sign of the Cross is the prayer to the Blessed Trinity.)

WE RESPOND ___ minutes

Connect to Life Ask the children to think of different times that they pray the Sign of the Cross. (Responses may include morning prayers, before and after meal prayers, and bedtime prayers, as well as in church.) Remind them: *Each time we pray the Sign of the Cross, we remember the Blessed Trinity.*

Pray Invite the children to gather in the prayer space. Pray together the Sign of the Cross.

Plan Ahead for Day 5

Catechist Goal: To review chapter ideas and their relationship to our faith life

Preparation: Make copies of *Sharing Faith with My Family*, guide page 31E.

Catechist Goal

• To review the chapter ideas that are key to growing as disciples of Jesus Christ

Our Faith Response

• To decide on ways to grow as disciples by living out what we have learned

Show What you Know

Invite the children to use a pencil to trace the *Key Words*. Encourage them to think about the letter sounds as they work. When every child has finished, ask volunteers to read the words and review the definitions.

Picture This

Read the question aloud. Invite the children to answer. Encourage children to add detail to their drawings.

Celebrate!

Begin the activity by reviewing the Sign of the Cross. Read aloud the first sentence of the activity instructions. Help the children to match the pictures to the appropriate words. Encourage the children to complete the activity alone or with a partner. When all have finished, pray the prayer together again.

Fast Facts

Ask a volunteer to read aloud the Fast Facts. Encourage the children to notice the Sign of the Cross at the beginning of Mass and to pray along!

Take Home

Remind the children that prayer is talking and listening to God and that they can pray alone or with others, including their family members. Invite the children to repeat the activity prayer after you. Encourage them to share the prayer with their families.

Discuss and send home copies of *Sharing Faith with My Family*, guide page 31E.

40 and **41**

Grade 1 Chapter 2

PROJECT

Show What you Know

Trace the Key Words. Talk about each one.

Blessed Trinity
prayer
Sign of the Cross

Picture This

Who is God's greatest gift? Draw him here.

Children should draw Jesus as a baby, child, or adult.

40   www.webelieveweb.com

DISCIPLE

Celebrate!

Draw a line to match the pictures to the words. Then, pray the Sign of the Cross.

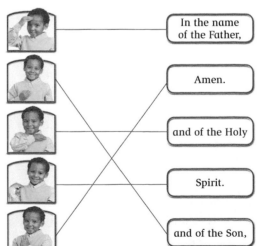

In the name of the Father,

Amen.

and of the Holy

Spirit.

and of the Son,

Fast Facts

Catholics begin the Mass by making the Sign of the Cross. This shows they believe in the Blessed Trinity.

Take Home

Prayer is listening to and talking to God. You can pray as a family. Together, say this prayer.

Thank you, God, for the gift of your Son, Jesus.

41

CHAPTER TEST

Circle the correct answer.

1. Is the Holy Spirit our Helper?

   (Yes)   **No**

2. Is prayer only talking to God?

   Yes   **(No)**

3. Did God keep his promise by sending his own Son, Jesus, to us?

   (Yes)   **No**

4. Is there only one God?

   (Yes)   **No**

5. Are we praying only to God the Father when we pray the Sign of the Cross?

   Yes   **(No)**

 Who are the Three Persons of the Blessed Trinity? God the Father, God the Son, and God the Holy Spirit

42

CHAPTER TEST

Read each test item aloud and allow time for the children to mark an answer. Decide whether the *Talk About It* activity will be a small group or whole class discussion. After you have finished, check the answers. Clarify any misconceptions.

Alternative Assessment

You may want the students to complete the following alternative-assessment activity.

Make your own copy of the three joined circles on page 37. Add words to tell what we believe about the Blessed Trinity.

Additional Testing

• Chapter 2 Test in *Assessment Book*, pages 5–6

• CD-ROM *Test Generator and Resource*: Use Chapter 2 Test or customize your own.

Review

Key Words

Review the definitions as they are presented in the chapter's *Key Word* boxes:

• Blessed Trinity (page 36)
• prayer (page 39)
• Sign of the Cross (page 39).

We Believe Statements

Review the four statements.

• God sent his own Son, Jesus, to us.
• Jesus is God's greatest gift.
• There are Three Persons in One God.
• The Sign of the Cross is a prayer to the Blessed Trinity.

To use the Chapter 2 Study Guide, visit

www.webelieveweb.com

Chapter 3 — Jesus Grew Up in a Family

Overview

In Chapter 2 the children learned about the Three Persons of the Blessed Trinity. In this chapter the children will learn how Jesus grew up as part of a family.

Doctrinal Content	For Adult Reading and Reflection *Catechism of the Catholic Church*	
The children will learn:		Paragraph
• God chose Mary to be the Mother of his Son.		484
• Jesus was born in Bethlehem.		525
• Jesus lived in Nazareth with Mary and Joseph.		532
• The Holy Family obeyed God the Father and prayed to him.		531

Key Words

Christmas (p. 47)
Holy Family (p. 48)

Catechist Background

What childhood memories do you have of experiencing God's presence in your family?

Go to **www.webelieveweb.com**, Catechist/Teacher, We Believe Correlations for this chapter's correlation to:
• Six Tasks of Catechesis
• Catholic Social Teaching.

Artists throughout the centuries have been fascinated by the Annunciation. Their depictions of the angel Gabriel's appearance to the Virgin Mary have helped us to appreciate her willing cooperation with God's plan. She had been chosen by God to give birth to his only Son. Mary said yes to God's request. She gave birth to Jesus in Bethlehem, the city of David, because her husband Joseph belonged to the messianic lineage of King David.

After fleeing to Egypt because of a threat from King Herod, Mary and Joseph returned and settled in Nazareth. Within this loving Jewish family, Jesus "grew and became strong, filled with wisdom" (Luke 2:40). The Holy Family lived as devout Jews, praying daily and worshiping in the local synagogue as well as in the Temple in Jerusalem.

The Holy Family prayed to God and showed love for God and one another. They obeyed the laws of their country. We can act in the same way within our own families. Many of the children may live in different types of families. Your challenge as a catechist is to make room for all their families when you talk of loving God and one another within families.

How can you promote the virtues of the Holy Family within all families?

43A

Lesson Planning Guide

Lesson Focus	Presentation	Materials

Day 1

page 43
 **We Gather in Prayer**

pages 44–45
God chose Mary to be the Mother of his Son.

📖 *Luke 1:26–35, 37*

- Pray for families.
- 🏃 Do the **We Gather** picture study.
- Present the **We Believe** text about Mary being chosen by God.
- Discuss the **We Respond** question.

For the prayer space: small table, table cloth, figures of Jesus, Mary, and Joseph

- colored pencils
- copies of reproducible master *What's the Word?*, guide page 43F

Day 2

pages 46–47
Jesus was born in Bethlehem.

📖 *Luke 2:1–7*

- Discuss the **We Gather** questions.
- Present the **We Believe** text and the Scripture story about the birth of Jesus.
- Share responses to the **We Respond** question.
- Read and discuss the *As Catholics* text.

- state map that shows your town or city

Day 3

pages 48–49
Jesus lived in Nazareth with Mary and Joseph.

- Follow the **We Gather** directives and discuss.
- Read and discuss the **We Believe** text about the Holy Family.
- Discuss the **We Respond** questions.
- 🏃 Choose ways to help in a family.
- Pray quietly.

- crayons or colored pencils
- chart paper and marker
- globe or world map

Day 4

pages 50–51
The Holy Family obeyed God the Father and prayed to him.

- 🏃 Do the **We Gather** activity.
- Present the **We Believe** text about the Holy Family's obedience to God.
- Discuss the **We Respond** question.
- Pray a prayer before meals.

- crayons or colored pencils
- copies of Reproducible Master 3, guide page 43G
- snack food for "A Biblical Snack" (See *Teaching Tip,* page 50.)

Day 5

pages 52–53
Project Disciple

page 54
Chapter 3 Test

- Complete the **Project Disciple** activities.
- Explain the *Take Home* activity.
- Discuss/send home **Sharing Faith with My Family**, guide page 43E.
- Complete **Chapter 3 Test**.
- Work on *Alternative Assessment* activity.

- pencils
- crayons or colored pencils
- copies of **Sharing Faith with My Family** reproducible master, guide page 43E

For additional ideas, activities, and opportunities: Visit Sadlier's  www.WeBelieveweb.com

43B

Chapter Story

When Jamie arrived home from school last week, her mom said, "Jamie, I have great news. Your dad's boss wants him to work in another city for the next few months. And we are going to go with him."

Jamie did not know what to say so she went to her room. Jamie thought, "If we go to live in another city, I won't be able to visit Aunt Olivia." Jamie's aunt Olivia was her dad's sister. She and Jamie did many fun things together.

Then Jamie thought, "What about soccer?" Soccer was her favorite sport, and her dad was going to be the coach of her team. Jamie decided that she really did not want to live in another place, even for a few months.

Then Jamie heard her dad calling her. "I guess you've heard the news, Jamie," Dad said.

"I heard, Dad," Jamie answered. "Do they play soccer where we are going to live?" she asked.

"Of course they do," Dad said. "We'll be living near a park. And I will still be able to help coach." Then Jamie asked, "What about Aunt Olivia? Can she come with us?"

Dad answered, "Your aunt has to stay here because of her job. But I think she can come to visit us."

Jamie thought about what her dad said. She knew her mom and dad loved her. She trusted them. She knew that they would do what was best for the family. She could join a soccer team and meet new friends. And Aunt Olivia would visit. Jamie hugged her mom and dad. She said, "I guess going to live in another city is not so bad, just for the next few months. I guess we better start packing."

▶ *Imagine you are Jamie. What would you have thought when you first heard the news? What would help change your mind?*

FAITH and MEDIA

▶ If you have the children do the "YES" cheer activity (Day 1 *Activity Bank*), record the children cheering. Play the audio or video occasionally throughout the year to remind the children that we try to do what God wants everyday.

▶ If you choose to do the newspaper headline activity (Day 2 *Activity Bank*), you might remind the children that newspapers—like books, videos, messengers, and the Internet—are examples of media. Newspapers are yet another way to tell stories and send messages. Together, brainstorm ways that people send and receive messages today.

CHAPTER PROJECT: HOLY FAMILY FIGURES

Have the children work in groups of three. Provide construction paper, glue, buttons, fabric, yarn and empty paper rolls (three rolls per group). Have the children use the materials to make figures of Mary, Joseph, and Jesus when he was six years old.

After the children have made the figures, have the groups use the figures to act out the Holy Family working or having fun together. Display the figures in your prayer space.

PROJECT DISCIPLE

Pray
Learn
Celebrate
Share
Choose
Live

Additional Activities

Fast Facts

Materials needed: 6-inch by 6-inch square of white felt for each child, fabric markers

Explain that in many families, a quilt is a special treasure. Explain that it is made up of many shapes that are sewn together to make one whole quilt. Share pictures of quilts as examples. Distribute a felt square to each child and help each write his or her family name along the bottom. Encourage the children to draw a family portrait in their squares. Assemble the finished squares into a quilt using fabric tape or thread. Display the quilt as you discuss the similarities and differences among their squares. Talk about their pictures coming together in one special quilt.

What's *the* Word?

(Use on Day 1.)

Materials needed: copies of reproducible master, guide page 43F

Explain to the children that they will be doing an activity to remember the story of the angel coming to Mary. Distribute the Scripture reproducible master. Choose three volunteers to read the parts of Reader 1, Reader 2, and Angel. Ask the other children to follow along as the story is read.

Celebrate!

Compile pictures of items that are associated with Christmas, a birthday celebration, or both. Suggestions include: an unlit candle, a cupcake, a balloon, an ornament, a wrapped gift, a star, a family, etc. Give an item to each child. Then do a class sorting activity. Establish and label a place for each category: *Christmas*, *Birthday*, or *Both*. Ask each child to take turns deciding where to place his or her item. Discuss as a class how celebrating Christmas and a birthday are alike and different.

Make *it* Happen

Materials needed: colored pencils

Make a class picture book. Make copies of a blank page with the title: *A picture of a way _____'s family is like the Holy Family.* Distribute a copy to the children and help them write their first names on the line. Then ask the children to illustrate a way their family is like the Holy Family. Bind the book and add it to the classroom library for the children to enjoy.

Meeting Individual Needs
Children with Tactile-Motor Needs

Have the children who have tactile-motor needs use large crayons for drawing. Assign peer helpers to assist the children for writing and art activities.

We Believe Resources

- Grade 1 *Review & Resource Book*, pages 10–12
- Grade 1 *Family Book*, pages 11–13
- Grade 1 *Assessment Book*, pages 7–8
- Grade 1 CD-ROM *Test Generator and Resource*: Use Chapter 3 Test or customize your own.
- **www.webelieveweb.com**

SHARING FAITH
with My Family

Sharing What I Learned

Look at the pictures below. Use each picture to tell your family what you learned in this chapter.

Family Travels

Many times the Holy Family traveled together.
Put this prayer card in a convenient place.
Say the prayer together when you begin your trips.

Holy Family, be with us as we travel.
We believe that:

- all God's ways are beautiful.

- all his paths lead us to peace and happiness.

Visit Sadlier's

www.WeBelieveweb.com

Connect to the Catechism
For adult background and reflection, see paragraphs 484, 525, 531, and 532.

PROJECT DISCIPLE

Name _____

What's *the* Word?

Reader 1: God loved Mary very much. God chose Mary to be the Mother of his Son.

Reader 2: One day God sent an angel to tell Mary the Good News.

Angel: "The Lord is with you." (Luke 1:28)

Reader 1: Mary was wondering about what the angel said.

Angel: "Do not be afraid, Mary." (Luke 1:30)

Reader 2: The angel told Mary that she was going to have a son. He told Mary that she was to name the child Jesus.

Angel: "The child to be born will be called holy, the Son of God." (Luke 1:35)

Reader 1: Mary said that she would do as God asked.

Make a prayer card. Add your favorite food.
Share the prayer with your family.

Grace Before Meals

Bless us, O Lord,
and these your gifts
which we are about to
receive from your goodness.
Through Christ our Lord.
Amen.

✝ We Gather in Prayer

Leader: Let us stand and pray together. For our families, that we may all keep growing in God's love, we pray,

All: God, please help us to share your love.

Leader: For families who are going to welcome new babies soon, we pray,

All: God, please help them to grow in your love.

Leader: For families who do not have everything they need to live, we pray,

All: God, please help us to take care of them.

43

PREPARING TO PRAY

The children ask God to help all families grow in his love.

• Prepare the children to pray the responses by reading them aloud and have the children repeat the words.

• If time permits, have each child draw a picture of her or his family.

The Prayer Space

• Place a small table in your prayer space and cover it with a cloth. On the table place the figures of Jesus, Mary, and Joseph from a Christmas crèche.

📖 **This Week's Liturgy**
Visit **www.webelieveweb.com** for this week's liturgical readings and other seasonal material.

Lesson Plan

We Gather in Prayer ___ minutes

✝ Pray

• Ask the children to open their books to page 43 and look at the photograph. If the children have drawn pictures of their families, explain that you would like them to hold their pictures this way as they walk to the prayer space. Then have them place their pictures on the prayer table.

• Pray the Sign of the Cross and begin to read the prayer. Read all the children's responses and have them repeat the words.

Family Connection Update

Invite the children to share their family prayer experiences.

Catechist Goal

• To recall that God chose Mary to be the Mother of his Son

Our Faith Response

• To believe in God's Word as Mary did

Lesson Materials

• colored pencils

• copies of reproducible master *What's the Word?*, guide page 43F

Teaching Tip

In the Time of Jesus

Children of this age do not have a developed sense of the past. While presenting this chapter, help the children compare and contrast daily life in the time of Jesus and the present time. In each illustration point out the dress, means of travel, and things in the market and in the home of the Holy Family.

God chose Mary to be the Mother of his Son.

WE GATHER

✝ *God, we need your love and your care.*

Look at each picture.
If it shows people today, circle NOW.
If it shows people in the time of Jesus, circle THEN.

NOW

(THEN)

(NOW)

THEN

44

Lesson Plan

WE GATHER ____ minutes

✝ **Pray** Pray the Sign of the Cross and the *We Gather* prayer.

Focus on Life Ask the children to look at the pictures on page 44. Point to each picture and ask the children to describe what is happening. Remind the children that families in the time of Jesus may have looked or dressed differently, but they acted in ways that showed love and care just as our families do. Share the *Chapter Story* on guide page 43C.

WE BELIEVE ____ minutes

Read Scripture Have the children listen as you read aloud the Scripture story. Stress the following points:

• *The angel told Mary that she was going to be the Mother of God's only Son.*

• *God wanted Mary to name the baby Jesus.*

• *Mary is the mother of Jesus. She did what God wanted her to do.*

Act Out the Event Remind the children that the angel was God's messenger who brought news to Mary. Divide the class into pairs. Have the children act out the meeting between the angel and Mary. Tell them to make sure to express Mary's surprise at seeing the angel and her happiness at being chosen to be the mother of Jesus.

WE BELIEVE

God loved Mary very much.
Mary always did what God wanted.

📖 Luke 1:26–35, 38

Read Along

One day God sent an angel to a young girl named Mary. The angel told her not to be afraid. The angel told her that she was going to have a son. Mary was also told to name the child Jesus.

The angel said to Mary, "Therefore the child to be born will be called holy, the Son of God." (Luke 1:35)

Mary told the angel that she would do what God wanted.

Mary is the Mother of God's only Son, Jesus.
Jesus loves his mother.
He wants us to love her, too.

WE RESPOND

Mary did what God asked of her.
We can, too.
What is one thing God asks you to do today?

Ask Mary for help. Pray together:
Holy Mary, Mother of God, pray for us.

45

ACTIVITY BANK

Multiple Intelligences
Bodily-Kinesthetic

Invite the children to do a cheer about doing what God wants. Have the children make up actions to do while cheering the following words. You may want to ask a few children to lead the cheer.

What did Mary say to God? **YES!**
Give me a Y—Y!
Give me an E—E!
Give me an S—S!
What did Mary say to God? **YES!**
Mary said YES to God!

What should we say to God each day? **YES!**
Give me a Y—Y!
Give me an E—E!
Give me an S—S!
What should we say to God? YES
We should say YES to God each day!

Scripture
Interpersonal, Linguistic

For a Scripture activity, see *What's the Word?*, guide page 43F.

Quick Check

✔ *What did God ask Mary to do?* (God asked Mary to be the Mother of his only Son, Jesus.)

✔ *What did Mary tell the angel?* (Mary said she would do what God wanted.)

WE RESPOND ___ minutes

Connect to Life Invite the children to identify some things God asks us to do every day. (Obey our parents; treat others kindly; pray; do our best in school.)

Then have the children consider how they would answer the *We Respond* question.

Pray Invite the children to pray the *We Respond* prayer.

Plan Ahead for Day 2

Catechist Goal: To tell the story of Jesus' birth

Preparation: Have a map of your state available.

45

Catechist Goal

• To tell the story of Jesus' birth

Our Faith Response

• To share the story of Jesus' birth with family and friends

 **Christmas**

Lesson Materials

• state map that shows your town or city

As Catholics...

Las Posadas

After you have presented the lesson, read the *As Catholics* text aloud. Direct attention to the picture on page 47. Explain that this is a *Las Posadas* procession.

Jesus was born in Bethlehem.

WE GATHER

✝ *God our Father, thank you for Jesus, your Son.*

Where do you live?
Have you lived in other places?

WE BELIEVE

Mary married a man named Joseph. They lived in the town of Nazareth. Mary was going to have a baby. Mary and Joseph were waiting for Jesus to be born.

 Luke 2:1–7

Read Along

During that time a new rule was made. All men had to go back to the town of their father's family. They had to sign a list and be counted.

Joseph was from the town of Bethlehem. So he and Mary had to go there.

When Mary and Joseph got to Bethlehem, it was very crowded. They looked for a place to stay. There was no room for them anywhere. At last, they found a place where animals were kept. They rested there. Later that night, Mary had a baby boy.

"She wrapped him in swaddling clothes and laid him in a manger, because there was no room for them in the inn." (Luke 2:7)

46

Lesson Plan

WE GATHER ___ minutes

✝ **Pray** Pray together the Sign of the Cross and the *We Gather* prayer.

Focus on Life Read the *We Gather* questions. On a state map point to the place where you live. Tell the children that some people live in cities and others live in small towns, or suburbs. Some people live on farms or ranches far away from towns or cities. Help the children describe the place where they now live. Ask volunteers to tell about other places where they have traveled to or lived. Ask: *How did you travel there?*

WE BELIEVE ___ minutes

Read the Text Read aloud the *We Believe* statement and the first *We Believe* paragraph. Explain: *Nazareth was a small town, which was far away from the city of Bethlehem. Mary and Joseph had to go to Bethlehem before Jesus was born. They had to travel by walking or riding on a donkey.*

Share a Scripture Story Ask the children to look at the illustration on page 46 as you read the story. When you are finished reading, ask: *How do you think Mary and Joseph felt when Jesus was born?*

God the Father loved us so much. He sent his Son into the world. At **Christmas** we celebrate the birth of Jesus.
One way we celebrate is by sharing the story of what happened when Jesus was born.

WE RESPOND

What would you tell your family and friends about the birth of Jesus?

Christmas the time when we celebrate the birth of Jesus

As Catholics...

Each year during the nine days before Christmas, Catholics in Mexico and other countries act out the story of Mary and Joseph on their way to Bethlehem. People take part in this outdoor play called *Las Posadas*. In English these words mean "The Inns." The actors who play Mary and Joseph go from house to house. But no one will let them in until the last day. Then the person playing the innkeeper lets them in. Then the rest of the people enter and celebrate the birth of Jesus.

How do you celebrate the birth of Jesus?

Children asking for 'posada' (La procesion)/© 2009 Banco de Mexico Diego Rivera Frida Kahlo Museums Trust, Mexico, D.F./Artists Rights Society (ARS)

47

ACTIVITY BANK

Scripture
The Christmas Story
To help the children visualize the Christmas story, have them dramatize it. Designate a certain corner of the room as Nazareth where Mary and Joseph began their journey and another point as Bethlehem where Jesus was born. Select children to portray Joseph, Mary, the innkeeper, and animals in the manger. Act as narrator for the play and have the children dramatize the action.

Curriculum Connection
Language Arts
Activity Materials: used front pages of newspapers, drawing paper, markers
With the children make up front-page headlines announcing the birth of Jesus. Print the headlines on drawing paper. Glue or tape them over the lead headline on the newspaper sheet. For every headline that you write, ask artists to draw a picture that you can also put on the newspaper.

Talk About Christmas Read aloud the *We Believe* text on page 47. Explain that we share the story of Jesus' birth by singing carols, by acting in plays, and by drawing pictures.

Quick Check
✔ *What do we celebrate on Christmas?* (We celebrate the birth of Jesus Christ on Christmas.)

✔ *Where was Jesus born?* (Jesus was born in Bethlehem.)

WE RESPOND ___ minutes
Connect to Life Invite the children to think about the way they would answer the *We Respond* question. Then ask for volunteers to share their answers.

Pray Gather in the prayer space. Pray together: *God our Father, thank you for Jesus, your Son.*

Plan Ahead for Day 3
Catechist Goal: To present that Jesus lived in Nazareth with Mary and Joseph

Preparation: Have a globe or world map available.

Catechist Goal

• To present that Jesus lived in Nazareth with Mary and Joseph

Our Faith Response

• To look to the Holy Family as an example of family life

 **Holy Family**

Lesson Materials

• chart paper and marker
• globe or world map
• crayons or colored pencils

Teaching Tip

Working in Pairs

For some discussions have the children share responses with partners. Sharing with one person may be more comfortable for the children who are shy. Try to pair children whose personalities or talents complement each other.

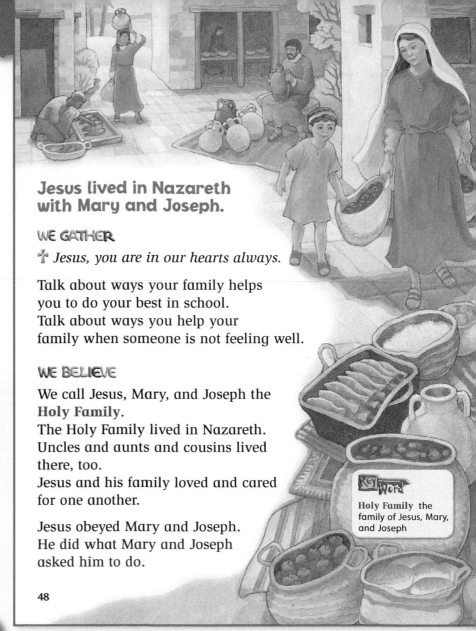

Jesus lived in Nazareth with Mary and Joseph.

WE GATHER

✝ *Jesus, you are in our hearts always.*

Talk about ways your family helps you to do your best in school.
Talk about ways you help your family when someone is not feeling well.

WE BELIEVE

We call Jesus, Mary, and Joseph the **Holy Family**.
The Holy Family lived in Nazareth.
Uncles and aunts and cousins lived there, too.
Jesus and his family loved and cared for one another.

Jesus obeyed Mary and Joseph.
He did what Mary and Joseph asked him to do.

Holy Family the family of Jesus, Mary, and Joseph

48

Lesson Plan

WE GATHER ____ minutes

✝ **Pray** Pray together the Sign of the Cross and the *We Gather* prayer.

Focus on Life Assign sets of partners. Read the first *We Gather* discussion directive. Ask the partners to discuss this point. Repeat this process for the second directive.

WE BELIEVE ____ minutes

Preview On a globe or world map, point to the town of Nazareth in the northern part of Israel. Read the *We Believe* statement. Explain: *Nazareth is a town in the country of Israel.*

Story Board Ask for a volunteer to read the first two *We Believe* paragraphs. Then invite the children to look at the pictures on these pages. Write the title "The Holy Family" on a large sheet of chart paper. Ask the children to think about ways that Jesus, Mary, and Joseph possibly worked and had fun together. Record the children's responses on the chart paper to make a story board about the Holy Family. Use the chart to review important concepts with the children. Stress the following points.

• *When Jesus was a child, he lived in Nazareth with Mary and Joseph.*

• *Jesus, Mary, and Joseph were a happy family who loved each other.*

• *Jesus obeyed his parents because he loved them very much.*

WE RESPOND

Think about ways Jesus, Mary, and Joseph helped one another. What are ways you will help your family?

🌑 Read the following sentences. Color the heart only if it is next to a way you can help your family.

❤ Take turns choosing TV programs.

🤍 Make fun of people.

❤ Play fair.

❤ Obey my parents or those who care for me.

🤍 Be mean to my brothers, sisters, or friends.

Pray quietly.

Jesus, help me to be like you. I want to help my family, too.

49

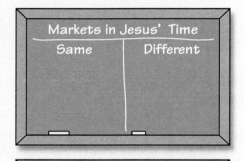

ACTIVITY BANK

Curriculum Connection

Social Studies

Direct attention to the illustration of the market on page 48 and the workshop on page 49. Help the children compare markets and workshops of Jesus' day with those of today. Draw a chart on the board for each place and list the children's responses.

Markets in Jesus' Time	
Same	Different

Workshops in Jesus' Time	
Same	Different

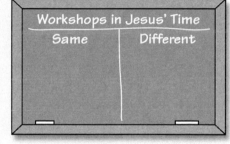

Quick Check

✔ *Who belonged to the Holy Family?* (Jesus, Mary, and Joseph belonged to the Holy Family.)

✔ *Where did the Holy Family live?* (The Holy Family lived in Nazareth.)

WE RESPOND _____ minutes

Connect to Life Have the children look at the pictures on these pages. Ask: *How are Jesus, Mary, and Joseph helping each other?* After a brief discussion, help the children with the activity. Read each sentence and then ask: *Should you color the heart for this sentence? Why or why not?*

Pray Invite the children to gather in the prayer space. Pray together the *We Respond* prayer. These words may be sung to the first two lines of "Twinkle, Twinkle, Little Star." Encourage the children to pray this prayer each day.

Plan Ahead for Day 4

Catechist Goal: To describe how the Holy Family obeyed God and prayed to him

Preparation: Make copies of Reproducible Master 3, guide page 43G.

49

Catechist Goal

• To describe how the Holy Family obeyed God and prayed to him

Our Faith Response

• To obey God and pray to him as the Holy Family did

Lesson Materials

• copies of Reproducible Master 3

• crayons or colored pencils

Teaching Tip

A Biblical Snack

Explain to the children: *People in Jesus' time ate some of the same foods as we do today. They ate bread, cheese, nuts, raisins, olives, and grapes.* After presenting the lesson, invite the children to share "a biblical snack." Before eating, pray the prayer before meals on page 51.

The Holy Family obeyed God the Father and prayed to him.

WE GATHER

✝ *Jesus, Mary, and Joseph, please help our families to love God.*

Imagine that the Holy Family is coming to visit. Draw a picture to show your family getting ready.

WE BELIEVE

Jesus, Mary, and Joseph believed
in the one, true God.
They loved God very much.
They obeyed God's laws.
They helped each other at home.
They helped other people.
They obeyed the laws of their country.

50

Lesson Plan

WE GATHER ___ minutes

✝ **Pray** Ask the children to quiet themselves for prayer. Then pray the Sign of the Cross and the *We Gather* prayer.

Focus on Life Invite the children to do the *We Gather* drawing activity. To help them get started, ask the following questions:

• *What foods would you make?*

• *How would you decorate?*

• *Who else would you invite?*

Invite them to share their feelings about this imagined visit. Tell the children that in this lesson they will learn more about the Holy Family.

WE BELIEVE ___ minutes

Act It Out Have volunteers take turns introducing the members of the Holy Family to the group.

The Holy Family and Us Read aloud the *We Believe* statement. Then tell the children that after you read each *We Believe* sentence on page 50, you want them to point to themselves and say: *And we do, too.*

Then read the paragraph on page 51. Ask the children: *When does your family join other families to pray?* Help them to conclude that we do this at Mass on Sundays.

The Holy Family prayed to God.
They prayed every morning and
every night.
They joined other Jewish families
for prayer each week.
They listened to stories about
God and his people.

WE RESPOND

When does your family pray together?
Share this prayer at your family meals.

Bless us, O Lord,
and these your gifts
which we are about to
receive from your goodness.
Through Christ our Lord.
Amen.

51

ACTIVITY BANK

Multiple Intelligences
Musical

Teach the children the following
words to sing to the tune of "Here
We Go 'Round the Mulberry Bush."

The Holy Family loved God very
 much,
loved God very much,
loved God very much.
The Holy Family loved God very
 much.
They prayed to him each day.

Ask the children to make up their
own verses. Encourage the children to
share the song with their families.

Quick Check

✔ *In whom did Jesus, Mary, and Joseph believe?* (They
believed in the one, true God.)

✔ *How did the Holy Family show their love for God?*
(They obeyed him; they prayed; they cared for one
another.)

WE RESPOND   ___ minutes

Connect to Life Read the *We Respond* question and
ask the children to think quietly about their answers.
Suggest to the children that they can pray before meals

with their families. Distribute copies of Reproducible
Master 3. Help the children make the prayer card.
Encourage them to put their prayer cards on the table
where they share their family meals.

Pray Remind the children that we receive all good
things, including food, from God. Pray together the
prayer before meals.

Plan Ahead for Day 5

Catechist Goal: To review chapter ideas and
their relationship to our faith life

Preparation: Make copies of *Sharing Faith
with My Family*, guide page 43E.

Catechist Goal

• To review the chapter ideas that are key to growing as disciples of Jesus Christ

Our Faith Response

• To decide on ways to grow as disciples by living out what we have learned

Show What *you* Know

Remind the children that some letters are short and some are tall. Review the chapter's *Key Words*. Ask the children to write the words into the word shapes. Help children who need assistance. Then discuss the definitions.

Picture This

Ask children to recall what they learned about Jesus. Point out the first picture as you read the line below it. Note the empty frame and read the line below it. Finally, read the third line as you point out the third picture. Ask the children: *How can you fill in this picture story?* Conclude that the children will draw a picture in the second box.

Celebrate!

Explain that this activity is a chart. Read the instruction line and recreate the chart on the board. Provide examples before the children begin.

Reality Check

Read the instruction line. Invite the children to check one, some, or all of the ways and to write an additional way beside the final box. Encourage them to remember these ways during the week.

Take Home

Briefly discuss what the children learned about the Holy Family. Ask them to share this information with their families.

Discuss and send home copies of *Sharing Faith with My Family,* guide page 43E.

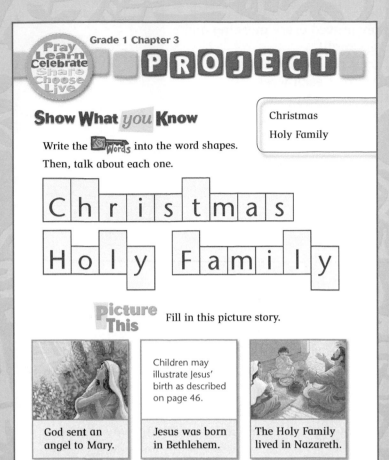

Pray Learn Celebrate Share Choose Live

Grade 1 Chapter 3

PROJECT

Christmas
Holy Family

Show What *you* Know

Write the Key Words into the word shapes. Then, talk about each one.

Christmas

Holy Family

Picture This   Fill in this picture story.

| God sent an angel to Mary. | Children may illustrate Jesus' birth as described on page 46.

Jesus was born in Bethlehem. | The Holy Family lived in Nazareth. |

52   www.webelieveweb.com

DISCIPLE

Pray Learn Celebrate Share Choose Live

Celebrate!

Complete the chart. Use words or pictures.

What are some ways you celebrate your birthday?	What are some ways you celebrate Jesus' birth?
Possible responses: attend a party with family and friends; eat cake with candles; play games; open gifts; sing; pray	Possible responses: attend a party with family and friends; exchange gifts; eat special food; pray; go to Mass

Reality Check

Check your favorite ways to help your family.

❏ Clean my room

❏ Listen

❏ Be kind

❏ Pray for my family members

_____

Possible responses: care for siblings;

❏ help with chores; obey parents

(your own way)

Take Home

Gather some family magazines. Find pictures of families doing things together. Make a collage of the different things that *your* family members do together. Talk about ways your family is like the Holy Family.

53

CHAPTER TEST

Circle the correct answer.

1. Jesus was born in _____.

   (Bethlehem)   Nazareth

2. When Jesus was growing up, the Holy Family lived in _____.

   Bethlehem   (Nazareth)

3. We celebrate the birth of Jesus on _____.

   (Christmas)   Easter

4. Mary _____ did what God asked her to do.

   (always)   never

5. Jesus, Mary, and _____ were members of the Holy Family.

   the angel   (Joseph)

What are some of the things the Holy Family did together? Possible responses: obeyed God's laws; helped each other at home; helped others; prayed together and with other families; listened to stories about God

54

Chapter 3 • Day 5

CHAPTER TEST

Read each test item aloud and allow time for the children to mark an answer. Decide whether the *Talk About It* activity will be a small group or whole class discussion. After you have finished, check the answers. Clarify any misconceptions.

Alternative Assessment

You may want the students to complete the following alternative-assessment activity.

Make a booklet. Show the ways the Holy Family showed love for each other and God.

Additional Testing

• Chapter 3 Test in *Assessment Book*, pages 7–8

• CD-ROM *Test Generator and Resource*: Use Chapter 3 Test or customize your own.

Review

Review the definitions as they are presented in the chapter's *Key Word* boxes:

• Christmas (page 47)
• Holy Family (page 48).

We Believe Statements

Review the four statements.

• God chose Mary to be the Mother of his Son.
• Jesus was born in Bethlehem.
• Jesus lived in Nazareth with Mary and Joseph.
• The Holy Family obeyed God the Father and prayed to him.

To use the Chapter 3 Study Guide, visit

www.webelieveweb.com

Overview

In Chapter 3 the children learned about the Holy Family. In this chapter the children will learn that Jesus worked among the people, sharing God's love.

Doctrinal Content	For Adult Reading and Reflection *Catechism of the Catholic Church*
The children will learn:	Paragraph
• John the Baptist helped people to get ready for Jesus.	535
• Jesus shared God's love with all people.	542
• Jesus teaches that God watches over us and cares for us.	305
• Jesus helped all those in need.	544

trust (p. 61)

Catechist Background

How can you prepare the way of the Lord for your children?

Each year in the Advent readings we hear the commanding voice of John the Baptist:

"Prepare the way of the Lord" (Luke 3:4). As the herald of the Messiah's coming, John opened hearts to the repentance and compassion that Jesus embodied.

Identified by John as "the Lamb of God" (John 1:29), Jesus announced the coming of the Kingdom of God for all people. Indeed, the Kingdom comes in Jesus himself. Jesus identified himself with the hungry, homeless, the sick, and imprisoned. He kept company with sinners, enabling them to experience God's mercy and forgiveness. Our own experience of Jesus should cause us to grow in generosity to others, especially the poor and the disadvantaged.

By the witness of his own life, Jesus taught his followers to trust in divine providence and to work

Go to **www.webelieveweb.com**, Catechist/ Teacher, We Believe Correlations for this chapter's correlation to:
- Six Tasks of Catechesis
- Catholic Social Teaching
- *Catechetical Formation in Chaste Living.*

to advance God's Kingdom of peace and justice. When John the Baptist's followers asked Jesus whether he was the Messiah, Jesus responded by describing his work.

"Go and tell John what you hear and see: the blind regain their sight, the lame walk, lepers are cleansed, the deaf hear, the dead are raised, and the poor have the good news proclaimed to them" (Matthew 11:4–5). These works of reaching out in love to those in need identify Christ and his followers in every generation. It is the way Jesus works among the people today.

How do you experience Jesus' call in your own life?

Lesson Planning Guide

Lesson Focus	Presentation	Materials

Day 1

page 55
✝ **We Gather in Prayer**

pages 56–57
John the Baptist helped people to get ready for Jesus.

🎵 Celebrate in song that Jesus is with us.
- Discuss the **We Gather** questions.
- Read the **We Believe** text introducing John the Baptist.

🏃 Do the **We Respond** activity.

For the prayer space: "Welcome, Jesus" sign, picture or statue of an adult Jesus, plant

🎵 "Jesus in the Morning," #3, Grade 1 CD

Day 2

pages 58–59
Jesus shared God's love with all people.

📖 *Luke 19:1–5*

- Follow the **We Gather** directive and discuss questions.
- Present the **We Believe** text about Jesus' teachings.
- Read the Scripture story about Zacchaeus.

🏃 Act out the Scripture story.

- Share responses in **We Respond**.

- costumes (optional)
- plant from prayer space
- copies of reproducible master *What's the Word?*, guide page 55F

Day 3

pages 60–61
Jesus teaches that God watches over us and cares for us

📖 *Luke 12:22–24*

- Share responses in **We Gather**.
- Read the Scripture story about God's care for us in **We Believe**.
- Discuss the **We Respond** question.

🎵 Sing a song about trust in God.

- Read and discuss the *As Catholics* text.

- crayons or colored pencils

🎵 "People Worry," Paule Freeburg and Christopher Walker, #4, Grade 1 CD
- copies of Reproducible Master 4, guide page 55G

Day 4

pages 62–63
Jesus helped all those in need.

📖 *Matthew 20:29–33*

- Discuss the **We Gather** questions.
- Read the Scripture story in **We Believe** about Jesus healing people.
- Share responses in **We Respond**.

🏃 Do the matching activity.

- costumes (optional)
- colored pencils or crayons

Day 5

pages 64–65
Project Disciple

page 66
Chapter 4 Test

- Complete the **Project Disciple** activities.
- Explain the *Take Home* activity.
- Discuss/send home **Sharing Faith with My Family**, guide page 55E.
- Complete **Chapter 4 Test**.
- Work on *Alternative Assessment* activity.

- pencils
- crayons or colored pencils
- copies of **Sharing Faith with My Family** reproducible master, guide page 55E

For additional ideas, activities, and opportunities: Visit Sadlier's **www.WeBelieve.web.com**

55B

Chapter Story

During dinner Justin told his family exciting news. He said, "The mayor of our city is coming to our school. The principal, Mrs. Garvey, announced it this morning. She told us that everyone would be part of getting ready for our visitor."

Every night Justin told his family what his class had done to prepare for their special visitor. Justin said, "Mrs. Santos taught my class a song about our city that we will sing for the mayor."

Justin's sister said, "My friend, Anita, was chosen to read her poem, 'My City Is Pretty.'"

The next day at school Miss Chen had Justin's class draw pictures of their city to hang in the school halls.

Justin loved to draw. He decided to draw the city at night. He drew the stars and moon in the sky. He drew tall buildings with lights shining from the windows.

The day of the mayor's visit was finally here. The school band played to welcome her. The mayor visited each classroom. Justin's class sang their song. Justin was thrilled that he was able to shake the mayor's hand. Miss Chen took a picture of the entire class with the mayor. Justin could not wait to get home to tell his family about everything that happened.

▶ *What is one of your favorite ways of making a guest feel welcomed?*

FAITH and MEDIA

▶ On Day 3, after reading the *As Catholics* text about quiet times for prayer and discussing special places to pray, explain: *Today we can even find special "places" to pray on the Internet.* If possible, show the class one of the prayer pages designed especially for young children.

Notes on links found:

_____

_____

_____

_____

_____

_____

_____

_____

_____

_____

_____

_____

_____

CHAPTER PROJECT: STORYBOARDS ABOUT JESUS

At the end of each day's lesson, help the children to make a storyboard about the Scripture story or the lesson's main idea. Divide a large sheet of poster board into four sections. Have volunteers draw a picture in each section. Draw speech balloons for the main characters. Have the children tell you the words to write in each balloon. Display the storyboards in the prayer space.

PROJECT DISCIPLE

Pray
Learn
Celebrate
Share
Choose
Live

Additional Activities

Make *it* Happen

Materials needed: drawing paper, colored pencils or crayons

Organize a card making activity in which the children each decorate a card for someone who is sick in a local children's hospital or nursing home. Help each child to write a message on the front of the card. Encourage the children to decorate the cards with bright colors and drawings. Then collect the cards and send them to the chosen recipients. Remember not to put any identifying or personal information on the children's cards. Congratulate the children on doing something to care for those who are sick or sad.

What's *the* Word?

(Use on Day 2.)

Materials needed: copies of reproducible master, guide page 55F

Distribute the Scripture reproducible master. Explain to the children that they will be doing an activity to remember the story of Zacchaeus. Choose four volunteers to read the parts of Reader 1, Reader 2, Zacchaeus, and Jesus. Ask the other children to follow along as the story is read.

More *to* Explore

Ask the children to remember ways that Jesus cared for all people. Then as a class, plan to make a special effort through the week to help others like Jesus did. At the end of each day, make time for the children to relate true stories from their day about school mates who acted like Jesus. You might give an example such as, "Today Nicholas helped me to clean up a container of art materials that I spilled." Allow the children to share these stories and reinforce good behavior.

Make *it* Happen

Help the children to act out scenarios in which they share God's love. Divide the children into small groups and provide them with real life situations that are relatable to first graders. Ask the children to act out their scenario for the class. Then have a class discussion about each scenario and how each showed ways to share God's love.

Meeting Individual Needs
Children with Auditory Needs

Make an audio recording of the Scripture stories in this chapter. Make it available to those children who would benefit from listening to these stories at a higher volume level.

We Believe Resources

- Grade 1 *Review & Resource Book*, pages 13–15
- Grade 1 *Family Book*, pages 14–16
- Grade 1 *Assessment Book*, pages 9–10
- Grade 1 CD-ROM *Test Generator and Resource*: Use Chapter 4 Test or customize your own.
- **www.webelieveweb.com**

SHARING FAITH
with My Family

Sharing What I Learned

Look at the pictures below. Use each picture to tell your family what you learned in this chapter.

Loving Others Day by Day

Put a weekly calendar on your refrigerator door. Each day, have the members of your family write how they showed love that day. Then read about the love your family shared!

Sunday
Monday
Tuesday
Wednesday
Thursday
Friday
Saturday

Visit Sadlier's

www.WEBELIEVEweb.com

Connect to the Catechism
For adult background and reflection, see paragraphs 535, 542, 305, and 544.

PROJECT DISCIPLE

Pray
Learn
Celebrate
Share
Choose
Live

Name _____

What's *the* Word?

Reader 1: Jesus shared God's love with all people.
He showed respect for poor people and rich people.
He was kind to people no matter how they looked.

Reader 2: One day Jesus was visiting a town.
Many people waited to see Jesus.
A very rich man named Zacchaeus wanted to see Jesus, too.

Zacchaeus: I am so short. I will never see Jesus.
I am going to climb a tree and sit in the branches.

Reader 1: Zacchaeus climbed the tree and waited.
When Jesus came to the tree, he stopped.

Reader 2: Jesus looked up. He spoke to the rich man.

Jesus: "Zacchaeus, come down quickly, for today I must stay at your house." (Luke 19:5)

Read the message on the medallion.

Color the medallion and cut it out.

Your teacher will help you to prepare it to wear.

Share the message with family and friends.

I am important to God.

Jesus Works Among the People

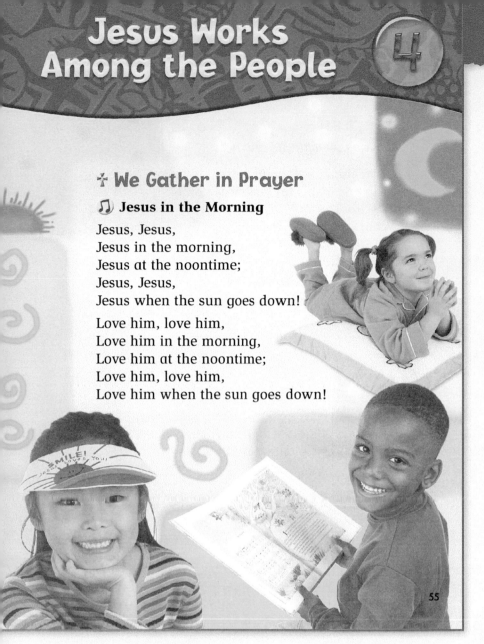

✝ **We Gather in Prayer**

🎵 **Jesus in the Morning**

Jesus, Jesus,
Jesus in the morning,
Jesus at the noontime;
Jesus, Jesus,
Jesus when the sun goes down!

Love him, love him,
Love him in the morning,
Love him at the noontime;
Love him, love him,
Love him when the sun goes down!

PREPARING TO PRAY

The children will sing a song to celebrate that Jesus is with us each day.

• Play the song "Jesus in the Morning," #3, Grade 1 CD. Make up actions. Have the children practice singing and doing the actions.

The Prayer Space
• Display a "Welcome, Jesus" sign.

• Cover the prayer table with a bright cloth. On the table place a picture or statue of an adult Jesus and a plant.

📖 **This Week's Liturgy**
Visit **www.webelieveweb.com** for this week's liturgical readings and other seasonal material.

Lesson Plan

We Gather in Prayer ___ minutes

✝ **Pray**

• Invite the children to gather in the prayer space. Ask the children to think about the different times of the day—morning, afternoon, and night. Stress: *Jesus is with us all through the day and the night.*

• Pray together the Sign of the Cross.

• Sing "Jesus in the Morning" and do the prayer actions.

Family Connection Update

Invite the children to share their family discussions about sharing God's love with people who are sick.

Catechist Goal

• To tell how John the Baptist helped people to get ready for Jesus

Our Faith Response

• To identify ways of welcoming Jesus into our lives

Teaching Tip

Teaching Tools: Illustrations

Use the illustrations that appear in the text to help the children to understand each lesson that is presented. For this lesson, explain that the illustration shows a desert. Point out: *Very few people live in deserts. Deserts do not have much water.* Explain that John went to the desert for quiet time away from people. He wanted to pray to get himself ready to welcome Jesus.

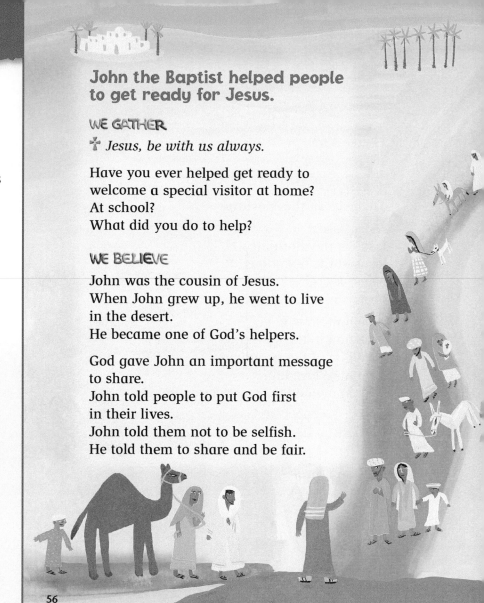

John the Baptist helped people to get ready for Jesus.

WE GATHER

✝ *Jesus, be with us always.*

Have you ever helped get ready to welcome a special visitor at home?
At school?
What did you do to help?

WE BELIEVE

John was the cousin of Jesus.
When John grew up, he went to live in the desert.
He became one of God's helpers.

God gave John an important message to share.
John told people to put God first in their lives.
John told them not to be selfish.
He told them to share and be fair.

56

Lesson Plan

WE GATHER ___ minutes

✝ **Pray** Pray together the Sign of the Cross and the *We Gather* prayer.

Focus on Life Read the *We Gather* questions. Have volunteers share their responses. Have the children imagine that you are going to have a special visitor in the classroom. Ask: *What will have to be done to get ready?* Share the *Chapter Story* on guide page 55C. Tell the children that in this lesson they will learn how John the Baptist helped people get ready for Jesus.

WE BELIEVE ___ minutes

Learn About John the Baptist Ask the children to look at the illustration as you read aloud the first two *We Believe* paragraphs. Stress:

• *God wanted John to share an important message.*

• *John told people to put God first in their lives.*

Write *John the Baptist* on the board. Then read the *We Believe* paragraph on page 57. Explain that John's message was: *Jesus is the person God promised to send. John wanted the people to know that they would soon be able to see and hear this person. They could get ready by sharing and by being kind and fair to others.*

Many people heard John's message.
John, called John the Baptist, was
getting the people ready.
They were getting ready to welcome
Jesus, the Son of God, into their lives.
Jesus would show them the way God
wanted them to live.

WE RESPOND

You need to be ready to
welcome Jesus every day.

Circle one way you can
welcome Jesus.

Share with my friends.

Say my prayers.

Be fair when I play.

Say "please" and "thank you."

Help my family at home.

What other ways can you
welcome Jesus?

57

ACTIVITY BANK

Multiple Intelligences
Intrapersonal
Activity Materials: container of sand,
water

Remind the children that people
went to the desert to hear John talk.
Place a container of sand on the
prayer table. Explain that this sand
stands for the sand in a desert. Have
the children take turns coming to the
prayer table. For each child wet the
sand a little. Have the child draw a
heart in the sand as he or she prays
quietly: *Jesus, I welcome you.* Then
run a piece of paper over the sand to
prepare for the next child.

Quick Check

✔ *How were John and Jesus related?* (John and Jesus
were cousins.)

✔ *What did John the Baptist do?* (John helped the
people get ready for Jesus.)

WE RESPOND ___ minutes

Connect to Life Emphasize that we should always
be prepared to welcome Jesus into our own lives
because he loves us and wants what is best for us. Then
read the ways of welcoming Jesus in the *We Respond*
activity. Read the list a second time, and then have the

children circle one way that they can welcome Jesus.
Explain that all the ideas are ways of welcoming Jesus,
but everyone can welcome Jesus in his or her own way.
Then ask volunteers to share their answers to the *We
Respond* question.

Pray Pray the following words and have the children
repeat them: *Jesus, we welcome you into our hearts.*

Plan Ahead for Day 2

Catechist Goal: To explain that Jesus shared
God's love with all people

Preparation: Make copies of *What's the
Word?*, guide page 55F.

Catechist Goal

• To explain that Jesus shared God's love with all people

Our Faith Response

• To share God's love as Jesus did

Lesson Materials

• costumes and props (optional)

• copies of reproducible master *What's the Word?*, guide page 55F

Teaching Tip

Costumes

Invite the children to bring in old sheets, towels, and pieces of fabric to use for costumes for Scripture plays. Stress with the children that they need to ask their parents for permission. Keep the costumes in a storage container in your classroom. Wash the costumes after each use.

Jesus shared God's love with all people.

WE GATHER

✝ *Jesus, welcome into our lives.*

Think about the people you see in your town.
What are they like? What do they do?

WE BELIEVE

When Jesus was a grown-up, he left his home in Nazareth.
He went from town to town teaching people.
He told them about God and his great love.

Jesus treated all people with respect. He shared the news of God's love with everyone. He shared with

• children and parents

• farmers and fishermen

• poor people and rich people

• those who were sick and those who were healthy.

58

Lesson Plan

WE GATHER ___ minutes

✝ **Pray** Pray together the Sign of the Cross and the *We Gather* prayer.

Focus on Life Ask the children to close their eyes and think about the people whom they see often. Then discuss the *We Gather* questions. Help the children to conclude that in most towns there are people of all different ages. Explain: *Some are poor, some are rich, some are healthy, and some are sick. Some are helpers. Some work outside and some work inside.*

WE BELIEVE ___ minutes

Read the Text Read aloud the *We Believe* statement. Then read aloud the first two *We Believe* paragraphs.

Walking with Jesus Place the children in small groups, asking each group to represent the different kinds of people that Jesus helped. Ask them to pantomime their roles of farmers, fishermen, adults, children, and people who are sick. Walk to each group, telling the children that Jesus (role-played by you) is there to help them. Have each group stop what they are doing and follow Jesus as you go to the next group. When all the groups are following you, gather in the prayer space to listen to a story about Jesus.

Share a Scripture Story Read the story of Zacchaeus. Explain: *Some people did not like Zacchaeus, but Jesus stopped to talk to him anyway. Jesus knew Zacchaeus needed God's love like everyone else.*

Here is a story about someone Jesus met.

📖 Luke 19:1–5

Read Along

One day Jesus visited a town called Jericho. A large crowd gathered to see Jesus. A very rich man named Zacchaeus wanted to see Jesus, too. Zacchaeus was so short that he could not see above the heads of the other people. He climbed a tree and sat in the branches so that he could see Jesus.

When Jesus came to the tree, he looked up. He said, "Zacchaeus, come down quickly, for today I must stay at your house." (Luke 19:5)

Zacchaeus was very happy. Jesus was coming to his house. Jesus knew that Zacchaeus needed to hear the news of God's love, too.

WE RESPOND

🧍 Act out the story of Zacchaeus. What did you learn about Jesus from this story?

Thank Jesus for sharing God's great love.

59

Chapter 4 • Day 2

ACTIVITY BANK

Curriculum Connection
Language Arts
Activity Materials: writing paper

Ask the children to think about what might have happened after Jesus spoke to Zacchaeus. Discuss the following question.

• *How do you think Zacchaeus prepared for Jesus' visit?*

After sharing some ideas, invite the children to write a continuation of the story.

Scripture
Linguistic, Interpersonal

For a Scripture activity, see *What's the Word?*, guide page 55F.

Quick Check

✔ *How did Jesus treat people?* (Jesus treated people with respect.)

✔ *What happened at the end of the story of Zacchaeus?* (Jesus called Zacchaeus down from a tree. Jesus asked to go to Zacchaeus' house for dinner.)

WE RESPOND   ___ minutes

Connect to Life Prepare the children to act out the story of Zacchaeus. You may want to provide costumes for the dramatization. Ask a volunteer to play the part of Zacchaeus. Using the plant on the prayer table, have the child hold it in front of his face and peek out. Have

another child lead the remaining children toward the hiding Zacchaeus. Ask the leading child to say the words that Jesus spoke to Zacchaeus. Invite the children to share responses to the *We Respond* question. Tell them to think about the happiness Zacchaeus felt when Jesus called to him. Stress: *Jesus treated Zacchaeus with respect.*

Pray Invite the children to gather at the prayer table. Have them pray with you: *Thank you, Jesus, for sharing God's love.*

Plan Ahead for Day 3

Catechist Goal: To emphasize that God watches over us and cares for us

Preparation: Make copies of Reproducible Master 4, guide page 55G.

59

Catechist Goal

• To emphasize that God watches over us and cares for us

Our Faith Response

• To name ways in which God watches over us

 **trust**

Lesson Materials

• crayons or colored pencils
• copies of Reproducible Master 4
• Grade 1 CD

As Catholics...

Quiet Times for Prayer

   After you have presented the lesson, read the *As Catholics* text. Tell the children that Jesus prayed often. Remind them that praying is talking and listening to God. Invite volunteers to share their favorite places to pray.

Jesus teaches that God watches over us and cares for us.

WE GATHER

✝ *God, we need your love always.*

What are some things that are important to you?
Show how you take care of one of them.

WE BELIEVE

Jesus wanted people to know about God. He wanted everyone to know that God takes care of them.

Luke 12:22–24

Read Along
One day Jesus was teaching. He pointed to the birds flying above the crowd. Jesus said that the birds did not have to worry about food. God cares for the birds. Jesus told the crowd that God cares for people even more! He said, "How much more important are you than birds!" (Luke 12:24)

60

Lesson Plan

WE GATHER _____ minutes

✝ **Pray** Pray together the Sign of the Cross and the *We Gather* prayer.

Focus on Life Ask the children to think about the *We Gather* question. Have volunteers take turns showing how they take care of one thing. Tell them some of the things that are important to you and how you take care of them. Tell the children that in this lesson they will learn that God is taking care of us, even when we are not aware of it.

WE BELIEVE _____ minutes

Share a Scripture Story Read aloud the *We Believe* statement and the first paragraph. Have the

children look at the illustration. Ask: *Have you ever watched how birds collect food or build their nests? How do they do these things?* Then explain: *God cares for and watches over every creature on earth.*

Read the Scripture story. Stress: *Jesus wanted the people to understand that God, who took care of the birds, would take care of us even more.*

Do an Activity Distribute copies of Reproducible Master 4. Provide time for the children to color their medallions and then cut them out. Punch a hole at the top of each medallion and string a piece of yarn through the hole. Tie the ends of the yarn together and place the medallion over the child's head. Allow the children to wear their medallions throughout the day.

Do you know how important we are to God?
God watches over us all the time.
He loves and takes care of us even when we do not know it.
When we believe someone loves us, we **trust** them.
Jesus tells us to trust God.

WE RESPOND

How does God watch over you?

Key Word
trust to believe in someone's love for us

🎵 **People Worry**

People worry about this and that.
People worry about this and that!
But Jesus tells us, "Don't worry.
Don't worry about this and that!"

God knows ev'rything we need,
 just believe, just believe.
God takes care of ev'ryone.
Trust in God, trust in God.

As Catholics...

We all need to take quiet time to pray to God. We can praise God. We can thank God. We can ask God for help. Before Jesus began to teach, he went into the desert. He went there to pray to God.

Where is your special place to pray?

61

ACTIVITY BANK

Multicultural Connection

Eye of God (Ojo de Dios)
Activity Materials: (for each child) string or yarn in several colors, 2 popsicle or craft sticks, glue, safety scissors

Explain to the children that the Huichol Indians of Mexico and the Aymara Indians of Bolivia weave brightly colored yarn on a simple cross frame of sticks to make a design called "Ojo de Dios" or "Eye of God." The design reminds us that God looks with love on people everywhere. Tell the children to glue the two craft sticks together in the form of a cross. Show them how to take one color of yarn and wrap it over and around one stick, then over and around the next, over and around the next, and so on until the string runs out. Take a different colored string and tie it onto the first one with a tight knot. Repeat wrapping with the new color until the sticks are completely covered.

Remember the Key Word Write the word *trust* on the board. Help the children remember the definition by repeating it together.

Quick Check

✔ *What does trust mean?* (It means to believe in someone's love for us.)

✔ *When does God watch over us?* (God watches over us all the time.)

WE RESPOND _____ minutes

Connect to Life Ask volunteers to share ways that God watches over us. Remind the children of the many gifts God gave them—the people in their lives, their homes, the food they eat, and the education they are receiving. Emphasize: *God does this because he loves each of us.*

Learn a Song Play "People Worry," #4, Grade 1 CD. Play it again and have the children join in singing.

Pray Invite the children to stand, gather in the prayer space, and sing "People Worry."

Plan Ahead for Day 4

Catechist Goal: To highlight that Jesus helped all those in need

Preparation: Provide costumes and props for the Scripture story dramatization.

Catechist Goal

• To highlight that Jesus helped all those in need

Our Faith Response

• To name ways in which we can help others as Jesus did

Lesson Materials

• colored pencils or crayons

• costumes and props (optional)

Teaching Tip

Capitalization

First graders are learning that certain words in our language are capitalized. They will see during the year that there are many words in their religion book that are capitalized. Explain: *We always use capital letters for the first letters of the names God the Father, Jesus, and the Holy Spirit.*

Jesus helped all those in need.

WE GATHER

✝ *Jesus, thank you for teaching that God cares for us.*

How do you know that someone loves and cares for you?
What does the person say?
What does the person do?

WE BELIEVE

Jesus cared for all people.
He welcomed and blessed the children.
He comforted people who were sad or afraid.

Jesus helped the poor.
He fed the hungry.
He healed many people who were sick.
He loved everyone, even those who did not like him.

62

Lesson Plan

WE GATHER   ___ minutes

✝ **Pray** Lead the children in praying the Sign of the Cross and the *We Gather* prayer.

Focus on Life Read the *We Gather* questions. Invite the children to share their responses. Tell the children that in this lesson they will learn about ways Jesus showed his love.

WE BELIEVE   ___ minutes

Read the Text Read aloud the *We Believe* statement and the first two paragraphs. Stress:

• *Jesus helped many people.*

• *Jesus loved everyone, even those who did not like him.*

Talk About the Picture Ask the children to look at the picture of Jesus on these pages. Ask: *How is Jesus showing God's love?* Then read the Scripture story.

📖 Matthew 20:29–33

Read Along
One day a large crowd was following Jesus. Two blind men heard that Jesus was passing by. They cried out to him for help. Jesus stopped and asked, "What do you want me to do for you?" They answered him, "Lord, let our eyes be opened." (Matthew 20:32–33)

Then Jesus touched their eyes. Right away the two men could see. They began to follow Jesus.

WE RESPOND

What do you think the two men said after Jesus healed them?

🕊 Finish this prayer. Match each picture to the right words.

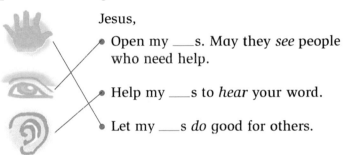

Jesus,

• Open my ___s. May they *see* people who need help.

• Help my ___s to *hear* your word.

• Let my ___s *do* good for others.

63

ACTIVITY BANK

Catholic Social Teaching
Call to Family, Community, and Participation
Activity Materials: video camera, poster board, crayons

Make a video to share with the children's ward of a community hospital. Check with the hospital's administration before sending.

On a sheet of poster board, print: *Get Well.* Have artists in the group draw a picture on the poster. Then use the poster as a backdrop when you record each child saying a brief get-well message: (*Hope you're feeling better soon; we're praying for you; get well as soon as possible.*)

Quick Check

✔ *What kind of things did Jesus do to help people?* (Possible responses are listed on page 62.)

✔ *What did the two men do after Jesus healed them?* (They followed him.)

WE RESPOND ___ minutes

Connect to Life Read the *We Respond* question. Ask volunteers to act out the story. They should also act out what the men said after Jesus healed them.

Read each sentence of the prayer. Pause to allow the children time to draw a line from the sentence to the appropriate drawing.

Pray Pray the prayer on page 63. For the first prayer sentence, have the children point to their eyes; second sentence, point to their ears; the third sentence, hold out their hands.

Plan Ahead for Day 5

Catechist Goal: To review chapter ideas and their relationship to our faith life

Preparation: Make copies of *Sharing Faith with My Family*, guide page 55E.

Catechist Goal

• To review the chapter ideas that are key to growing as disciples of Jesus Christ

Our Faith Response

• To decide on ways to grow as disciples by living out what we have learned

Show What you Know

Review the definition of the *Key Word trust.* Then ask the children to write a sentence using the word.

What Would you do?

Read aloud the first paragraph. Draw attention to the picture. Ask: *What did you learn from the children's facial expressions?* Then read the instruction line. Invite children to write what Henry could say to Jess. When they have finished, review all responses.

Make it Happen

Read the activity instructions. Brainstorm a list of possible responses on the board. Allow children time to draw their responses. Encourage them to tell about what they have drawn.

Pray Today

Read aloud the instruction line. Invite children to think quietly about a person they will pray for. They may think of or write a prayer. Encourage them to share the prayer with their families.

Take Home

Remind the children that one way Jesus showed God's love was by caring for people who were sick. Read the bulleted list in *Take Home.* Encourage the children to talk to their family members about caring for the sick as a way to share God's love.

Discuss and send home copies of *Sharing Faith with My Family,* guide page 55E.

64 and **65**

Grade 1 Chapter 4

PROJECT

Show What you Know

Write a sentence using the Word **trust.** Possible responses:

Jesus tells us to trust God. We trust God.

To trust is to believe in someone's love for us.

What Would you do?

Jess spilled her snack during snack time. She felt sad and hungry. Henry wanted to help Jess.

In the ⬭ write what Henry could say to Jess.
Possible responses:

Don't be sad. I will share my snack with you.

64   www.webelieveweb.com

DISCIPLE

Make it Happen

Jesus shared the news of God's love with everyone. Draw one way you can share the news of God's love.

Possible drawings: share a story about Jesus; treat others with respect; tell others that God loves us

Pray Today

Praying for people is another way to help and love them. Think of someone you know who needs your love. Say a prayer for this person.

↳ **DISCIPLE CHALLENGE** Pray your prayer with friends and family.

Take Home

Circle one way your family can share God's love with people who are sick:
• praying for or with them
• cheering them up
• listening to them
• reading Bible stories to them.

• _____
(another way)

65

CHAPTER TEST

Circle the correct answer.

1. Was Zacchaeus the cousin of Jesus?

Yes   (No)

2. When we trust God, do we believe in his love for us?

(Yes)   No

3. Did Jesus treat all people with respect?

(Yes)   No

4. Did Jesus show God's love by healing the sick?

(Yes)   No

5. Did Jesus stay in Nazareth all his life on earth?

Yes   (No)

What did John the Baptist tell people? Possible responses: to put God first in their lives; not to be selfish; to share and be fair

66

CHAPTER TEST

Read each test item aloud and allow time for the children to mark an answer. Decide whether the *Talk About It* activity will be a small group or whole class discussion. After you have finished, check the answers. Clarify any misconceptions.

Alternative Assessment

You may want the students to complete the following alternative-assessment activity.

Tell and draw some of the ways Jesus showed people God's love.

Additional Testing

• Chapter 4 Test in *Assessment Book*, pages 9–10

• CD-ROM *Test Generator and Resource*: Use Chapter 4 Test or customize your own.

Review

Review the definition as it is presented in the chapter's *Key Word* box:

• trust (page 61).

We Believe Statements

Review the four statements.

• John the Baptist helped people to get ready for Jesus.

• Jesus shared God's love with all people.

• Jesus teaches that God watches over us and cares for us.

• Jesus helped all those in need.

To use the Chapter 4 Study Guide, visit

www.webelieveweb.com

Chapter 5 · Jesus Teaches Us About Love

Overview

In Chapter 4 the children learned that Jesus worked among the people. In this chapter the children will learn about love and how Jesus wants us to live our daily lives.

Doctrinal Content	For Adult Reading and Reflection *Catechism of the Catholic Church*
The children will learn:	Paragraph
• Many people wanted to follow Jesus.	544–546
• Jesus taught the Great Commandment.	2055
• Jesus taught us to love God, ourselves, and others.	1931
• Jesus taught us that all people are our neighbors.	1931

commandments (p. 71)

Catechist Background

What does Jesus teach about love?

Go to www.webelieveweb.com, Catechist/ Teacher, We Believe Correlations for this chapter's correlation to:
• Six Tasks of Catechesis
• Catholic Social Teaching.

During his public mission on earth, Jesus often used parables to teach God's message of love. The people who came to Jesus heard simple stories drawn from daily life that served as invitations to enter God's Kingdom. For example, he spoke of the person who sells all he has in order to buy the field in which a treasure is buried (Matthew 13:44).

At the heart of Jesus' life and teaching was the Great Commandment requiring love of God, of oneself, and of one's neighbor. His disciples were to express that love by obeying the commandments and by living the Beatitudes.

This requirement to love means that followers of Jesus must treat everyone as a neighbor. In the parable of the good Samaritan, the lawyer who asks Jesus "And who is my neighbor?" is led to the conclusion that the neighbor is the one who treated the victim with compassion. Jesus says, "Go and do likewise" (Luke 10:29, 37). Christians may not discriminate against any person or group in serving those in need.

In the Gospel of John we are reminded that living Jesus' teaching about love is the very identity of his disciples. Jesus declares, "This is how all will know that you are my disciples, if you have love for one another" (John 13:35).

How will you become more conscious of those in need? What will be your response?

Lesson Planning Guide

Lesson Focus	Presentation	Materials
Day 1		
page 67 **We Gather in Prayer** **pages 68–69** *Many people wanted to follow Jesus.*	• Pray for Jesus' blessing. • Discuss the We Gather questions. • Read the We Believe text about Jesus' travels and teachings. Do the We Respond activity.	For the prayer space: a large poster with the Great Commandment printed on it, statue or picture of Jesus, Bible • pencils or crayons
Day 2		
pages 70–71 *Jesus taught the Great Commandment.*  *Matthew 22:37, 39*	• Discuss the We Gather questions. • Present the Great Commandment in We Believe. • Share responses in We Respond. • Pray together. • Read and discuss the *As Catholics* text.	• Bible • highlighter or crayon • copies of reproducible master *What's the Word?*, guide page 67F
Day 3		
pages 72–73 *Jesus taught us to love God, ourselves, and others.*	• Share responses in We Gather. • Read about and discuss sharing love. Do the We Respond picture study activity. • Pray together.	• crayons or colored pencils • Bible
Day 4		

pages 74–75
 Jesus taught us that all people are our neighbors.

  *Luke 10:30–35*
	• Discuss the We Gather questions.
	 • Read the Scripture story in We Believe.
	 • Share responses in We Respond.
	  Sing a song about being a neighbor.
		• construction paper, scissors (optional)
		 • colored pencils or crayons
		  "Good Neighbors," #5, Grade 1 CD
		 • copies of Reproducible Master 5, guide page 67G

Day 5		
pages 76–77 **Project Disciple** **page 78** **Chapter 5 Test**	• Complete the Project Disciple activities. • Explain the *Take Home* activity. • Discuss/send home Sharing Faith with My Family, guide page 67E. • Complete Chapter 5 Test. • Work on *Alternative Assessment* activity.	• pencils • crayons or colored pencils • copies of Sharing Faith with My Family reproducible master, guide page 67E

For additional ideas, activities, and opportunities: Visit Sadlier's **www.WeBelieve.web.com**

Enrichment Ideas

Chapter Story

Jeremy's family was new to the neighborhood. Jeremy's parents were very happy to have a new home but Jeremy was upset. He did not think he would find friends like he had in his old neighborhood.

One day not long after they had moved, Jeremy's sister Jessica was outside in the front yard. A girl from the neighborhood walked up to Jessica and introduced herself. Jeremy pretended not to notice, but he made sure he stayed on the front porch. He hoped that maybe the girl had brothers, or knew some other boys in the neighborhood who could be his friends.

The girls went up on the porch. "Tisha, this is my little brother, Jeremy," Jessica said.

"Hi," he mumbled.

Tisha thought that Jeremy looked lonely. She took Jeremy by the hand. "Let's go to my house so you can meet my brother. He's the same age as you are."

Jessica and Jeremy first asked their mom if they could go to Tisha's. Their mom said yes so they went with Tisha to meet her brother.

Tisha introduced Jeremy to her brother, Matt. Matt was friendly. He invited Jeremy to play his new game.

On the way home, Jessica said to Jeremy, "What a great day! We both have new friends."

Jeremy answered, "Maybe Tisha and Matt can come to our house on Saturday. Let's go ask Mom."

▶ *Do you like to make new friends? Tell why or why not.*

FAITH and MEDIA

▶ Remember the power of educational video in your planning and teaching. Supplementing a lesson with video is a way to add multimedia to your classroom experience. Always preview videos before use in the classroom. A suggested video for this chapter is *The Story of the Good Samaritan* in The Beginner's Bible series, Sony Wonder (30 minutes).

Note here any other videos you may find helpful:

_____
_____
_____
_____
_____
_____
_____
_____
_____

CHAPTER PROJECT: LEARNING LOG

By keeping a daily log the children can document and reinforce their knowledge of the chapter content. Provide children with a sheet of drawing paper. Demonstrate how to fold the sheet to make a small booklet. Have children print their names and label "Day 1" through "Day 4." Name the booklet: "What I Learned About Jesus." After each day's lesson, provide the children with time to write about or draw what they learned on the appropriate log page. Invite the children to take their logs home and share them with their families at the end of the week.

PROJECT DISCIPLE

Pray
Learn
Celebrate
Share
Choose
Live

Additional Activities

What's the Word?

(Use on Day 2.)

Materials needed: copies of reproducible master, guide page 67F

Distribute copies of the Scripture reproducible master. Explain to the children that they will be doing an activity to remember the story of the Great Commandment. Choose four volunteers to read the parts of Reader 1, Reader 2, Man, and Jesus. Ask the other children to follow along as the story is read.

More to Explore

Tell the children that Jesus taught that we are all neighbors. As you begin your lessons for this chapter, set up a display of picture books about different cultures of people and a globe. Invite the children to read about their neighbors in other countries and to find these countries on the globe.

Fast Facts

Materials needed: ink pad, drawing paper, colored pencils

Ask the children: *Do you know why a thumbprint is special?* Explain to the children that every thumbprint is different. Explain that no one has a thumbprint exactly like theirs. Tell the children that they will be making a picture of themselves using their thumbprints. Show the children a finished thumbprint self-portrait as an example. Invite the children to come up one at a time. Show them how to press their thumbs onto the ink pad and transfer the print onto the paper. After the children wash their thumbs they can complete the self-portrait with the thumbprint as their head. When all drawings are complete, display them on a wall under the title: *We are friends of Jesus!*

Make it Happen

Have the children work in pairs. Ask each pair to prepare a role-play of people showing respect for one another. Have the children present their role-plays to the class.

Meeting Individual Needs
Children with Visual Needs

Seat the children with visual needs where they can best see the board or other teaching focus point. Make sure the children have pencils with thick, dark lead, which will allow them to see more clearly what they write. Also make sure you write large enough on the board for the children to see. Use the school copy machine to make enlarged copies of any material you distribute.

We Believe Resources

- Grade 1 *Review & Resource Book*, pages 16–18
- Grade 1 *Family Book*, pages 17–19
- Grade 1 *Assessment Book*, pages 11–12
- Grade 1 CD-ROM *Test Generator and Resource*: Use Chapter 5 Test or customize your own.
- **www.webelieveweb.com**

SHARING FAITH
with My Family

Sharing What I Learned

Look at the pictures below. Use each picture to tell your family what you learned in this chapter.

Good Neighbors

Talk together about ways family members can be good neighbors this week. Choose one or two of these ways. Write them below.

_____

_____

_____

Visit Sadlier's

www.WEBELIEVEweb.com

 Connect to the Catechism
For adult background and reflection, see paragraphs 544–546, 2055, and 1931.

PROJECT DISCIPLE

Pray
Learn
Celebrate
Share
Choose
Live

Name _____

What's *the* Word?

Reader 1: One day a group who studied God's laws went to talk to Jesus. One man asked Jesus a question.

Man: "Teacher, which commandment in the law is the greatest?" (Matthew 22:36)

Reader 2: Jesus answered the student.

Jesus: "You shall love the Lord, your God, with all your heart, with all your soul, and with all your mind."
(Matthew 22:37)

Reader 1: Then Jesus continued with these words.

Jesus: "You shall love your neighbor as yourself."
(Matthew 22:39)

Reader 2: We call this commandment the Great Commandment.

Work as a neighbor. Write another verse for the song.

♪ **Good Neighbors**

(Go 'Round and 'Round the Village)

Let's try to be good neighbors!

Let's try to be good neighbors!

Let's try to be good neighbors

As Jesus wants us to.

_____

_____

_____

_____

Jesus Teaches Us About Love

✝ We Gather in Prayer

Leader: • Jesus, you blessed the children who came to see you. We ask you to bless us now.

All: • Jesus, bless our eyes so we may see your love.

• Jesus, bless our ears so we may hear your words of love.

• Jesus, bless our hands so we may share your love.

• Jesus, bless our mouths so we may tell others about your love.

• Jesus, fill our hearts with love.

67

PREPARING TO PRAY

The children ask Jesus to bless them so that they may experience his love and share it with others.

• Read aloud the words of the prayer. Have the children make up actions for each prayer verse.

The Prayer Space

• On a sheet of poster board, print the Great Commandment. Display the poster in the prayer space.

• On the prayer table, place a statue or picture of Jesus and an open Bible.

📖 **This Week's Liturgy**

Visit **www.webelieveweb.com** for this week's liturgical readings and other seasonal material.

Lesson Plan

We Gather in Prayer ____ minutes

✝ Pray

• Invite the children to gather together in the prayer space.

• Invite the children to pray the Sign of the Cross. Then begin the prayer.

• Have the children do the appropriate action for each prayer verse.

• (Option) Conclude the prayer by singing together "Jesus in the Morning," #3 on the Grade 1 CD. The words are on page 55 of the children's books.

Family Connection Update

Invite the children to share their family discussions about our neighbors living in other countries.

Catechist Goal

• To recount that many people wanted to follow Jesus

Our Faith Response

• To listen to Jesus and follow him

Teaching Note

Group Skits

Asking children to act out what they are studying is an interesting and effective way to reinforce learning. These dramatic activities work best, however, when they are carefully organized. Before placing children into groups, explain the instructions clearly, so all the children understand what is expected of them. Communicate your expectations explicitly, so the children know what behaviors are and are not acceptable. Assign a time limit to the children so they will stay focused.

Many people wanted to follow Jesus.

WE GATHER

✝ *Jesus, bless us.*

Think about the people you know. Who do you like to spend time with? Why?

WE BELIEVE

Jesus traveled from place to place. News about him spread everywhere. Many people went looking for Jesus.

When Jesus taught, crowds of people would come to hear him. One day Jesus even had to get on a boat so all the people could see and hear him.

Why did crowds of people come to Jesus? The people needed him to:

• make them feel better

• teach them to pray

• tell them the Good News about God's love

• tell them how to live a better life.

68

Lesson Plan

WE GATHER ___ minutes

✝ **Pray** Invite the children to pray together the Sign of the Cross and the *We Gather* prayer.

Focus on Life Ask the children to share answers to the *We Gather* questions. You might want to contribute a story about someone with whom you like to spend time. Tell them about the special qualities of this person. Share the *Chapter Story* on guide page 67C. Tell the children that in this lesson, they will learn why people like to spend time with Jesus.

WE BELIEVE ___ minutes

Read the Text Invite a volunteer to read aloud the *We Believe* statement. Ask the children to pay close

attention as you read aloud the *We Believe* section. Emphasize:

• *More and more people began to hear about Jesus and what he taught about God and love.*

• *Jesus wanted people to know that God cared about all of them.*

• *Jesus made everyone feel special.*

Use the Illustration Have the children look at the illustration on these pages. Ask volunteers to share their responses to the following questions.

• *What do you think Jesus is saying?*

• *What do you think the people will say about Jesus when they go home?*

After spending time with Jesus, people came to know what God's love was like.
Jesus made everyone feel special.

WE RESPOND

How can you spend time with Jesus?

Circle each thing you can do.

- Pray.
- Listen to a story about Jesus.
- Share Jesus' love with others.

69

Quick Check

✔ *Why did crowds of people come to hear Jesus?* (Jesus taught them to pray, told them the Good News of God's love, and told them how to live better lives.)

✔ *How did Jesus make people feel?* (Jesus made people feel special.)

WE RESPOND _____ minutes

Connect to Life Read the *We Respond* question. Have the children circle the ways they can spend time with Jesus.

Pray Remind the children: *God loves us and wants us to be happy.* Invite them to stand as you pray: *Jesus, we are your friends.*

Plan Ahead for Day 2

Catechist Goal: To present that Jesus taught the Great Commandment

Preparation: Make copies of *What's the Word?*, guide page 67F.

Catechist Goal

• To present that Jesus taught the Great Commandment

Our Faith Response

• To identify ways of showing love for God

 commandments

Lesson Materials

• highlighters or crayons

• copies of reproducible master *What's the Word?*, guide page 67F

As Catholics...

After you have presented the lesson about the Great Commandment, read aloud the *As Catholics* text. Explain to the children that praying a morning offering is a way that they can say good morning to God and thank him each day.

Jesus taught the Great Commandment.

WE GATHER

✝ *Jesus, we want to follow you.*

What is one of your family's rules? How does keeping this rule help you and your family?

WE BELIEVE

Commandments are laws or rules given to us by God. These laws help us to live as God wants us to.

Jesus taught us the Great Commandment. He said,

"You shall love the Lord, your God, with all your heart, with all your soul, and with all your mind. You shall love your neighbor as yourself." (Matthew 22:37, 39)

70

Lesson Plan

WE GATHER ___ minutes

✝ **Pray** Invite the children to make the sign of the cross. Pray together the *We Gather* prayer.

Focus on Life Ask the children to name some of the class rules that they follow. Then invite the children to share their responses to the *We Gather* questions on page 70. Help the children to conclude that keeping rules helps us to be peaceful and to be safe. Tell the children that in this lesson they will learn about the Great Commandment.

WE BELIEVE ___ minutes

Read about God's Laws Write the word *commandments* on the board. Then read the first two *We Believe* sentences. Stress: *God gives us laws because he loves us. He wants us to live in peace.*

The Great Commandment Read aloud the Great Commandment, pausing after each phrase to have the children repeat it. Then invite the children to highlight the words in their texts.

Then read the first paragraph on page 71 and the list of ways we show our love for God.

When we follow this commandment, we do what God wants us to do. We love God, ourselves, and others.

We show God our love in these ways.

- We do what God wants us to do.
- We go to Mass on Sunday.
- We pray to God everyday.
- We make the Sign of the Cross with respect.

Key Word
commandments laws or rules given to us by God

WE RESPOND
What are other ways you can show your love for God?

Pray these words.
My God, I offer you today all I think and do and say.

As Catholics...
When we wake up in the morning, we can pray to God. This shows how important God is to us. There are special prayers we say to offer God our whole day. We call these prayers morning offerings. You can say the prayer on this page as a morning offering.

71

Chapter 5 • Day 2

ACTIVITY BANK

Prayer
Prayer Cards
Activity Materials: construction paper, hole puncher, string, crayons or markers

Help the children make prayer cards. Have them copy the *We Respond* prayer on a piece of construction paper. You might want to use a hole puncher to make a hole at the top of each card. Show the children how to attach a string. Encourage the children to hang the cards in their rooms to remind them to pray a morning offering every day.

Scripture
Linguistic, Interpersonal
For a Scripture activity, see *What's the Word?*, guide page 67F.

Quick Check

✔ *What are the commandments?* (The commandments are laws or rules given to us by God.)

✔ *How do we follow the Great Commandment?* (We love God with all our heart, mind, and soul, and we love our neighbors as ourselves.)

WE RESPOND ___ minutes

Connect to Life Have the children look at the photos on page 70. Ask: *How are the people showing their love for God?* Then read the *We Respond* question.

Have volunteers share their responses. Suggest that two ways are showing love for ourselves and love for others.

Pray Gather the children into a circle in the prayer space. Invite them to stand quietly and think about what they learned in this lesson. Then help them pray the prayer together.

Plan Ahead for Day 3

Catechist Goal: To highlight that Jesus taught us to love God, ourselves, and others

Preparation: Provide magazine photos of people taking care of themselves and others (option).

71

Catechist Goal

• To highlight that Jesus taught us to love God, ourselves, and others

Our Faith Response

• To identify ways of loving others as Jesus did

Teaching Tip

Learn to Listen

Point out to the children that one simple way to help others is to be a good listener. Tell them that sometimes people need to talk about things and they need someone to listen. Help the children understand what it means to be a good listener. Explain and model these tips:
• *Look at the person when he or she is talking to you; do not turn away.*
• *Stay quiet and listen carefully; do not talk when the other person is talking.*

Jesus taught us to love God, ourselves, and others.

WE GATHER

✝ *God the Father, God the Son, and God the Holy Spirit, help us.*

You show love for yourself when you eat the right foods.
What other things can you do to show that you love yourself?

WE BELIEVE

When we learn about Jesus' teaching, we learn about love. God made us to show us his love. We show God we love ourselves when we take care of ourselves. We can share our love with others, too.

Lesson Plan

WE GATHER ___ minutes

✝ **Pray** Read the *We Gather* prayer aloud and invite the children to repeat it.

Focus on Life Read the *We Gather* question aloud. Brainstorm ideas that show that the children love themselves. (Suggestions: exercising, keeping clean, getting enough sleep, looking both ways before crossing the street, taking medicine when they are sick, asking for help when needed, and taking care of their books and toys.) Write all responses on the board. Tell the children that in this lesson they will learn what Jesus taught us about love.

WE BELIEVE ___ minutes

Read the Text Read aloud the *We Believe* paragraphs. Emphasize: *You have the ability to love others as Jesus wants.*

Act It Out Ask: *What would it be like if everyone in the world obeyed the Great Commandment?* Divide the class into two groups. One group acts out following the Great Commandment in the classroom, and the other group acts out following the Great Commandment at recess or at lunchtime. Help each group make up a short skit demonstrating ways they show their love for others in each environment.

Jesus showed us how to love people.
He was kind.
He listened to people's problems.
He cared for all people.
Jesus wants us to act as he acted.
We do this when we love God, ourselves,
and others.

WE RESPOND

Say a prayer to Jesus. Ask Jesus to help
you to love others as he did.

Look at the pictures. Color the
star beside the pictures that show
people acting as Jesus did.

73

ACTIVITY BANK

Scripture

Great Commandment Mobile
Activity Materials: plastic or wire
hangers, yarn, triangles cut from
light-colored construction paper
(3 for each child), hole puncher,
markers or crayons

Give three triangles to each child.
Write on the board: *Love God. Love
myself. Love others.* Have the children copy a different one of these
sentences on one of the triangles. On
the back of each triangle invite the
children to draw a picture to show
what the sentence on the other side
means to them. After the children
have completed their drawings, use
a hole puncher to make a hole at the
top of each triangle. Give each child
a piece of yarn to pass through the
hole and help them to attach each of
the triangles onto a plastic or wire
hanger. Explain that their mobile
will help them to remember the
Great Commandment.

Quick Check

✔ *How do we show God that we love ourselves?* (We
take care of ourselves.)

✔ *What did Jesus do to show people he loved them?*
(He was kind, listened to problems, and cared for
them.)

WE RESPOND   ___ minutes

Connect to Life Read aloud the directions for the
We Respond activity. Talk about what is happening in
each picture. Allow time for the children to complete
the activity independently. When they have finished,
invite the children to share their chosen pictures.

Pray Have the children gather in the prayer space.
Invite them to pray quietly, asking Jesus to help them
show love for all people. Conclude by praying *Amen*
together.

Plan Ahead for Day 4

Catechist Goal: To introduce that Jesus
taught us that all people are our neighbors

Preparation: Make copies of Reproducible
Master 5, guide page 67G.

Catechist Goal

• To introduce that Jesus taught us that all people are our neighbors

Our Faith Response

• To identify ways of being a good neighbor to others

Lesson Materials

• construction paper
• scissors
• Grade 1 CD
• copies of Reproducible Master 5

Teaching Note

Child Safety

Stress that the children should always ask their parents' or guardians' permission before they help someone in their neighborhood. They should never go to someone else's home or yard without their caretaker's knowledge.

Jesus taught us that all people are our neighbors.

WE GATHER

✜ *Jesus, help us to love others as you did.*

Who are your neighbors? How do you help them?

WE BELIEVE

After Jesus taught the Great Commandment, someone asked who our neighbors are. Jesus answered by telling this story.

📖 Luke 10:30–35

Read Along

One day a man was walking down the road. Robbers hurt him and took his money. They left the man on the side of the road.

A priest walked by the person who was hurt. He did not stop to help. Then another religious leader passed and saw the hurt man. But he kept walking. Finally, a man from the country called Samaria stopped to help him. He rubbed oil on the man's cuts and covered them with bandages. The Samaritan brought the hurt man to a roadside inn.

The next day the Samaritan had to leave. He said to the innkeeper, "Take care of him. If you spend more than I have given you, I shall repay you on my way back." (Luke 10:35)

74

Lesson Plan

WE GATHER ___ minutes

✜ **Pray** Pray the Sign of the Cross and the *We Gather* prayer.

Focus on Life Encourage the children to share their responses to the first *We Gather* question. Then invite them to respond to the second question. (Possible responses: helping elderly people in their gardens; doing an errand with their parents to help a neighbor) Share a story about a time that you helped someone. Ask the children to share ideas about the ways to be good neighbors to their classmates. Tell the children that in this lesson they will learn what it means to be a good neighbor.

WE BELIEVE ___ minutes

Clarify the Term Read aloud the *We Believe* statement on page 74. Tell the children that you will read a Bible story. The hero of the story is a Samaritan. Explain: *He is called a Samaritan because he comes from a place called Samaria.*

Read Read aloud the story of the good Samaritan. Then ask:

• *How did the man from Samaria help?* (He rubbed oil on the man's cuts, covered him with bandages, took him to an inn.)

• *Who acted the way Jesus would have?* (the man from Samaria)

Then read the explanation of why Jesus uses this story.

Which man was a good neighbor?
The good neighbor was the man
from Samaria.
We call him the good Samaritan.
He cared for and helped the hurt man.

Jesus told this story to help us
understand that:

- all people are our neighbors

- we are to be good neighbors to
everyone.

WE RESPOND

How can you be a good neighbor in
your school or neighborhood this week?

Stand and shake hands with those who
are near you.

🎵 **Good Neighbors**
(*"Go 'Round and 'Round the Village"*)

Let's try to be good neighbors!
Let's try to be good neighbors!
Let's try to be good neighbors
as Jesus wants us to.

75

ACTIVITY BANK

Curriculum Connection
Art
Activity Materials: brown paper
sandwich bags, colored pencils,
crayons, construction paper, brown
or black yarn, glue

Have the children display their
understanding of the good Samaritan
story by acting it out with puppets.
Help the children make simple puppets out of brown paper bags. Have
them draw the face of a character on
the bottom of the bag, and draw the
body on the side of the bag. Have
groups of children, using their puppets and their own words, retell the
Samaritan story.

Offer a Hand Have the children trace one of their
hands on construction paper. After they cut out the hand
print, they should label it "I'll lend you a hand!" You may
want the children to tape the hand print to their desks or
display them on a bulletin board. Explain: *The hand print
is a reminder to be a loving, helpful person each day.*

Quick Check

✔ *What did the good Samaritan do for the injured man?*
(He nursed his wounds, took him to an inn, made
sure he was taken care of.)

✔ *What did Jesus teach us by telling the good Samaritan
story?* (All people are our neighbors; we are to be
good neighbors to everyone.)

WE RESPOND
_____ minutes

Connect to Life Encourage the children to share
ideas of ways they can practice being a good neighbor.

Distribute Reproducible Master 5. Play "Good
Neighbors," #5 on the Grade 1 CD. Help the children
write another verse for the song.

Pray Sing the song as a conclusion to today's lesson.

Plan Ahead for Day 5

Catechist Goal: To review chapter ideas and
their relationship to our faith life

Preparation: Make copies of *Sharing Faith
with My Family,* guide page 67E.

Catechist Goal

• To review the chapter ideas that are key to growing as disciples of Jesus Christ

Our Faith Response

• To decide on ways to grow as disciples by living out what we have learned

Show What you Know

Read the question. Ask the children to write the *Key Word* on the line.

What Would you do?

Ask children to look at the maze. Explain that there is only one way to get through it from start to finish. The goal is to get to Jesus. Note that the signs are clues. Allow children time to complete the maze. If you can, make a transparency of the maze, or use your interactive whiteboard to complete it as a class.

Make it Happen

Review that there are many ways to be good neighbors. Explain that the good neighbor chart has two columns. Ask the children to circle one of the choices from each column. Explain that the person they circled from the first column and the action they circled from the right column is one way to be a good neighbor. Talk about the ways the family in the picture is showing love for God and one another.

Take Home

Remind children that all people are our neighbors. Tell them to ask their families to find out more about neighbors through library books or the Internet, or by watching videos about people in other parts of the world.

Discuss and send home copies of *Sharing Faith with My Family*, guide page 67E.

Grade 1 Chapter 5

PROJECT

Show What you Know

What are the laws or rules given to us by God?

commandments

What Would you do?

Follow the path that will bring you closer to Jesus. Use the sign posts to help you.

76 www.webelieveweb.com

DISCIPLE

Make it Happen Be a good neighbor. Circle one item from each column and do it today.

Who will you help?	What will you do?
A classmate	Be kind
A family member	Share a story about Jesus
Someone you know in your parish	Teach him or her a prayer

DISCIPLE CHALLENGE How are the family members in the picture showing their love for God and one another?
Possible responses: The family members are sharing a story about Jesus. They are listening.

Take Home

Jesus taught us that we are all neighbors. We can show love for our neighbors. With your family, learn more about your neighbors who are from or living in other countries.

77

CHAPTER TEST

Circle the correct answer.

1. Jesus taught us that _____ people are our neighbors.

   (all)   some

2. _____ people came to hear Jesus.

   (Many)   Few

3. We show God our love when we _____.

   hurt others   (love ourselves)

4. Commandments are _____ given to us by God.

   (laws)   tests

5. Jesus _____ people's problems.

   forgot about   (listened to)

 What did Jesus teach us in the story of the good Samaritan? Possible responses: all people are our neighbors; we are to be good neighbors to everyone

78

CHAPTER TEST

Read each test item aloud and allow time for the children to mark an answer. Decide whether the *Talk About It* activity will be a small group or whole class discussion. After you have finished, check the answers. Clarify any misconceptions.

Alternative Assessment

You may want the students to complete the following alternative-assessment activity.

Draw pictures of or write about ways we show our love for God and others.

Additional Testing

• Chapter 5 Test in *Assessment Book*, pages 11–12

• CD-ROM *Test Generator and Resource*: Use Chapter 5 Test or customize your own.

Review

Review the definition as it is presented in the chapter's *Key Word* box:

• commandments (page 71).

We Believe Statements

Review the four statements.

• Many people wanted to follow Jesus.

• Jesus taught the Great Commandment.

• Jesus taught us to love God, ourselves, and others.

• Jesus taught us that all people are our neighbors.

To use the Chapter 5 Study Guide, visit

www.webelieveweb.com

The Church Year

By means of the yearly cycle the Church celebrates the whole mystery of Christ, from his incarnation until the day of Pentecost and the expectation of his coming again.

(Norms Governing Liturgical Calendars, 17)

Overview

In this chapter the children will learn about the Church year.

For Adult Reading and Reflection
You may want to refer to paragraph 1168 of the *Catechism of the Catholic Church*.

Catechist Background

Go to **www.webelieveweb.com**, Catechist/ Teacher, We Believe Correlations for this chapter's correlation to the Six Tasks of Catechesis.

W hat seasons of the Church year do you celebrate in a special way?

The annual cycle of liturgical seasons makes present to us the mysteries of redemption that we celebrate. By opening "up to the faithful the riches of her Lord's powers and merits," the Church encourages us to take hold of these riches in our own lives and to be "filled with saving grace" (CCC 1163).

The Triduum is at the heart of the liturgical year. On these days, we celebrate the Passion, Death, and Resurrection of Jesus Christ. On Easter itself, the greatest feast, the Church rejoices in the Lord's victory over death and his gift of new life to all believers. The joyful celebration of the Easter season extends until Pentecost Sunday.

During all the liturgical seasons, each Sunday is a celebration of the Lord's Resurrection, a "little Easter." Every week we gather in liturgical assembly to celebrate the Liturgy of the Word and the Liturgy of the Eucharist. Here we meet the risen Lord who strengthens us to be his disciples in our world today.

In each liturgical season, the liturgy empowers us to move beyond the limits of historical time and place and enter into God's time of salvation. We are present to Jesus' Death and Resurrection, present to his mercy and compassion, present to his challenges and his call to us in the here and now. In the liturgy we learn to know and love Jesus. We find that, "Jesus Christ is the same yesterday, today, and forever" (Hebrews 13:8).

I n what way will you enter into the celebration of the Church year?

Lesson Planning Guide

Lesson Focus	Presentation	Materials
Day 1		
Guide page 79C **Guide and Text page 79** **Introduce the Season**	• Read the *Chapter Story*. • Introduce the Church year. • Proclaim words on the banner.	
Day 2		
Guide and Text pages 80–81 **We Gather**	• Share responses to the We Gather question. • Present the We Believe text listing the special times in the Church year.	
Day 3		
Guide and Text page 82 **We Believe** **We Respond**	Do the We Respond thanking Jesus activity.	• crayons or colored pencils • Grade 1 CD
Day 4		
Text page 83 **Guide page 83–84** **We Respond in Prayer**	• Together follow Jesus through the Church year in prayer.	• prayer space items: pictures or statues of Jesus, sign with symbols of the seasons (guide page 83) ♫ "Jesus in the Morning," #3, Grade 1 CD
Day 5		
Text page 84 **Guide page 83–84, 84A** **Project Disciple**	• Complete the Project Disciple activities. Discuss the *Take Home* activity. • Complete the Reproducible Master 6 activity. See guide pages 79C and 84A. • Discuss/send home the Sharing Faith with My Family, guide page 84B.	• pencils • crayons or colored pencils • copies of Reproducible Master 6, guide page 84A • copies of Sharing Faith with My Family reproducible master, guide page 84B

For additional ideas, activities, and opportunities: Visit Sadlier's **www.WeBelieveweb.com**

Chapter Story

Sara was excited when she came home from school. She was going to visit her friend Theresa. Theresa had not been at school all week because she had broken her leg.

Sara's dad walked with Sara to Theresa's apartment. Theresa was sitting on the sofa with her leg stretched out. Sara sat beside her. Sara told her friend, "I really missed you at school today. We had music and gym class together. Mrs. Pollack told us to stand in a circle. Then she taught us to sing 'If You're Happy.' I was smiling a lot while I was singing. Mrs. Pollack said, 'You must really be happy about something, Sara. You're singing and clapping with your whole heart.'"

Theresa asked, "Why were you so happy singing the song, Sara?"

Sara answered, "I was happy because I know I was coming to visit you. Now you can show you are happy to see me by singing the song with me."

The two friends sang and clapped and laughed. When it was time for Sara to go, Theresa said, "I am so happy that you're my friend." Then Theresa clapped her hands twice and waved goodbye.

How did Sara and Theresa show their happiness? What are other ways we can show that we are happy? that we are friends?

PROJECT DISCIPLE
Additional Activities

Make it Happen

Distribute Reproducible Master 6, guide page 84A. Prepare the Grade 1 CD and have track #3, "Jesus in the Morning" ready.

Explain to the children that they are going to learn a song about praising Jesus through the whole Church year. Play the first verse of "Jesus in the Morning." Then play the second and third verses, allowing the children to practice and learn each verse.

As the music plays, ask the children to color the scene pictures on this reproducible master. Send the song home for the children to share with their family members and friends.

Picture This

Have the children work in small groups. Give each group a long sheet of paper on which to make a mural. Write on each mural paper *Jesus is with you always.* Then have the children in each group decorate their murals. Display the murals in places where they can be signs of cheer.

Praise to you, Lord Jesus Christ.

THE CHURCH YEAR

This chapter presents an overview of the Church Year.

SEASONAL CHAPTER 6

Catechist Goal

• To introduce the Church's celebration of the Church year

Our Faith Response

• To praise and thank God all through the Church year

An Online Resource

Celebrate the **Church year** *as a class, school, and/or a parish community.* Gather In My Name *events come complete with detailed leader's guides, preparation charts, handouts, promotional ideas, organizational materials, and much more. Go to:*

www.webelieveweb.com

Lesson Plan

Introduce the Season ___ minutes

• **Pray** the Sign of the Cross and the words *God, you are wonderful.*

• **Read** aloud the *Chapter Story* on guide page 79C. Discuss how Sara and Theresa showed that they were happy by laughing, clapping, and singing. Ask: *What are some other ways we show that we are happy? we are thankful?*

• **Have** the children open their texts to page 79. Ask them to look at the photograph and the art work on the page. Remind the children that God has given us many gifts. Ask: *How are the children showing God that they are happy and thankful for these gifts?*

• **Remind** the children that God's greatest gift to us is Jesus. Explain: *All through the year we remember and celebrate all that Jesus did for us.* Ask the children to stand, raise their arms in the air, and pray: *Praise to you, Lord Jesus Christ.*

Lesson Materials
- copies of Reproducible Master 6
- Grade 1 CD
- crayons or colored pencils

Teaching Tip

The Names of the Seasons

The children are just learning to identify the names of the seasons of the year: fall, winter, spring, summer. For this reason, it is recommended that you do not use the word *seasons* to refer to the special times the Church celebrates throughout the Church year.

The Church praises Jesus all year long.

WE GATHER

What does the word *praise* mean to you?

WE BELIEVE

All year long the Church gathers to thank God for his great love. Together, we praise God. We celebrate all that Jesus did for us.

80

Lesson Plan

WE GATHER ___ minutes

Focus on Life Read the *We Gather* question. Invite volunteers to share their responses. Help the children to conclude that when we praise someone, we tell them they are special and wonderful. Explain: *We tell someone that they have done something wonderful or have done something in a wonderful way.*

WE BELIEVE ___ minutes

• **Read** the *We Believe* statement in the banner at the top of page 80. Explain: *We are the Church. The Church is all the people who believe in Jesus and follow his teachings.*

• **Invite** the children to look at the photo on page 80. Ask: *What do you think the people in the photo are doing?* Stress that the people are together praising God the Father and Jesus. Then read aloud the *We Believe* paragraph on page 80.

Every year we have special times to praise and thank God. Each year we join together to celebrate these special times.

Read Along

Advent is a time of waiting. We wait and get ready for the coming of the Son of God.

Christmas is a time to celebrate the birth of the Son of God. We celebrate God's greatest gift to us, his Son, Jesus.

Lent is a time to remember all that Jesus has done for us. We get ready for the Church's great celebration.

The Three Days are the Church's greatest celebration. We remember and celebrate that Jesus died for us and rose to new life.

Easter is a time of great joy. We rejoice and celebrate that Jesus rose to new life.

Ordinary Time is when we celebrate everything about Jesus, especially his life and teachings.

Advent

Christmas

Ordinary Time

Ordinary Time

Lent

Three Days

Easter

THE CHURCH YEAR

81

ACTIVITY BANK

Multiple Intelligences
Spatial
Activity Materials: scissors, construction paper: tan, gray, or yellow

Make a copy of the chart on page 81 for each child. Help the children cut along the outside edge of the chart. Then have them glue the chart to a piece of construction paper. Tell them to write *The Church Year* above or below the chart. Then encourage the children to share the chart with their families.

• **Direct** the children's attention to the chart on page 81. Explain that the chart shows special times we praise and thank God.

• **Read** aloud the description of each season on page 81. Point out to the children where the season is on the chart border. Ask the children to say aloud what color is used for each season: Advent, purple; Christmas, white and gold; Ordinary Time, green; Lent, purple; the Three Days, white with red; Easter, white and gold.

Quick Check

✔ *When does the Church praise Jesus?* (The Church praises Jesus all year long.)

✔ *What does the Church do when we gather together?* (We praise and thank God; we celebrate all that Jesus did for us.)

81

CONNECTION

To Liturgy

The Mass is the Church's greatest celebration throughout the year. During the celebration we praise and thank God for his many gifts. You may want to teach the children the beginning of one of the Mass's prayers of praise.

"Glory to God in the highest,
    and on earth peace to people
        of good will.
We praise you,
we bless you,
we adore you,
we glorify you,
we give you thanks for your great
    glory,
Lord God, heavenly King,
O God, almighty Father."

The Church year helps us to follow Jesus. The different times help us remember and celebrate all that Jesus did for us. The times also help us remember that Jesus is with us today!

All during the year we thank Jesus for the gift of himself. We thank him for being with us always.

WE RESPOND

In the empty space, draw something or someone for whom you are thankful to Jesus.

82

Lesson Plan

WE BELIEVE (continued)

• **Read** aloud the two *We Believe* paragraphs on page 82. Have the children highlight or underline the first two sentences of the first paragraph.

• **Stress** the following points:
  ◆ Jesus is with us all during the year.
  ◆ Jesus is with us always.

WE RESPOND ___ minutes

Connect to Life Ask: *What are some things for which you are thankful?* Have volunteers share their responses.

Read the *We Respond* activity directions. While the children are drawing, you may want to play the songs that the children have learned (Grade 1 CD). When the children have finished drawing, ask them to share their pictures with the group.

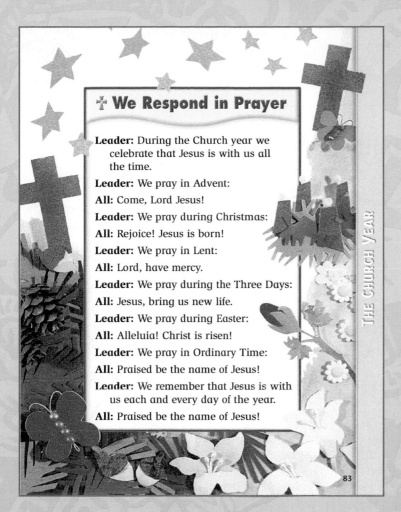

✝ We Respond in Prayer

Leader: During the Church year we celebrate that Jesus is with us all the time.

Leader: We pray in Advent:

All: Come, Lord Jesus!

Leader: We pray during Christmas:

All: Rejoice! Jesus is born!

Leader: We pray in Lent:

All: Lord, have mercy.

Leader: We pray during the Three Days:

All: Jesus, bring us new life.

Leader: We pray during Easter:

All: Alleluia! Christ is risen!

Leader: We pray in Ordinary Time:

All: Praised be the name of Jesus!

Leader: We remember that Jesus is with us each and every day of the year.

All: Praised be the name of Jesus!

83

THE CHURCH YEAR

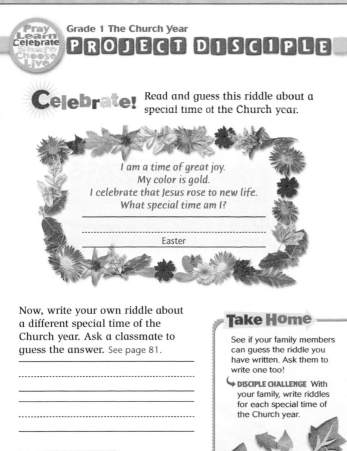

Pray
Learn
Celebrate
Share
Choose
Live

Grade 1 The Church Year

PROJECT DISCIPLE

Celebrate!
Read and guess this riddle about a special time of the Church year.

I am a time of great joy.
My color is gold.
I celebrate that Jesus rose to new life.
What special time am I?

Easter

Now, write your own riddle about a different special time of the Church year. Ask a classmate to guess the answer. See page 81.

_____
_____
_____
_____

Take Home

See if your family members can guess the riddle you have written. Ask them to write one too!

↳ **DISCIPLE CHALLENGE** With your family, write riddles for each special time of the Church year.

We Respond in Prayer (p. 83)

Prepare a sign with the name and symbol for each season (Advent, purple candle; Christmas, white/gold star; Ordinary Time, green leaves; Lent, purple cross; The Three Days, white cross outlined in red; Easter, white and yellow butterfly). Give the signs to volunteers. Gather the children into the prayer space with their books open to page 83. Read each prayer verse. Ask the child with the appropriate sign to hold it up for all to see.

📖 This Week's Liturgy
Visit **www.webelieveweb.com** for this week's liturgical readings and other seasonal material.

Project Disciple (p. 84)

Celebrate!

Explain to the children that a riddle is a puzzle that has several clues. Read aloud the clues. Ask the children to think about the answer and write it on the line. You may give a second example before asking the children to write their own Church year riddles. Refer the children to page 81 if needed. Collect the children's riddles. Read each aloud for the children to solve.

Take Home

Encourage the children to challenge their family members by writing additional riddles for each time of the Church year.

Discuss and send home copies of *Sharing Faith with My Family*, guide page 84B.

Project Disciple Additional Activities
See the activities suggested on page 79C of the guide.

Share this song with your family and friends.

Jesus in the Morning

Jesus, Jesus,
Jesus in the morning,
Jesus at the noon time;
Jesus, Jesus,
Jesus when the sun goes down!

Praise him, praise him,
Praise him during Advent,
Praise him during Christmas;
Praise him, praise him,
Praise him in Ordinary Time!

Praise him, praise him,
Praise him during Lent;
Praise him in the Three Days;
Praise him, praise him,
Praise him at Easter time!

SHARING FAITH
with My Family

Sharing What I Learned

Look at the pictures below. Use them to tell your family what you learned in this chapter.

A Family Prayer of Praise and Thanks

We praise you, Lord,
All through the year,
As seasons come and go.

We praise you, Lord,
For you are here
And with us now, we know.

Give praise and thanks to the Father!
Give praise and thanks to Jesus, his Son!
Give praise and thanks to the Holy Spirit!
Amen! Amen! Amen!

Visit Sadlier's

www.WeBelieveweb.com

Connect to the Catechism
For adult background and reflection, see paragraph 1168.

84B

Ordinary Time

Apart from those seasons having their own distinctive character, thirty-three or thirty-four weeks remain in the yearly cycle that do not celebrate a specific aspect of the mystery of Christ. Rather, especially on the Sundays, they are devoted to the mystery of Christ in all its aspects. This period is known as Ordinary Time.

(Norms Governing Liturgical Calendars, 43)

Overview

In this chapter the children will learn that we celebrate the life and teachings of Jesus in Ordinary Time.

For Adult Reading and Reflection
You may want to refer to paragraph 1163 of the *Catechism of the Catholic Church*.

Catechist Background

Go to **www.webelieveweb.com**, Catechist/Teacher, We Believe Correlations for this chapter's correlation to the Six Tasks of Catechesis.

How do Sundays make a difference in your week?

During the season of Ordinary Time, we celebrate the life and teachings of Jesus Christ. Ordinary Time is the only season that we celebrate twice during the year. The season of Ordinary Time that comes after Pentecost and before Advent is the longest season of the year. There are also some weeks of Ordinary Time between the seasons of Christmas and Lent.

Ordinary Time is named for the ordinal numbers that mark its Sundays. In Ordinary Time, the Gospel for that year (Matthew, Mark, or Luke) is read in consecutive order. These Gospels proclaim the events of Christ's ministry as well as his teachings and parables.

The key days of every season are Sundays. This is because Sunday is the day of Christ's Resurrection. Sunday is the day when the community of believers "encounters the risen Lord who invites them to his banquet" (CCC 1166). As Pope John Paul II wrote, "Weekly attendance at the Sunday Eucharist and the cycle of the liturgical year make it possible to give a rhythm to Christian life and to sanctify time, which the risen Lord opens to the blessed eternity of the kingdom" ("On Liturgical Reform," March 8, 1997). Each Sunday we gather as disciples ready to hear the Word of the Lord, to be nourished by his Body and Blood, and to encourage one another to love and serve the Lord.

When we gather to celebrate the Eucharist, we give thanks for the saving Passion, Death, and Resurrection of the Lord Jesus. We join in the rhythm of the season and sanctify our days in time. We also rejoice in Jesus' promise of life, now and forever.

How does participating in Sunday's celebration of the Eucharist give rhythm to your life?

Lesson Planning Guide

Lesson Focus	Presentation	Materials
Day 1 **Guide page 85C** **Guide and Text page 85** *Introduce the Season*	• Read the *Chapter Story.* • Introduce Ordinary Time. • Proclaim words of thanks.	
Day 2 **Guide and Text pages 86–87** *We Gather* *We Believe*	• Share responses to the We Gather question. 🏃 Do the picture-study activity about Jesus.	
Day 3 **Guide and Text page 88** *We Believe* *We Respond*	• Present the We Believe text explaining the special celebrations during Ordinary Time. 🏃 Do the We Respond activity about being a follower of Jesus.	• crayons or colored pencils
Day 4 **Text page 89** **Guide page 89–90** *We Respond in Prayer*	• Remember in prayer a special day that we honor all the saints. 🎵 Sing a song about being children of God.	🎵 "Children of God," Michael Lynch, #6, Grade 1 CD • prayer space items: green tablecloth, a Bible, a picture or statue of Jesus, green plant
Day 5 **Text page 90** **Guide page 89–90, 90A** *Project Disciple*	• Complete the Project Disciple activities. Discuss the *Take Home* activity. • Complete the Reproducible Master 7 activity. See guide pages 85C and 90A. • Discuss/send home the Sharing Faith with My Family, guide page 90B.	• pencils • crayons or colored pencils • copies of Reproducible Master 7, guide page 90A • copies of Sharing Faith with My Family reproducible master, guide page 90B

For additional ideas, activities, and opportunities: Visit Sadlier's **www.WeBelieveweb.com**

Chapter Story

During his family's picnic, Carlos talked to Belinda, his favorite cousin. Both children were in first grade but they belonged to different parishes and went to different schools.

Carlos told Belinda about his religion classes. He said, "Sometimes Mr. Stack comes to our class and asks us to help him act out Bible stories about Jesus. Mr. Stack brings a big suitcase filled with costumes and things he needs to tell stories."

Belinda asked, "What was your favorite story that Mr. Stack acted out?"

Carlos explained, "My favorite was the story of Jesus curing the blind men. We all helped act it out. Mr. Stack pretended he was Jesus walking down the road. Angel and Kyle pretended they were the blind men who called out to Jesus. They asked Jesus to heal them."

Belinda asked, "What did you do?"

"I was in the crowd. After the blind persons were healed, we all said, 'Ooh' and 'Ahh' in surprise," Carlos told his cousin.

Belinda told Carlos, "I would really like to watch and listen to Mr. Stack acting out stories about Jesus."

What story about Jesus would you like to help act out? Why?

PROJECT DISCIPLE
Additional Activities

Make *it* Happen

Distribute Reproducible Master 7, guide page 90A. Read the activity directions. Tell the children to ask you if they need help in spelling names. You may want to play instrumental music while the children are working.

After the children have finished writing, have them color the vine and leaves green. Then have them cut out the vines.

Use tape to attach the vines together. Hang the one vine you have made in the prayer space. At least once a week during Ordinary Time, have the children pray for the people whose names they have written on the vine.

Celebrate!

Plan a saints' prayer walk to have on or near All Saints' Day, November 1. Tell the children that they can dress as their favorite saints. During the walk have them sing "Children of God." Invite other groups of children to join your group for the prayer walk. After the walk, share a snack volunteers have prepared.

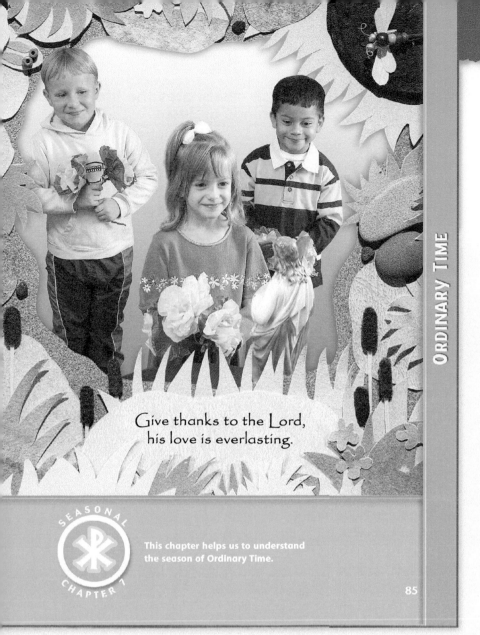

Give thanks to the Lord, his love is everlasting.

Catechist Goal

- To present Ordinary Time as the time when the Church celebrates the life and teachings of Jesus

Our Faith Response

- To discover ways to show we are followers of Jesus

An Online Resource

Celebrate **Ordinary Time** *as a class, school, and/or a parish community. Gather In My Name events come complete with detailed leader's guides, preparation charts, handouts, promotional ideas, organizational materials, and much more. Go to:*

www.webelieveweb.com

SEASONAL CHAPTER 7

This chapter helps us to understand the season of Ordinary Time.

85

Lesson Plan

Introduce the Season ___ minutes

- **Pray together:** *Jesus, thank you for showing us how to love God and others.*

- **Read** aloud the *Chapter Story* on guide page 85C. Assign partners. Have the partners discuss the question that follows the story.

- **Direct** the children to turn to page 81 in their books. Have them point to the Ordinary Time space after Easter. Ask: *What is the color of Ordinary Time?* (green)

Explain that in this chapter the children will learn how the Church celebrates Ordinary Time.

- **Direct** attention to the photo on page 85. Explain that the children are honoring Jesus. Ask: *What are other ways we can honor Jesus?* Have a few volunteers share their responses.

- **Pray** together the words below the photograph.

Lesson Materials
- copies of Reproducible Master 7
- children's books of saints
- Grade 1 CD
- scissors, tape, green crayons
- crayons or colored pencils

Teaching Tip
Marking Sundays

Explain to the children: *Long ago God asked his people to keep one day of the week as a holy day. For us Sunday is that day. Every Sunday we show God our love by doing special things.* Write *God's Day* in each Sunday space on the calendar page for the current month. Display the calendar where the children will see it often.

The Church celebrates the life and teachings of Jesus.

WE GATHER

We can put things in order by numbering them.

What is the biggest number of things that you have put in order?

WE BELIEVE

The Church has special times to celebrate. During Ordinary Time, we celebrate the life and teachings of Jesus. We try to follow him more closely each day. This season is called Ordinary Time because the Church puts the Sundays in number *order*.

Every Sunday of the year is a special day. Every Sunday we celebrate the Mass. We remember the things Jesus has done for us. We thank Jesus for the gift of himself.

86

Lesson Plan

WE GATHER ___ minutes

✝ **Pray:** *God, we love you.*

• **Focus on Life** Read the *We Gather* text. Invite volunteers to share their responses to the question. Then on the board write the letters of the alphabet in two columns, thirteen letters in a column. Point to each letter and ask the children to identify the ordinal number for the letter. Give the children the following example: *A is the first letter of the alphabet.* Write the ordinal number beside each letter. Tell the children: *First, second, fourteenth, and twenty first are examples of ordinal numbers.*

WE BELIEVE ___ minutes

• **Read** aloud the first *We Believe* paragraph. If you are presenting this lesson in Ordinary Time, identify the numbers of the previous and coming Sundays. (For example: *Last Sunday was the twenty-eighth Sunday of Ordinary Time.*)

• **Have** the children use a green crayon to underline the second sentence of the first paragraph. Explain: *Green is the color that stands for Ordinary Time.*

• **Ask** volunteers to read the last paragraph on page 86 and the first paragraph on page 87. Discuss with the children what we can do on Sundays to keep them as holy days.

We hear wonderful stories about

- Jesus' teaching, healing, and forgiving
- the first followers of Jesus
- the Holy Spirit helping the first members of the Church.

ORDINARY TIME

Look at the pictures on these pages. Which one shows Jesus teaching? Which one shows him healing? Which one tells us something about the first followers of Jesus?

✗ Share your answers.

87

ACTIVITY BANK

Faith and Media

Sunday Signs
Activity Materials: magazines, scissors, glue, sheets of poster paper, crayons

Tell the children that Sunday is a day for worshiping God, spending time with family, and resting. Have the children work in groups. Give each group a sheet of poster paper. Invite each group to make collages to illustrate appropriate activities for Sunday. Have them select pictures of people praying, singing, sharing a meal, napping, reading, and enjoying nature. Have someone in each group print a sentence about Sunday on the poster. For example: *Sunday is a special day for God and our families.* Display the posters in the neighborhood.

✗ **Direct** attention to the Scripture art. Have volunteers tell what Jesus is doing in each picture. If you have time, have the children act out each scene.

Quick Check

✔ *What do we do in Ordinary Time?* (We celebrate the life and teachings of Jesus.)

✔ *Why do we call this time "Ordinary Time"?* (The Church puts the Sundays in number order.)

CONNECTION

To Liturgy

Explain to the children: *The saints are a very important part of the Church. That is why we gather with our Church family on All Saints' Day to honor them. Together with the priest we celebrate Mass.* Tell the children that during Mass we listen to Jesus' teaching about ways we can live as children of God and followers of Jesus. Also explain that in some parishes, children dress up as their favorite saints and have a prayer walk before or after Mass.

Saints are followers of Jesus who loved him very much. The saints have died, but they now live forever with God. The lives of the saints show us how to be followers of Jesus.

We celebrate many special days during Ordinary Time. One of them is called All Saints' Day. It is celebrated on November 1.

WE RESPOND

Draw yourself here. Write one way you are a follower of Jesus.

88

Lesson Plan

WE BELIEVE (continued)

• **Invite** the children to look at the art on page 88. Explain that it shows some of the saints they have learned about in Kindergarten or will learn about this year. (The illustration shows the following saints from top to bottom: Mary, Saints Joseph, Frances of Rome, Peter, Francis of Assisi, Katharine Drexel, John Bosco, Patrick, Martin de Porres, Thérèse of Lisieux, and Rose of Lima.) Note that the children will learn more about the saints in Chapter 25.

• **Read** aloud the first paragraph on page 88. Ask the children to name their favorite saints. Then read the second *We Believe* paragraph.

WE RESPOND ___ minutes

• **Connect to Life** Ask a volunteer to read the activity directions. Give the children time to complete the activity. While the children are working, you may want to play the Grade 1 CD. When the children are finished drawing and writing, ask them to share their work with the persons sitting near them.

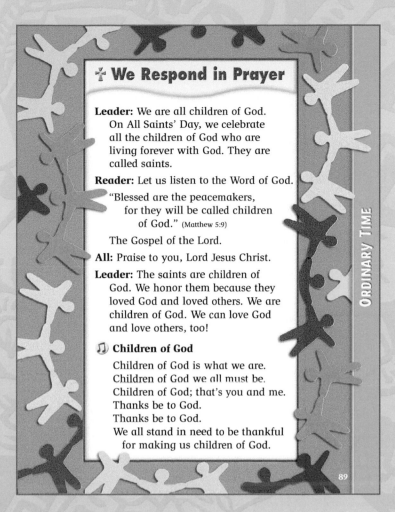

✝ We Respond in Prayer

Leader: We are all children of God. On All Saints' Day, we celebrate all the children of God who are living forever with God. They are called saints.

Reader: Let us listen to the Word of God.

"Blessed are the peacemakers, for they will be called children of God." (Matthew 5:9)

The Gospel of the Lord.

All: Praise to you, Lord Jesus Christ.

Leader: The saints are children of God. We honor them because they loved God and loved others. We are children of God. We can love God and love others, too!

🎵 **Children of God**

Children of God is what we are.
Children of God we all must be.
Children of God; that's you and me.
Thanks be to God.
Thanks be to God.
We all stand in need to be thankful for making us children of God.

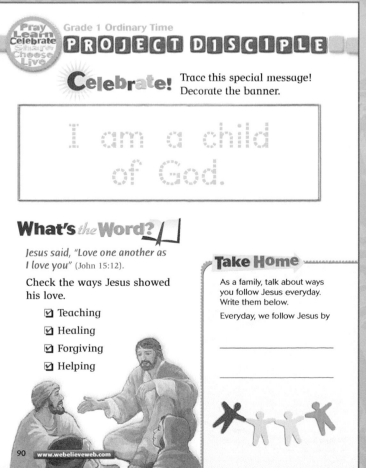

Pray Learn Celebrate Share Choose Live

Grade 1 Ordinary Time

PROJECT DISCIPLE

Celebrate! Trace this special message! Decorate the banner.

> I am a child of God.

What's *the* Word?

Jesus said, "Love one another as I love you" (John 15:12).

Check the ways Jesus showed his love.

☑ Teaching
☑ Healing
☑ Forgiving
☑ Helping

Take Home

As a family, talk about ways you follow Jesus everyday. Write them below.

Everyday, we follow Jesus by

_____

_____

We Respond in Prayer (p. 89)

Display a green plant, green tablecloth, a Bible, and a picture of Jesus in the prayer space. Invite the children into the prayer space with their books open to page 89. Explain that they will celebrate that the saints are part of the Church. Read the leader part and assign the reader part to a volunteer. Pause so the children can reflect on ways to be peacemakers. Sing "Children of God," #6 on the Grade 1 CD.

 This Week's Liturgy
Visit **www.webelieveweb.com** for this week's liturgical readings and other seasonal material.

Project Disciple (p. 90)

☀ Celebrate!

Read aloud the activity instructions and message. Instruct the children to trace the words and decorate the banner.

What's *the* Word?

Read aloud the instruction line and invite the children to check one, some, or all of the ways. Encourage them to remember all the ways Jesus showed his love.

Take Home

Encourage a class discussion about ways the children can follow Jesus every day. Ask the children to continue this discussion with their families.

Discuss and send home copies of *Sharing Faith with My Family*, guide page 90B.

Project Disciple Additional Activities See the activities suggested on page 85C of the guide.

Make a vine. Write your name on one of the leaves. On each of the other leaves write the name of a person who helps you grow close to Jesus. Color the leaves and vine green. Cut it out.

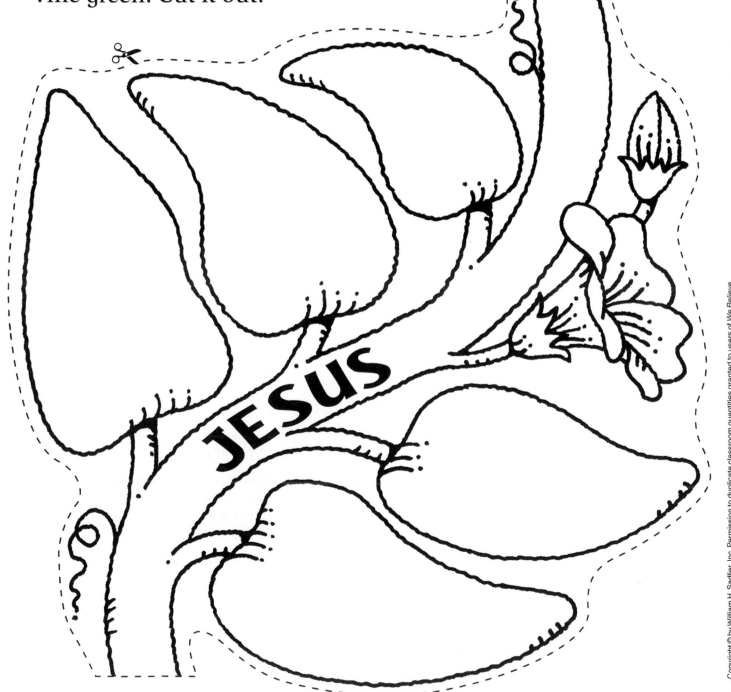

JESUS

Sharing What I Learned

Look at the pictures below. Use them to tell your family what you learned in this chapter.

Around the Table

On Sundays in Ordinary Time, we hear the teachings of Jesus. After Mass this Sunday, talk about the gospel reading that you listened to. What does Jesus teach us? How does he want us to live?

As a family decorate the words below. Together ask Jesus to help you put them into action.

LOVE ONE ANOTHER
AS I LOVE YOU.

John 15:12

Visit Sadlier's

www.WeBelieveweb.com

 Connect to the Catechism
For adult background and reflection, see paragraph 1163.

90B

ASSESSMENT

Unit 1 Test

Read aloud each set of test directions. You may also choose to read aloud each test item. Wait for a minute for the children to indicate their responses in writing before proceeding to the next item or set of directions.

Alternative Assessment

You may want the children to complete the following alternative-assessment activity.

Draw a picture. Show Jesus with his family. Tell what you know about Jesus' family.

Additional Testing

• Unit 1 Test in Grade 1 *Assessment Book*, pages 13–14

• Unit 1 Alternative Assessment in Grade 1 *Assessment Book*, page 27

• CD-ROM *Test Generator and Resource*: Use Unit 1 Test or customize your own.

Grade 1 Unit 1

UNIT TEST

Fill in the circle beside the correct answer.

1. The Bible is a special book about _____.
   - ● God
   - ○ trees

2. God sent his own Son, _____, to us.
   - ○ Joseph
   - ● Jesus

3. On Christmas, we celebrate the birth of _____.
   - ● Jesus
   - ○ Joseph

4. Jesus taught us that we should be good neighbors to _____.
   - ● everyone
   - ○ people we know

Circle the correct answer.

5. Was Jesus mean to people? Yes (No)

6. Did God create the world? (Yes) No

7. Did Jesus teach us that God watches over us and cares for us? (Yes) No

8. Was Zacchaeus Jesus' only follower? Yes (No)

continued on next page   91

Grade 1 Unit 1

Look at the two pictures below.
For each picture, write what Jesus is doing and saying. Possible responses:

9.

Jesus is saying, "Let the children come to me."

Jesus is welcoming the children.

Jesus is being a friend to the child.

10.

Jesus is saying, "What do you want me to do for you?"

Jesus is healing the sick man.

Jesus is touching the blind man's eyes so he can see.

92

---

91 and **92**

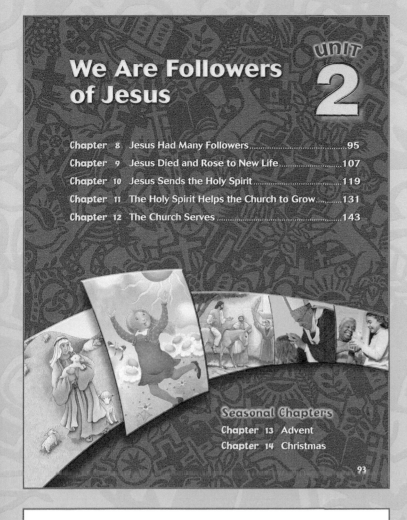

We Are Followers of Jesus

UNIT 2

Chapter 8 Jesus Had Many Followers 95

Chapter 9 Jesus Died and Rose to New Life 107

Chapter 10 Jesus Sends the Holy Spirit 119

Chapter 11 The Holy Spirit Helps the Church to Grow ... 131

Chapter 12 The Church Serves 143

Seasonal Chapters

Chapter 13 Advent

Chapter 14 Christmas

93

PROJECT DISCIPLE
DEAR FAMILY

In Unit 2 your child will grow as a disciple of Jesus by:

- appreciating that Jesus had many followers, and he taught them to pray
- understanding that Jesus died and rose to bring us new life
- learning that Jesus Christ sent the Holy Spirit to his followers
- hearing the story of Pentecost, and the ways the Holy Spirit helps the Church to grow
- recognizing that the pope and bishops lead the Church in caring for and serving others.

Celebrate!

This image is a model of the Temple in Jerusalem during Jesus' time. Jesus was Jewish, and so the roots of our Catholic faith are Jewish. If you have Jewish friends, invite them for a meal and celebrate your common heritage. Pray for all Jewish People.

Show That You Care

In Chapter 12 your child will learn about the pope and the bishops. Help your child to name the Church leaders. (Visit your parish Web site.)

Our pope is _____

Our bishop is _____

Our pastor is _____

Our parish ministers are _____

Together thank God for those who serve the Church today.

94

Reality Check

"Parents' respect and affection are expressed by the care and attention they devote to bringing up their young children and *providing for their physical and spiritual needs.*"

(*Catechism of the Catholic Church*, 2228)

Pray Today

Pray the Lord's Prayer together. Talk about the ways your family can help the Kingdom of God to grow. Remind your child that you always pray the Lord's Prayer at Mass on Sunday.

Fast Facts

The Church uses several symbols to represent the Holy Spirit: a flame, a dove, clouds and light, a hand, and others. In your church, look for any symbols for the Holy Spirit. Which symbol means the most to your family?

Take Home

Each chapter in your child's *We Believe* Grade 1 text offers a "Take Home" activity that invites your family to support your child's journey to more fully become a disciple of Christ.

Be ready for this unit's Take Home:

Chapter 8: Praying the Lord's Prayer together

Chapter 9: Praising God

Chapter 10: Joining the parish for breakfast

Chapter 11: Making a Holy Spirit poster

Chapter 12: Pledging to serve others

CLASS CONNECTION

Read aloud the unit title and the chapter titles. Ask the children: *What do you think you will be learning in this unit?* Invite a few volunteers to respond. Then explain to the children that they will be learning about Jesus' followers, the Holy Spirit, and the Church.

HOME CONNECTION

Project Disciple Dear Family

Sadlier *We Believe* calls on families to become involved in:

- learning the faith
- prayer and worship
- living their faith.

Highlighting of these unit family pages and the opportunities they offer will strengthen the partnership of the Church and the home.

For additional information and activities, encourage families to visit Sadlier's

www.WeBelieveweb.com

Chapter 8 Jesus Had Many Followers

Overview

In Chapter 5 the children learned that Jesus teaches us about love. In this chapter the children will learn about the people who followed Jesus and what they learned from him.

Doctrinal Content	For Adult Reading and Reflection *Catechism of the Catholic Church*
The children will learn:	Paragraph
• Jesus invited people to be his followers.	543
• Jesus' followers believed that he was the Son of God.	548
• Jesus showed his followers how to pray.	2759
• We pray the Lord's Prayer.	2776

Apostles (p. 97)
Lord's Prayer (p. 101)

Catechist Background

Go to **www.webelieveweb.com**, Catechist/Teacher, We Believe Correlations for this chapter's correlation to the Six Tasks of Catechesis.

How are you responding to Jesus' call?

The invitation Jesus gave to Peter and Andrew is amazing. "As he was walking by the Sea of Galilee, he saw two brothers, Simon who is called Peter, and his brother Andrew, casting a net into the sea; they were fishermen. He said to them, 'Come after me, and I will make you fishers of men.' At once they left their nets and followed him" (Matthew 4:18). Jesus spoke directly and they followed immediately! What we know and believe is that each of us, as a baptized Christian, is called in much the same way. Christ expects us to follow also, in whatever ways we can find to use the talents God has given us.

Later in the Gospel, we read that Jesus calmed the storm when his friends were afraid. (See Luke 8:22–25.) He took away their fear by giving them confidence in his power and by assuring them of his presence. Christ is here for us in the same way when we, too, ask for help.

In these incidents we see that Jesus called, he calmed, and very importantly, he also taught his disciples to pray. (See Matthew 6:5–8.) Jesus taught prayer first by his own example and then by his words. By your own prayer, you are leading in the manner that Jesus led his followers. Like him, you show both by example and by word.

These three incidents are models for each baptized person. As a catechist, you are following Christ by using your talents with your class, by asking for God's help when you need it, and by praying often.

How do you make prayer part of your life?

Lesson Planning Guide

Lesson Focus	Presentation	Materials

Day 1

page 95
**We Gather in Prayer**

pages 96–97
Jesus invited people to be his followers.

📖 *Matthew 4:18–20*

🎵 Gather together to pray in song.

🧍 Do the We Gather activity.

• Read the We Believe text about the invitation to be a follower of Jesus.

🧍 Answer Jesus' invitation.

• Reflect on the We Respond questions.

For prayer space: container of sand, shells, pebbles, toy sailboat (option)

🎵 "Jesus Wants to Help Us," Paule Freeburg and Christopher Walker, #7, Grade 1 CD

• costumes and props (option)
• copies of reproducible master *What's the Word*, guide page 95F

Day 2

pages 98–99
Jesus' followers believed that he was the Son of God.

📖 *Luke 8:22–25*

• Discuss the We Gather questions.
• Present the We Believe text about Jesus, the Son of God.
• Read the Scripture story about the storm at sea.

🧍 Act out the Scripture story.

• Share responses for We Respond.

• costumes and props

Day 3

pages 100–101
Jesus showed his followers how to pray.

📖 *Luke 11:1–2*

• Respond to the We Gather directives.
• Read and discuss the We Believe text about Jesus teaching us to pray.

🧍 Do the decorating activity.

• Discuss the We Respond questions.
• Read and discuss the *As Catholics* text.

• crayons or colored pencils

Day 4

pages 102–103
We pray the Lord's Prayer.

🧍 Do the We Gather drawing activity.

• Present the We Believe chart about the Lord's Prayer.

🧍 Make up actions for the prayer.

• Share responses for We Respond.
• Pray together.

• crayons or colored pencils
• copies of Reproducible Master 8, guide page 95G

Day 5

pages 104–105
Project Disciple

page 106
Chapter 8 Test

• Complete the Project Disciple activities.
• Explain the *Take Home* activity.
• Discuss/send home Sharing Faith with My Family, guide page 95E.
• Complete Chapter 8 Test.
• Work on *Alternative Assessment* activity.

• pencils
• crayons or colored pencils
• copies of Sharing Faith with My Family reproducible master, guide page 95E

For additional ideas, activities, and opportunities: Visit Sadlier's **www.WeBelieveweb.com**

95B

Enrichment Ideas

Chapter Story

One day in class Amy noticed that all of her classmates had blue envelopes on their desks. The envelopes all looked the same. Amy wondered what they might be.

During recess, Amy asked her friend, Tomás, about the blue envelopes. Tomás told her that the envelopes were invitations for Lisa's birthday party. Amy was upset that she did not receive an invitation. Lisa lived on her street, and Amy thought that they were good friends. "Maybe Lisa doesn't like me anymore," Amy thought.

By the end of the school day Amy still did not receive a blue envelope. Amy was putting on her coat when Lisa walked up to her.

"Hi Amy!" said Lisa. "I'm having a birthday party next Saturday afternoon. I wanted to give you your invitation in person because we are good friends. I really hope you can come. The party won't be any fun without you!"

Lisa gave the invitation to Amy. Amy smiled and said, "Thanks, Lisa! I can't wait to come to your party!"

Amy felt better. Lisa had not forgotten her. Amy and Lisa were still good friends.

▶ *Why do you think Lisa wanted to give Amy her invitation in person? How did this change Amy's feelings?*

FAITH and MEDIA

▶ On Day 1, after the class has sung the song "Jesus Wants to Help Us"—and especially if you plan to sing the song in the Day 1 *Activity Bank*—explain that songs are another example of media. People all over the world use songs to tell stories ("Mary Had a Little Lamb") and send messages ("Happy Birthday to You").

▶ On Day 3, consider supplementing the *Multicultural Connection* activity with a class visit to **www.webelieveweb.com** to listen to the Lord's Prayer. The Web site offers audio versions of many prayers. The children can quietly listen to the audio or may pray along.

CHAPTER PROJECT: WRITING SONG LYRICS

After you have presented Day 1's lesson, share the song lyrics from the Scripture activity in the *Activity Bank*. For Days 2 and 3, help the children write lyrics that retell the Scripture stories. Use the tune "Here We Go 'Round the Mulberry Bush" or another familiar tune. Record the children singing the songs and share the recording with a parish religious education group or senior-citizen group.

PROJECT DISCIPLE

Pray
Learn
Celebrate
Share
Choose
Live

Additional Activities

What's the Word?

(Use on Day 1.)

Materials needed: copies of reproducible master, guide page 95F

Distribute copies of the Scripture reproducible master. Explain to the children that they will learn a song about Jesus and the fishermen. Ask the children to repeat each verse after you sing it. Then sing the song together. Once the children have learned the words, invite them to make up actions for each verse.

Make it Happen

Dedicate some classroom wall space and write the title: *Jesus, I want to be your friend and follower. I can. . . .* Distribute a sentence strip to each child. Ask the children to finish the sentence by writing a word or phrase on the sentence strip. Display the sentence strips under the title. Remind the children to look at and read the responses throughout the week.

Picture This

Materials needed: poster paper divided into 3 sections, markers

Divide children into small groups and distribute a sheet of poster paper to each group. Explain that the children will design a cartoon strip of one of the stories about Jesus from the week's lessons. You may want to provide appropriate examples of cartoon strips. Assign each group a story: Matthew 2:18–20, Luke 8:22–25, or Luke 11:1–2. Help the children to plan out their cartoon strip before they begin their designs. Use the words *first*, *next*, and *last* to guide the retelling of the stories. Display the finished cartoons.

Pray Today

Make time throughout the week to pray the Lord's Prayer as a class. When you call the children together to pray, remind them that the Lord's Prayer is the prayer Jesus taught us.

Meeting Individual Needs
English Language Learners

Work closely with children who are learning English. Whenever possible use pictures to help the children with the meanings of difficult words and concepts.

We Believe Resources

- Grade 1 *Review & Resource Book*, pages 19–21
- Grade 1 *Family Book*, pages 24–26
- Grade 1 *Assessment Book*, pages 15–16
- Grade 1 CD-ROM *Test Generator and Resource*: Use Chapter 8 Test or customize your own.
- www.webelieveweb.com

SHARING FAITH
with My Family

Sharing What I Learned

Look at the pictures below. Use each picture to tell your family what you learned in this chapter.

For All to See and Pray

Pray the Lord's Prayer with your family.
Talk about what the words mean.

Our Father, who art in heaven,
hallowed be thy name;
thy kingdom come;
thy will be done on earth as it is in
  heaven.
Give us this day our daily bread;
and forgive us our trespasses
as we forgive those who trespass
  against us;
and lead us not into temptation,
but deliver us from evil.
Amen.

Visit Sadlier's

www.WeBelieveweb.com

Connect to the Catechism
For adult background and reflection,
see paragraphs 543, 548, 2759, and 2776.

PROJECT DISCIPLE

Pray
Learn
Celebrate
Share
Choose
Live

Name _____

What's *the* Word?

Sing this song to the tune of "Here We Go 'Round the Mulberry Bush." Make up actions to do while you sing.

Jesus saw two fishermen,
two fishermen, two fishermen.
Jesus saw two fishermen,
one day as he was walking.

Jesus called, "Come follow me."
"Come follow me." "Come follow me."
Jesus called, "Come follow me.
You can be my helpers."

Both men left their nets on shore,
their nets on shore, their nets on shore.
Both men left their nets on shore
to go and follow Jesus.

Name _____

Color the border of the chart.
Share the chart with your family and friends.

The Lord's Prayer	When we pray this prayer
Our Father, who art in heaven,	We praise God. We pray to God as our loving Father.
hallowed be thy name;	We say that God is holy. We honor and respect his name.
thy kingdom come; thy will be done on earth as it is in heaven.	We ask that all people will know and share God's love. This is what God wants for all of us.
Give us this day our daily bread;	We ask God to give us what we need. We remember all people who are hungry or poor.
and forgive us our trespasses as we forgive those who trespass against us;	We ask God to forgive us. We need to forgive others.
and lead us not into temptation, but deliver us from evil. Amen.	We ask God to keep us free from anything that goes against his love.

Jesus Had Many Followers

✝ We Gather in Prayer

🎵 Jesus Wants to Help Us

We believe Jesus wants to help us.
We believe Jesus wants to help us.
We believe that Jesus
always wants to help us.

When we pray, Jesus wants to hear us.
When we pray, Jesus wants to hear us.
We believe that Jesus
always wants to hear us.

95

PREPARING TO PRAY

The children will sing about their belief in Jesus.

• Play the song "Jesus Wants to Help Us," #7, Grade 1 CD. Have the children practice singing.

The Prayer Space

• Display things that remind the children of the chapter's Scripture stories: Jesus calls Peter and Andrew and Jesus calms a storm at sea. A container of sand, shells, pebbles, and a toy sailboat are recommended.

• On the prayer table, place an open Bible.

📖 **This Week's Liturgy**
Visit **www.webelieveweb.com** for this week's liturgical readings and other seasonal material.

Lesson Plan

We Gather in Prayer ___ minutes

✝ Pray

• Invite the children to gather in the prayer space.

• Begin by praying the Sign of the Cross. Then have the children sing "Jesus Wants to Help Us." When they have finished singing, ask the children to silently thank Jesus for helping us and for hearing our prayers.

Family Connection Update

Invite the children to share their family discussions about neighbors from or living in other countries.

Catechist Goal

• To introduce Jesus as a person who invited people to become his followers

Our Faith Response

• To accept Jesus' invitation to be his followers

 **Apostles**

Lesson Materials

• costumes and props (option)

• copies of reproducible master *What's the Word?*, guide page 95F

Teaching Note

Jesus' Followers

The concept of Jesus inviting people to be his followers is more fully developed in the Grade 2 *We Believe* text. For now, explain to the children that Jesus invited many people to be his followers. Some accepted Jesus' invitation, and some did not. Some followers traveled with Jesus most of the time; some went to see him when he was near their homes.

Jesus invited people to be his followers.

WE GATHER

✝ *Jesus, please help us to be your followers.*

🧒 Act out how you feel when you get a special invitation from a friend.

WE BELIEVE

Jesus invited people to come and be with him.
He asked people to be his followers.
Here is a story about our friend Jesus and his first followers.

📖 Matthew 4:18–20

Read Along

One day Jesus was walking by the sea. He saw two brothers fishing. Their names were Peter and Andrew.

Jesus invited Peter and Andrew to be his followers. "At once they left their nets and followed him." (Matthew 4:20)

96

Lesson Plan

WE GATHER ___ minutes

✝ **Pray** Invite the children to pray the Sign of the Cross and the *We Gather* prayer.

Focus on Life Ask the children to think about the way they feel when they receive a special invitation from a friend. Encourage volunteers to act out these situations. Share the *Chapter Story* on guide page 95C. Tell the children that in this lesson they will learn that Jesus asked people to be his followers.

WE BELIEVE ___ minutes

Invitation to Follow Read aloud the *We Believe* statement. Stress: *Jesus asked many people to be his followers.*

Share a Scripture Story Have the children look at the picture on pages 96 and 97. Ask: *What do you think Jesus is saying to the two fishermen?* Read the story. Explain: *Peter and Andrew had heard about Jesus who was going from village to village teaching. They were not just following a stranger whom they knew nothing about.*

Then read the *We Believe* text that follows the Scripture story. Stress:

• *Followers of Jesus learned from him.*

• *Followers of Jesus shared God's love with others.*

Act Out the Story If time permits, invite volunteers to act out the Scripture story. Have the children look at the picture on the pages. Ask some children to take the parts of the people sitting on the beach.

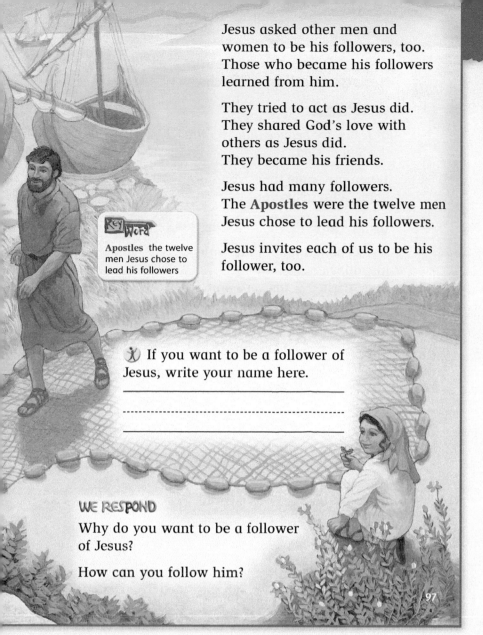

Jesus asked other men and women to be his followers, too. Those who became his followers learned from him.

They tried to act as Jesus did. They shared God's love with others as Jesus did. They became his friends.

Jesus had many followers. The **Apostles** were the twelve men Jesus chose to lead his followers.

Jesus invites each of us to be his follower, too.

Key Word
Apostles the twelve men Jesus chose to lead his followers

If you want to be a follower of Jesus, write your name here.

_____
- -
_____

WE RESPOND

Why do you want to be a follower of Jesus?

How can you follow him?

97

ACTIVITY BANK

Scripture
Musical, Bodily-Kinesthetic
For a Scripture activity, see *What's the Word?*, guide page 95F.

Present the Key Word Write the word *Apostles* on the board. Explain: *Peter and Andrew were two of Jesus' Apostles. They became leaders of Jesus' many followers.*

Do the Activity Ask: *Do you want to be a follower of Jesus?* Ask the children to write their names on the line provided.

Quick Check

✔ *What did Jesus invite people to do?* (Jesus invited people to be his followers.)

✔ *Who were the Apostles?* (They were the twelve men Jesus chose to lead his followers.)

WE RESPOND ___ minutes

Connect to Life Provide a minute of quiet time. Have the children reflect on the *We Respond* questions. Tell the children that they can be good friends to Jesus and to others by acting as Jesus did.

Pray Conclude the day's lesson by inviting the children to pray the following words aloud: *Jesus, thank you for calling me to follow you. Help me to act as you did and help me to be your friend.*

Plan Ahead for Day 2

Catechist Goal: To present that Jesus' followers believed that he was the Son of God

Preparation: Reflect on the *We Respond* questions.

Catechist Goal

• To present that Jesus' followers believed that he was the Son of God

Our Faith Response

• To show through prayer and action our belief in Jesus Christ as the Son of God

Lesson Materials

• costumes and props

Teaching Tip

When Accidents Happen

Sometimes in the children's enthusiasm in acting out stories or making gestures when praying, accidents may happen. For example, if a child knocks over something displayed, remain calm. After pausing for a moment help the child pick up the object. Then have everyone continue what they were doing.

Jesus' followers believed that he was the Son of God.

WE GATHER

✝ *Jesus, we believe that you are the Son of God.*

When are some times you need help? Who helps you?

WE BELIEVE

Jesus spent a lot of time with his followers.
They trusted Jesus very much.
Here is a story about a time when Jesus helped his followers.

📖 Luke 8:22–25

Read Along

One day Jesus was in a boat with his followers. He fell asleep. Soon a storm started rocking the boat. Jesus' followers were afraid. They woke Jesus up. They believed he would help them.

Jesus told the winds and waves to be still. Jesus' followers were amazed because the storm stopped. They asked, "Who then is this, who commands even the winds and the sea, and they obey him?" (Luke 8:25)

✸ Act out the story.

98

Lesson Plan

WE GATHER ___ minutes

✝ **Pray** Invite the children to stand to pray the *We Gather* prayer.

Focus on Life Ask the children to name different times when they need help and people who help them. Write the responses on the board or on chart paper. Tell the children that in this lesson they will learn that Jesus' followers trusted and believed in him.

WE BELIEVE ___ minutes

Share a Scripture Story Read the *We Believe* statement and the first *We Believe* paragraph. Tell the children that they will learn about an amazing thing that Jesus did to help his followers. Have the children

look at the pictures on the pages as you read the story dramatically.

Do the Activity Invite the children to act out the Scripture story. Ask for volunteers to play Jesus and his followers. Have the rest of the class form human "waves" as the story is acted out. Have the children playing the "waves" sit in a circle around Jesus and his followers. Tell each child to stand one-by-one, and throw his or her arms up in the air. As the children are acting like the "waves," have them make storm noises. Then the child portraying Jesus commands the wind and waves to be still. The children acting as the "waves" should stop their actions. Conclude the activity by reading aloud the last *We Believe* paragraph.

Jesus did amazing things to
help people.
Jesus calmed the storm.
He did many things that only God
can do.
Jesus' followers saw these things and
believed in him.
They believed Jesus was the Son of God.

WE RESPOND

Imagine that you were on that boat
with Jesus.
What would you have said to Jesus
after he calmed the storm?

What will you do to show that you
believe in Jesus?

Pray together.
Jesus, Son of God, we believe in you.

99

ACTIVITY BANK

Curriculum Connection
Art
Activity Materials: water color
paints, water color paper
Have the children work in pairs.
Ask one child in each pair to paint a
picture of the beginning of the story
of the storm in action. Then ask the
other partner to paint a picture of the
quiet sea after Jesus had calmed it.
When the partners have finished,
display the pairs of pictures in the
school hallway.

Quick Check

✔ *What did Jesus' followers believe?* (They believed that
Jesus was the Son of God.)

✔ *In the Scripture story, what did Jesus do for his
followers?* (He calmed the wind and waves.)

WE RESPOND ___ minutes

Connect to Life Read aloud the *We Respond* directive and question. Draw several speech balloons on the
board or on chart paper. Invite volunteers to share
what they would have said to Jesus after he calmed the
storm. Write these responses in the speech balloons.
Display the balloons in the prayer space. Ask the children to volunteer ways they can show they believe in

Jesus. Stress: *Sharing God's love with other people is one
way to show Jesus we believe in him.*

Pray Read the second *We Respond* question. Provide a
minute of quiet time in which the children can reflect
on their responses. Then read together the *We Respond*
prayer.

Plan Ahead for Day 3

Catechist Goal: To explore how Jesus taught
his followers to pray

Preparation: Reflect on the Scripture illustration on page 100.

Catechist Goal

• To explore how Jesus taught his followers to pray

Our Faith Response

• To pray as Jesus taught

 **Lord's Prayer**

Lesson Materials

• colored pencils or crayons

As Catholics...

The Title Lord

After you have presented the lesson, read aloud the *As Catholics* text. Remind the children to listen for the word *Lord* during next Sunday's Mass.

Jesus showed his followers how to pray.

WE GATHER

✝ *Jesus, you are always with us.*

Talk about something you have learned by listening to others.

Talk about something you have learned by watching other people.

WE BELIEVE

Jesus often prayed to God the Father. Sometimes Jesus prayed alone. Sometimes he prayed with other people.

Jesus' followers learned to pray by watching him pray. They learned to pray by listening to Jesus, too.

 Luke 11:1–2

Read Along

One day Jesus was praying. When he was finished, one of his followers asked him to teach the group to pray.

Jesus told his followers, "When you pray, say: 'Father, hallowed be your name.'" (Luke 11:2)

100

Lesson Plan

WE GATHER ___ minutes

✝ **Pray** Invite the children to pray the Sign of the Cross and the *We Gather* prayer.

Focus on Life Read the *We Gather* text. Invite volunteers to tell what they have learned by listening. List responses on the board. (Possible responses: words to a song, favorite stories, what to do at home and at school) Then invite volunteers to tell what they learn by watching other people. (Possible responses: how to make things, how to dance, how to play games) List responses on the board. Emphasize that we can learn many things by listening to and watching others. Tell the children that in this lesson they will learn that Jesus showed his followers how to pray.

WE BELIEVE ___ minutes

Read Scripture Invite the children to look at the picture of Jesus' followers watching him pray. Point out: *Sometimes Jesus prayed by himself; sometimes he prayed with others.* Then read the first two *We Believe* paragraphs and the Scripture passage.

Learn the Lord's Prayer Read each line of the Lord's Prayer; pause and have the children repeat the words.

Do the Activity Have the children decorate the border of the prayer.

We call the prayer Jesus taught his followers the **Lord's Prayer**.
We also call this prayer the Our Father.
Here are the words we pray.

> Our Father, who art in heaven,
> hallowed be thy name;
> thy kingdom come;
> thy will be done on earth as it is in heaven.
> Give us this day our daily bread;
> and forgive us our trespasses
> as we forgive those who trespass against us;
> and lead us not into temptation,
> but deliver us from evil.
> Amen.

Decorate the prayer frame.

WE RESPOND

Who teaches you to pray?
Why do you pray?

As Catholics...

Lord is another name for God. Jesus' followers sometimes called him Lord. We use the name *Lord* in many of our prayers. When we do this, we remember that Jesus is the Son of God.

During Sunday Mass, listen for the times we pray, "Lord."

101

ACTIVITY BANK

Liturgy
Liturgical Music
Activity Materials: musical recording of the Lord's Prayer

Tell the children that the Lord's Prayer is sometimes sung at Mass. If possible, play a musical recording of the prayer. Have the children listen; then play the recording again and invite them to sing along.

Multicultural Connection
Our Father
Activity Materials: chart or poster paper

Before the activity, write the first line of the Lord's Prayer in different languages. Then teach the children the phrase in the different languages. You may wish to use the following.

- Italian   *Padre Nostro* (Pa-dray Nō-strō)
- Spanish   *Padre Nuestro* (Pa-dray New-es-trō)
- Swahili   *Baba Yetu* (Ba-ba Yay-too)
- French   *Notre Pere* (Nō-tra Pear)

Quick Check

✔ *What did Jesus teach his followers to do?* (He taught them to pray.)

✔ *What prayer did Jesus teach his followers?* (He taught them the Lord's Prayer.)

WE RESPOND   __ minutes

Connect to Life Invite the children to answer the *We Respond* questions. Help the children to think about the people who teach them to pray. Ask volunteers to explain why people pray.

Pray Invite the children to bring their books with them and gather in the prayer space. Tell them: *Let us remember the people who teach us to pray as we pray the Lord's Prayer together.* Slowly read the prayer aloud as the children pray along.

Plan Ahead for Day 4

Catechist Goal: To teach the meaning of the words of the Lord's Prayer

Preparation: Make copies of Reproducible Master 8, guide page 95G.

Catechist Goal

• To teach the Lord's Prayer and the meaning of the words

Our Faith Response

• To pray the Lord's Prayer in a meaningful way

Lesson Materials

• colored pencils or crayons
• copies of Reproducible Master 8

Teaching Note

Sensitivity to Family Differences

For today's *We Gather* activity, the children are asked to draw a picture of their families praying. Be sensitive to the fact that some families may not pray together at home. Tell the children that they can draw a picture of their families praying at home or at church. Emphasize the idea that participating together at Mass is a way that they pray together with their families.

We pray the Lord's Prayer.

WE GATHER

✝ *Jesus, teach us to pray as you did.*

🧍 Draw a picture to show a time you prayed with your family.

WE BELIEVE

Jesus taught his followers the Lord's Prayer.

We can pray this prayer with others or by ourselves.

102

Lesson Plan

WE GATHER ___ minutes

✝ **Pray** Invite the children to pray the Sign of the Cross together. Then have the children repeat the *We Gather* prayer.

Focus on Life Ask the children to do the *We Gather* activity. You may want to suggest a few ideas for the drawing, such as praying before a family meal, at bedtime, or during Mass on Sunday. Invite volunteers to share their pictures and explain them. Tell the children that in this lesson they will learn the meaning of the words of the Lord's Prayer.

WE BELIEVE ___ minutes

Learn the Lord's Prayer Read aloud the *We Believe* opening sentences. Explain to the children that each verse of the Lord's Prayer is given with a brief explanation. Invite the class to read each verse of the prayer as it is given on the page. Then read aloud what we are saying when we pray these words. Invite the children to ask questions about each individual verse.

Do the Activity Point out to the children that along with saying the words, we can also use prayerful actions as we pray the Lord's Prayer. Encourage the children to give their ideas on some actions that can be done as they pray. Offer a few suggestions. For example, you might point upward for "Our Father, who art in heaven." Then place the palms of your hands together for "hallowed be thy name." When the children have decided on actions for the whole prayer, have them stand. Ask a few volunteers to lead the class. Together read the prayer aloud along with the prayerful actions.

The Lord's Prayer	When we pray this prayer:
Our Father, who art in heaven,	We praise God. We pray to God as our loving Father.
hallowed be thy name;	We say that God is holy. We honor and respect his name.
thy kingdom come; thy will be done on earth as it is in heaven.	We ask that all people will know and share God's love. This is what God wants for all of us.
Give us this day our daily bread;	We ask God to give us what we need. We remember all people who are hungry or poor.
and forgive us our trespasses as we forgive those who trespass against us;	We ask God to forgive us. We need to forgive others.
and lead us not into temptation, but deliver us from evil. Amen.	We ask God to keep us free from anything that goes against his love.

ⅹ̇ Make up actions for the Lord's Prayer.

WE RESPOND

When do you hear the Lord's Prayer prayed?
Gather in a circle. Pray the Lord's Prayer together.

103

ACTIVITY BANK

Multiple Intelligences
Verbal-Linguistic
Activity Materials: two pieces of poster board, marker, scissors

Have prepared two copies of the Lord's Prayer written on poster board. Then cut the poster boards into six sections. Follow the sections presented in the lesson. Divide the class into two groups. Give each group a set of the six scrambled strips. Explain to the children that they have to arrange the Lord's Prayer strips in the correct order. Whichever group completes the task correctly reads the prayer aloud. Allow the other group to continue until the Lord's Prayer is completed.

Quick Check

✔ *Who taught his followers the Lord's Prayer?* (Jesus taught us the Lord's Prayer.)

✔ *When we pray the Lord's Prayer, what do we ask God?* (We ask God to give us what we need; to forgive us; to keep us from anything that goes against his love.)

WE RESPOND   __ minutes

Connect to Life Invite volunteers to answer the *We Respond* question. Explain: *We pray the Lord's Prayer with our parish family at Mass. We can pray the Lord's Prayer with others or by ourselves. For example, you may pray it upon waking up or before going to bed, before going to* school, *or when you are sad or afraid.* Stress: *Praying this prayer at any time will bring you closer to God.*

Distribute copies of Reproducible Master 8. Have the children color the border of the chart. Encourage the children to show the chart to their families.

Pray Gather the children in a circle. You might want the children to hold hands as they pray the Lord's Prayer.

Plan Ahead for Day 5

Catechist Goal: To review chapter ideas and their relationship to our faith life

Preparation: Make copies of *Sharing Faith with My Family,* guide page 95E.

Catechist Goal
• To review the chapter ideas that are key to growing as disciples of Jesus Christ

Our Faith Response
• To decide on ways to grow as disciples by living out what we have learned

Show What you Know

Read aloud the activity instruction. Point out the two *Key Words* in the box to the right of the activity. Read aloud each question, allowing time for the children to write the appropriate *Key Word* on the line provided. Ask volunteers to share the answers. Clarify any misconceptions.

Pray Today
Read the opening line. Ask a volunteer to read the prayer while the children listen and look at the photo. Discuss the way the prayer shows trust in God.

What's the Word?

Read aloud the paragraph. Together, brainstorm and make a list of things that people need. You may consider an alternate list of things that people *want* if you find that some of the suggestions are not needs. Then ask the children to complete the activity individually.

Make it Happen

Read aloud the instruction line and the possible choices (the checklist). Have children check the ways and write a way to follow Jesus. Encourage them to do these things during the week.

Take Home

Encourage the children to relate the stories about Jesus from the week's lessons to their families. Remind them to pray the Lord's Prayer with them, too!

Discuss and send home copies of *Sharing Faith with My Family*, guide page 95E.

Grade 1 Chapter 8

PROJECT

Show What you Know

Apostles
Lord's Prayer

Write the that answers each question.

What is the prayer Jesus taught his followers?

Lord's Prayer

Who are the twelve men Jesus chose to lead his followers?

Apostles

Pray Today
Many fishermen in France pray this prayer. It shows they trust God.

*Dear God,
be good to me.
The sea is so wide,
and my boat is so small.*
(Fishers of Brittany, France)

104 www.webelieveweb.com

DISCIPLE

What's the Word?

Jesus taught us to pray the Lord's Prayer. Part of this prayer is, "Give us this day our daily bread." When we pray these words, we are praying for the needs of all people. Draw some things that people need today.

Possible drawings: food; water; shelter; love; family and friends; the sun; the rain

Make it Happen

Finish this message to Jesus. As your friend and follower, I can
❑ share my toys.
❑ pay attention in school.
❑ say my prayers.
❑ help a friend.

Possible responses: help my family;
❑ care for my pet; be kind to others
(your own way)

Take Home
Share the stories about Jesus you have learned this week. Pray the Lord's Prayer together as a family. Talk about what the words mean.

105

CHAPTER TEST

Circle the correct answer.

1. The _____ of Jesus learned from him.

   teachers   (followers)

2. Jesus' followers believed that he was _____.

   (the Son of God)   an Apostle

3. Jesus taught his followers the _____.

   Sign of the Cross   (Lord's Prayer)

4. The _____ men Jesus chose to lead his followers were the Apostles.

   (twelve)   ten

5. Jesus _____ prayed to God the Father.

   never   (often)

 What did Jesus do to help his followers in the storm? calmed the storm

106

CHAPTER TEST

Read each test item aloud and allow time for the children to mark an answer. Decide whether the *Talk About It* activity will be a small group or whole class discussion. After you have finished, check the answers. Clarify any misconceptions.

Alternative Assessment

You may want the students to complete the following alternative-assessment activity.

> *Write sentences or draw pictures about Jesus' first followers. What did they see? What did they hear?*

Additional Testing

• Chapter 8 Test in *Assessment Book*, pages 15–16

• CD-ROM *Test Generator and Resource*: Use Chapter 8 Test or customize your own.

Review

Review the definitions as they are presented in the chapter's *Key Word* boxes:

• Apostles (page 97)
• Lord's Prayer (page 101).

We Believe Statements

Review the four statements.

• Jesus invited people to be his followers.
• Jesus' followers believed that he was the Son of God.
• Jesus showed his followers how to pray.
• We pray the Lord's Prayer.

To use the Chapter 8 Study Guide, visit

www.webelieveweb.com

Overview

In Chapter 8 the children learned about Jesus' followers and what he taught them. In this chapter the children learn that Jesus loves us and that he died on the cross and rose to new life for us.

Doctrinal Content	For Adult Reading and Reflection *Catechism of the Catholic Church*
The children will learn:	Paragraph
• Jesus told his followers that he loved and cared for them.	754
• Many people gathered to welcome and praise Jesus.	559
• Jesus taught in the Temple in Jerusalem.	584
• Jesus died and rose.	638

Temple (p. 113)
Easter Sunday (p. 115)

Catechist Background

What gives you hope?

Go to **www.webelieveweb.com**, Catechist/ Teacher, We Believe Correlations for this chapter's correlation to:
• Six Tasks of Catechesis
• *Catechetical Formation in Chaste Living.*

One important aspect of Jesus' message, that he loves us and cares for us, is captured in the story of the Good Shepherd. (See John 10:1–18.) This story was one to which the people of Jesus' day could relate. It contains a profound message of someone who watches over us and will even sacrifice his life for us. As Jesus taught this lesson of his ultimate love, people's hearts were uplifted and they found hope. It was this hope in Jesus that drew people to welcome him into Jerusalem with palms and shouts of "Hosanna!" The people were joyful because they had hope in their hearts.

The angel who met the women at the empty tomb on Easter morning repeated a message of love and hope. He told the women not to be afraid. We, too, believe Christ is with us as he promised. We do not have to give in to fear but can always find the hope that comes from faith.

Truly it is what happened between those two events of Palm Sunday and Easter Sunday that is so amazing. Jesus did what he said the Good Shepherd was willing to do. He gave his own life for us. How easily we say, "Jesus rose again on the third day." But it is the miracle of miracles. He rose again. And because of that, we will too.

The promise of Eternal Life enables Christians to be persons of hope. Every day of our lives we face that challenge. We can be hopeful because we have faith in what Jesus did for us. This gives us joy and peace in our hearts. When our own joyful hope shines through, we give a powerful message to the children in our care. This is what a Christian believer is like!

How does your belief in the Resurrection of Christ affect your daily life?

Lesson Planning Guide

Lesson Focus	Presentation	Materials

Day 1

page 107
We Gather in Prayer

pages 108–109
Jesus told his followers that he loved and cared for them.

📖 *John 10:2, 14*

- Praise and thank Jesus in prayer.
- Discuss the picture and answer the **We Gather** question.
- Read the **We Believe** text about Jesus our Good Shepherd.
- 🕴 Do the activity to show ways to love.
- Discuss the **We Respond** question.

For the prayer space: a Bible, a cross, palm branches, a picture of Jesus, the Good Shepherd (option)

- crayons or colored pencils

Day 2

pages 110–111
Many people gathered to welcome and praise Jesus.

📖 *John 12:12–13*

- 🕴 Do the **We Gather** activity.
- Read the Scripture story in **We Believe** to introduce the events of Palm Sunday.
- Share responses for **We Respond**.
- 🕴 Do the activity about praising Jesus.
- Read and discuss the *As Catholics* text.

- crayons or colored pencils, scissors
- copies of Reproducible Master 9, guide page 107G

Day 3

pages 112–113
Jesus taught in the Temple in Jerusalem.

📖 *Luke 21:37–38*

- Share responses for **We Gather**.
- Read and discuss the **We Believe** text about the Temple in Jerusalem.
- 🎵 Sing a song about the house of God.
- 🕴 Make up actions for the song.
- Discuss the **We Respond** question.

- 🎵 "In the House of God," Christopher Walker, #8, Grade 1 CD
- globe or world map
- pictures of Jerusalem and the Temple in the time of Jesus (option)

Day 4

pages 114–115
Jesus died and rose.

📖 *John 19:18, 25, 30, 42*
Matthew 28:1–7

- Follow the **We Gather** directive and discuss the question.
- Read the Scripture stories in **We Believe** about Jesus' Death and rising.
- Share responses for **We Respond**.
- 🕴 Do the activity to celebrate Jesus' love.

- crayons or colored markers
- Grade 1 CD (option)
- copies of reproducible master *What's the Word?*, guide page 107F

Day 5

pages 116–117
Project Disciple

page 118
Chapter 9 Test

- Complete the **Project Disciple** activities.
- Explain the *Take Home* activity.
- Discuss/send home **Sharing Faith with My Family**, guide page 107E.
- Complete **Chapter 9 Test**.
- Work on *Alternative Assessment* activity.

- pencils
- copies of **Sharing Faith with My Family** reproducible master, guide page 107E

For additional ideas, activities, and opportunities: Visit Sadlier's **www.WEBELIEVEweb.com**

Enrichment Ideas

Chapter Story

Yoshi was very excited. His Aunt Kaya was coming to visit. Aunt Kaya lived far away in the country of Japan.

Yoshi's family had many things to do to get ready for their visitor. Yoshi helped his parents clean the apartment. He picked up his toys and put them away. Yoshi wanted everything to look beautiful for his aunt.

The smell in the kitchen was delicious. Yoshi's mom made Aunt Kaya's favorite dessert—chocolate cake. When the cake cooled, Yoshi put icing on it.

Then Yoshi and his dad drove to the airport to pick up his aunt. In one of the airport shops, Yoshi's dad bought flowers to give to Aunt Kaya. He told Yoshi that he could give the flowers to his aunt as soon as she arrived. Yoshi couldn't wait!

Yoshi and his dad waited a long time. Aunt Kaya's flight was delayed. But then they heard that the plane was landing. After about thirty minutes they saw Aunt Kaya walking toward them. Yoshi hugged his aunt and gave her the flowers. Aunt Kaya said, "Yoshi, thank you for making me feel so welcome." Yoshi told his aunt, "We have more surprises at home."

▶ *How do you think Yoshi's aunt felt about her welcome?*

FAITH and MEDIA

▶ If you do this week's *Chapter Project: Proclaim the Good News*, remind the children that news bulletins are examples of media. You might also want to post the finished series of news bulletins on a bulletin board.

▶ On Day 3, after reading about Jesus' teaching in the Temple in Jerusalem, you might want to visit the Internet. As a class locate a site to see pictures of what archaeologists think the Temple might have looked like.

▶ On Day 2, if you do the "Bumper Stickers for Jesus" activity (*Activity Bank*), remind the children that bumper stickers are another example of media.

CHAPTER PROJECT: PROCLAIM THE GOOD NEWS

Have the children work together to prepare a "Good News Bulletin" proclaiming how much Jesus loves us. Have the children form four groups. Each day invite one of the groups to print important words from the day's lesson on chart paper. Then have the group decide on a scene or scenes that represent what they have learned in the lesson. Ask artists in the group to draw a picture or pictures of the scene(s) chosen. When all four groups have had a turn, compile their efforts in order into a class "Good News Bulletin." Display the bulletin in the classroom or hallway to share the Good News with other classes.

PROJECT DISCIPLE

Pray
Learn
Celebrate
Share
Choose
Live

Additional Activities

What's *the* Word?

(Use on Day 4.)

Materials needed: copies of reproducible master, guide page 107F

Distribute copies of the Scripture reproducible master. Explain to the children that they will do an activity to remember the story of Jesus rising to new life. Choose eight volunteers to read the parts of Readers 1–6, the Angel, and the Women. Ask the other children to play the part of All. Encourage the children to read their parts dramatically and imagine that they were truly present on the day Jesus rose.

Picture This

Help the children to compare Jesus and a shepherd by completing a graphic organizer as a class. Write *Shepherds* and *Jesus* on the board. List the attributes of each under the titles. Then discuss as a class the similarities between shepherds and Jesus, our Good Shepherd.

More *to* Explore

Prepare a slide show of images or a video that shows the city of Jerusalem at the time of Jesus and today. (Travel Web sites may be helpful.) Explain to the children that many Catholics still visit this part of the world. Encourage them to ask family members and friends if they have ever visited this part of the world.

Make *it* Happen

Materials needed: drawing paper, colored pencils or crayons

Remind the children that the Church teaches us that we should respect all workers. Make a list of people in the school or community who care for and protect the people. You may refer to the *Reality Check* activity on Day 5 and include other examples. When the list is complete, distribute drawing paper to the children. Encourage the children to make a thank you card for one of the people named. Be sure the children do not include identifying or personal information. Send the cards to the appropriate recipients.

Meeting Individual Needs
Children Who Are Visual Learners

Ask the children who are visual learners to describe what they see in each illustration of the chapter. Point out to all the children that studying the pictures will help them to remember the concepts presented.

We Believe Resources

- Grade 1 *Review & Resource Book*, pages 22–24
- Grade 1 *Family Book*, pages 27–29
- Grade 1 *Assessment Book*, pages 17–18
- Grade 1 CD-ROM *Test Generator and Resource*: Use Chapter 9 Test or customize your own.

- **www.webelieveweb.com**

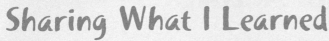
Sharing What I Learned

Look at the pictures below. Use each picture to tell your family what you learned in this chapter.

  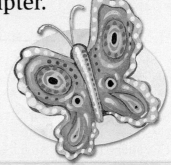

Family Prayer Table

Set up a prayer table in your home. Place the table in a space where the family can easily gather or where people can pray by themselves. Look at the photo for ideas.

Invite the family to gather at the prayer table each night this week. Pray in your own words. Thank Jesus for all he has done for us.

Together, write your own family prayer here:

_____

_____

Visit Sadlier's

www.WEBELIEVEweb.com

 Connect to the Catechism
For adult background and reflection, see paragraphs 754, 559, 584, and 638.

PROJECT DISCIPLE

Pray
Learn
Celebrate
Share
Choose
Live

Name _____

What's *the* Word?

Reader 1: It was Sunday, the third day after Jesus died.

Reader 2: Something wonderful happened!

Reader 3: Early that morning women went to visit Jesus' tomb.

Reader 4: They saw an angel sitting in front of it.

Angel: "Do not be afraid!" (Matthew 28:5)

Reader 5: The angel told the women that Jesus had risen.

Reader 6: The women ran to tell Jesus' other followers the Good News.

Women: Jesus is risen from the dead!

All: Alleluia! Alleluia!

Name _____

Read the word on the palm branch.

Color the palm branch.

Cut it out.

Use the branch as you praise God together.

Hosanna

✝ We Gather in Prayer

Leader: Jesus, today we gather together to pray to you.

All: Jesus, we believe in you.

Leader: Jesus, you are wonderful.

All: Jesus, we praise you.

Leader: Jesus, you have done so much for us.

All: Jesus, we thank you.

Leader: Jesus, we want to follow you.

All: Jesus, help us to be your followers.

107

PREPARING TO PRAY

The children will praise and thank Jesus.

• Choose a child to be the leader of prayer. Help this child prepare.

The Prayer Space

• Display a picture of Jesus, the Good Shepherd. (option)

• Place a Bible, a cross, and palm branches on the prayer table.

📖 **This Week's Liturgy**

Visit **www.webelieveweb.com** for this week's liturgical readings and other seasonal material.

Lesson Plan

We Gather in Prayer ___ minutes

✝ Pray

• Invite the children to bring their books and gather in the prayer space. Ask the children to open their books to page 107. Have them look at the stained-glass window of Jesus as they pray.

• Ask the leader to begin and then have the children join in saying the prayer.

• After the children pray the last response, pray together the Lord's Prayer.

Family Connection Update

Invite the children to share the times when their families prayed the Our Father together.

Catechist Goal

• To explain Jesus' message of love and care for his followers

Our Faith Response

• To love and care for others as Jesus does

Lesson Materials

• crayons or colored pencils

Teaching Tip

Listening

Show the children how to be good listeners. Be sure that you are giving the children your undivided attention when they speak to you. Establish eye contact and maintain a posture that indicates you are an active and involved listener. Have the children practice following your example.

Jesus told his followers that he loved and cared for them.

WE GATHER

✝ *Jesus, help us to love and care for others.*

Look at the picture. What is happening?

WE BELIEVE

Jesus was a good teacher.
He wanted his followers to understand what he was teaching.
He talked about things they knew about.

📖 John 10:2,14

Read Along

One day Jesus was talking about shepherds. He said, "I am the good shepherd, and I know mine and mine know me." (John 10:14)

Jesus' followers knew all about shepherds.
Shepherds stay with their sheep night and day.
They take care of many sheep.
They know each of their sheep.
They do everything they can to keep each one safe.

108

Lesson Plan

WE GATHER ___ minutes

✝ **Pray** Invite the children to pray the Sign of the Cross together and say the *We Gather* prayer.

Focus on Life Ask the children: *Have you ever cared for an animal? Did you give the pet food and water? What did you do to keep the animal safe?* Ask the children to describe the picture on page 108. Point out that at the time that Jesus lived, many men were shepherds. Explain: *Shepherds were responsible for the sheep that lived in the hills outside of the villages and towns. They took very good care of the animals.* Tell the children that in this lesson they will learn how Jesus took care of his followers.

WE BELIEVE ___ minutes

Understand Jesus the Teacher Read the *We Believe* statement at the top of page 108. Point out: *Jesus loves us and wants to take care of us. Jesus is always with us.* Read aloud the first *We Believe* paragraph. Discuss what it means to be a teacher. Explain: *Jesus used stories to teach a lesson. In his stories he used words and things that his followers knew about.*

Read Scripture Have the children listen as you read the Scripture story. Ask: *Why did Jesus call himself the good shepherd?*

Then continue reading the last two *We Believe* paragraphs. Have the children highlight the similarities between shepherds and Jesus.

Jesus is our Good Shepherd.
He is with us night and day.
He knows each one of us.
He loves us very much.
He shows us ways to love
God and others.

Follow the path that shows ways to love God and others.

What signs did you follow along the way?

WE RESPOND

How is Jesus like a shepherd to us?

109

ACTIVITY BANK

Multiple Intelligences
Interpersonal, Verbal-Linguistic

Have the children work in groups. Select one child to be a reporter. The other children will pretend to be shepherds. Have the reporter interview the shepherds about their jobs. Questions might be:

• *How long have you been a shepherd?*

• *Why did you become a shepherd?*

• *What is the hardest part of your job?*

• *What do you enjoy the most?*

Encourage the members of each group to respond. Invite the children to share the group interview with the entire class.

Do the Activity Explain the directions for the *We Believe* activity. Read the different signs on the path. Be sure the children understand their meanings.

Quick Check

✔ *What did Jesus tell us about himself in the Bible story?* (He is the Good Shepherd.)

✔ *Why did Jesus tell us he was the Good Shepherd?* (He wanted us to know that he is with us night and day; he knows each one of us; he loves us very much.)

WE RESPOND _____ minutes

Connect to Life Read the *We Respond* question and discuss the children's answers. Help them make the connection between a shepherd caring for his sheep and Jesus caring for us.

Pray Invite the children to gather in the prayer space. Pray the following prayer once. Then have the children repeat it after you. *Dear Jesus, thank you for being our Good Shepherd.*

Plan Ahead for Day 2

Catechist Goal: To tell the story of Jesus' welcome into Jerusalem

Preparation: Make copies of Reproducible Master 9, guide page 107G.

Catechist Goal

• To tell the story of Jesus' welcome into Jerusalem

Our Faith Response

• To name ways we can praise Jesus

Lesson Materials

• copies of Reproducible Master 9
• crayons or colored pencils, scissors

As Catholics...

We Pray Hosanna

After you have presented the lesson, read aloud the *As Catholics* text. In a missalette find the words we pray at the beginning of the eucharistic prayer of Mass. Read the words aloud to the children. Ask them to join in praying these words next Sunday at Mass.

Many people gathered to welcome and praise Jesus.

WE GATHER

✝ *Jesus, we praise you.*

🧍 Imagine special visitors are coming to your school.
Act out how you will welcome them.

WE BELIEVE

Jesus visited many towns.
People welcomed him in different ways.
Some began to believe in Jesus.
They believed that Jesus was sent by God.

110

Lesson Plan

WE GATHER   ___ minutes

✝ **Pray** Invite the children to pray the Sign of the Cross and the *We Gather* prayer.

Focus on Life Talk about the anticipation the children feel when a visitor is coming. Ask: *What do you do to make the visitor feel welcomed?* List the children's responses on the board. Share the *Chapter Story* on guide page 107C. Tell the children that in this lesson they will learn about the ways people welcomed Jesus to Jerusalem.

WE BELIEVE   ___ minutes

Read Scripture Invite the children to look at the picture on these two pages. Explain that the people are welcoming Jesus. Have the children look at the picture

as you read the Scripture story. When you are finished, ask: *What did the people do to welcome Jesus?* (They ran to meet him. They waved palm branches.) Also ask: *What did the people say?* (They shouted, "Hosanna.")

Explain: *The Jewish people celebrate special feasts. During these times, they pray and remember God's goodness and love. In this story the Jews were gathering to celebrate their special celebration of Passover. Families came to Jerusalem from all over to be together and worship God.*

Words of Praise Read the last *We Believe* paragraph. Point out that *Hosanna* is a word of praise. Ask the children: *When do you hear this word prayed?* (at Mass on Sunday) Then invite the children to show ways they would praise Jesus if he was entering their neighborhood.

📖 John 12:12–13
Read Along
Many people were in Jerusalem for a feast. They heard that Jesus was near the city, so they ran out to meet him. They waved palm branches in the air. They shouted,
"Hosanna!
Blessed is he who comes in the name of the Lord." (John 12:13)

As Catholics...

During every Mass we pray Hosanna. We pray the same words the people did when they welcomed Jesus to Jerusalem. We show that we believe Jesus is the Son of God.

At Mass next week, praise Jesus for all he has done for us.

Hosanna is a word of praise.
The people that day were happy to see Jesus.
They shouted Hosanna to praise him.
They waved palm branches, too.

WE RESPOND

When do you praise Jesus?

🧍 Show some ways we can praise Jesus.

111

ACTIVITY BANK

Evangelization
Bumper Stickers for Jesus
Activity Materials: bumper stickers, strips of paper for bumper stickers, crayons or markers

Explain to the children what a bumper sticker is. Give the children examples of slogans and phrases that you have seen on bumper stickers or show them bumper stickers you have brought in. Now encourage them to think of short phrases that can give people a message about Jesus. Print the messages on strips of paper. Have volunteers decorate the bumper stickers. Post the bumper stickers around the room.

Do the Activity Distribute copies of Reproducible Master 9. Have the children say the word *Hosanna* and then color the palm branch and cut it out. Explain that the children will use the palm branch for the closing prayer.

Quick Check

✔ *Who did the people believe sent Jesus?* (They believed God sent Jesus.)

✔ *What word did the people shout to praise Jesus?* (They shouted Hosanna.)

WE RESPOND ___ minutes

Connect to Life Read the *We Respond* question. Discuss the different times and places that the children

praise Jesus. Explain: *We can praise God with others or by ourselves.* Then ask volunteers to show ways we can praise Jesus. (Gestures: raise arms in the air; have a prayer walk; sing. Words: Alleluia; Hosanna; We praise you.)

Pray Ask the children to gather in the prayer space carrying their palm branches. Have them wave the branches in the air and repeat several times: *Jesus, we love and praise you.*

Plan Ahead for Day 3

Catechist Goal: To explain how Jesus taught in the Temple in Jerusalem

Preparation: Have available Grade 1 CD.

Catechist Goal

• To explain how Jesus taught in the Temple in Jerusalem

Our Faith Response

• To listen to Jesus our teacher

 **Temple**

Lesson Materials

• world map or globe
• pictures of Jerusalem and the Temple during Jesus' time (option)
• Grade 1 CD

Teaching Tip

Participation in Discussions

When you ask a question, pause for a moment to allow all the children time to think about their responses. Encourage all to listen attentively as each child shares a response. Affirm and thank the children for participating in the discussion.

Jesus taught in the Temple in Jerusalem.

WE GATHER

✝ *Jesus, we want to listen to your teaching.*

Where do you live?
Talk about the cities or towns that are nearby.
Do you ever go to these places?
Why?

WE BELIEVE

Jerusalem is an important city to Jews.
They go there for special feasts.
They go there to pray.

Jerusalem was very important in Jesus' time, too.
Jesus went to Jerusalem.
He taught the people there.

The **Temple** was the holy place in Jerusalem where the Jewish People prayed.

📖 Luke 21:37–38

Read Along
During the week before Jesus died, he taught in the Temple area every day. "And all the people would get up early each morning to listen to him." (Luke 21:38)

112

Lesson Plan

WE GATHER ___ minutes

✝ **Pray** Invite the children to pray the Sign of the Cross and the *We Gather* prayer.

Focus on Life Read aloud the *We Gather* questions and directive. Discuss the children's responses. Ask: *In what ways are cities the same today as they were in the time of Jesus?* (Many people live there. There is a lot of noise. There are large buildings.) Tell the children that in this lesson they will learn about Jerusalem and its importance to Jews and to Jesus.

WE BELIEVE ___ minutes

Locating Jerusalem Show the children a globe or map of the world. Locate your city and then show where Jerusalem is. Read aloud the *We Believe* statement at the top of page 112. If possible show the children pictures of Jerusalem and the Temple as they looked in the time of Jesus.

Learn About Jerusalem Read aloud the *We Believe* text. As you read the text, emphasize:

• *Jerusalem is an important city where Jewish people go to celebrate and pray to God.*

• *The Temple was a holy place in Jerusalem where the Jewish People prayed.*

Read Scripture Ask the children to look at the picture on the pages as you read aloud the Scripture story. Ask: *Why do you think so many people went to hear Jesus teach?* (Possible responses: Jesus taught them about God's love; Jesus was a good teacher.)

Key Word
Temple the holy place in Jerusalem where the Jewish People prayed

WE RESPOND

Where do you go to pray and listen to Jesus' teaching?

🎵 **In the House of Our God**

In the House of our God,
in the House of our God,
we give praise to the Lord
in the House of our God.

🧍 Make up actions for the song.

113

ACTIVITY BANK

Multicultural Connection
Churches Around the World
Activity Materials: pictures of Catholic churches from around the world, globe or map of the world

Gather pictures of Catholic churches that are located in different countries. As you show each picture, point out on a globe or map where the church is located. Explain that the one thing that all churches have in common is that people can go there to pray to God and to hear God's Word.

Quick Check

✔ *Why is the city of Jerusalem important?* (Jewish people go there for special feasts and to pray.)

✔ *Where did Jesus teach in Jerusalem?* (Jesus taught in the Temple in Jerusalem.)

WE RESPOND ___ minutes

Connect to Life Read the *We Respond* question. Discuss the variety of times and places where people can pray. Point out to the children that they should be with a grown-up family member or teacher when they go to church to pray.

Learn a Song Play "In the House of Our God," #8, Grade 1 CD. Play it again and have the children join in singing. As a class, make up some simple hand motions that will express the words of the song. Practice them with the music.

Pray Explain that singing is a form of prayer. Gather the children in the prayer space to praise God by singing "In the House of Our God."

Plan Ahead for Day 4

Catechist Goal: To teach the love Jesus showed by dying and rising to new life

Preparation: Make copies of *What's the Word?*, guide page 107F. Be prepared to share a time when someone showed they loved you.

Catechist Goal

• To teach the love Jesus showed by dying and rising to new life

Our Faith Response

• To celebrate that Jesus died and rose so that we could live in God's love

 Easter Sunday

Lesson Materials

• crayons or colored markers
• Grade 1 CD (option)
• copies of reproducible master *What's the Word?*, guide page 107F

Teaching Note

Presenting the Death and Resurrection of Jesus Christ

Some catechetical leaders recommend that with young children we not overemphasize the Death of Jesus on the cross. We always balance the story of Jesus' Death with the story of the Resurrection. For this lesson do not elaborate on either scriptural account. Emphasize that Jesus showed his love for us by dying and rising to bring us new life.

Jesus died and rose.

WE GATHER

✝ *Jesus, thank you for your great love.*

Think about the people who love you very much.
How do they show their love for you?

WE BELIEVE

Jesus showed his love in many ways.
He cared for people.
He listened to them.
He shared God's love with them.

Jesus showed his love in a special way.
Jesus died so that all people could live in God's love.

📖 John 19:18, 25, 30, 42

Read Along

Jesus was nailed to a cross. Jesus' mother and a few followers were with him. Jesus died on the cross. After he died, some of his followers placed his body in a tomb.

114

Lesson Plan

WE GATHER — minutes

✝ **Pray** Invite the children to pray the Sign of the Cross and say together the *We Gather* prayer.

Focus on Life Read the *We Gather* text. Discuss these ideas. Provide a minute of silence for the children to reflect on how people show their love for them. Then discuss how people can show their love. Encourage the children to understand that a show of love does not have to mean giving presents. Explain: *We can show love by listening, by helping, by praying.* Tell the children that in this lesson they will learn that Jesus died and rose so that all people can live in God's love.

WE BELIEVE — minutes

Read the Text Read aloud the first two *We Believe* paragraphs. Discuss how much Jesus must have loved us to die on the cross for us.

Share Scripture Stories Read aloud the first Scripture story. Discuss the feelings Jesus' mother and friends must have felt when he died. Then read the second Scripture story. Ask the children how they think Jesus' mother and friends felt when they found out that he had risen from the dead. Explain: *This is why we celebrate Easter Sunday. We are celebrating and praising Jesus because he has risen from the dead.*

On the third day after Jesus died, something wonderful happened.

📖 Matthew 28:1–7

Read Along
Early on Sunday morning, some women went to visit Jesus' tomb. They saw an angel sitting in front of the tomb. The angel said, "Do not be afraid!" (Matthew 28:5)

The angel told the women that Jesus had risen to new life. He told them to go tell the other followers.

Jesus died and rose to bring us new life. **Easter Sunday** is the special day we celebrate that Jesus Christ rose to new life. We pray Alleluia.
Alleluia is another special word of praise.

WE RESPOND

How does your family celebrate Easter Sunday?

✖ Celebrate what Jesus did for us.
Color the Alleluia garden.

Key Word
Easter Sunday the special day we celebrate that Jesus Christ rose to new life

115

Activity Bank

Multiple Intelligences
Intrapersonal
Activity Materials: drawing paper, markers or crayons
Have the children fold a piece of drawing paper to make a greeting card. On the cover have them draw a picture that represents Jesus' love for us. Show them where to write a note inside thanking Jesus for dying and rising to new life.

Curriculum Connection
Language Arts
Activity Materials: large piece of white paper, marker, crayons
Ask the children to think about what love is. Under the words "Love Is," print their responses on the board. When you finish, you will have a "Love is . . ." poem. Recopy the words and display it in the prayer space.

Scripture
Interpersonal, Linguistic
For a Scripture activity, see *What's the Word?*, guide page 107F.

Learn About Easter Read the last *We Believe* paragraph. Stress: *Jesus died and rose to bring us new life.* Point out the *Key Word* and its definition. Ask: *What word do we use to praise Jesus?* (Alleluia)

Quick Check
✔ *Why did Jesus die on the cross?* (Jesus died so that all people could live in God's love.)
✔ *What is Easter Sunday?* (It is the special day we celebrate that Jesus rose to new life.)

WE RESPOND ___ minutes

Connect to Life Invite the children to share their answers to the *We Respond* question. Discuss the importance of joining with our parish family at Mass to celebrate Easter Sunday. Emphasize: *Jesus wants us to celebrate that he rose to bring us new life.*

Praising Jesus Invite the children to complete the *We Respond* activity. As the children work, you may want to play the recording of "Jesus in the Morning," #3, Grade 1 CD.

Pray Gather the children in the prayer space. Invite the children to raise their arms in a gesture of praise. Pray together: *Alleluia! Alleluia! Alleluia!*

Plan Ahead for Day 5

Catechist Goal: To review chapter ideas and their relationship to our faith life

Preparation: Make copies of *Sharing Faith with My Family*, guide page 107E.

115

Catechist Goal

• To review the chapter ideas that are key to growing as disciples of Jesus Christ

Our Faith Response

• To decide on ways to grow as disciples by living out what we have learned

Show What *you* Know

Explain to the children that they will draw a line to correctly match the two sentence parts. Have them do so. Review the activity as a class once all have finished.

Celebrate!

Read the instructions and choices. Encourage the children to circle all the ways that they can celebrate that Jesus died and rose for us.

picture This

Remind the children of the story Jesus told his followers about the shepherd. Read the question and instruct the children to finish the sentence.

Reality Check

Explain to the children that this activity is a check list. After reading the paragraph and all the choices, instruct the children to check all the boxes that name people who help protect and care for them. Brainstorm names of others who help us. Consider saying a prayer to thank God for these important people.

Take Home

Encourage the children to teach these words of praise to their family members and to pray them together.

Discuss and send home copies of *Sharing Faith with My Family*, guide page 107E.

Grade 1 Chapter 9

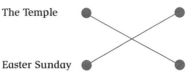
PROJECT

Show What *you* Know

Match the sentence parts.

The Temple — is the special day we celebrate that Jesus Christ rose to new life.

Easter Sunday — was the holy place in Jerusalem where the Jewish People prayed.

Celebrate!

Circle the ways you can celebrate that Jesus died and rose for us.

Pray   **Praise**   **Sing**

116   www.webelieveweb.com

DISCIPLE

picture This
What does this stained glass window show?

Jesus is our

_____

Good Shepherd

Reality Check

The Church teaches us to respect all workers. People work in our neighborhood to protect and care for us. Who helps to protect and care for you?

☑ Police officers

☑ Firefighters

☑ People who keep my neighborhood clean

☑ People in my parish and school

Take Home

What are the two words of praise you learned in this chapter?

Hosanna

_____

Alleluia

Say these words as a family.

117

CHAPTER TEST

Circle the correct answer.

1. The word people used to praise Jesus as he entered Jerusalem was _____.

   (Hosanna)   Alleluia

2. The _____ was the holy place in Jerusalem where the Jewish People prayed.

   Mountain   (Temple)

3. _____ died and rose to bring us new life.

   (Jesus)   Peter

4. _____ is the special day we celebrate that Jesus Christ rose to new life.

   (Easter Sunday)   Christmas Day

5. The city of Jerusalem was _____ in the time of Jesus.

   not important   (very important)

 Why did Jesus call himself the Good Shepherd? Possible responses: he is always with us; he knows each of us; he loves us very much

118

Chapter 9 • Day 5

CHAPTER TEST

Read each test item aloud and allow time for the children to mark an answer. Decide whether the *Talk About It* activity will be a small group or whole class discussion. After you have finished, check the answers. Clarify any misconceptions.

Alternative Assessment

You may want the students to complete the following alternative-assessment activity.

What are some things Jesus did to show his love for us? Draw or write your answer.

Additional Testing

• Chapter 9 Test in *Assessment Book*, pages 17–18

• CD-ROM *Test Generator and Resource*: Use Chapter 9 Test or customize your own.

Review

Review the definitions as they are presented in the chapter's *Key Word* boxes:

• Temple (page 113)
• Easter Sunday (page 115).

We Believe Statements

Review the four statements.

• Jesus told his followers that he loved and cared for them.
• Many people gathered to welcome and praise Jesus.
• Jesus taught in the Temple in Jerusalem.
• Jesus died and rose.

To use the Chapter 9 Study Guide, visit

www.webelieveweb.com

Overview

In Chapter 9 the children learned that Jesus died and rose to new life. In this chapter the children will learn that Jesus sent the Holy Spirit to his followers.

Doctrinal Content	For Adult Reading and Reflection *Catechism of the Catholic Church*
The children will learn:	Paragraph
• The risen Jesus visited his followers.	641
• Jesus Christ promised that the Holy Spirit would come to his followers.	729
• The Holy Spirit was sent to Jesus' followers.	730
• The Holy Spirit is the Third Person of the Blessed Trinity.	732

Pentecost (p. 125)

Catechist Background

Go to **www.webelieveweb.com**, Catechist/ Teacher, We Believe Correlations for this chapter's correlation to:
- Six Tasks of Catechesis
- *Catechetical Formation in Chaste Living.*

What helps you overcome fear?

What a wonderful story we have in the surprise breakfast Jesus prepares for his followers! (See John 21:2–12.) Having spent a frustrating night fishing without any results, the disciples heeded Jesus' advice to put their nets down on the other side. There they caught so many fish they could not pull in the net. When they came to shore, they saw Jesus with a charcoal fire and bread and fish prepared for them. Who would not take delight in such a surprise picnic on the seashore?

This wonderful event is filled with meaning. It was the risen Lord's third appearance, and we read in the Gospel, "Jesus came over and took the bread and gave it to them, and in like manner the fish" (John 21:13). He was feeding them as he said. And he would continue to feed not only them but us.

This story is part of the promise of Jesus not to abandon his followers. When he first appeared after his Resurrection, he told his disciples to not be afraid. Now he comes to feed them. Also, he promises the Holy Spirit will come to be with them when he returns to his Father. The Holy Spirit came dramatically the first time. Fear disappeared. There was no doubt that Jesus kept his promise.

And it is just as true today. Christ continues to nourish us in many ways: in the Eucharist, in his presence in each of us, and, since the first Pentecost, in the abiding presence of the Holy Spirit. All we need to do is open our hearts and open our eyes to see that this is true.

When do you recognize the presence of the Holy Spirit in your own life?

Lesson Planning Guide

Lesson Focus	Presentation	Materials

page 119
✠ **We Gather in Prayer**

pages 120–121
The risen Jesus visited his followers.

📖 *John 21:2–12*

- Celebrate Jesus' rising by singing and listening to Scripture.
- Follow the **We Gather** directive and respond to the questions.
- Present the Bible story about the risen Jesus visiting his followers.
- 🧍 Do the **We Believe** activity.
- Do the role-playing **We Respond** activity.

For the prayer space: picture of Jesus, Alleluia sign, candle with paper flame

🎵 "Sing for Joy," Bernadette Farrell, #9, Grade 1 CD
- strip of paper with message "You are special," one for each child, tape
- copies of Reproducible Master 10, guide page 119G

pages 122–123
Jesus Christ promised that the Holy Spirit would come to his followers.

- Share responses for **We Gather**.
- Read and discuss the **We Believe** text about the promise of the Holy Spirit.
- 🧍 Draw or write an answer to the **We Respond** question.

- colored pencils or crayons
- copies of reproducible master *What's the Word?*, guide page 119F

pages 124–125
The Holy Spirit was sent to Jesus' followers.

📖 *Acts of the Apostles 2:1–4*

- Share responses for **We Gather**.
- Read the Scripture story in **We Believe** about the coming of the Holy Spirit.
- 🧍 Share the tunes for the **We Respond** activity.
- Read and discuss the *As Catholics* text.

pages 126–127
The Holy Spirit is the Third Person of the Blessed Trinity.

- Do the picture study and answer the **We Gather** question.
- Present the **We Believe** text about prayers to the Blessed Trinity.
- 🧍 Follow the **We Respond** directive to pray together using actions.

pages 128–129
Project Disciple

page 130
Chapter 10 Test

- Complete the **Project Disciple** activities.
- Explain the *Take Home* activity.
- Discuss/send home **Sharing Faith with My Family**, guide page 119E.
- Complete **Chapter 10 Test**.
- Work on *Alternative Assessment* activity.

- pencils
- crayons or colored pencils
- copies of **Sharing Faith with My Family** reproducible master, guide page 119E

For additional ideas, activities, and opportunities: Visit Sadlier's **www.WeBelieveweb.com**

119B

Chapter Story

Anna's grandma lived close to Anna's family. Anna and her grandma did many things together. Anna's favorite thing to do with her grandma was to feed the ducks in the park pond. They would go to the pond and throw little pieces of bread to the ducks.

One day Anna's grandma talked to her on their way to the park. She said, "Anna, my bones and muscles hurt me when it is cold outside. I'm going to move to a place where it is warmer. We won't be able to see each other very often. But I want you to remember how much I love you, even when I am not with you. When you miss me, you can think about the special times we spent together, especially feeding the ducks."

On the day after Grandma moved, Anna was very sad. Anna's dad saw her and sat down to talk to her. He gave Anna a gift bag. He said, "Anna, Grandma left this gift for you."

Anna looked in the bag. She was surprised to see what Grandma had given to her. She said, "Look, Dad! Grandma gave me a loaf of bread. Will you take me to the park? I can feed the ducks. When I come home, I can write a note to Grandma to thank her for the great surprise."

▶ *Why did Anna think her grandma's gift was a great surprise?*

FAITH and MEDIA

▶ On Day 4, consider supplementing the *Multicultural Connection* activity with a class visit to **www.webelieveweb.com** to listen to the Sign of the Cross. The Web site offers audio versions of many prayers. The children can quietly listen to the audio or may pray along.

▶ If you do the poster-message activity (Day 3 *Activity Bank*), stress that posters are a media source.

CHAPTER PROJECT: HOLY SPIRIT BOOKMARK

Make patterns for children to trace bookmarks. Give each child a sheet of yellow construction paper. Have him or her use a pattern to trace the outline of two or three bookmarks on the sheet. Help the children cut out the bookmarks. Ask them to draw and color a flame and write *Holy Spirit* on each bookmark. Suggest that the children give one of the bookmarks to a family member or friend. Explain: *Keep one bookmark to place in your Bible or* We Believe *book.*

PROJECT DISCIPLE

Pray
Learn
Celebrate
Share
Choose
Live

Additional Activities

What's *the* Word?

(Use on Day 2.)

Materials needed: copies of reproducible master, guide page 119F

Distribute copies of the Scripture reproducible master. Explain to the children that they will do an activity to remember the story of Jesus promising to send the Holy Spirit to his followers. Choose seven volunteers to read the parts of Readers 1–7. Ask the other children to follow along. Consider discussing how the children feel about Jesus' words, "I am with you always."

What Would *you* do?

Materials needed: paper plate for each child, craft sticks, colored pencils

Distribute a paper plate and a craft stick to each child. Invite the children to imagine that they are Jesus' followers who waited for Jesus to send the Holy Spirit to help them. On one side of the plate, ask the children to draw a face showing how Jesus' friends might have felt before the Holy Spirit came. One the other side, have them draw a face showing how Jesus' friends might have felt after. Help the children affix the craft sticks to the plates to complete their masks.

Celebrate!

Materials needed: costumes, nets, video camera (option)

Plan a class reenactment of the Scripture story on page 120. Assign acting roles of Peter and Jesus' followers. If possible, use costumes and simple nets for the fishermen. Assign readers to retell the story. Try to involve all the children who want to participate. If possible, use a video camera to record the performance. Then, invite parents, family members, or another class to visit the classroom to watch the video (or a live performance) and enjoy a "breakfast" with the children.

Picture This

When discussing the Holy Spirit as the Third Person of the Blessed Trinity, have the Blessed Trinity images from Chapter 2 available. Remind the children that we use the images of the three intertwined circles, the equilateral triangle, or the shamrock to help us remember that there are Three Persons in One God.

Meeting Individual Needs
Children with Attention Deficit Disorder

Help the children complete activities successfully by breaking down directions into steps. Have the children complete each step before they go on with the next. You may also consider pairing a child with attention deficit disorder with another child who could help him or her follow the directions.

We Believe Resources

- Grade 1 *Review & Resource Book*, pages 25–27
- Grade 1 *Family Book*, pages 30–32
- Grade 1 *Assessment Book*, pages 19–20
- Grade 1 CD-ROM *Test Generator and Resource*: Use Chapter 10 Test or customize your own.
- www.webelieveweb.com

Sharing What I Learned

Look at the pictures below. Use each picture to tell your family what you learned in this chapter.

Sharing a Bible Story

Share the story about Jesus' visit with his followers on the beach. (See page 120 of the student book.) Talk about what it must have been like to be with Jesus that morning.

Messages of God's Love

Make fish like the one on this page. Have each family member write a message on a fish about Jesus or the Holy Spirit. An example is *Jesus is with us always.*

Hide the fish in places where other family members will find them during the week. At the end of the week, gather to read all the messages.

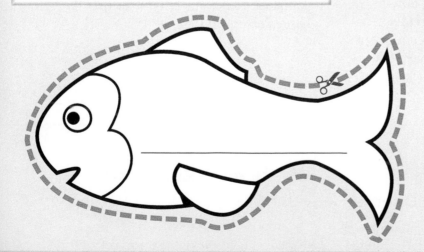

Visit Sadlier's

www.WE BELIEVE web.com

Connect to the Catechism
For adult background and reflection, see paragraphs 641, 729, 730, and 732.

119E

PROJECT DISCIPLE

Pray
Learn
Celebrate
Share
Choose
Live

Name _____

What's *the* Word?

Reader 1: After Jesus rose from the dead, he visited his followers.

Reader 2: After forty days it was time for him to return to his Father in Heaven.

Reader 3: He asked his close followers to come to a mountain.

Reader 4: There Jesus told them what he wanted them to do.

Reader 5: Jesus said to go to all the lands to tell the people about him.

Reader 6: Jesus told his followers that he would send the Holy Spirit to help them.

Reader 7: Jesus said, "I am with you always."

(Matthew 28:20)

119F

Name

Read the message on the fish.

Color the fish and cut it out.

Punch a hole in the fish.

Put a string through the hole.

Hang the fish in a place where you
will see the message often.

Jesus is always with us

Jesus Sends the Holy Spirit

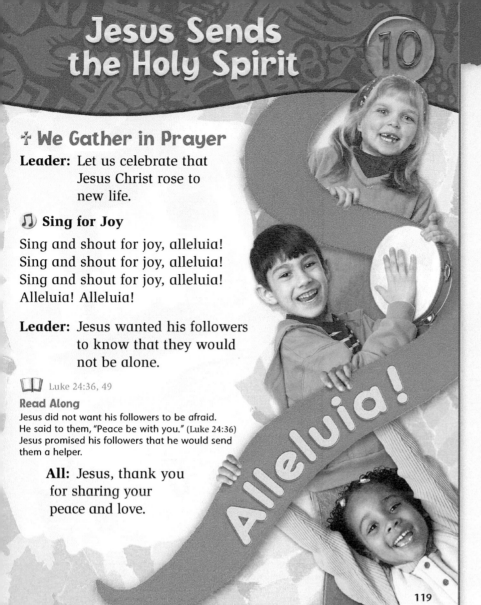

✝ We Gather in Prayer

Leader: Let us celebrate that Jesus Christ rose to new life.

🎵 **Sing for Joy**

Sing and shout for joy, alleluia!
Sing and shout for joy, alleluia!
Sing and shout for joy, alleluia!
Alleluia! Alleluia!

Leader: Jesus wanted his followers to know that they would not be alone.

📖 Luke 24:36, 49

Read Along
Jesus did not want his followers to be afraid. He said to them, "Peace be with you." (Luke 24:36) Jesus promised his followers that he would send them a helper.

All: Jesus, thank you for sharing your peace and love.

Alleluia!

119

PREPARING TO PRAY

The children will sing a joyful song and listen to Scripture.

• Go over the words to "Sing for Joy," #9, Grade 1 CD. Have the children practice singing the song. Make up gestures for the words of the song. Have the children practice them.

• Choose a child to be the reader, and have him or her practice reading the passage from Luke.

The Prayer Space

• Gather the following items for the prayer table: picture of Jesus to represent that Jesus is always with us; sign reading *Alleluia* to represent our joy that Jesus rose to new life at Easter; candle with a paper flame to represent the Holy Spirit.

 This Week's Liturgy
Visit **www.webelieveweb.com** for this week's liturgical readings and other seasonal material.

Lesson Plan

We Gather in Prayer ___ minutes

✝ Pray

• Invite the children to the prayer space by saying: *We gather in prayer*.

• Pray the Sign of the Cross.

• Sing "Sing for Joy," using the joyful gestures you have prepared.

• Read the Scripture story and invite the children to respond in prayer.

Family Connection Update

Invite the children to share their family experiences of praising God.

Catechist Goal

• To highlight that the risen Jesus visited his followers

Our Faith Response

• To express our joy in the risen Jesus' presence

Lesson Materials

• surprise messages (See *Focus on Life*)
• crayons or colored pencils
• copies of Reproducible Master 10
• scissors, hole punch, yarn or string

Teaching Tip

A Surprise Visitor

Invite your principal or a priest from the parish to pay a surprise visit to your class. Ask the visitor to read the Scripture story on page 120. Have the visitor discuss the story with the children.

The risen Jesus visited his followers.

WE GATHER

✝ *Alleluia, Jesus is risen!*

Think of a time when someone surprised you. How did they surprise you? What did you do?

WE BELIEVE

Jesus wanted his followers to know that he had risen. So he visited them. Here is a story about one of his visits.

📖 John 21:2–12

Read Along

One night Peter and some of Jesus' other followers went fishing. They were on the boat all night, but they did not catch any fish. Early the next morning, Jesus' followers saw someone on the shore. The person called out. He told them to put their nets into the water again.

Jesus' followers put the nets back into the water. They were surprised when they saw the nets filled with fish. They suddenly knew that the person on the shore was Jesus.

Peter was excited. He jumped into the water and swam to shore. The other followers came in the boat. Jesus said to them, "Come, have breakfast." (John 21:12)

120

Lesson Plan

WE GATHER ___ minutes

✝ **Pray** Invite the children to pray the Sign of the Cross and say together the *We Gather* prayer.

Focus on Life Before class begins, tape a colored strip of paper titled, "You are special" on each child's desk. Before you begin presenting the *We Gather* section, ask: *How did you feel when you saw the surprise message taped on your desks?* Then read aloud the *We Gather* directive and questions. Pause for a minute to allow the children time to think about their responses. Invite volunteers to share their responses. Ask volunteers to share stories about surprises that they have received. Tell the children that in this lesson they will learn that Jesus surprised his followers by visiting them after he had risen from the dead.

WE BELIEVE ___ minutes

Share a Scripture Story Read aloud the *We Believe* statement and the first paragraph. Explain to the children that they will now hear a story about the way that Jesus surprised his followers. Ask the children to look at the picture as you read aloud the Scripture story. If you have invited a guest, have him or her read the story.

Do the Activity Read the *We Believe* activity directions. Allow time for the children to complete the activity. Read aloud the sentences as the children number them. Then ask volunteers to retell the story in their own words.

ⓧ Number these sentences 1, 2, 3, 4 to retell the story.

_____3_____ The followers knew the person was Jesus. They went back to shore.

_____4_____ Jesus asked his followers to have breakfast with him.

_____1_____ Jesus' followers went fishing but did not catch any fish.

_____2_____ Someone on shore called out and told them to put their nets in again. They caught many fish.

WE RESPOND

ⓧ Imagine that your class is having breakfast with Jesus. Act out what you would say and do.

121

ACTIVITY BANK

Catholic Social Teaching
Call to Family, Community, and Participation
Activity Materials: copies of Reproducible Master 10, scissors

Invite another class to visit. Have the children prepare activities for the visit, one activity being the acting out of the Scripture story. Also have extra copies of Reproducible Master 10 available. Ask the children to color and cut out the fish to give to their visitors. After sharing the Scripture story during the visit, have the children present the fish to their visitors. Surprise both groups by preparing a snack to share.

Quick Check

✔ *What surprise did Jesus' followers receive when they were fishing one night?* (Their nets were filled with fish; Jesus was waiting for them on the shore.)

✔ *Why did Jesus visit his followers?* (He wanted them to know he had risen.)

WE RESPOND   ___ minutes

Connect to Life Read the *We Respond* directives. Assign the children to small groups. Ask the children in each group to act out what they would say and do if they were having breakfast with Jesus. Invite the groups to share their skits with the entire class. Point out that the followers of Jesus may have said and done some of the same things when they had breakfast with Jesus.

Do the Activity Distribute copies of Reproducible Master 10. Read the directions. Help the children make their fish or send the sheet home for the children to do the activity with their families.

Pray Remind the children that the followers of Jesus were very happy to see him. Invite the children to shout the word "Alleluia" three times in thanksgiving for the risen Jesus.

Plan Ahead for Day 2

Catechist Goal: To describe how the Holy Spirit would help Jesus' followers

Preparation: Make copies of *What's the Word?*, guide page 119F. Prepare for reading the *Chapter Story*, guide page 119C.

Catechist Goal

• To describe how the Holy Spirit would help Jesus' followers

Our Faith Response

• To ask the Holy Spirit to help us tell others about Jesus

Lesson Materials

• colored pencils or crayons
• copies of reproducible master *What's the Word?*, guide page 119F

Teaching Note

Jesus' Promise

Jesus' promise to send the Holy Spirit is further developed in the *We Believe* Grades 2 and 3 texts. When studying the Grade 3 text, the children will learn that the word *Ascension* means Jesus' returning to his Father in heaven.

Jesus Christ promised that the Holy Spirit would come to his followers.

WE GATHER

✝ *Jesus, help us to remember you always.*

Think about your family and friends. Why do you like to be with them?

Share ways you can remember them when they are not with you.

WE BELIEVE

The risen Christ was going to return to the Father in Heaven. He did not want his followers to feel sad without him.

Jesus wanted his followers to remember him. He wanted them to tell others about God's love. He promised that the Holy Spirit would come to be with them.

122

Lesson Plan

WE GATHER ___ minutes

✝ **Pray** Provide the children with a few moments of silence to think about Jesus. Then read the *We Gather* prayer and invite the children to repeat the words.

Focus on Life Read aloud the *We Gather* directives and questions. Then invite volunteers to share their responses. Share the *Chapter Story*, guide page 119C. Emphasize the way Anna will remember what she did with her grandmother. Tell the children that in this lesson they will learn that Jesus promised to send the Holy Spirit to his followers to help them remember him.

WE BELIEVE ___ minutes

Talk about Jesus' Promise Tell the children that Jesus' friends liked to be with him, too. They wanted to remember Jesus. Read aloud the *We Believe* statement and the first two *We Believe* paragraphs. Point out:

• *Jesus wanted his friends to remember him.*

• *Jesus promised to send the Holy Spirit to his followers.*

Stress: *After Jesus made the promise to send the Holy Spirit, he returned to his Father.*

The Holy Spirit would help Jesus' followers to:

- remember the things Jesus had said and done
- love others as Jesus had taught them
- tell others about Jesus.

After he made this promise, Jesus returned to his Father.

WE RESPOND

Ask the Holy Spirit to help you remember Jesus each day.

What is one thing you want to tell someone about Jesus? Draw or write your answer here. Who will you tell this to today?

123

ACTIVITY BANK

Multiple Intelligences

Interpersonal

Activity Materials: poster board or chart paper, marker

Tell the children that we can also make a promise to Jesus. On a piece of poster board or chart paper, develop with the children a class "Promise to Jesus." The "Promise" can include ways the children will show their love for God and others. After writing the class promise, display it in the prayer space. From time to time during the coming months, read the promise and ask the children to continue doing what they have said.

Scripture

Interpersonal, Linguistic

For a Scripture activity, see *What's the Word?*, guide page 119F.

Quick Check

✔ *Who did Jesus promise to send to his followers?* (Jesus promised to send the Holy Spirit.)

✔ *What would the Holy Spirit help Jesus' followers do?* (The Holy Spirit would help them to remember the things Jesus had said and done, love others as Jesus had taught them, tell others about Jesus.)

WE RESPOND ___ minutes

Connect to Life Remind the children that the Holy Spirit helped Jesus' followers tell others about him. Discuss with the children what they might like to tell

others about Jesus. Have the children complete the *We Respond* activity. Invite volunteers to share their writings or drawings. Ask the children to name the person with whom they would share this.

Pray Invite the children to repeat these words: *Holy Spirit, please help me to remember Jesus.*

Plan Ahead for Day 3

Catechist Goal: To present the coming of the Holy Spirit at Pentecost

Preparation: Prepare a dramatic reading of the Scripture story, Acts of the Apostles 2:1–4.

Catechist Goal

• To present the coming of the Holy Spirit at Pentecost

Our Faith Response

• To share the joy that Jesus' followers felt on Pentecost

 **Pentecost**

As Catholics...

Symbol of the Holy Spirit

After you have presented the lesson, read aloud the *As Catholics* text. Ask the children to discuss why they think a picture of a flame or fire is a good way to remind us of the Holy Spirit.

The Holy Spirit was sent to Jesus' followers.

WE GATHER

✝ *Holy Spirit, be with us.*

Think of a time when you waited for someone to keep a promise. What did you do while you were waiting?

WE BELIEVE

After Jesus returned to Heaven, his followers went to Jerusalem. They stayed together in a house there. They prayed and waited for the Holy Spirit.

Here is what happened when the Holy Spirit came to Jesus' followers.

 Acts of the Apostles 2:1–4

Read Along

Early one morning, Jesus' followers were together in one place. Jesus' mother, Mary, was with them. Suddenly, they heard a sound like a strong wind. Then they saw what looked like flames of fire over each of them. "And they were all filled with the holy Spirit." (Acts of the Apostles 2:4)

124

Lesson Plan

WE GATHER ___ minutes

✝ **Pray** Have the children sing the *We Gather* prayer verse to the tune of "Mary Had a Little Lamb."

Holy Spirit, be with us,
be with us, be with us.
Holy Spirit, be with us
at home, at school, at play.

Focus on Life Read the *We Gather* directive and question. Invite volunteers to share what they did while they were waiting for someone to keep a promise. Tell the children that in this lesson they will learn how the Holy Spirit came to the waiting followers of Jesus.

WE BELIEVE ___ minutes

Think About the Followers Read the *We Believe* statement and the first paragraph. Explain: *Jesus' followers remembered that he promised to send the Holy Spirit to them. They went to Jerusalem to pray and wait together.*

Share the Scripture Story Have the children listen as you read the story from the Acts of the Apostles. Tell the children that you will reread the story. Explain: *When I say the word* suddenly, *make strong wind noises.* Then reread the story allowing the children to make the sound of strong winds.

Learn About Pentecost Read the last *We Believe* paragraph and introduce the *Key Word.* Draw nine

Pentecost is the day the Holy Spirit came to Jesus' followers.
We celebrate Pentecost fifty days after Easter Sunday.
On this day we celebrate the coming of the Holy Spirit.
Every day we remember that the Holy Spirit is with us.

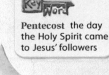

Pentecost the day the Holy Spirit came to Jesus' followers

WE RESPOND

How do you think Jesus' followers felt on Pentecost?

Work with a partner. Make up a special tune or beat for this prayer.

You came on Pentecost.
You came to be with us.
Holy Spirit, we thank you
For coming to be with us.

As Catholics...

The Holy Spirit helps us to share God's love with others. God's love brings light and warmth to the world. This is why the Church often uses a picture of a flame or fire to remind us of the Holy Spirit. Fire gives us light and warmth.

Remember to pray to the Holy Spirit often.

125

ACTIVITY BANK

Faith and Media
Poster Messages
Activity Materials: poster board, construction paper, scissors, glue, markers

Explain to the children that posters are media. Have the children form three groups. Give each group a sheet of poster board. Tell the children in each group to make a poster that has the message: *The Holy Spirit is with us.* Have the children draw pictures or cut paper decorations to put on their posters. Display the posters in the parish church or parish center.

---

blank lines on the board for each letter of the *Key Word.* Challenge the children to guess all the correct letters of the word. Have the children explain in their own words the meaning of *Pentecost.*

Quick Check

✔ *What did Jesus' followers do after Jesus returned to heaven?* (Jesus' followers returned to Jerusalem to pray and wait together.)

✔ *What is Pentecost?* (Pentecost is the day the Holy Spirit came to Jesus' followers.)

WE RESPOND ___ minutes

Connect to Life Read aloud the *We Respond* question. Invite the children to share their responses. Then

read the words to the prayer about Pentecost and the Holy Spirit. Help the children to make up a tune or special beat for the prayer. Note that the words may be sung to the tune of "The Farmer in the Dell."

Pray Have the children look at the flame on the prayer table and think about Jesus' followers at Pentecost. Then invite them to say a silent prayer of thanks to Jesus for sending us the Holy Spirit.

Plan Ahead for Day 4

Catechist Goal: To review that the Holy Spirit is the Third Person of the Blessed Trinity

Preparation: Think of actions to express praise to the Blessed Trinity.

Catechist Goal

• To review that the Holy Spirit is the Third Person of the Blessed Trinity

Our Faith Response

• To recognize that the Holy Spirit is always with us

Teaching Tip

Praying with Actions

Provide as large a space as possible when children are asked to make up actions for prayers and to do the actions while praying. Push desks together or to the sides of the room. Also consider praying outdoors or in the school gymnasium.

The Holy Spirit is the Third Person of the Blessed Trinity.

WE GATHER

✝ *God the Holy Spirit, we love you.*

Look at the pictures.
What prayer do you think the children are saying?

WE BELIEVE

The Sign of the Cross is a prayer to the Blessed Trinity.

God the Father is the First Person of the Blessed Trinity.
God the Son is the Second Person of the Blessed Trinity.
God the Holy Spirit is the Third Person of the Blessed Trinity.

It is important for us to remember that the Holy Spirit is God.
The Holy Spirit is always with us.

126

Lesson Plan

WE GATHER ___ minutes

✝ **Pray** Remind the children that the Holy Spirit listens to our prayers. Pray the Sign of the Cross and the *We Gather* prayer.

Focus on Life Have the children study the pictures on page 126. Then ask them to share answers to the *We Gather* question. Tell the children that in this lesson they will learn a special prayer to the Blessed Trinity.

WE BELIEVE ___ minutes

Review Ask the children to share what they have learned about the Blessed Trinity. (See Chapter 2 in the pupil's text.) Have volunteers write on the board the names of the Three Persons of the Blessed Trinity.

Practice the Sign of the Cross Invite a volunteer to reread the first *We Believe* sentence. Stress: *The Sign of the Cross is a very important prayer that reminds us of the Blessed Trinity.* Review with the children how to make the sign of the cross. Encourage the children to practice praying the Sign of the Cross.

Learn a Prayer to the Blessed Trinity Draw a circle on the board or on chart paper. Tell the children: *A circle does not have a beginning or an end. That's why looking at a circle reminds us of God the Father's, God the Son's, and God the Holy Spirit's love for us.* Then read aloud the Glory to the Father prayer. Reread the prayer, asking the children to draw an imaginary circle in the air as they repeat each line after you.

Here is a prayer we say to praise the Blessed Trinity.
In the prayer, *glory* is another word for praise.

Glory be to the Father
and to the Son
and to the Holy Spirit
as it was in the beginning
is now, and ever shall be
world without end.
Amen.

WE RESPOND

Together think of actions to use when you pray these words of praise.

Pray this prayer together now with actions.

127

ACTIVITY BANK

Multicultural Connection

The Sign of the Cross in Different Languages

The Sign of the Cross is a special prayer to the Blessed Trinity said by Catholics around the world. Help the children appreciate the universality of the Catholic Church and all the many different people who make up the Catholic family by teaching them the Sign of the Cross in different languages. For example, in Spanish the Sign of the Cross is prayed,

- *En el nombre del Padre,*
  (En el nom-bray del Pa-dray)

- *y del Hijo,*
  (ē del ē-yō)

- *del Espiritu Santo.*
  (del E-spear-ē-too Sahn-tō)

Amen.

Quick Check

✔ *Who are the Three Persons of the Blessed Trinity?*
(The Three Persons of the Blessed Trinity are God the Father, God the Son, and God the Holy Spirit.)

✔ *What prayers can we say to the Blessed Trinity?*
(We can pray the Sign of the Cross and the Glory to the Father.)

WE RESPOND ___ minutes

Connect to Life Have the children think of actions to accompany the prayer, Glory to the Father. Give the children time to practice the actions in small groups.

Pray Pray together Glory to the Father with actions.

Plan Ahead for Day 5

Catechist Goal: To review chapter ideas and their relationship to our faith life

Preparation: Make copies of *Sharing Faith with My Family,* guide page 119E.

Chapter 10 • Day 5

Catechist Goal
• To review the chapter ideas that are key to growing as disciples of Jesus Christ

Our Faith Response
• To decide on ways to grow as disciples by living out what we have learned

Show What you Know
Remind the children that some letters are short and some are tall. Review the chapter's *Key Word*. Ask children to look at the short and tall letters in the word and write them into the word shape.

Reality Check
Ask a volunteer to read aloud the activity question. You may want to direct the children to reread page 123 of their text to remember ways the Holy Spirit helps followers of Jesus. Then allow the children to complete the activity.

Picture This
Note that the Church often uses a picture of a flame or fire to remind us of the Holy Spirit. (God's love brings light and warmth to the world.) Read the instructions and have children complete the activity.

Make it Happen
As a prayer to the Blessed Trinity, children may name the Sign of the Cross or the prayer on page 127. Say both prayers aloud. Encourage the children to teach the prayers to a friend.

Take Home
Encourage the children to do the *Take Home* activity with their family.

Discuss and send home copies of *Sharing Faith with My Family*, guide page 119E.

128 and 129

Grade 1 Chapter 10

PROJECT

Show What you Know
Use the word shape to write the Key Word. It is the day the Holy Spirit came to Jesus' followers.

Pentecost

P e n t e c o s t

Reality Check
What can the Holy Spirit help you to do today?
- ☑ Remember the things Jesus said and did
- ☑ Love others as Jesus taught
- ☑ Tell others about Jesus
- ☑ Tell others about God's love

128 www.webelieveweb.com

DISCIPLE

Picture This
Draw a flame of fire over each of Jesus' followers to remind you that the Holy Spirit came upon them.

Make it Happen
Name a prayer to the Blessed Trinity.
↳ DISCIPLE CHALLENGE
Say it.
Teach it to your friend.

Take Home
In many parishes, people join one another for breakfast after Sunday Mass. They talk with people they know. They meet new people. Check your parish bulletin or Web site to see if your parish does this. If so, plan to join in as a family.

129

CHAPTER TEST

Circle the correct answer.

1. Did Jesus visit his followers after he rose from the dead?

(Yes)   No

2. Did Jesus promise that the Holy Spirit would come to his followers?

(Yes)   No

3. Was Christmas the day the Holy Spirit came to Jesus' followers?

Yes   (No)

4. Is the Holy Spirit the Third Person of the Blessed Trinity?

(Yes)   No

5. Did Jesus want his followers to forget him?

Yes   (No)

 What did the Holy Spirit help Jesus' followers to do? Possible responses: remember the things Jesus said and did; love others as Jesus taught them; tell others about Jesus

130

CHAPTER TEST

Read each test item aloud and allow time for the children to mark an answer. Decide whether the *Talk About It* activity will be a small group or whole class discussion. After you have finished, check the answers. Clarify any misconceptions.

Alternative Assessment

You may want the students to complete the following alternative-assessment activity.

What happened on Pentecost? Draw a picture. Write a sentence to tell about your picture.

Additional Testing

• Chapter 10 Test in *Assessment Book*, pages 19–20

• CD-ROM *Test Generator and Resource*: Use Chapter 10 Test or customize your own.

Review

Review the definition as it is presented in the chapter's *Key Word* box:

• Pentecost (page 125).

We Believe Statements

Review the four statements.

• The risen Jesus visited his followers.

• Jesus Christ promised that the Holy Spirit would come to his followers.

• The Holy Spirit was sent to Jesus' followers.

• The Holy Spirit is the Third Person of the Blessed Trinity.

To use the Chapter 10 Study Guide, visit

www.webelieveweb.com

Overview

In Chapter 10 the children learned that Jesus sent the Holy Spirit to be with his followers. In this chapter the children will learn how the Holy Spirit helps the Church to grow.

Doctrinal Content	For Adult Reading and Reflection *Catechism of the Catholic Church*
The children will learn:	Paragraph
• The Church began on Pentecost.	767
• The first members of the Church did many things together.	2624
• The Holy Spirit helped the Church to grow.	768
• The Holy Spirit helps the Church today.	798

Church (p. 133)

Catechist Background

What qualities are most outstanding in your parish community?

Go to **www.webelieveweb.com**, Catechist/ Teacher, We Believe Correlations for this chapter's correlation to:
- Six Tasks of Catechesis
- Catholic Social Teaching.

On Pentecost the Holy Spirit did not come gently and quietly. The Holy Spirit came as a strong wind bringing strength, courage, and so many other gifts to Jesus' followers. Disciples of Christ, members of his Church, were not to be a weak and cowardly community. The Holy Spirit was here to help the disciples to be strong in faith, responsible, and caring. The Holy Spirit was among Jesus' followers to help them do the right thing. And they did.

The members of the Church community in those early years took care of one another, not out of fear but out of faith and love. The Holy Spirit gave them the courage to follow Jesus' words and example. They shared all they had with one another so that no one was in need. They ate and prayed together and met to share the Good News. Their numbers grew. Others saw the followers and heard about Christ. Many came to believe and wanted to join the early Church community.

What joy and courage we can take from our own conviction that Christ did not send the Holy Spirit only to those first followers. The Holy Spirit is with the Church today just as on that first Pentecost. It is up to us to discover how the Holy Spirit can help us to become a strong and caring community of believers.

How does the Holy Spirit work through you?

Lesson Planning Guide

Lesson Focus	Presentation	Materials

Day 1

page 131
 We Gather in Prayer

pages 132–133
The Church began on Pentecost.

 *Acts of the Apostles
2:36–38, 41*

- Pray to the Holy Spirit.
- Respond to the **We Gather** question.
- Read the **We Believe** text about the beginning of the Church.
- Respond to the **We Respond** question.
- Complete the drawing activity.

For the prayer space: large flame, Bible opened to Acts of the Apostles 2:36–41; four paper plates faces: happy, sad, brave, tired

- crayons or colored pencils
- copies of reproducible master *What's the Word?*, guide page 131F

Day 2

pages 134–135
The first members of the Church did many things together.

- Do the **We Gather** role-play activity.
- Read and discuss the **We Believe** text about the first members of the Church.
- Sing about the first Church members.
- Write more verses to the song.
- Discuss the **We Respond** question.

- "The First Church Members," #10, Grade 1 CD
- copies of Reproducible Master 11, guide page 131G

Day 3

pages 136–137
The Holy Spirit helped the Church to grow.

- Share responses for **We Gather**.
- Present the **We Believe** text about the first members of the Church.
- Complete the activity.
- Read the **We Respond** directive and respond in prayer.
- Read and discuss the *As Catholics* text.

- colored pencils

Day 4

pages 138–139
The Holy Spirit helps the Church today.

- Sing the **We Gather** song.
- Present the **We Believe** text about the Church today.
- Share responses for **We Respond**.
- Sing together.

- "Share the Light," Bernadette Farrell, #11, #12, Grade 1 CD

Day 5

pages 140–141
Project Disciple

page 142
Chapter 11 Test

- Complete the **Project Disciple** activities.
- Explain the *Take Home* activity.
- Discuss/send home **Sharing Faith with My Family**, guide page 131E.
- Complete **Chapter 11 Test**.
- Work on *Alternative Assessment* activity.

- pencils
- copies of **Sharing Faith with My Family** reproducible master, guide page 131E

For additional ideas, activities, and opportunities: Visit Sadlier's  www.WeBelieveweb.com

131B

Enrichment Ideas

Chapter Story

Antonio had just finished all of his homework. He was looking forward to watching his favorite television show. When the program started, his mother came into the room. She said, "Antonio, I am going to take a meal to Mrs. Farrell. She came home from the hospital today. I would like you to come with me. Mrs. Farrell would like to see you."

"I'm tired and I just want to sit and watch television," mumbled Antonio.

As Antonio watched his show, the doorbell rang. He could hear his father at the door talking to someone. A man at the door was saying, "I have a flat tire and I can't drive my car. Could you help me?" Antonio's father called, "Antonio, I will be right outside. This man needs me to help him."

A few minutes later Antonio's little brother, Mario, ran into the room and asked, "Antonio, can you help me put my toys away? Mommy said I can't go bike riding unless I clean up." Antonio yelled at him, "Leave me alone!"

Some time later Antonio noticed how quiet the house was. He thought about his mom and dad going out of their way to help other people. Then he thought about his brother. Instead of helping out, Antonio was sitting all by himself.

So Antonio ran upstairs to Mario's room. He said, "Mario, I'm sorry I yelled before. I'll help you pick up your toys." Together they cleaned the room and then went outside to ride their bicycles. Antonio felt better. He realized that helping someone helps you to be happy.

▶ *Why did Antonio change his mind and decide to help?*

FAITH and MEDIA

▶ On Day 4, after singing "Share the Light" with the children, you might show the class how we can share Jesus' love with someone by sending that person prayers and greetings in an e-card such as those found on the program's Web site.

▶ The first members of the Church lived like a family. View some television programs or movies to find examples of families who share and work together. Explore the ways that the families keep a happy and peaceful home. What makes these families the same? What are some differences between the families in the media and our own families?

CHAPTER PROJECT: SHARING VINE

In this chapter the children learn how the Holy Spirit helps the Church to grow. Discuss the ways the first members of the Church shared. Make a "Sharing Vine" with the children. Cut small strips of construction paper. When a child is kind and shares something with another child, ask the child to take a strip of paper and write the sharing act on the paper. Use glue, tape, or a stapler to attach the pieces of paper together to form a vine. Display the vine in the prayer space and continue to add to it each day. Decide on a day to celebrate with a sharing and caring party.

PROJECT DISCIPLE

Additional Activities

What's the Word?

(Use on Day 1.)

Materials needed: copies of reproducible master, guide page 131F

Distribute the Scripture reproducible master. Explain to the children that they will be doing an activity to remember the story of the day the Church began. Choose three volunteers to read the parts of Readers 1–3. Ask the other children to follow along.

Pray Today

Materials needed: flames cut out of poster/cardboard, paint, brushes, markers

Allow each child to paint a flame cut-out using fiery colors. Once dry, encourage each child to write a prayer to the Holy Spirit on the flame using a marker. Provide prompts if children need assistance in beginning their prayers. Encourage the children to display the flame in a place that will remind them to pray to the Holy Spirit often.

More to Explore

Invite several guest speakers to visit the classroom and speak to the children about what the Church means to them. If possible, include a parish priest. In advance of the presentations help the children to think of questions to ask the speakers. You might also want to give a copy of these questions to the speakers so they can prepare for the session. Allow time for the questions after each presentation.

Question Corner

Make a class picture book. Run off a copy of a blank page with the title: *A picture of a way _____'s family is like the first Church members.* Distribute copies to the children and help them write their first names on the line. Then ask the children to illustrate a way their family is like the first Church members. Bind the book and add it to the classroom library for the children to enjoy.

Meeting Individual Needs
Children Who Are Shy

When children are going to work in pairs, try to assign a shy child and an outgoing child as partners. Circulate among the pairs to measure the balance of the participation. Stop to help partners who are having problems communicating with each other.

We Believe Resources

- Grade 1 *Review & Resource Book*, pages 28–30
- Grade 1 *Family Book*, pages 33–35
- Grade 1 *Assessment Book*, pages 21–22
- Grade 1 CD-ROM *Test Generator and Resource*: Use Chapter 11 Test or customize your own.
- **www.webelieveweb.com**

Sharing What I Learned

Look at the pictures below. Use each picture to tell your family what you learned in this chapter.

A Prayer Card

Cut out the prayer card. Ask each person in your family to write his or her initials on the flame. Pray to the Holy Spirit often.

Fold

All: Holy Spirit, we ask for your help.

Child: When we are excited or happy,

Child: When we are sad or lonely,

Child: When we are tired or afraid,

All: Holy Spirit, fill our hearts with love.

Visit Sadlier's
www.WeBelieve.web.com

Connect to the Catechism
For adult background and reflection, see paragraphs 767, 2624, 768, and 798.

PROJECT DISCIPLE

Name _____

What's *the* Word?

Reader 1: It was fifty days after Jesus rose from the dead.

Reader 2: Peter and other followers had received the Gift of the Holy Spirit that morning.

Reader 3: They left the house where they were staying. Peter talked to the crowds of people in the streets.

Reader 1: Peter told the people to become followers of Jesus. He told them that they would receive the Holy Spirit.

Reader 3: That day about three thousand people became followers of Jesus. We call this day Pentecost. It was the day the Church began.

Name _____

Share this song with your family and friends.

🎵 **The First Church Members**

("Here We Go 'Round the Mulberry Bush")

We can act like the first
    Church members,
the first Church members,
the first Church members,
We can act like the first
    Church members.
We can follow their example.

The Holy Spirit Helps the Church to Grow

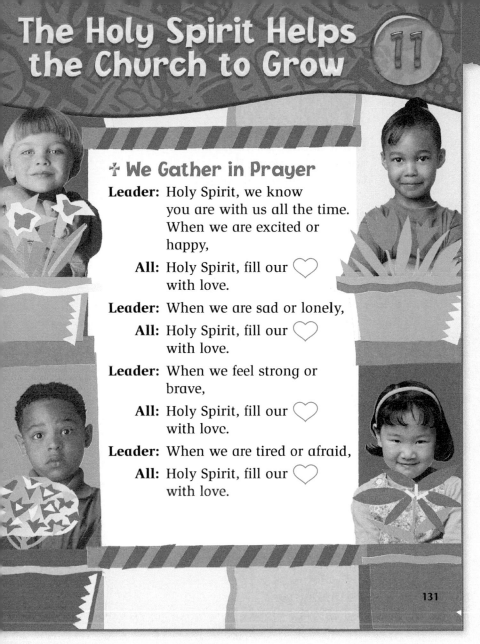

✝ We Gather in Prayer

Leader: Holy Spirit, we know you are with us all the time. When we are excited or happy,

All: Holy Spirit, fill our ♡ with love.

Leader: When we are sad or lonely,

All: Holy Spirit, fill our ♡ with love.

Leader: When we feel strong or brave,

All: Holy Spirit, fill our ♡ with love.

Leader: When we are tired or afraid,

All: Holy Spirit, fill our ♡ with love.

131

PREPARING TO PRAY

The children will ask the Holy Spirit to help them.

• Make four paper-plate faces to represent the facial expressions of feelings mentioned in the prayer: happiness, sadness, brave feelings, tiredness or fear. Give a plate to each of four volunteers. Point out to each child the part of the prayer at which he or she should hold up the plate.

• Show the children how to cross their arms over their hearts each time they pray the response.

The Prayer Space

• Display a large flame to represent the Holy Spirit.

• On the prayer table place the Bible opened to the story of what Peter did on Pentecost (Acts of the Apostles 2:36–41).

 This Week's Liturgy
Visit **www.webelieveweb.com** for this week's liturgical readings and other seasonal material.

Lesson Plan

We Gather in Prayer ___ minutes

✝ Pray

• Invite the children to pray the Sign of the Cross. Then have the prayer leader begin to pray. Ask the children to respond: *Holy Spirit, fill our hearts with love.*

• Cue the children with the paper-plate faces to hold them in the air during the appropriate prayer part.

• When you have finished praying, display the plate faces in the prayer space.

Family Connection Update

Invite the children to share their family experiences of joining with their parish.

Catechist Goal

• To explain how the Church began on Pentecost

Our Faith Response

• To identify why Pentecost is a special day to us

 **Church**

Lesson Materials

• crayons or colored pencils

• copies of reproducible master *What's the Word?*, guide page 131F

Teaching Tip

Uppercase C and Lowercase C

After you have presented the lesson, have the children highlight the word *Church* in the last *We Believe* paragraph and in the *Key Word* box. Point out that we begin *Church* with an uppercase C when we are talking about all the people who belong to the Church. We use a lowercase c when we are talking about the building where we gather to pray.

The Church began on Pentecost.

WE GATHER

✝ *Jesus, we believe in you.*

Think about something exciting that happened to you.
Who did you tell about it?

WE BELIEVE

On Pentecost Jesus' followers were excited.
The Holy Spirit had come to them.
They left the house where they were staying.
They wanted to tell people what had happened.

132

Lesson Plan

WE GATHER ___ minutes

✝ **Pray** Begin the lesson by praying the Sign of the Cross and the *We Gather* prayer.

Focus on Life Read the *We Gather* directive and question. Pause briefly to allow children time to think about their responses. Present a few situations to the class. For each have them discuss how and with whom they would share the news. Situations:

• *Your soccer team won the championship game.*

• *Your favorite aunt and cousins are coming to visit.*

Tell the children that in this lesson they will learn about the way the Church began.

WE BELIEVE ___ minutes

Review Ask: *What happened on Pentecost?* (The Holy Spirit came to Jesus' followers.) Remind the children that Jesus' followers were in Jerusalem when the Holy Spirit came.

Learn About the Church Have the children look at the picture on the page. Explain: *Many people were in Jerusalem on Pentecost.* Then read the first *We Believe* paragraph and the Scripture story.

Explain: *Many people received the Holy Spirit that day. They became Jesus' followers. This is how the Church began.*

📖 Acts of the Apostles 2:36–38, 41

Read Along

On Pentecost, Peter and the other Apostles told people about Jesus. Peter told the people to believe in Jesus. He asked them to become Jesus' followers. If they did this, they would receive the Holy Spirit.

That day about three thousand people received the Gift of the Holy Spirit. They became followers of Jesus.

This was the beginning of the Church.

The **Church** is all the people who believe in Jesus and follow his teachings.

Key Word

Church all the people who believe in Jesus and follow his teachings

WE RESPOND

Why is Pentecost a special day?

🧍 Add yourself to the picture. Pretend you are in the crowd. Tell what you are seeing and hearing.

133

ACTIVITY BANK

Curriculum Connection

Language Arts

Activity Materials: large index cards (4" × 6"), sample postcard, crayons or markers

Have the children think about ways that we tell people good news. Bring in a sample postcard to show the children what postcards look like. Ask the children to pretend that they were present at the first Pentecost. Provide each student with one large index card. Have the children write a postcard to a friend to tell the news of Pentecost. Have them decorate the front of the postcard with a flame. On the back of the card, have the children write the good news about the Holy Spirit.

Scripture

Interpersonal, Linguistic

For a Scripture activity, see *What's the Word?*, guide page 131F.

Remember the Key Word On the board write the word *Church* in large letters. Ask the children to tell you what they think the word *Church* means. Read aloud the last *We Believe* paragraph. Have the children stand, point to themselves, and say: *We are the Church.*

Quick Check

✔ *What did Peter do after he received the Holy Spirit on Pentecost?* (He told people about Jesus, told them to believe in Jesus, and asked them to become Jesus' followers.)

✔ *What is the Church?* (The Church is all the people who believe in Jesus and follow his teachings.)

WE RESPOND ⎯ minutes

Connect to Life Invite the children to share their answers to the *We Respond* question. Explain that Pentecost is like the Church's birthday, which makes it a very important day of celebration. Then ask the children to draw a picture of themselves as if they were part of the crowd on the first Pentecost.

Plan Ahead for Day 2

Catechist Goal: To relate what the first members of the Church did together

Preparation: Make copies of Reproducible Master 11, guide page 131G.

Catechist Goal

• To relate what the first members of the Church did together

Our Faith Response

• To name ways we as members of the Church can work together

Lesson Materials

• chart paper
• Grade 1CD
• copies of Reproducible Master 11

Teaching Note

The Early Church

In the early days of the Church, the early Christians met and worshiped in one another's homes since they had no official place of worship. Many different houses were used for worship. The first Christians were a close group and considered themselves a family. They turned to each other for both spiritual and material help.

The first members of the Church did many things together.

WE GATHER

✝ *Holy Spirit, make us one in Jesus.*

🧍 Act out some things your family does together.

WE BELIEVE

The first members of the Church were like a close family.

They talked about Jesus' teachings. They learned together about ways to follow Jesus. They shared their money. They shared the things they had. They ate their meals together. They praised God together.

134

Lesson Plan

WE GATHER
___ minutes

✝ **Pray** Invite the children to pray the *We Gather* prayer. Read it together three times. Have the children hold hands and listen carefully for the word *one* as they repeat the prayer.

Focus on Life Have the children think about their families. Read aloud the *We Gather* direction. Invite volunteers to act out what they do with their families. Encourage the other children to guess the activity. Have the children give ideas of what families do together. List their ideas on the board or chart paper. Tell the children that in this lesson they will learn that the first members of the Church were like a close family.

WE BELIEVE
___ minutes

Learn About the First Church Members As you read the *We Believe* text, have the children repeat the sentences one at a time. Have the children look again at their list of ideas of what families do together. Have them compare their list with the things the first members of the Church did.

Sing the Song Play the song "The First Church Members," #10 on the Grade 1 CD. Go over the words with the children. Ask the children to share their ideas for actions to go along with the song. For example, have them pretend to pass food to the person standing next to them as they sing, "shared their things." Gather the children in the prayer space. Have them stand in a circle, arms length apart. Invite them to use

♫ **The First Church Members**

("Here We Go 'Round the Mulberry Bush")

The first Church members shared
    their things,
shared their things, shared their things.
The first Church members shared
    their things
And we can do the same.

Sing this song again using these words:

The first Church members prayed
    together.

Together make up more
verses for this song.

WE RESPOND

How can you live like the first
Church members lived?

ACTIVITY BANK

Meeting Individual Needs
Children Who Are Gifted and Talented
Activity Materials: drawing paper
Have the children do an acrostic, using the letters of Church or Holy Spirit. For each letter have the children write one thing the first Church members did together.

```
_____  C _____
_____  H _____
_____  U _____
_____  R _____
_____  C ared for the sick.
_____  H _____
```

the actions as they sing the song. Then together make up additional verses for the song. As you make up the other verses, try to incorporate other motions as well.

Quick Check

✔ *What were the first members of the Church like?* (The first members of the Church were like a close family.)

✔ *What were some of the things that the first members of the Church did together?* (Possible responses include what is listed in the first *We Believe* paragraph.)

WE RESPOND ___ minutes

Connect to Life Have the children take a minute to think about their answer to the *We Respond* question.

Then invite them to share their answers.

Pray Distribute copies of Reproducible Master 11. Read the song verse on the sheet. Sing the song verse together. Encourage the children to show the sheet to their families and to share ways that they can follow the example of the first Church members. Pray by singing the verse.

Plan Ahead for Day 3

Catechist Goal: To examine the ways the Holy Spirit helped the Church to grow

Preparation: On the board or chart paper, draw a tree with many leaves.

Catechist Goal

• To examine the ways the Holy Spirit helped the Church to grow

Our Faith Response

• To pray to the Holy Spirit when we need help

Lesson Materials
• colored pencils

As Catholics...

Saint Peter and Saint Paul

After you have presented the lesson, read the *As Catholics* text to the children. Remind them that Saint Peter was with Jesus from the beginning of his mission. Tell the children that Saint Paul traveled all over the world building the Church. Explain: *You can read more about these saints' brave acts in the book of the Bible called the Acts of the Apostles.*

The Holy Spirit helped the Church to grow.

WE GATHER

✟ *Holy Spirit, help us to tell others about Jesus.*

Name some people who help you to believe in Jesus.

WE BELIEVE

The first members of the Church were filled with the Holy Spirit.

With the help of the Holy Spirit, they:
• believed in Jesus
• told everyone what Jesus had done for them
• shared God's love with others
• helped those who were poor or sick
• tried to be kind and fair to everyone.

Every day more and more people became members of the Church.

136

Lesson Plan

WE GATHER ___ minutes

✟ **Pray** Invite the children to pray the *We Gather* prayer on page 136. Divide the class into three groups. Have the first group pray with you. Then invite the second group to join in, then the third group.

Focus on Life On the board or chart paper, draw a tree with many branches and leaves. Read the *We Gather* directive. Invite each child to respond with at least one name. Write these names on the leaves of the branches. Add a few of your own. Then invite the children to look at all of the people who help them. Tell the children that in this lesson they will learn that the Holy Spirit helped the Church to grow.

WE BELIEVE ___ minutes

The Church Grows Read aloud the *We Believe* statement and the text. Have the children look at the pictures on pages 136 and 137. Ask: *What do you think it would have been like to have spent time with the first members of the Church?* Explain that when people heard about Jesus and saw how happy and loving the first members of the Church were, they wanted to be members, too.

Do the Activity Read the directions for the *We Believe* activity. Have the children follow these directions to find the missing word. Invite a volunteer to read the completed sentence.

Q G A R M O S W

The Holy Spirit helps the Church to

G _ R _ O _ W _ .

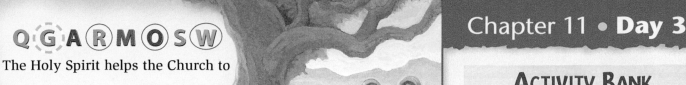

👤 Read the sentence above.
What word is missing?
Circle every other letter.
Use the letters in the circles
to write the missing word.

WE RESPOND

Together the first members
of the Church prayed and
asked the Holy Spirit to be
with them.

Say a prayer to ask the
Holy Spirit to be with you.

As Catholics...

After the Church began, Paul
became a member, too. Like Peter,
he told everyone he met about
Jesus. Paul taught that all people
were welcome in the Church.

On June 29, the Church honors
Saint Peter and Saint Paul. On this
day, we remember that Peter and
Paul helped the Church to grow.

You can learn more about Saint
Peter and Saint Paul in the Bible.

137

ACTIVITY BANK

Multiple Intelligences
Bodily-Kinesthetic
Activity Materials: index cards, construction paper, markers, art supplies
    Divide your class into five groups.
On each index card write a different
way that the Holy Spirit helped the
first members of the Church. Give a
card to each group with one of the
following:

• *The Holy Spirit helped them to
believe in Jesus.*
• *The Holy Spirit helped them to tell
everyone what Jesus had done for
them.*
• *The Holy Spirit helped them to
share God's love with others.*
• *The Holy Spirit helped them help
those who were poor and sick.*
• *The Holy Spirit helped them try to
be kind and fair to everyone.*

    Invite the groups to come up with
a short skit to act out. You may wish
to have available construction paper
and other art supplies for them to
make props. Have each group act out
its skit in front of the class.

Quick Check

✔ *Who helped the first members of the Church believe in
Jesus?* (The Holy Spirit helped the first members of
the Church.)

✔ *How did the Holy Spirit help members of the Church?*
(Possible responses are those listed in the *We Believe*
text.)

WE RESPOND ___ minutes

Connect to Life Read the *We Respond* text. Dim or
turn off the overhead lights. Provide a few minutes of
quiet time. Invite the children to pray quietly to ask the
Holy Spirit to be with them.

Pray Using the *We Believe* bulleted list, extend the
prayers. Have the children pray aloud: *Holy Spirit, help
us share God's love. Help us to help those who are poor or
sick. Help us to be kind and fair to everyone.*

Plan Ahead for Day 4

Catechist Goal: To highlight the ways that
the Holy Spirit helps the Church today

Preparation: Have Grade 1 CD available.

Catechist Goal

• To highlight ways that the Holy Spirit helps the Church today

Our Faith Response

• To use the Holy Spirit's help to live as Jesus taught us

Lesson Materials

• Grade 1 CD

Teaching Tip

Working in Groups

When children work together in groups, provide incentive for the members of the group to work peacefully and keep focused. Draw several happy faces on index cards. When you see a group working nicely together, give the group a happy-face card. When the activity is over, ask the groups to hold up their cards. Affirm the children in these groups for working well together. Then collect the cards to use again.

The Holy Spirit helps the Church today.

WE GATHER

✝ *God, may we grow in your love.*

🎵 **Share the Light**

Share the light of Jesus.
Share the light that shows the way.
Share the light of Jesus.
Share God's spirit today.
Share God's spirit today.

WE BELIEVE

The Holy Spirit is always with the Church.
We are members of the Church.
The Holy Spirit helps us to know that Jesus loves us.
The Holy Spirit helps us to live as Jesus taught us.

138

Lesson Plan

WE GATHER _____ minutes

✝ **Pray** Invite the children to pray the Sign of the Cross and the *We Gather* prayer.

Focus on Life Invite the children to read the words to the *We Gather* song, "Share the Light," #11 on the Grade 1 CD. Have them listen to the song and then join in and sing. Point out that light often brings brightness if we are in the dark and happiness if we are afraid. Explain: *The light of Jesus can bring brightness and happiness to our lives.* You may want to read the *Chapter Story* on guide page 131C at this time. Tell the children that in this lesson they will learn that the Holy Spirit helps us to live as Jesus taught us.

WE BELIEVE _____ minutes

Learn About the Church Today Read aloud the *We Believe* statement and the first *We Believe* paragraph. Ask: *How does the Holy Spirit help us in the Church today? How is the Church like one big family?*

The Holy Spirit Is with Us Have the children form small groups. Ask the children in the groups to look at the photos on pages 138 and 139. Invite the groups to name ways the Holy Spirit is helping the people in the photos. (Possible responses: page 138 left, sharing time and things and following the rules when playing with others; page 138 right, sharing and caring for others who are poor; page 139, praying)

With the help of the Holy Spirit we:
- pray
- share with others
- care for those who are poor or sick
- show respect for all people
- learn more about Jesus and the Church
- follow the rules when working and playing with others.

WE RESPOND

What can you and your family do to live as Jesus taught us?

♫ Share the Light

Share the love of Jesus.
Share the love that shows the way.
Share the love of Jesus.
Share God's spirit today.
Share God's spirit today.

139

ACTIVITY BANK

Parish
Plan a Special Day
Activity Materials: large chart paper, poster board, and markers

Organize a "Kindness Day." Involve the children in planning a day on which they will focus on doing kind acts. Have them brainstorm ways they can help people in their school and parish. Some suggestions: have a canned food drive or clothing drive; make cards or draw pictures for the home-bound and the elderly of the parish. Invite the children to make posters to tell the rest of the school and parish about "Kindness Day."

Quick Check

✔ *Who helps the members of the Church to live as Jesus taught?* (The Holy Spirit helps members of the Church live as Jesus taught.)

✔ *How does the Holy Spirit help us?* (Possible responses are those listed in the *We Believe* text.)

WE RESPOND ___ minutes

Connect to Life Read aloud the *We Respond* question. Invite volunteers to share their answers. Ask: *Why do you think it is important for your family to love, share, and work together?* Discuss the children's responses.

Pray Gather the children in the prayer space. Sing the song, "Share the Light," #12 on the Grade 1 CD. You might want to repeat the *We Gather* verse, #11 on the CD along with the *We Respond* verse.

Plan Ahead for Day 5

Catechist Goal: To review chapter ideas and their relationship to our faith life

Preparation: Make copies of *Sharing Faith with My Family*, guide page 131E.

Catechist Goal

• To review the chapter ideas that are key to growing as disciples of Jesus Christ

Our Faith Response

• To decide on ways to grow as disciples by living out what we have learned

Show What you Know

Review the definition of the *Key Word* with the children. Ask the children to trace the word in each statement. Have them take turns reading them aloud.

Fast Facts

Use the following pronunciation key to teach the children to say "thank you" in many languages.
Korean: kam sa ham ni da (kahm-sah-hahm-nee-dah)
Polish: dziekuje (jehn-koo-yeh)
Spanish: gracias (grah-see-ahs)
Swahili: ashante (ah-sahn-tay)
Tongan: malo malo (mah-loh mah-loh)

Reality Check

Read the activity question and choices. Circulate among the children to provide assistance in completing the activity.

Make it Happen

Allow children to work with a partner to add actions to the "Share the Light" song from page 139. Let children perform their work for the class and for their families.

Take Home

Encourage the children to do the *Take Home* activity with their families.

Discuss and send home copies of *Sharing Faith with My Family*, guide page 131E.

140 and **141**

Grade 1 Chapter 11

PROJECT

Show What you Know

Trace the Word in every faith statement. Think about what it means.

The Church began on Pentecost.

The first members of the Church did many things together.

The Holy Spirit helped the Church to grow.

The Holy Spirit helps the Church today.

Fast Facts

Here are some ways to thank members of the Church all over the world.

thank you	English
kam sa ham ni da	Korean
dziekuje	Polish
gracias	Spanish
ahsante	Swahili
malo malo	Tongan

140 www.webelieveweb.com

DISCIPLE

Reality Check
How are your family members like the first Church members?

❑ We talk about Jesus' teachings.
❑ We learn about ways to follow Jesus.
❑ We share our money.
❑ We share our things.
❑ We eat together.
❑ We praise God together.

Make it Happen

Make up prayer actions to the "Share the Light" song you learned. Then, teach it to your friend.

Now, pass it on!

Take Home

Make a poster with your family to show how the Holy Spirit is with the Church today. Use pictures from a magazine or draw your own. Write words to go with your pictures.

141

CHAPTER TEST

Circle the correct answer.

1. The Church began on _____.

   (Pentecost)   Easter

2. The first members of the Church _____.

   did not share   (shared many things)

3. The _____ is all the people who believe in Jesus and follow his teachings.

   Holy Spirit   (Church)

4. The Holy Spirit helps us to live as _____ taught us.

   the crowd   (Jesus)

5. The first members of the Church were _____ the Holy Spirit.

   (filled with)   tired of

What does the Holy Spirit help us to do? Possible responses: pray; share with others; care for people who are poor or sick; show respect for all people; learn more about Jesus and the Church; follow the rules when working and playing with others

142

Chapter 11 • Day 5

CHAPTER TEST

Read each test item aloud and allow time for the children to mark an answer. Decide whether the *Talk About It* activity will be a small group or whole class discussion. After you have finished, check the answers. Clarify any misconceptions.

Alternative Assessment

You may want the students to complete the following alternative-assessment activity.

> *Make a poster to show how the Holy Spirit is with the Church today. Write words to go with the pictures.*

Additional Testing

• Chapter 11 Test in *Assessment Book*, pages 21–22

• CD-ROM *Test Generator and Resource*: Use Chapter 11 Test or customize your own.

Review

Review the definition as it is presented in the chapter's *Key Word* box:

• Church (page 133).

We Believe Statements

Review the four statements.

• The Church began on Pentecost.

• The first members of the Church did many things together.

• The Holy Spirit helped the Church to grow.

• The Holy Spirit helps the Church today.

To use the Chapter 11 Study Guide, visit

www.webelieveweb.com

Overview

In Chapter 11 the children learned how the Holy Spirit helped the Church grow. In this chapter they will learn that Jesus appointed the Apostles to care for the Church, and how the pope and bishops care for the Church today.

Doctrinal Content	For Adult Reading and Reflection *Catechism of the Catholic Church*
The children will learn:	Paragraph
• The Apostles led and cared for the Church.	858
• The bishops lead and care for the Church.	862
• The pope leads and cares for the whole Church.	881
• The Church serves others.	1942

Catechist Background

What activities define your life?

Go to **www.webelieveweb.com**, Catechist/ Teacher, We Believe Correlations for this chapter's correlation to:
- Six Tasks of Catechesis
- Catholic Social Teaching
- *Catechetical Formation in Chaste Living.*

When we reflect on the life of Christ, it is clear how he spent his years of public ministry. Jesus proclaimed the Good News, the Word of God. Jesus prayed and worshiped. Jesus served others and he formed a community. Today the Church continues this same work of Christ: proclaiming the Word, praying and worshiping, serving others, and building a community.

Just as Jesus our Savior proclaimed the Good News in words and in action, the Church also studies and explains Scripture, teaches about God's love in preaching, in catechesis, and in the example it gives in action.

Jesus prayed to and worshiped God. The Church today keeps the celebration of the Eucharist at the heart of its life. It celebrates the sacraments and over the centuries has provided many forms of prayer, both private and communal.

Jesus served others. He was a servant-leader who responded to the needs, problems, and sufferings of others. Today ministry to all people but especially to the needs of the poor and suffering is the highest priority of the servant Church.

Jesus gathered a community around him and that caring community continued to grow. Building up the community of the Body of Christ is also a work of the Church today. Just as the Apostles led the early Church to do these same things, the role of the pope and bishops today in leading and caring for the Church is to continue this same mission.

How do you participate in the mission of Christ through Word, worship, service, and community?

Lesson Planning Guide

Lesson Focus	Presentation	Materials

Day 1

page 143
✝ **We Gather in Prayer**

pages 144–145
The Apostles led and cared for the Church.

📖 *Matthew 16:18*

🎵 Sing a song about being the Church.
- Share responses for **We Gather**.

🧍 Find the meaning of the name Peter.
- Present the Bible story in **We Believe** about Saint Peter.
- Reflect on the **We Respond** question.

For the prayer space: poster board with title "We Are the Church," parish bulletin, illustrated Bible

🎵 "We Are the Church," Christopher Walker, #13, Grade 1 CD

Day 2

pages 146–147
The bishops lead and care for the Church.

- Follow the **We Gather** directives.
- Read and discuss the **We Believe** text about the bishops.

 Do the picture-study activity.
- Answer the **We Respond** question.
- Pray to the Holy Spirit.

- chart paper, markers
- copies of Reproducible Master 12, guide page 143G
- crayons or colored pencils

Day 3

pages 148–149
The pope leads and cares for the whole Church.

🧍 Do the **We Gather** matching activity.
- Share responses to the question.
- Present the **We Believe** text about the pope.
- Discuss the **We Respond** question.
- Read and discuss the *As Catholics* text.

- world map

Day 4

pages 150–151
The Church serves others.

📖 *John 13:15*

🧍 Complete the **We Gather** activity.
- Present the **We Believe** text about serving others.

 Do the picture-study activity.
- Discuss the **We Respond** question.

- construction-paper hearts
- crayons or colored pencils
- copies of reproducible master *What's the Word?*, guide page 143F

Day 5

pages 152–153
Project Disciple

page 154
Chapter 12 Test

- Complete the **Project Disciple** activities.
- Explain the *Take Home* activity.
- Discuss/send home **Sharing Faith with My Family**, guide page 143E.
- Complete **Chapter 12 Test**.
- Work on *Alternative Assessment* activity.

- pencils
- crayons or colored pencils
- copies of **Sharing Faith with My Family** reproducible master, guide page 143E

Enrichment Ideas

Chapter Story

Last Thursday morning the Perez children were in the kitchen. Their dad came and talked to them.

"Your mother is not feeling well today," he said. "She needs to rest quietly, so let's try to not disturb her. I'm going to make breakfast while you get ready for school. And April, since you're the oldest, I'm going to ask you to help out the most."

April told her dad, "I'll try to do my best, Dad."

The children went back to their rooms. "Who will help me practice my spelling words?" asked Raul. "Mom always asks me my spelling words before I go to school."

"I will," said April. "That's what big sisters are for."

"Who's going to tie my shoes and comb my hair?" asked Maria. "I don't want to be late for preschool. I better ask Mommy to do that before she goes to sleep."

"No," said Raul. "I'll help you. Remember, Dad said not to bother Mom today."

That evening as Mr. Perez and the children sat down to dinner, Mrs. Perez came into the kitchen. Everyone called out together, "Hi, Mom! How are you feeling? We're so glad you're out of bed!"

"I thought I smelled something tasty," she said. "Who made this yummy dinner?"

"Dad did," Raul replied. "And he made breakfast, too. Maria helped me clear the table after breakfast, and April did the dishes. She helped me with my spelling words, too. I tied Maria's shoes and combed her hair. Are you feeling better, Mom?"

"I sure am," said Mrs. Perez. "And it makes me feel even better to know that I have such a helpful family!"

▶ *How did Mrs. Perez's family help to make her feel better?*

FAITH and MEDIA

▶ On Day 2, after discussing how bishops lead and care for the Church, consider visiting your diocesan Web site with the class.

▶ On Day 3, after talking about the pope and reading the *As Catholics* text about the Vatican, you might visit the Vatican Web site with the children.

▶ On Day 5, after reading about Mother Teresa, consider showing the children a video about her life or visiting an appropriate Web site.

CHAPTER PROJECT: CARING FOR THE COMMUNITY

Divide a large sheet of paper into four sections. Label the sections *Family, School, Church,* and *Neighborhood.* Throughout the week, discuss with the children how they can show God's love by serving the people in each of these groups. Write their ideas in the appropriate space on the paper, or invite them to draw pictures of their ideas. As a class, choose one of the ideas to carry out together. Some examples might include: cleaning up the school playground; planting flowers in a church flower bed; helping parents set the table before dinner; collecting food for the food pantry; or delivering handmade cards to a senior-citizen center.

PROJECT DISCIPLE

Pray
Learn
Celebrate
Share
Choose
Live

Additional Activities

Picture This

Help the children understand the role of the pope and bishop in the Church. Complete a graphic organizer as a class to show the relationship among the leaders of the Church. You might include the responsibilities of each.

Make it Happen

Materials needed: hearts made of craft foam, hole puncher, yarn

Punch a hole in the top of the craft foam hearts. Distribute several hearts to each child, along with a length of yarn. Remind the children that Jesus told his followers to help people who were poor, sick, or hungry. Invite the children to write on each heart one thing they can do to help others. Then help them string the hearts onto the yarn to make a necklace. Encourage the children to wear or to display the necklace to remind them to help others.

What's the Word?

(Use on Day 4.)

Materials needed: copies of reproducible master, guide page 143F, colored pencils

Distribute the Scripture reproducible master. Read aloud the quote to the children. Invite them to design a poster using pictures that show what the words mean. Encourage them to make colorful artwork. Display the posters around the classroom or school.

Pray Today

Allow the children some quiet time. Encourage them to talk to Jesus quietly. Invite them to tell Jesus how they feel about serving others as he did.

Meeting Individual Needs
Children with Auditory Needs

Place children with auditory needs in a location where you will be clearly visible to them. Be sure to face the children when you speak. Speak slowly and enunciate clearly. Ask all the children to do the same when they are speaking.

We Believe Resources

- Grade 1 *Review & Resource Book*, pages 31–33
- Grade 1 *Family Book*, pages 36–38
- Grade 1 *Assessment Book*, pages 23–24
- Grade 1 CD-ROM *Test Generator and Resource*: Use Chapter 12 Test or customize your own.
- **www.webelieveweb.com**

Sharing What I Learned

Look at the pictures below. Use each picture to tell your family what you learned in this chapter.

Talking Together

Talk together about the way your family would feel if you could meet the pope. Write a question that your family would like to ask the pope.

_____

_____

_____

A Prayer for the Church

Pray this prayer together.

Holy Spirit, watch over (name), our pope.
Protect and bless (name), our bishop.
Holy Spirit, bless all people, old and young, rich and poor, those who live nearby and those who live far away, the sick and the healthy.
We ask you to hear our prayer.

Visit Sadlier's

www.WeBelieveweb.com

 Connect to the Catechism
For adult background and reflection, see paragraphs 858, 862, 881, and 1942.

PROJECT DISCIPLE

Name _____

What's *the* Word?

Make a poster to show what Jesus wanted his Apostles and us to do.

Jesus said, "I have given you a model to follow, so that as I have done for you, you should also do" (John 13:15).

Name _____

Find the missing word to complete the sentence. Use green to color all the **X** spaces. Use blue to color all the **O** spaces.

Bishops lead and care for the _____.

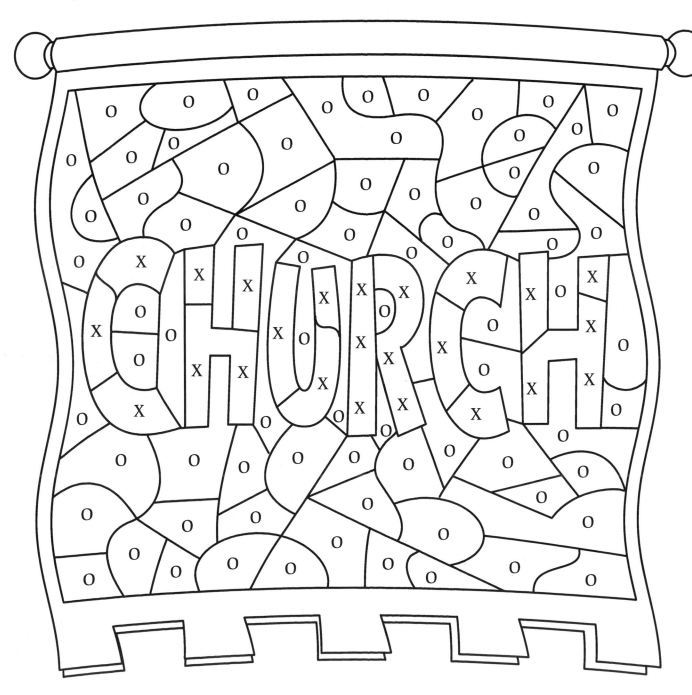

✝ **We Gather in Prayer**

🎵 **We Are the Church**

We are the Church,
happy to be
the children in God's family.

We are following Jesus.
We are following Jesus.
Everyone old and young.
Everyone weak and strong.
We are following Jesus.

143

PREPARING TO PRAY

The children pray by singing about belonging to the Church.

• Read the words to the song, "We Are the Church" on page 143. Then play the song #13 on the Grade 1 CD. Have the children practice singing this song for the opening prayer.

• On a sheet of poster board, print "We Are the Church." Ask the children to take turns writing their names on the poster. Have them name some of the people who are leaders in your parish. Write these leaders' names on the poster.

The Prayer Space

• On the prayer table open an illustrated Bible to a story about Jesus and the Apostles serving others.

• Display the poster "We Are the Church" and a parish bulletin.

📖 **This Week's Liturgy**
Visit **www.webelieveweb.com** for this week's liturgical readings and other seasonal material.

Lesson Plan

We Gather in Prayer ___ minutes

✝ **Pray**

• Invite the children to gather in the prayer space.

• Pray the Sign of the Cross.

• Ask the children to join hands to form a circle, and then sing "We Are the Church," #13, Grade 1 CD.

• Go around the circle and say each child's name. After you say each name, ask the other children to say: *You are the Church.*

Family Connection Update

Invite the children to share their experiences of working on a "Holy Spirit is with the Church" poster.

Catechist Goal

• To describe how the Apostles led and cared for the Church

Our Faith Response

• To share our love for Jesus as the Apostles did

Lesson Materials

• chart paper

• crayons or colored pencils

Teaching Note

The Apostle Peter

Peter was one of the first disciples called by Jesus. Peter often was the spokesperson for the other Apostles. Peter's given name at birth was Simon. Jesus named him *Cephas,* the Aramaic word for "rock." We are more familiar with the Greek translation, Peter.

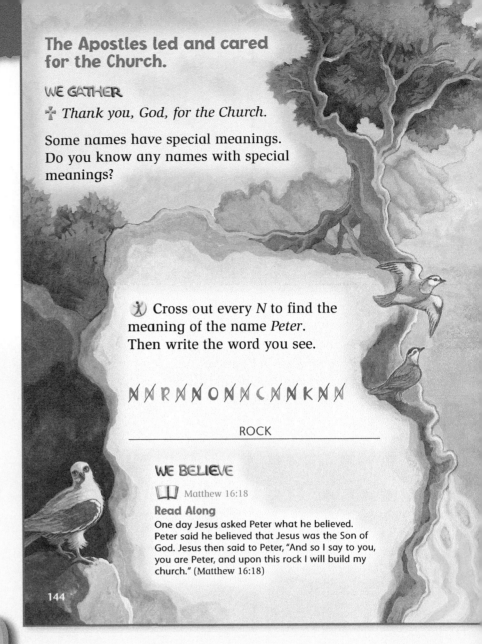

The Apostles led and cared for the Church.

WE GATHER

✝ *Thank you, God, for the Church.*

Some names have special meanings. Do you know any names with special meanings?

Cross out every *N* to find the meaning of the name *Peter.* Then write the word you see.

ⵍ ⵎ ⵏ ⵎ Ⲟ ⵎ ⵉ ⵎ Ⲕ ⵎ ⵎ

ROCK

WE BELIEVE

📖 Matthew 16:18

Read Along

One day Jesus asked Peter what he believed. Peter said he believed that Jesus was the Son of God. Jesus then said to Peter, "And so I say to you, you are Peter, and upon this rock I will build my church." (Matthew 16:18)

144

Lesson Plan

WE GATHER

— minutes

✝ **Pray** Pray the Sign of the Cross and the *We Gather* prayer.

Focus on Life Read the *We Gather* question. Share the meanings of a few names with the children. For example, *John* means "gift of God," and *Olivia* means "peaceful." Explain the directions for the *We Gather* activity. Write the activity letters on the board. Invite a volunteer to cross out the **Ns**. Ask the class to read together the word that tells what Peter means. Share the *Chapter Story* on guide page 143C. Ask: *Did April do what her dad asked her to do?* Tell the children that in this lesson they will learn that Peter and the Apostles led the early Church.

WE BELIEVE

— minutes

Talk About Leaders Read aloud the *We Believe* statement at the top of page 144. Ask the children to share what they know about the Apostles.

Sharing Scripture Read aloud the Scripture story about Jesus choosing Peter to be the leader of the Church. Ask the children: *Why do you think Jesus gave Peter a name meaning "rock"?* Make a word web on chart paper. Write the word *rock* in the middle of the web as you say the word. Ask the children to name words they think of when they hear the word *rock.* Write the related words in the web. (Possible responses: hard, ground, strong) Read aloud the words in the word web. Explain: *Jesus wanted Peter to be strong in his faith.*

Before Jesus died, he asked the Apostles to lead and care for all of his followers. He chose the Apostle Peter to be the leader of all the Apostles.

The Holy Spirit helped Peter and all the Apostles to lead the Church. Their belief in Jesus stayed strong. They shared their love for Jesus with others.

Peter and the Apostles went to faraway lands. They went to teach people about Jesus. Many of these people became members of the Church. Peter and the other Apostles worked to help the Church grow.

WE RESPOND

How can you share your love for Jesus with others?

145

ACTIVITY BANK

Church
Make a Rock Garden
Activity Materials: a large stone for each child, paint, paintbrushes, newspaper, potting soil, large plastic container, artificial flowers

Give each child a large stone and a paintbrush. Invite the children to choose a color to paint their stones. When the paint has dried, have them print their family names on the stones. They may also add other decorations if there is room. When all the children are finished, use the stones to make a rock garden in the prayer space. Put potting soil in a large plastic container. Put the children's rocks in the soil. Insert artificial flowers in the soil around the rocks. Explain: *When you look at the rock garden, remember that our families are part of the Church and that they help the Church to grow.*

Read the Text Read aloud the *We Believe* text. Remind the children that after Jesus returned to heaven, he sent the Holy Spirit. Stress the following points:

• *The Holy Spirit helped the Apostles to remember Jesus.*

• *The Apostles showed their love for Jesus by teaching other people about him.*

Quick Check

✔ *Who did Jesus choose to be the leader of the Apostles?* (Jesus chose Peter.)

✔ *How did the Apostles show their love for Jesus?* (They showed their love by teaching the people about Jesus, sharing their love for Jesus with others, and working to help the Church grow.)

WE RESPOND ___ minutes

Connect to Life Provide a minute of quiet time. Invite the children to reflect on their responses to the *We Respond* question.

Pray Ask the children to pray the following after you: *Jesus, help us to be strong in our love for others.*

Plan Ahead for Day 2

Catechist Goal: To explain the role of bishops to lead and care for the Church

Preparation: Make copies of Reproducible Master 12, guide page 143G.

Catechist Goal

- To explain the role of bishops to lead and care for the Church

Our Faith Response

- To ask the Holy Spirit to help our bishops

Lesson Materials

- copies of Reproducible Master 12
- crayons or colored pencils
- chart paper, markers

Teaching Tip

Graphic Organizer

Make the following graphic illustration in your presentation of this lesson.

- Draw a figure to represent the bishop.
- Draw small churches around the bishop.

The bishops lead and care for the Church.

WE GATHER

✝ *Holy Spirit, please be with the Church.*

Think about your school.
Name some people who lead and care for the students.

WE BELIEVE

Jesus chose the Apostles to lead the Church. In later years, the Apostles chose other men to lead the Church.

These men took the place of the Apostles. They were the new leaders of the Church. They did the work the Apostles had done. They worked together to lead the Church. These leaders became known as bishops.

146

Lesson Plan

WE GATHER _____ minutes

✝ **Pray** Invite the children to pray the Sign of the Cross and the *We Gather* prayer on page 146. Softly repeat the prayer several times.

Focus on Life Invite the children to name people who lead and care for the students of the school. Ask: *How do they lead and care for you?* (Possible responses: principal sets the rules to keep us safe; teachers help the children learn about God's love; custodians keep the school clean; the school nurse takes care of the children when they are sick.) Tell the children that in this lesson they will learn how bishops lead and care for the Church.

WE BELIEVE _____ minutes

Illustrate the Text Read aloud the *We Believe* statement. Draw a stick figure on the board and explain that the figure represents Jesus. Point to the Jesus drawing as you read the first *We Believe* sentence.

Draw twelve figures around Jesus and explain that the figures stand for the Apostles. Then read the second sentence. Draw other figures around the Apostles and label them as bishops and the people of the Church.

Read aloud the remaining *We Believe* paragraphs. Help the children to understand that bishops lead and care for the Church by teaching people about Jesus and the Church, praying with the people, and caring for their needs.

Bishops still lead and care for the
Church today.
They teach about Jesus and
the Church.
They pray with the people in
their care.

Bishops take care of each diocese.
A diocese is made up of many
members of the Church.
A bishop leads and cares for
the people of his diocese.

Look at the pictures on this page.
Talk about ways the bishops are
leading and caring for the
members of the Church.

WE RESPOND

Who is your bishop?

Say a prayer and ask the
Holy Spirit to help him.

147

ACTIVITY BANK

Church
Thanking the Bishop
Activity Materials: white construction paper, crayons or markers,
envelopes, your bishop's address
  Have the children make thank-you
cards for their bishop. Fold pieces of
white construction paper in half.
Have the children draw a picture on
the front of the card. Then help them
write a thank-you message on the
inside of the card. Collect and write a
cover letter to include with the package of cards. Send the package to the
bishop's office.

Mission
Praying for Others
  Remind the children that their
bishop often prays with members of
the Church. Organize the children
into small groups and invite them to
think of a person or group of people
for whom they would like to pray.
Then have them write a brief prayer
and pray it together as a group.

Define Diocese Help the children to understand
that many parishes make up a diocese, and the bishop
is the leader of the diocese. Use the graphic organizer
idea suggested in the Teaching Tip on guide page 146.
Distribute copies of Reproducible Master 12. Allow the
children to follow the directions and complete the
sentence (Church).

Do the Activity Discuss the pictures on page 147.
Help the children to identify what the bishops are doing
in each picture. (top: bishop is teaching; bottom, bishop
is visiting and talking.)

Quick Check

✔ *Who did the Apostles choose to lead and care for the
  Church?* (The Apostles chose bishops to lead and
  care for the Church.)

✔ *What does a bishop do?* (A bishop leads and cares
  for the people of his diocese.)

WE RESPOND ___ minutes

Connect to Life Remind the children of their
bishop's name and where he lives. Explain to the children that their pastor lets the bishop know what is
happening in their parish community. Together pray
for the bishop of your diocese.

Plan Ahead for Day 3

Catechist Goal: To tell how the pope leads
and cares for the whole Church

Preparation: Have available a globe or world
map.

Catechist Goal
• To tell how the pope leads and cares for the whole Church

Our Faith Response
• To welcome the pope's leadership of the Church

Lesson Materials
• world map

As Catholics...

The Vatican

After you have presented the lesson, read the *As Catholics* text to the children. Ask: *Why do you think the pope speaks to the people each week?* (The pope teaches people about Jesus and the Church.)

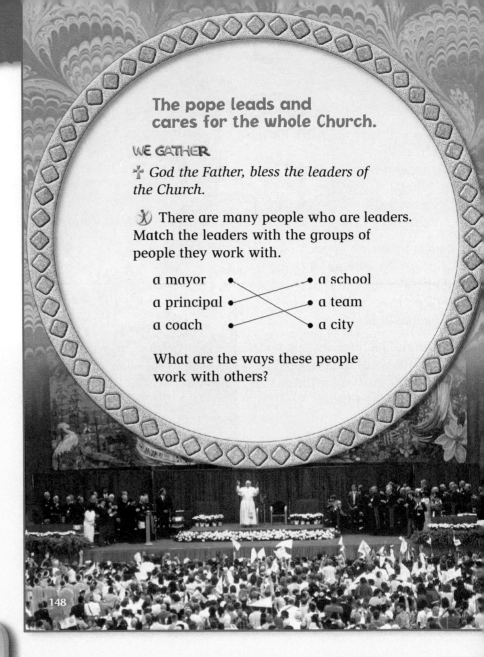

The pope leads and cares for the whole Church.

WE GATHER

✝ God the Father, bless the leaders of the Church.

There are many people who are leaders. Match the leaders with the groups of people they work with.

a mayor — a school
a principal — a team
a coach — a city

What are the ways these people work with others?

148

Lesson Plan

WE GATHER ___ minutes

✝ **Pray** Invite the children to pray together the Sign of the Cross and the *We Gather* prayer on page 148.

Focus on Life Help the children to do the *We Gather* matching activity. Encourage the children to share their answers to the question following the activity. Help the children to identify various ways that mayors, principals, and coaches lead the people with whom they work. Tell the children that in this lesson they will learn about the pope, who leads the whole Church.

WE BELIEVE ___ minutes

Preview Read aloud the *We Believe* statement. Remind the children: *Jesus chose Peter to be the leader of*

the Apostles. It was Peter's work to watch over the Apostles and help them teach others about Jesus. Ask: *Who does the Apostles' work today?* (bishops) Explain that the bishops need someone to be their leader. Stress: *The pope was chosen to be the leader of the bishops, and he helps to care for the whole Church.*

Use a Map Read aloud the first *We Believe* paragraph. Use a world map to show the children Rome, Italy. Explain: *The pope lives in the Vatican. The Vatican is in Rome, Italy.* Then help the children understand that the pope leads the whole Church. Point to different places around the world. As you point to each country, explain: *The pope watches over and cares for the Church in this country.*

WE BELIEVE

The pope is the Bishop of Rome in Italy. He takes the place of Saint Peter. Just like Saint Peter, he leads and cares for the whole Church.

The pope works together with all the bishops.

- He prays for and takes care of the Church.
- He teaches what Jesus taught.
- He visits people all over the world.
- He helps people everywhere.
- He cares for those in need.

The Holy Spirit helps the pope to be a good leader.
The Holy Spirit helps the pope to care for the Church.

WE RESPOND

Imagine that the pope will be coming to visit your city or town. You have the chance to meet him. What do you think he might say to you?

Pope Francis

As Catholics...

The pope lives in the Vatican in Rome, Italy. The main church building of the Vatican is called Saint Peter's. It is named for Peter, the first leader of the Church.

People who are visiting from all over the world gather outside Saint Peter's every Wednesday. There the pope speaks about Jesus and the Church.

Find out the name of the pope.

149

ACTIVITY BANK

Curriculum Connection
Language Arts
Activity Materials: sentence strips with sentences on the *We Believe* list, drawing paper, crayons or markers, book-binding materials

Have the children make a class book about the pope. On sentence strips write the *We Believe* sentences that list the responsibilities of the pope. Divide the children into small groups. Give one of the sentence strips to each group. Explain that the children are to draw and color a picture that illustrates the group's sentence. After they complete the picture, they are to write the sentence under their picture. Collect all of the pictures and bind them together to form a book. Ask the children to decide on a title for the book. Then invite one child from each group to design the cover. Gather the children in the prayer space and read the book aloud.

Quick Check

✔ *Who leads and cares for the whole Church?* (The pope leads and cares for the whole Church.)

✔ *What are some ways that the pope leads and cares for the Church?* (The pope works with all of the bishops. He prays for the Church and teaches what Jesus taught.)

WE RESPOND — minutes

Connect to Life Read the *We Respond* question and invite the children to share their responses. Emphasize: *The pope loves and prays for people around the world. He wants the members of the Church to know that Jesus loves and cares for them.*

Pray Ask the children to gather in the prayer space. Pray together: *Holy Spirit, guide the leaders of the Church.*

Plan Ahead for Day 4

Catechist Goal: To explore the ways the Church serves others

Preparation: Make copies of *What's the Word?*, guide page 143F. Have available construction-paper hearts.

Catechist Goal

• To explore the ways the Church serves others

Our Faith Response

• To choose ways of serving others as members of the Church

Lesson Materials

• construction-paper hearts
• crayons or colored pencils
• copies of reproducible master
What's the Word?, guide page 143F

Teaching Note

Stewardship

During this lesson as you explore caring for others with the children, encourage them to think about caring for the earth and all people. Explain that when we work to make the earth a safe place to live, we also serve one another.

The Church serves others.

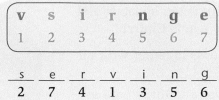

WE GATHER

✝ *Jesus, help us love all the people of the world.*

🏃 Use the code to fill in the correct letters.

v	s	i	r	n	g	e
1	2	3	4	5	6	7

<u>s</u> <u>e</u> <u>r</u> <u>v</u> <u>i</u> <u>n</u> <u>g</u>
 2   7   4   1   3   5   6

is another word for caring and helping.

WE BELIEVE

Jesus showed his followers ways to serve others.
He fed people who were hungry.
He spent time with people who needed him.
He took care of people who were sick.
He shared God's love with everyone.

Jesus said, "As I have done for you, you should also do." (John 13:15)

150

Lesson Plan

WE GATHER ___ minutes

✝ **Pray** Point out that God loves all people from all over the world. Emphasize that God asks us to love all people, too. Pray together the Sign of the Cross and the *We Gather* prayer on page 150.

Focus on Life Read the directions for the *We Gather* activity. Help the children complete the puzzle. Have a volunteer read the sentence adding the missing word. Ask: *How do parents and teachers serve?* (They teach children and keep them safe.) *How can children serve their parents and teachers?* (They can respect and listen to them.) Reread the *Chapter Story* on guide page 143C. Ask: *How did the Perez children love and serve their family?* Tell the children that in this lesson they will learn how the Church serves others.

WE BELIEVE ___ minutes

Act It Out Read aloud the *We Believe* statement and the first *We Believe* paragraph. Invite the class to play a game of charades. Write on the board the four ways Jesus served others. Invite a volunteer to choose one way and act it out. Encourage the rest of the class to guess the way being acted out.

Read aloud the verse, John 13:15. Stress: *We should care for one another as Jesus cares for us.* Distribute cut-out hearts, one for each child. Have the children copy the Bible verse onto the heart. Encourage the children to display the hearts in their homes to remind their families of Jesus' teaching. Then read the remaining *We Believe* text with the children.

Members of the Church serve others.
Look at the pictures on these pages.
They show members of the Church.
How are they doing what
Jesus did?

We show our love for God
when we serve others.

👤 Which pictures show
how you and your family
can love and serve others?
Put a ♡ beside them.

WE RESPOND

What can you do in your
school to serve one another?

151

ACTIVITY BANK

Multicultural Connection
Missions
Activity Materials: computer
Type *Catholic Missions* into your
Internet safe search engine to find
many missionaries serving others
around the world. Visit some of the
sites with the children to learn about
special projects the missionaries are
doing in other countries and see pictures of the Church caring for people
all over the world.

Family
Family Service Project
Inform parents that the children
are learning about serving others.
Suggest that families participate
together in a community service project. Suggest specific community
needs, such as a neighborhood soup
kitchen. Invite families to visit the
class to share their experiences after
completing their family project.

Scripture
Spatial, Interpersonal
For a Scripture activity, see *What's
the Word?*, guide page 143F.

Do the Activity Read the directions for the *We
Believe* activity. As the children look at the pictures, help
them identify what the members of the Church are
doing. Have the children complete the activity. Have
volunteers share times when they and their families
have done the acts of service depicted in the pictures.
Then ask the children to name other ways they and
their families show God's love by serving others.

Quick Check

✔ *What does the Church do for others?* (The Church
   serves others by helping and caring for them.)

✔ *How can we show our love for God?* (We show our
   love for God by serving others.)

WE RESPOND _____ minutes

Connect to Life Read the *We Respond* question.
Brainstorm with the children ways they can serve one
another in school. List on the board the children's
ideas. (Possible responses: befriend new students; share
school supplies.)

Pray Ask the children to join hands to form a circle.
Pray aloud together: *Jesus, help us to serve _____.*

Plan Ahead for Day 5

Catechist Goal: To review chapter ideas and
their relationship to our faith life

Preparation: Make copies of *Sharing Faith
with My Family*, guide page 143E.

151

Catechist Goal

• To review the chapter ideas that are key to growing as disciples of Jesus Christ

Our Faith Response

• To decide on ways to grow as disciples by living out what we have learned

Show What *you* **Know**

Help the children to unscramble the *Key Words.* Discuss ways people have led and cared for the Church.

Picture This   Encourage the children to think about ways they can serve as members of the Church. Circulate as the children work and offer encouragement.

Saint Stories   Read aloud the story of Blessed Teresa of Calcutta. Invite the children to review ways that Mother Teresa and the Missionaries of Charity serve others.

More *to* **Explore**

Guide the children in discovering the name of their bishop and the pope if they do not already know. Visit **www.vatican.va** or your diocesan Web site.

Take Home

Remind the children that being a member of the Church means serving others! Encourage the children to sign the pledge card with their family members and to make a plan about serving others.

Discuss and send home copies of *Sharing Faith with My Family,* guide page 143E.

Pray Learn Celebrate Share Choose Live

PROJECT

Show What *you* **Know**

Unscramble the words below. How have these people led and cared for the Church?

plostAse	hopsib	oppe
_____	_____	_____
Apostles	bishop	pope

✝ **Picture This**   You are a member of the Church. Draw a picture of a way you can serve others.

Possible drawings: visit someone who is sick; donate food to a collection for the hungry; help family members; respect classmates and friends

---

DISCIPLE

Pray Learn Celebrate Share Choose Live

Saint Stories   Blessed Teresa of Calcutta was known as Mother Teresa. She cared for people in India who were sick and homeless. She and her helpers fed people. They gave them a place to stay. Mother Teresa's helpers are called the Missionaries of Charity. They care for people in cities all over the world.

More *to* **Explore**

What is the name of your bishop? What is the name of the pope? Find out!

Take Home

Talk with your family about ways you can serve others. Make a plan!

↳ **DISCIPLE CHALLENGE**
Print your family name on the pledge card. Ask each family member to sign it.

The _____ Family pledges to serve others.

_____

_____

_____

CHAPTER TEST

Circle the correct answer.

1. Did Jesus choose Peter to be the leader of the Apostles?

(**Yes**)   **No**

2. Do we serve others by caring for and helping them?

(**Yes**)   **No**

3. Is the pope the leader of your town?

Yes   (**No**)

4. Do the bishops do the work the Apostles did?

(**Yes**)   **No**

5. Does the pope only care about some of the members of the Church?

Yes   (**No**)

 What are some ways the Church loves and serves others? Possible responses: feeding people who are hungry; spending time with people; caring for the sick; sharing God's love with others

154

CHAPTER TEST

Read each test item aloud and allow time for the children to mark an answer. Decide whether the *Talk About It* activity will be a small group or whole class discussion. After you have finished, check the answers. Clarify any misconceptions.

Alternative Assessment

You may want the students to complete the following alternative-assessment activity.

Draw or write the answer. Members of the Church serve one another. How does the pope serve? How do the bishops serve? How do we serve?

Additional Testing

• Chapter 12 Test in *Assessment Book*, pages 23–24

• CD-ROM *Test Generator and Resource*: Use Chapter 12 Test or customize your own.

Review

We Believe Statements

Review the four statements.

• The Apostles led and cared for the church.

• The bishops lead and care for the Church.

• The pope leads and cares for the whole Church.

• The Church serves others.

To use the Chapter 12 Study Guide, visit

www.webelieveweb.com

Advent

Advent has a twofold character: as a season to prepare for Christmas when Christ's first coming to us is remembered; as a season when that remembrance directs the mind and heart to await Christ's Second Coming at the end of time.

(Norms Governing Liturgical Calendars, 39)

Overview

In this chapter the children will learn that Advent is the season in which we get ready to celebrate Jesus Christ's birth at Christmas.

Catechist Background

Is there anything for which you are waiting or longing?

The Church celebrates Advent as a season of joyful preparation for the coming of the Lord. We prepare for Christmas when we celebrate that the only Son of God came to live among us on earth. We prepare for Christ's second coming at the end of time. "When the Church celebrates *the liturgy of Advent* each year, she makes present this ancient expectancy of the Messiah, for by sharing in the long preparation for the Savior's first coming, the faithful renew their ardent desire for his second coming." (*CCC* 524)

The Prologue of John's Gospel proclaims the Son of God as the light that overcomes our darkness. "The true light, which enlightens everyone, was coming into the world." (John 1:9) In that light, symbolized by the candles on our Advent wreaths,

For Adult Reading and Reflection
You may want to refer to paragraph 524 of the *Catechism of the Catholic Church.*

Go to www.webelieveweb.com, Catechist/ Teacher, We Believe Correlations for this chapter's correlation to:
- Six Tasks of Catechesis
- Catholic Social Teaching.

we see the unmistakable signs of God's love around and within us.

Jesus Christ, the greatest sign of God's love for humanity and all creation, is "the final event towards which all the events of salvation history converge" (*General Directory for Catechesis,* 40; see Luke 24–27). During the four weeks of Advent, we respond to this gift of our loving God by joyfully expecting the feast of his Nativity and by keeping watch for Christ's future coming. Having received the greatest gift of all in Jesus, we express our thanks by giving of ourselves to family, friends, and those in need.

How will you give of yourself during Advent?

Lesson Planning Guide

Lesson Focus	Presentation	Materials
Day 1		
Guide page 155C **Guide and Text page 155** **Introduce the Season**	• Read the *Chapter Story*. • Introduce the Advent season. • Ask Jesus to be with us.	
Day 2		
Guide and Text pages 156–157 **We Gather** **We Believe**	• Discuss the We Gather questions. • Present the We Believe text about Advent. • Complete the Advent wreath activity.	• crayons or colored pencils
Day 3		
Guide and Text page 158 **We Believe** **We Respond**	♪ Sing a song for Advent. • Present the We Respond text. • Brainstorm ways to share Jesus' light. Do the drawing activity.	• "Advent Song," Mary Lu Walker, #14, Grade 1 CD • colored pencils or crayons
Day 4		
Text page 159 **Guide page 159–160** **We Respond in Prayer**	• Listen to Scripture. ♪ Respond to the reading in song.	• prayer space items: large star, purple tablecloth, battery-operated candle, Bible, globe • two flashlights ♪ "Jesus, Come to Us," David Haas, #15, Grade 1 CD
Day 5		
Text page 160 **Guide pages 159–160, 160A** **Project Disciple**	• Complete the Project Disciple activities. Discuss the *Take Home* activity. • Complete the Reproducible Master 13 activity. See guide pages 155C and 160A. • Discuss/send home Sharing Faith with My Family, guide page 160B.	• pencils • crayons or colored pencils • copies of Reproducible Master 13, guide page 160A • copies of Sharing Faith with My Family reproducible master, guide page 160B

For additional ideas, activities, and opportunities: Visit Sadlier's **www.WeBelieve.web.com**

Chapter Story

When Maura came home from school, she was upset. Maura's dad asked, "What's the matter, Maura?"

Maura explained, "Today everyone at school was talking about seeing their grandparents at Thanksgiving. I told them that we don't see Granna and Grandda very much because they live in Ireland. Mrs. Cruz showed everybody where Ireland was on the map. She said, 'Maura's grandparents live across the Atlantic Ocean.' Everyone said that was really far away."

Maura asked her dad, "When are we going to see Granna and Grandda? When Granna called on my birthday she said that they would visit soon."

Maura's dad smiled and said, "I have good news. Grandda and Granna are coming to visit at Christmas."

Maura asked, "How long do we have to wait until Christmas?"

Maura's dad said, "Well, Christmas is four weeks from now. It may be hard to wait, but the time will go quickly. We have a lot to do in order to get ready for their visit. What do you think we should do first?"

What do you think Maura said?

PROJECT DISCIPLE
Additional Activities

Celebrate!

Distribute Reproducible Master 13, guide page 160A, along with purple construction paper. Explain to the children: *You are going to make an Advent wheel.* Have the children color and cut out the wheels, glue them to the construction paper, and punch holes through the center of the wheels. After the children cut out the pointers, help them use brad fasteners to attach the pointers to the wheels. Explain: *Put your Advent wheel in a place where you will see it every day. Move the pointer on the wheel each day of Advent. Mark the space for every day you share Jesus' light.*

Make *it* Happen

Help the children make prayer cards to send to senior citizens of the parish. On the front of the card have the children decorate a star-filled sky. On the inside encourage them to write the prayer *Come, Lord Jesus! Be with us.* Ask the pastoral assistant or parish priests to distribute the cards.

Come, Lord Jesus!
Be with us.

SEASONAL
CHAPTER 13

This chapter prepares us to celebrate the season of Advent.

ADVENT

155

Catechist Goal

• To present that Advent is the time we get ready to celebrate Jesus' birth at Christmas

Our Faith Response

• To think of ways we can share Jesus' light with others

Gather In My Name
Whole Community Catechesis

An Online Resource

Celebrate **Advent** *as a class, school, and/or a parish community. The* Gather in My Name *events come complete with detailed leader's guides, preparation charts, handouts, promotional ideas, organizational materials, and much more. Go to:*

www.webelieveweb.com

Lesson Plan

Introduce the Season ___ minutes

• **Pray:** *Jesus, we love you.*

• **Introduce Advent** Share the *Chapter Story* on guide page 155C. Discuss with the children what Maura can do to get ready for her grandparents' Christmas visit.

• **Write** the word *Advent* on the board. Explain that the word comes from a word that means "coming." Tell the children: *In Advent we get ready for the coming of God's Son, Jesus.*

• **Invite** the children to look at the photograph on page 155. Ask: *What do you think the children are doing?* Help the children conclude that the people are waiting for something to happen or a visitor.

• **Pray** Read the prayer below the photograph. Explain: *Come, Lord Jesus is a special Advent prayer of the Church.*

Chapter 13 • Advent

Lesson Materials
- copies of Reproducible Master 13
- Grade 1 CD
- crayons or colored pencils
- scissors, glue, purple construction paper, brad fasteners

Teaching Note

Presenting the Chapter

Present this chapter during the first week of Advent. On a monthly calendar, mark each day of Advent with a purple dot or star. Call the children's attention to the calendar each time you meet during the season.

WE GATHER

Think about a time your family was waiting to celebrate a special day.

What did you do?

How did you feel?

WE BELIEVE

The Church has a special time of waiting. Each year we wait for the coming of the Son of God. This waiting time is called Advent.

The word *Advent* means "coming." Each year during Advent we prepare. We get ready for the coming of God's Son, Jesus. We get ready to celebrate his birth at Christmas.

There are four weeks in Advent. The Church celebrates these four weeks in different ways. One way is by lighting candles on an Advent wreath.

156

Lesson Plan

WE GATHER
_____ minutes

Focus on Life Read the *We Gather* text. Discuss the children's responses to the questions. Have volunteers act out what they did while they were waiting to celebrate a special day.

WE BELIEVE
_____ minutes

• **Read** the first two *We Believe* paragraphs. Have the children highlight or underline the last two sentences of the second paragraph.

• **Explain** to the children that the season of Advent begins on a Sunday, four weeks before Christmas. Read the third *We Believe* paragraph on page 156.

• **Direct** the children's attention to the Advent wreath on page 157. Read the first paragraph on page 157. Ask: *How many purple candles are there?* (three) Explain that purple is the Advent color. Tell the children: *The rose candle is lit on the third Sunday of Advent. Rose is a color of joy. When we light the rose candle we are happy that we will celebrate Christmas soon.*

On the Advent wreath there is one candle for each week. The light from the candles reminds us that Jesus is the Light of the World.

We pray as we light the candles on the Advent wreath. We remember that Jesus is with us. We prepare to celebrate his birth at Christmas.

Color the flames on each candle on the Advent wreath.

157

ACTIVITY BANK

Multiple Intelligences
Interpersonal and Intrapersonal
Activity Materials: index cards with a star drawn on each card (one for each child), gift box or bag

Explain to the children that one way we share Jesus' light with others is by praying for them. Give an index card to each child. Have the children write their names on the cards.

Collect the cards and put them in a gift box or bag. Each week of Advent have each child draw a card from the box. Explain that the name on the card is the name of the person for whom the child will pray for during the coming week. Stress: *Do not tell anyone for whom you are praying.*

Collect the cards again to keep for the following week. Before picking cards the next week, have the pray-ers identify themselves to the children for whom they prayed during the previous week.

Have the children color the flames of the Advent wreath candles.

Quick Check

✔ *What do we get ready for in Advent?* (We get ready for the coming of God's Son, Jesus. We get ready to celebrate his birth at Christmas.)

✔ *What does the light from the Advent wreath candles remind us of?* (Jesus is the Light of the World.)

CONNECTION

To Catholic Social Teaching

Option for the Poor and Vulnerable

One of the first feast days during the Advent season is the feast of Saint Nicholas, December 6. Saint Nicholas was a bishop of the Church in the fourth century. He taught people to be kind to children, especially to the children who were poor. There is a story about him helping a poor man who had three daughters. He left bags of money for the family at night so no one would know that he was the person giving the money.

Tell the children the story of Saint Nicholas. Plan with the group one way you can follow his example. One idea is to collect money to buy special treats to give to families in need.

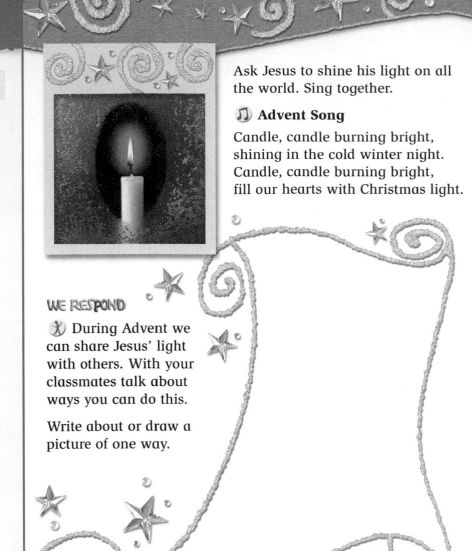

Ask Jesus to shine his light on all the world. Sing together.

♫ Advent Song

Candle, candle burning bright,
shining in the cold winter night.
Candle, candle burning bright,
fill our hearts with Christmas light.

WE RESPOND

During Advent we can share Jesus' light with others. With your classmates talk about ways you can do this.

Write about or draw a picture of one way.

158

Lesson Plan

WE BELIEVE (continued)

• **Ask** the children to look at the photo on page 158. Play "Advent Song," #14 on the Grade 1 CD. Have the children sing the song together.

WE RESPOND ___ minutes

Connect to Life Read the *We Respond* text. On chart paper, draw a star. Discuss with the children ways we can share Jesus' light during Advent. On the chart paper write the ways the children suggest. Display the chart in the prayer space during the season of Advent.

Read the activity directions. Give the children time to complete the activity. Ask them to share their work with the children who are sitting near them.

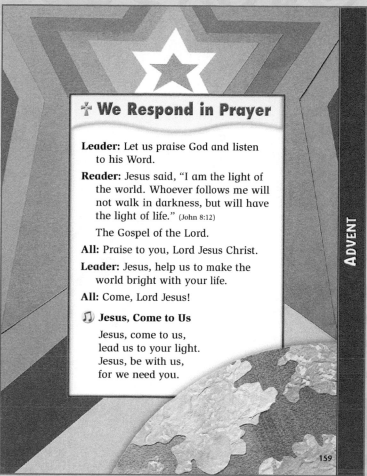

✝ We Respond in Prayer

Leader: Let us praise God and listen to his Word.

Reader: Jesus said, "I am the light of the world. Whoever follows me will not walk in darkness, but will have the light of life." (John 8:12)

The Gospel of the Lord.

All: Praise to you, Lord Jesus Christ.

Leader: Jesus, help us to make the world bright with your life.

All: Come, Lord Jesus!

🎵 **Jesus, Come to Us**

Jesus, come to us,
lead us to your light.
Jesus, be with us,
for we need you.

ADVENT

159

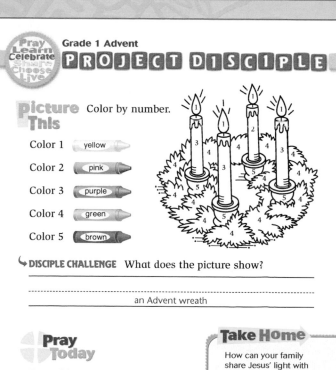

Grade 1 Advent

PROJECT DISCIPLE

Pray Learn Celebrate Share Choose Live

Picture This   Color by number.

Color 1 — yellow
Color 2 — pink
Color 3 — purple
Color 4 — green
Color 5 — brown

↳ **DISCIPLE CHALLENGE**   What does the picture show?

an Advent wreath

Pray Today

Trace this prayer.

Pray it during Advent to show you are waiting for Jesus.

Come, Lord Jesus!

Take Home

How can your family share Jesus' light with others? Decide on one way and make it happen during the Advent season.

160   www.webelieveweb.com

We Respond in Prayer (p. 159)

Display a large star, a battery-operated candle, a Bible, and a globe on a purple cloth on the prayer table. Choose a prayer leader and a reader and allow preparation time. Turn off the overhead lights and light the candle. Ask the children to think about God's gifts that give us light. Have two children with flashlights lead a procession to the prayer space. Together pray the Sign of the Cross and the prayer. Then sing "Jesus, Come to Us," #15 on the Grade 1 CD.

📖 **This Week's Liturgy**

Visit **www.webelieveweb.com** for this week's liturgical readings and other seasonal material.

Project Disciple (p. 160)

Picture This   Read aloud the activity instructions and invite children to complete the activity individually. Complete the Disciple Challenge together. Ask the children which week of Advent the wreath is celebrating.

Pray Today   Ask a volunteer to read the activity instructions. Have each child trace the prayer and then pray with a friend.

Take Home

Have the class discuss ways they can share Jesus' light. Ask the children to continue this discussion with their families.

Discuss and send home copies of *Sharing Faith with My Family*, guide page 160B.

Project Disciple Additional Activities See the activities suggested on page 155C of the guide.

Name _____

Make an Advent wheel.

1. Cut out the wheel and the pointer.

2. Move the pointer each day of Advent.

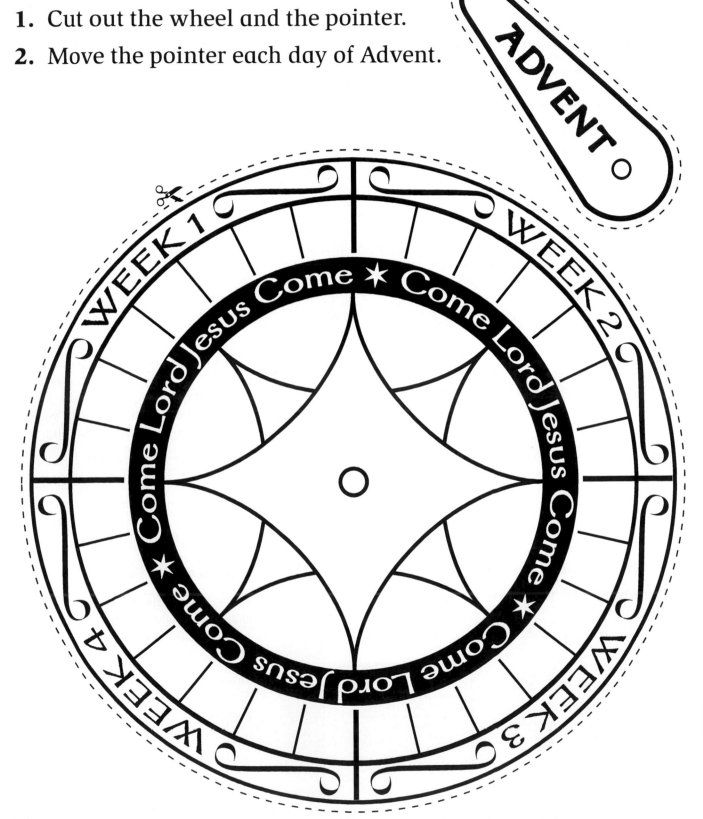

SHARING FAITH
with My Family

Sharing What I Learned

Look at the pictures below. Use each picture to tell your family what you learned in this chapter.

Advent Prayer Partners

Ask each member of your family to write his or her name on a slip of paper. Then have each person choose a name. That person is your Advent "prayer partner." Pray especially for your prayer partner. Make that person a special card for Christmas.

Family Prayer

Keep a candle on the table when you share family meals. Before each meal, ask a grown-up to light the candle. Then pray together, "Come, Lord Jesus."

Visit Sadlier's

www.WeBelieveweb.com

Connect to the Catechism
For adult background and reflection, see paragraph 524.

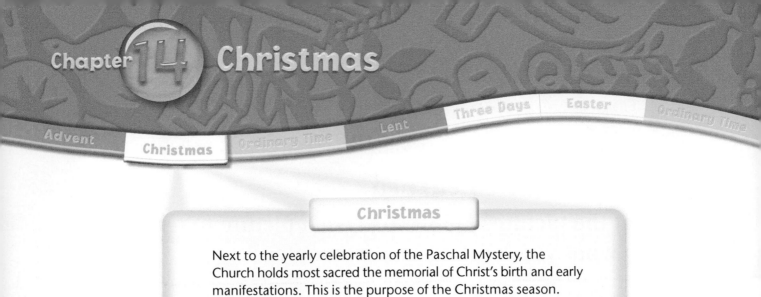

Christmas

Next to the yearly celebration of the Paschal Mystery, the Church holds most sacred the memorial of Christ's birth and early manifestations. This is the purpose of the Christmas season.

(Norms Governing Liturgical Calendars, 32)

Overview

In this chapter the children will learn that at Christmas the Church celebrates the birth of Jesus.

For Adult Reading and Reflection
You may want to refer to paragraph 463 of the *Catechism of the Catholic Church.*

Go to **www.webelieveweb.com**, Catechist/ Teacher, We Believe Correlations for this chapter's correlation to:
- Six Tasks of Catechesis
- Catholic Social Teaching.

Catechist Background

What was your most memorable celebration of Christmas? Why?

In some of our cultural settings, we are apt to think of Christmas as one single day rather than an entire season. For the Church, however, Christmas Day is a beginning: the beginning of the Christmas season.

For about two weeks we celebrate the mystery of the Incarnation, the coming of the Word made flesh to us. As we profess in the Nicene Creed,

". . . for our salvation,
   he came down from heaven,
and by the Holy Spirit was incarnate of the
   Virgin Mary,
   and became man."

Each day of the Christmas season renews the celebration of the birth of Jesus Christ. In the northern hemisphere, the Christmas season is a celebration of light at the darkest time of the year. The traditional Christmas lights of this season remind us that Jesus, "the light [which] shines in the darkness," (John 1:5) is the true light that enlightens our lives every day of this season and throughout the year. Jesus truly is light for all people.

The feasts of this season reflect the light of Christ, each in its own way. As we celebrate the feasts of the Holy Innocents, the Holy Family, the Solemnity of Mary, Mother of God, the Epiphany, and the Baptism of the Lord, we rejoice in the everlasting truth that Jesus Christ is our light and our life. Each day of the Christmas season we have reason to sing: "Today is born our Savior, Christ the Lord" (Christmas antiphon).

Throughout the Christmas season how will you celebrate that Jesus Christ is our light and our life?

Lesson Planning Guide

Lesson Focus	Presentation	Materials
Day 1		
Guide page 161C **Guide and Text page 161** **Introduce the Season**	• Read the *Chapter Story*. • Introduce the Christmas season. • Proclaim words on the banner.	♫ "Jesus Come to Us," David Haas, #15, Grade 1 CD
Day 2		
Guide and Text pages 162–163 **We Gather** **We Believe**	• Share responses to the We Gather question. • Present the We Believe text. 🏃 Act out the Scripture story about Mary and Joseph's journey to Bethlehem.	• costumes and props (optional)
Day 3		
Guide and Text page 164 **We Respond**	🏃 Do the We Respond activity about choosing acts of love as gifts.	• crayons or colored pencils
Day 4		
Text page 165 **Guide page 165–166** **We Respond in Prayer**	• Rejoice in Jesus and proclaim Scripture. ♫ Respond in song.	• prayer space items: white table-cloth, Christmas-stable figurines, chart paper titled: *We Pray at Christmas for* ♫ "Joy to the World," #16, Grade 1 CD • bells
Day 5		
Text page 166 **Guide pages 165–166, 166A** **Project Disciple**	• Complete the Project Disciple activities. Discuss the *Take Home* activity. • Complete the Reproducible Master 14 activity. See guide pages 161C and 166A. • Discuss/send home Sharing Faith with My Family, guide page 166B.	• pencils • copies of Reproducible Master 14, guide page 166A • copies of Sharing Faith with My Family reproducible master, guide page 166B

For additional ideas, activities, and opportunities: Visit Sadlier's **www.WeBelieveweb.com**

Chapter Story

This year Vincent helped his parents and his older sister to set up the family's nativity scene. When they were finished working, Vincent's mother told this story.

"A very, very long time ago a man we know today as Saint Francis of Assisi lived in a small town in Italy. Francis loved God very much. He wanted to show God his thanks by being kind and helpful to all God's creatures. Crowds often gathered to hear Francis talk. They listened to Francis tell them about all the loving things Jesus said and did."

"One year on the day before Christmas, Francis planned a special surprise. That night Francis gathered the townspeople and asked them to follow him. Everyone stopped at a stable. Inside the stable were people pretending to be Mary and Joseph. Their baby boy was inside the manger, the box from which animals ate. Then Francis led a donkey and oxen into the stable. He began to tell the townspeople the story of Jesus' birth in a stable in Bethlehem."

When Vincent's mother finished telling the story, she explained, "After Saint Francis set up the stable, the custom of setting up stable scenes at Christmas spread all over the world. Looking at the scenes helps up to remember and celebrate Jesus' birth."

How has Saint Francis's surprise helped people?

PROJECT DISCIPLE
Additional Activities

Celebrate!

Have available paper cups filled with sand (one for each child) and craft sticks (3 for each child). Distribute copies of Reproducible Master 14, guide page 166A. Explain: *During the Christmas season we celebrate the Epiphany, the feast of the three kings. The kings traveled many miles in the desert to visit Jesus in Bethlehem.* Then read the Scripture story (Matthew 2:1–11). After the children color and cut out the figures of the kings, help them glue the figures to craft sticks. Distribute the sand-filled cups and ask the children to insert the figures into the cups. Explain: *We celebrate the feast of the three kings on January 6 or on the second Sunday after Christmas. Take your cup home and put it in a place away from the manger. Each day during the Christmas season, move the kings closer to your manger scene.*

Pray Today

Bring the children to visit the manger or nativity scene in your parish church. Allow the children to pray quietly. Then sing "Joy to the World" or another familiar Christmas hymn together.

"For a child is born to us, a son is given us."

Isaiah 9:5

SEASONAL
CHAPTER 14

This chapter addresses the entire Christmas season.

161

Chapter 14 • Christmas

Catechist Goal

• To highlight the Christmas season as the time in which we celebrate the birth of the Son of God

Our Faith Response

• To show our joy during the Christmas season

Gather In My Name

Whole Community Catechesis

An Online Resource

Celebrate **Christmas** *as a class, school, and/or a parish community. The* Gather in My Name *events come complete with detailed leader's guides, preparation charts, handouts, promotional ideas, organizational materials, and much more. Go to:*

www.webelieveweb.com

Lesson Plan

Introduce the Season ___ minutes

• **Put** a white tablecloth on the prayer table. Give volunteers Christmas-stable figurines. Ask all the children to walk prayerfully to the prayer space as you sing together "Jesus, Come to Us," #15 on the Grade 1 CD. (See pupil's text, page 159.) Help the children arrange the figurines on the prayer table.

• **Invite** the children to sit quietly and listen to a special Christmas story. Read the *Chapter Story* on guide page 161C and discuss the children's responses to the question.

• **Explain** that Christmas is the season in which we celebrate God's greatest gift to us, Jesus. Tell the children that white and gold are the colors of the season.

• **Proclaim** the Scripture passage on the banner.

Lesson Materials

- costumes and props (optional)
- Grade 1 CD
- copies of Reproducible Master 14
- crayons
- scissors, glue, craft sticks (three for each child)
- cups filled with sand (one for each child)

Teaching Note

When to Present the Lesson

Because you will not meet with the children during most of the Christmas season, present this lesson during the week before Christmas. Emphasize that Christmas is not just one day we celebrate, but it is a season that lasts about two weeks.

At Christmas the Church celebrates the birth of Jesus.

WE GATHER

What do you think of when you think of Christmas?

WE BELIEVE

Christmas is a special time. During Christmas, we celebrate the birth of the Son of God. We celebrate God's greatest gift to us, his Son, Jesus.

Act out this Christmas play.

Narrator: Before Jesus was born, the ruler wanted to count all the people. Each man had to go back to the town his family came from to be counted. Joseph's family was from Bethlehem. So Joseph and Mary made the long journey to Bethlehem.

Joseph: Here we are, Mary! We're finally in Bethlehem! You must be very tired.

Mary: I'm all right, Joseph. It was a long journey. It will be so good to rest!

Joseph: Here is an inn. Maybe we can stay here.

162

Lesson Plan

WE GATHER ___ minutes

Focus on Life Read the *We Gather* question. Have a few volunteers share their responses.

Write the word *Christmas* on the board or on chart paper. Ask: *What word do you see at the beginning of this word?* Have a volunteer come to the board and circle the word *Christ*.

WE BELIEVE ___ minutes

- **Read** aloud the first *We Believe* paragraph. Explain: *One of the ways we celebrate the birth of Jesus is by acting out the Bible story.*

- **Choose** volunteers for the roles of Mary, Joseph, the innkeeper, and the innkeeper's wife. Provide time for these children to prepare their parts. As these children are getting ready, ask the others to turn to page 46. Have them look at the picture of Joseph and Mary traveling to Bethlehem.

Innkeeper: Not another traveler! What do you want?

Joseph: We need a place to stay.

Innkeeper: Sorry, there's no room left.

Joseph: Please, sir. My wife needs a place to rest. We're going to have a baby soon.

Innkeeper's Wife: We do have a place where the animals are kept. I put down fresh straw this morning. At least you can try to keep warm there.

Mary: Thank you for your kindness. May God bless you!

Narrator: So Joseph and Mary stayed there. Joseph made a place for the baby in the animals' feedbox. It is called a manger. He filled the manger with clean straw.

That night, Jesus was born. Mary and Joseph were filled with joy. They wrapped the baby in swaddling clothes and laid him in the manger.

Read Along

During Christmas, we sing with joy. Jesus has brought light and love into the world. He is with us now and forever.

Christmas is a time to honor the Holy Family. We remember the love of Mary and Joseph. We remember their love and care for Jesus.

163

CHRISTMAS

ACTIVITY BANK

Multiple Intelligences
Bodily-Kinesthetic, Musical
Activity Materials: costumes and props, material for scenery

Have the children present the play to other groups in the parish. Ask the children who are artistic to help you prepare the scenery. Provide practice time each day for a few days before the presentation.

After the presentation, invite both the actors and the audience to sing a few familiar Christmas carols together.

• **Read** the words of the play once. Then give the characters appropriate costumes and props to use for acting out their parts. Invite the other children to pretend they are animals in the stable. Have them gather around Mary and Joseph as you read the narrator's words on page 163.

• **Explain** that Christmas is not just one day. Tell the children: *Christmas is a time that is about two weeks long.* Then read the text in the *Read Along* box on page 163. Stress: *Jesus is with us now and forever.*

Quick Check

✔ *What do we celebrate at Christmas?* (Accept reasons given on page 162.)

✔ *At Christmas, what do we remember about the Holy Family?* (We remember the love of Mary and Joseph. We remember their love and care for Jesus.)

CONNECTION

To Liturgy

Explain: *During the Christmas season, we celebrate special feast days. One of these days is the feast of the Holy Family. We celebrate this feast on the Sunday after Christmas day.*

Tell the children that when we gather for Mass on this day, we listen to a story about the Holy Family. The priest blesses the families who are in church, and we pray together for families throughout the world.

Ask the children to do something special for their families on the feast of the Holy Family. A few ideas are given in the *We Respond* activity on page 164.

WE RESPOND

Christmas is a time to share God's love with family and friends. Each thing you do for others can be a gift.

🧑 Color each gift box that shows a way you can share God's love. Then add your own way.

Each day during this time of year try to do these things.

Help keep my home clean.

Pray for my family.

Get along with everyone.

Share my things.

164

Lesson Plan

WE RESPOND   ___ minutes

Connect to Life Remind the children that Christmas time lasts for about two weeks. Read the *We Respond* paragraph. Stress: *We do not stop being kind and helpful after Christmas day.*

🧑 **Read** the directions for the *We Respond* activity. Then ask a volunteer to read the words written on each gift box on page 164. Ask volunteers to share other ways we can share God's love. Write these ways on the board or on chart paper.

• **Play** a recording of Christmas carols as the children are working. Assist anyone who needs help with writing or spelling. When the children have completed the activity, invite volunteers to share the ways they have written.

• **Pray** together: *Jesus, help us to share God's love with family and friends.*

✝ We Respond in Prayer

Leader: Let us give thanks for the Son of God brings light and love into the world. Rejoice in the Lord always.

All: Rejoice in the Lord always.

Reader: Let us listen to a reading from the Bible.

"The people who walked in darkness
    have seen a great light;
Upon those who dwelt in the land
    of gloom
    a light has shone.
You have brought them abundant joy
    and great rejoicing." (Isaiah 9:1–2)

The word of the Lord.

All: Thanks be to God.

🎵 **Joy to the World**

Joy to the world!
The Lord is come;
Let earth receive her King;
Let ev'ry heart prepare him room,
And heav'n and nature sing,
And heav'n and nature sing,
And heav'n, and heav'n and nature sing.

CHRISTMAS

165

Pray / Learn / Celebrate / Share / Choose / Live

Grade 1 Christmas

PROJECT DISCIPLE

Fast Facts

During Christmas, many people use a nativity scene to remind them of Jesus' birth.

↳ **DISCIPLE CHALLENGE** Can you find the Holy Family in the nativity scene? Circle Jesus, Mary, and Joseph.

Question Corner What are some ways your family celebrates Christmas?

- ❏ Exchange gifts to show our love
- ❏ Share special meals
- ❏ Decorate our home
- ❏ Pray
- ❏ Celebrate Jesus' birth
- ❏ Set up a nativity scene
- ❏ Go to Mass

Take Home

As a family, think of a special way you can share God's love with others during Christmas.

We Respond in Prayer (p. 165)

Display Christmas-stable figurines and chart paper that reads *We Pray at Christmas for* on a white cloth on the prayer table. Choose a volunteer to be the prayer leader and allow preparation time. Together, pray the Sign of the Cross and the prayer. Distribute bells to volunteers and instruct the children to ring the bells after each line of the song. Sing together "Joy to the World," #16 on the Grade 1 CD. Ask the children to share names of people or groups for whom they would like to pray. Write the names on the chart paper.

📖 This Week's Liturgy

Visit **www.webelieveweb.com** for this week's liturgical readings and other seasonal material.

Project Disciple (p. 166)

Fast Facts Read aloud the fact. Ask the children if any of their families set up a manger or nativity scene. Read the challenge activity. Help the children to find the Holy Family in the photo.

Question Corner Read the question and choices aloud to the children. Encourage them to check any of the ways their families celebrate Christmas.

Take Home

Invite children to talk with their families about a way they can share God's love during the Christmas season.

Discuss and send home copies of *Sharing Faith with My Family*, guide page 166B.

Project Disciple Additional Activities See the activities suggested on page 161C of the guide.

165 and **166**

Name _____

Color the figures of the three kings.
Cut out the figures and attach them
to craft sticks.

SHARING FAITH
with My Family

Sharing What I Learned

Look at the pictures below. Use each picture to tell your family what you learned in this chapter.

For All to See and Pray

Color the holly leaves on the wreath green. Color the berries red. Then pray this blessing with your family.

God our Father, bless our wreath. The green leaves remind us that your love never ends. Its red berries remind us that Jesus died and rose for us. Thank you for sending Jesus, your Son, to be with us always. Amen.

Visit Sadlier's

www.WeBelieveweb.com

 Connect to the Catechism
For adult background and reflection, see paragraph 463.

166B

Unit 2 • Unit Review

ASSESSMENT

Unit 2 Test

Read aloud each set of test directions. You may also choose to read aloud each test item. Wait for a minute for the children to indicate their responses in writing before proceeding to the next item or set of directions.

Alternative Assessment

You may want the children to complete the following alternative-assessment activity.

Draw a picture of a way the Holy Spirit helps the Church today.

Additional Testing

• Unit 2 Test in Grade 1 *Assessment Book*, pages 25–26

• Unit 2 Alternative Assessment in Grade 1 *Assessment Book*, page 28

• Semester Test (Units 1–2) in Grade 1 *Assessment Book*, pages 29–30

• CD-ROM *Test Generator and Resource*: Use Unit 2 Test or customize your own.

Grade 1 Unit 2

UNIT TEST

Fill in the circle beside the correct answer.

1. Jesus taught his followers how to _____.
   ● pray   ○ read

2. Jesus told us that he was the _____.
   ○ pope   ● Good Shepherd

3. The Church is all the people who believe in _____ and follow his teachings.
   ○ Peter   ● Jesus

Circle the correct answer.

4. Is the Holy Spirit the Third Person of the Blessed Trinity?   (Yes)   No

5. Did Jesus choose John to be the leader of the Apostles?   Yes   (No)

6. Did Jesus' followers believe he was the Son of God?   (Yes)   No

continued on next page   167

Grade 1 Unit 2

Match each sentence to the correct picture.

7.
8.
9.
10.

Jesus invited people to be his followers.

Jesus taught his followers to pray.

The first members of the Church shared God's love with others.

The Holy Spirit came to Jesus' followers on Pentecost.

168

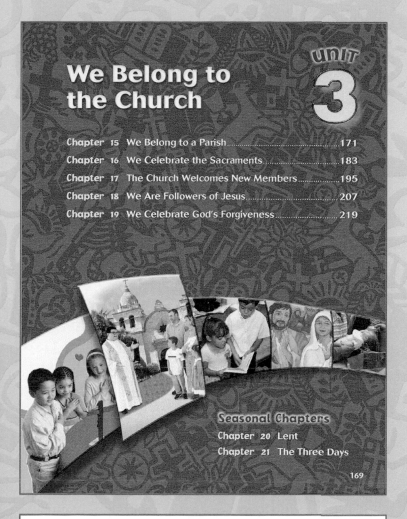

We Belong to the Church

UNIT 3

Chapter 15 We Belong to a Parish 171

Chapter 16 We Celebrate the Sacraments 183

Chapter 17 The Church Welcomes New Members 195

Chapter 18 We Are Followers of Jesus 207

Chapter 19 We Celebrate God's Forgiveness 219

Seasonal Chapters

Chapter 20 Lent

Chapter 21 The Three Days

169

PROJECT DISCIPLE

Pray Learn Celebrate Share Choose Live

DEAR FAMILY

In Unit 3 your child will grow as a disciple of Jesus by:

- appreciating the parish family and the ways the parish works and worships together
- celebrating God's love in the sacraments that Jesus gave us
- welcoming new members of the Church who receive Baptism
- choosing to act as "children of the light" by showing Christ to others
- understanding that God is always ready to forgive us and that he asks us to forgive others.

Question Corner Which sacraments have your family members received?

Baptism _____

Confirmation _____

Penance _____

Eucharist _____

Matrimony _____

Holy Orders _____

Anointing of the Sick _____

Give thanks to Jesus for all the sacraments.

170

Reality Check

The Christian family "is a community of faith, hope, and charity; it assumes singular importance in the Church."
(*Catechism of the Catholic Church*, 2204)

More to Explore

Chapter 15 focuses on the parish. Name your parish. What other parishes do you know about? You might check your diocesan Web site. Talk about other parishes you have belonged to and the parishes in the neighborhoods around yours. How does your parish work with other parishes? Help your child to feel the connections we all have as Catholics.

Make it Happen

Talk about God's love and forgiveness. Remind your child how important forgiveness is in our relationship with God and with others. Is there anyone you need to say "I am sorry" to? Is there anyone you need to say "I forgive you" to? Make it happen!

Take Home

Each chapter in your child's *We Believe* Grade 1 text offers a "Take Home" activity that invites your family to support your child's journey to more fully become a disciple of Christ.

Be ready for this unit's Take Home:

Chapter 15: Helping people who are hungry

Chapter 16: Singing at Mass

Chapter 17: Finding holy water in your parish church

Chapter 18: Praying to Jesus, the Light of the World

Chapter 19: Forgiving others in the family

Unit 3 ● Unit Opener

CLASS CONNECTION

Read aloud the unit title and the chapter titles. Ask the children: *What do you think you will be learning in this unit?* Invite a few volunteers to respond. Then explain to the children that they will be learning about celebrating the sacraments with our parish and being followers of Jesus.

HOME CONNECTION

Project Disciple Dear Family

Sadlier *We Believe* calls on families to become involved in:

- learning the faith
- prayer and worship
- living their faith.

Highlighting of these unit family pages and the opportunities they offer will strengthen the partnership of the Church and the home.

For additional information and activities, encourage families to visit Sadlier's

www.WeBelieveweb.com

169 and 170

Chapter 15 We Belong to a Parish

Overview

In Chapter 12 the children learned about the structure of the Catholic Church. In this chapter the children will learn about the parish community and its activities.

Doctrinal Content	For Adult Reading and Reflection *Catechism of the Catholic Church*
The children will learn:	Paragraph
• Our parish is like a family.	2179
• We gather together to worship.	2182
• We work together as a parish.	2179
• Our parish helps many people.	2444

Key Words

parish (p. 173)
worship (p. 175)
pastor (p. 176)

Catechist Background

How does your family help you to grow in faith?

Go to **www.webelieveweb.com**, Catechist/ Teacher, We Believe Correlations for this chapter's correlation to:
• Six Tasks of Catechesis
• Catholic Social Teaching.

Just as we have a biological or adopted family that helps form us from infancy to maturity, so we have a family of faith that helps us in our spiritual growth. As Catholics, we experience that community of faith most intimately in a local congregation called the parish. It is at the level of the parish that most of our Christian formation takes place. The parish is where the community initiates people into the faith, gathers together for liturgical celebrations, teaches and hands on the faith, and practices works of charity by helping others in need.

A primary task of the parish is to worship. When we gather together to worship, we are gathering together to give thanks and praise to our God. This act is the basis of who we are as Catholics. "The liturgy is the summit toward which the activity of the Church is directed; it is also the fount from which all her power flows" (Constitution on the Sacred Liturgy, paragraph 10).

Although it is the source and summit of all we do, the liturgy is not the only work of the parish community. In the parish we also evangelize and teach, provide for the poor, care for those who are grieving and suffering, and engage in works of social justice that impact the world in which we live.

To help the parish in its mission, the bishop appoints a priest, called the pastor, to lead the local community. In addition to the pastor and priests, the parish has other leaders who serve the people. Lay and religious, paid and volunteer, it takes many people working together to help the parish community fulfill its mission.

How do you help your parish to form others in faith?

Lesson Planning Guide

Lesson Focus	Presentation	Materials
Day 1		
page 171 ✚ **We Gather in Prayer** **pages 172–173** *Our parish is like a family.*	• Pray the Lord's Prayer. 👥 Do the **We Gather** role-play activity. • Read the **We Believe** text about belonging to a parish. • Discuss the **We Respond** question. 👥 Complete the parish membership card.	For the prayer space: statue of Jesus, Bible opened to a book of the New Testament, cutout figures, sign that has the name of your parish
Day 2		
pages 174–175 *We gather together to worship.*	👥 Do the **We Gather** connect-the-dots activity. • Read and discuss worshiping with our parish community. • Discuss the **We Respond** question. 🎵 Pray by singing.	🎵 "Open Our Hearts," Christopher Walker, #17, Grade 1 CD • copies of reproducible master *What's the Word?*, guide page 171F
Day 3		
pages 176–177 *We work together as a parish.*	• Discuss the **We Gather** question. • Present the **We Believe** text. 👥 Write the name of the pastor. • Read the **We Respond** directive and share responses to the question. • Read and discuss the *As Catholics* text.	• index cards • copies of Reproducible Master 15, guide page 171G
Day 4		
pages 178–179 *Our parish helps many people.*	👥 Act out situations in **We Gather**. • Present the **We Believe** text about ways parishioners help one another. 👥 Do the **We Respond** activity. • Pray together for all those in need.	• crayons or colored pencils
Day 5		
pages 180–181 **Project Disciple** **page 182** **Chapter 15 Test**	• Complete the **Project Disciple** activities. • Explain the *Take Home* activity. • Discuss/send home **Sharing Faith with My Family**, guide page 171E. • Complete **Chapter 15 Test**. • Work on *Alternative Assessment* activity.	• pencils • crayons or colored pencils • copies of **Sharing Faith with My Family** reproducible master, guide page 171E

For additional ideas, activities, and opportunities: Visit Sadlier's **www.WE BELIEVE web.com**

Enrichment Ideas

Chapter Story

Paula came running into the apartment holding a piece of paper. "Look, Mom!" Our parish is having a special talent night."

Mrs. Barowski took the flyer from Paula and read the announcement. "All members of Saint Simon's Parish are invited to join in Talent Night."

"Mom, can we be part of the show? I want to dance with my friend, Mia. We learned a tap dance that we have been practicing for months. And Mom, you have to sing. You have such a beautiful voice."

"I guess I could, Paula. I'll ask Aunt Teresa to play the piano while I sing. Why don't you go tell your brother what we are planning? Maybe he would like to play his guitar with his friends."

Paula knocked on her brother's door. She told him about talent night. She said, "Mom is even going to sing. So, Kenny, you have to be in the show, too. Then our whole family will be taking part."

"What could I do?" Kenny asked.

"You could ask Enrique, Frank, and Sal to play the guitar with you. You are always sitting in here playing together."

Kenny said, "I don't know if we are good enough to perform in front of everybody."

Just then Mrs. Barowski came into Kenny's room. She said, "The show is not for musical stars. It is a night when our family can share our special gifts. It is a night for fun and to enjoy with our parish. Invite your friends over here and practice together. You will be wonderful."

▶ *Would you like your family to take part in a parish talent night? Why or why not?*

FAITH and MEDIA

▶ On Days 1 and 2 you might bring copies of the parish bulletin to class and visit the parish Web site (if your parish has one) with the children. Remind them that parish bulletins and parish Web sites are both examples of media: The parish uses them to send messages to the members of the parish family and also to tell others about the many things that go on in the parish each week.

▶ On Day 4, as the children record get-well greetings (see guide page 179), you might remind them that sending such messages is another example of the use of media.

CHAPTER PROJECT: PARISH FAMILY GUESTS

During the week invite some of the people of the parish (a priest, deacon, the director of religious education, a person from the parish leadership team) to come and talk to the class. Ask each guest to tell the children what her or his role is. Also ask each guest to stress with the children how important they are to the parish. Provide time for the children to ask questions of the speakers. Also provide time for the children to tell the guests what they are learning about the Church. The children could also sing some of the songs they have been learning.

PROJECT DISCIPLE

Pray
Learn
Celebrate
Share
Choose
Live

Additional Activities

What's *the* Word?

(Use on Day 2.)

Materials needed: copies of reproducible master, guide page 171F, colored pencils or crayons

Distribute copies of the Scripture reproducible master. Ask a volunteer to read the Scripture quote. As a class, brainstorm a list of people who gather together as parish. Then invite children to draw pictures of people in their individual parishes.

Question Corner

If children in the classroom are members of different parishes, challenge them to interview each other about their parishes. Encourage children to think of questions to ask a person who belongs to a different parish and allow time for the children to talk together about similarities and differences among their parishes. Invite children to continue the discussion with friends and family members outside of the classroom.

Picture This

Materials needed: mural paper, paint

Prepare a long sheet of mural paper and paints. Write the words *We Belong to a Parish* on the paper. Divide children into small groups and invite each child to paint his or her self-portrait onto the mural. Display the finished mural in the classroom or school.

Show What *you* Know

Materials needed: drawing paper, colored pencils or crayons, computer (option), voice recorder (option)

Make a class picture book or presentation about the parish. Ask each child to write a descriptive sentence about the parish on a blank sheet of drawing paper or type it into a computer paint program. Invite the children to illustrate their sentences. When all drawings are completed, bind the pages into classroom book about the parish or create a presentation on the computer. Ask each child to read his or her sentence into the voice recorder and embed these into the presentation (option). Share the book as a class.

Meeting Individual Needs
Children with Developmental Needs

Children with developmental needs may experience frustration at not being able to process information at the same rate as their classmates. You can help them by providing them with a preview of the lesson content. For example, tell the children with developmental needs the *We Gather* question before you teach that part of the lesson. Help the children to think of some answers they can share when you ask the question in class.

We Believe Resources

- Grade 1 *Review & Resource Book*, pages 34–36
- Grade 1 *Family Book*, pages 43–45
- Grade 1 *Assessment Book*, pages 31–32
- Grade 1 CD-ROM *Test Generator and Resource*: Use Chapter 15 Test or customize your own.
- **www.webelieveweb.com**

SHARING FAITH
with My Family

Sharing What I Learned

Look at the pictures below. Use each picture to tell your family what you learned in this chapter.

Parish Helpers

Talk about the people who help your parish family. Talk about what they do to help. Together make a thank-you card or sign to send to one of these helpers. Use this space to plan what you will write.

_____

_____

We Belong

Pray this prayer every day this week.

God, thank you for our parish family.
Help us to join together to share your love.

Visit Sadlier's

www.WeBelieveweb.com

Connect to the Catechism
For adult background and reflection, see paragraphs 2179, 2182, and 2444.

PROJECT DISCIPLE

Pray
Learn
Celebrate
Share
Choose
Live

Name _____

What's *the* Word?

Jesus said, "Where two or three are gathered together in my name, there am I in the midst of them."
(Matthew 18:20)

Draw a picture to show who gathers together in your parish. Remember that Jesus is with you when you gather.

Name _____

Decorate this thank-you card. Send it to
a special parish helper.

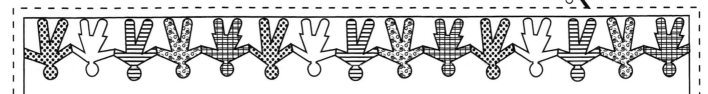

Fold

THANK YOU

We Belong to a Parish

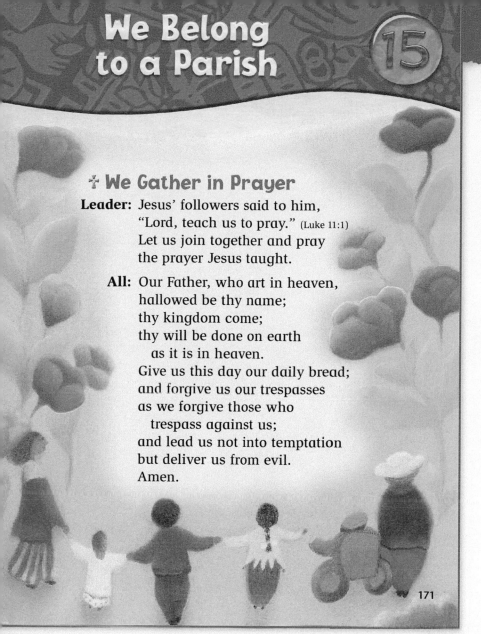

✝ We Gather in Prayer

Leader: Jesus' followers said to him, "Lord, teach us to pray." (Luke 11:1) Let us join together and pray the prayer Jesus taught.

All: Our Father, who art in heaven, hallowed be thy name; thy kingdom come; thy will be done on earth as it is in heaven. Give us this day our daily bread; and forgive us our trespasses as we forgive those who trespass against us; and lead us not into temptation but deliver us from evil. Amen.

171

PREPARING TO PRAY

The children will join together to pray the Lord's Prayer.

• Prepare cutout figures of four people. On each cutout print one of these phrases: *Praise and thank God; Share God's love; Follow Jesus;* and *Help others.*

• Print the name of your parish on a sheet of poster board or chart paper. Invite the children to write their names on the poster.

The Prayer Space
• Display the cutout figures and name chart you have made.

• On the prayer table place a statue of Jesus and a Bible opened to one of the books of the New Testament.

📖 This Week's Liturgy
Visit **www.webelieveweb.com** for this week's liturgical readings and other seasonal material.

Lesson Plan

We Gather in Prayer ___ minutes

✝ Pray

• Explain to the children that you will be the prayer leader. Remind them that the Lord's Prayer is the special prayer Jesus taught us.

• Invite the children to gather in the prayer space.

• Pray the Sign of the Cross and then read the words of the leader.

• Ask the children to join hands to form a circle. Pray the Lord's Prayer together.

Family Connection Update
Invite the children to share their family experiences of serving others.

Catechist Goal

• To show that the parish is like a family

Our Faith Response

• To identify the things we do in our parish

 **parish**

Teaching Tip

Reading Paragraphs

In the children's books, the *We Believe* text of Units 3 and 4 is presented in paragraph format. Review what a paragraph is by pointing out that it is made up of individual sentences. You may want to pair the children who have advanced reading skills with the children who have difficulty reading. When you are reading paragraphs aloud, give all the children guidance in following along.

Our parish is like a family.

WE GATHER

✝ *God, thank you for the Church.*

🧑 Act out some ways families spend time together.

WE BELIEVE

We belong to the Catholic Church. We are Catholics. We belong to a parish.

Lesson Plan

WE GATHER ___ minutes

✝ **Pray** Pray together the Sign of the Cross and the *We Gather* prayer.

Focus on Life Ask the children to name ways that families spend time together. List these ways on the board. If necessary, suggest activities such as eating meals together, watching television, going to Mass, or playing a game together. Have the children work in small groups to act out a family spending time together. Read the *Chapter Story* on guide page 171C. Tell the children that in this lesson they will learn about ways that parish communities are like families.

WE BELIEVE ___ minutes

Review Ask a few volunteers to share what they have learned about the Church. Remind the children that the Church is all the people who believe in Jesus and follow his teachings.

Learn About the Parish Print the word *parish* on the board. Read aloud the *We Believe* statement. Explain: *A parish is a group of Catholics who join together to share God's love.* Read aloud the *We Believe* paragraphs.

Then direct attention to the photographs on these pages. Have the children stand, point to themselves, and say: *We are part of our parish. We join together to share God's love.*

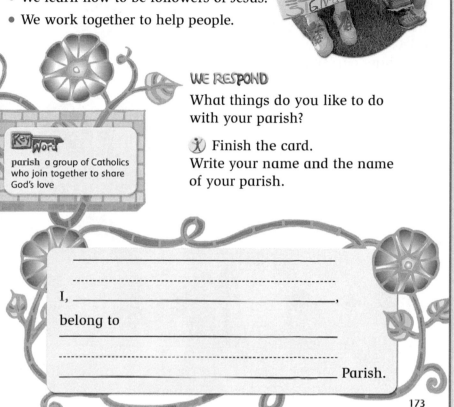

A **parish** is a group of Catholics who join together to share God's love. They pray, celebrate, and work together. The people who belong to a parish are like a family.

We do many things with our parish.
- We praise and thank God.
- We share God's love with others.
- We learn how to be followers of Jesus.
- We work together to help people.

Key Word
parish a group of Catholics who join together to share God's love

WE RESPOND

What things do you like to do with your parish?

🏃 Finish the card.
Write your name and the name of your parish.

_____

I, _____,

belong to

_____

_____ Parish.

173

ACTIVITY BANK

Multiple Intelligences
Interpersonal
Have the children work in pairs. Have each set of partners act out a situation in which one tells a friend who is not a member of the parish what a person can do with the parish community. These conversations should include the activities mentioned in *We Believe*.

Parish
Singing About the Parish
Activity Materials: Grade 1 CD, words for "We Are the Church," page 143 of the children's text
Play the recording of "We Are the Church," #13 on the Grade 1 CD. Have the children sing along. Then have the children sing the song again; replacing the word *Church* with the word *parish*.

Quick Check

✔ *What is a parish?* (A parish is a group of Catholics who join together to share God's love.)

✔ *What do we do with our parish?* (Possible responses are listed in the third *We Believe* paragraph.)

WE RESPOND ___ minutes

Connect to Life Read the *We Respond* question. Pause briefly to allow all the children time to reflect. Then invite volunteers to share their responses. List their ideas on the board. (Possible responses: participate at Mass, go to a pancake breakfast, or attend an annual parish fair)

Ask the children to complete the activity by writing the name of their parish on the card provided.

Pray Lead the children in praying: *Jesus, thank you for our parish. Help us love one another as members of a family. Amen.*

Plan Ahead for Day 2

Catechist Goal: To explain that the parish joins together to celebrate God's love

Preparation: Make copies of *What's the Word?*, guide page 171F.

Catechist Goal

• To explain that the parish joins together to celebrate God's love

Our Faith Response

• To thank and praise God at Mass and in our work

Key Word **worship**

Lesson Materials

• colored pencils or crayons

• Grade 1 CD

• copies of reproducible master *What's the Word?*, guide page 171F

Teaching Tip

Learning Tools

Two learning tools that both children and adults enjoy using are the television and the computer. Both tools include programs for lifetime learning. Provide opportunities for the children to use these tools in religion class. See *Faith and Media* suggestions on the *Enrichment* pages of the guide. Encourage the children to use these tools at home with parental or other adult supervision.

We gather together to worship.

WE GATHER

✝ *O God, we give you thanks and praise.*

🧍 Find out where these people are going. Connect the dots.

WE BELIEVE

Our parish joins together to celebrate God's love. We **worship** God. We give him thanks and praise.

Every week we gather to worship God in our parish church. Our parish church is a holy place. God is with us there in a special way.

174

Lesson Plan

WE GATHER _____ minutes

✝ **Pray** Ask the children to hold up their arms in a gesture of praise. Then pray together the *We Gather* prayer.

Focus on Life Ask the children to complete the *We Gather* activity. When they have finished connecting the dots, ask the children to share how they feel when they gather with other people in the parish church. Tell the children that in this lesson they will learn that a parish joins together to celebrate God's love.

WE BELIEVE _____ minutes

Learn About Worship Read aloud the *We Believe* statement. Print the word *worship* on the board.

Point out that when we worship God, we thank him and we praise him. Explain: *When we thank God, we tell him that we appreciate all that he does for us. When we praise God, we tell him that he is wonderful and good.*

Then read aloud the first two *We Believe* paragraphs. Emphasize that God is with our parish when we gather to worship him.

Discuss the Picture Direct attention to the photograph on page 175. Ask: *What do you think the members of the parish are doing?* Help the children to conclude that they are worshiping God by singing. Explain: *One way to praise God is by singing.*

Look at the picture.
Talk about what you see.

WE RESPOND

How does your parish worship God?

🎵 Open Our Hearts

God, we come to worship you:

Chorus
Open our hearts to listen to you.
Open our hearts to listen to you.

God, your love is always true:
(Chorus)

Key Word
worship to give God thanks and praise

175

ACTIVITY BANK

Liturgy
Songs of Worship
Activity Materials: missalette, drawing paper, crayons or markers
Remind the children about the songs and hymns your parish sings at Mass. Use the missalette as a resource book. Ask the children to name their favorite songs and tell why they are their favorites. Also encourage the children to ask the members of their families to name their favorites. As a class choose one favorite song. Have the children illustrate the lyrics of the song.

Scripture
Intrapersonal, Spatial
For a Scripture activity, see *What's the Word?*, guide page 171F.

Quick Check

✔ *What do we do when we worship God?* (We give God thanks and praise.)

✔ *Why is our parish church a holy place?* (God is with us there in a special way.)

WE RESPOND ___ minutes

Connect to Life Read aloud the *We Respond* question. Ask the children to talk about different ways to thank and praise God.

Play "Open Our Hearts," #17 on the Grade 1 CD. Have the children read the words quietly as they listen to the recording. Then invite the children to join you as you sing the song. Ask the children to cross their arms over their hearts when they sing, "Open our hearts." Have them hold one hand behind an ear when they sing "listen to you."

Pray Sing together "Open Our Hearts."

Plan Ahead for Day 3

Catechist Goal: To introduce the people who work together as a parish

Preparation: Make copies of Reproducible Master 15, guide page 171G.

Catechist Goal

• To introduce the people who work together as a parish

Our Faith Response

• To express gratitude for our parish leaders and helpers

 **pastor**

Lesson Materials

• index cards

• copies of Reproducible Master 15

As Catholics...

Catechists

After presenting the lesson, read aloud the *As Catholics* text. Tell the children that dedicated adults taught you about the Catholic faith. Then ask: *Who teaches you the Catholic faith?* Emphasize that growing in knowledge and faith is something we need to do our entire lives.

We work together as a parish.

WE GATHER

✝ *Jesus, please help the members of our parish.*

Who are some of the people you know in your parish?

WE BELIEVE

The leader of a parish is called the **pastor**. The pastor is a priest.

The pastor leads us in worship. He teaches us about Jesus. He helps us to care for one another.

🧍 Who is the pastor of your parish? Write his name here.

_____

- -

_____

Sometimes the parish has a deacon. He helps the pastor.

Other leaders in the parish work with the pastor, too. Together they help the parish family.

pastor the priest who is the leader of the parish

176

Lesson Plan

WE GATHER _____ minutes

✝ **Pray** Begin by praying together the *We Gather* prayer. Then ask volunteers to complete the prayer with specific examples, such as *Jesus, please help the members of our parish to be safe as they drive their cars.* Print the children's prayers on index cards and place the cards on the prayer table.

Focus on Life Ask the children to name some of the people they know in the parish. Explain: *Many people help the parish to be a family or community of faith.* Tell the children that in this lesson they will learn about the pastor, the leader of the parish, and the ways other leaders in the parish work with him.

WE BELIEVE _____ minutes

Do the Activity Read the *We Believe* statement together. Ask the children to think about ways in which the people of the parish can work together. Read aloud the first two *We Believe* paragraphs. Then ask the children to name the pastor of their parish. Print his name on the board. Have the children write the pastor's name in their texts.

Introduce the Pastor Arrange for the pastor or another priest of your parish to visit during this lesson. Invite him to give a brief talk about his duties as pastor and to name the other members of his parish team. As he explains, print the titles of the other team members on chart paper and add a brief description of their roles. When the pastor has finished speaking, have the children thank him for visiting the class.

Many people work together in our parish. Some help us to worship God. Some teach us about God. Some work with us to care for those who are sick or in need.

ACTIVITY BANK

Parish
Greetings
Activity Materials: drawing paper, crayons or colored pencils, voice recorder or video camera (option)

Plan to send greeting cards to another first grade religion class. Talk with the parish's director of religious education. Explain to this person that your class would like to communicate with the group of first graders in the parish program.

Distribute drawing paper for the children to illustrate some of the things that they have learned this year about Jesus and the Church.

If a video camera is available, invite the class to deliver a message to the parish group. As a class decide on the message. Have the children say the message together. Then invite the children to introduce themselves as they hold up their drawings. Have each child give a brief explanation of her or his drawing.

WE RESPOND

Talk about ways you thank the pastor of your parish.

Other people work in and help lead your parish. How can you thank them?

As Catholics...

Catechists teach the Catholic faith to the children, youth, and adults of the parish. They are very important people in the parish. They teach about Jesus and the Church. They help us to be friends and followers of Jesus.

Who teaches you about the Catholic faith?

177

Review the Members of the Parish Team
Read aloud the last two *We Believe* paragraphs. Review the list of the parish helpers. Encourage the children to ask questions about each of the members of the team.

Quick Check

✔ *Who is the leader of your parish?* (The leader of our parish is the pastor.)

✔ *What do other members of the parish do?* (Other members of the parish help us to worship God, teach us about God, and care for those who are sick or in need.)

WE RESPOND ___ minutes

Connect to Life Help the children to think about and name ways to thank the pastor and other parish leaders. As the children name ways to thank these people, list the ideas on the board.

Distribute copies of Reproducible Master 15. Have each child make a thank-you card to send to a parish helper.

Pray Invite the children to pray: *Jesus, thank you for all the people of our parish.*

Plan Ahead for Day 4

Catechist Goal: To explore ways our parish helps people

Preparation: Decide on a service project that your class can work on together.

Catechist Goal

• To explore ways our parish helps people

Our Faith Response

• To join our parish family in helping others

Lesson Materials

• crayons or colored pencils

Teaching Tip

Classroom Helpers

Explain to the children: *When you take care of the classroom, you are helping to take care of the parish.* In assigning the children to do classroom chores (cleaning erasers, taking messages to the office), try to include all the children at different times. Keep track of the children who have done jobs so you will know who is waiting to be assigned. Most children will accept gladly the responsibility of taking care of their classroom.

Our parish helps many people.

WE GATHER

✝ *Jesus, help our parish to do your work.*

🧍 How would you help? Act out what you can do.

• Your friend forgot his lunch.
• Your sister spilled milk on the table.
• Your friend fell and got hurt.

WE BELIEVE

In our parish we help one another. We try to spend time with our parish family. We may join them for picnics or dinners. We help people of our parish who are in need.

Our parish helps other people, too. We gather food and clothes for those who are poor. We send money to those who are in need.

178

Lesson Plan

WE GATHER ___ minutes

✝ **Pray** Invite the children to pray the Sign of the Cross together and the *We Gather* prayer on page 178.

Focus on Life Invite the children to do the *We Gather* activity. Read aloud each situation and have volunteers act out what they would do. When you have finished, ask the children to suggest other occasions when they could help someone. Tell the children that in this lesson they will learn some important ways the parish helps people.

WE BELIEVE ___ minutes

Learn About the Parish's Work Read the *We Believe* statement aloud. Point out to the children that the parish helps many people in order to show God's great love and care for all his children. Explain: *When we show our love for others, we show God that we love him, too.* Read the *We Believe* paragraphs. Stress the main ideas:

• *The parish helps people in the parish family who are in need.*

• *The parish helps people in need throughout the world.*

Act It Out Have the children look at the photographs on pages 178–179. Invite volunteers to act out what the people in the pictures might be saying or doing.

Our parish cares for those who are sick. People from the parish visit them. We can pray for them. We can also send them cards.

WE RESPOND

🧍 Circle one way you will help your parish this week.

- Join in singing and praying.
- Keep the parish buildings neat and clean.
- Pray for my parish.
- Be kind and friendly.

Together say a prayer for all those who are in need.

ACTIVITY BANK

Catholic Social Teaching

Call to Family, Community, and Participation

Activity Materials: voice recorder

Involve the children in making a special get-well greeting. Teach them the following words to the tune of "Mary Had a Little Lamb."

*Thinking of you is what we do,
what we do, what we do.
Praying for you is our gift to you,
and hope you'll feel better soon.*

After practicing the song, record the children's voices. After the song, have the children say their name with a message: For example, *feel better; get well soon; we love you.* When everyone has had a turn to record a message, upload the recordings. Burn them onto a CD and ask a priest or pastoral minister to take it when he or she visits the people who are sick. Ask the person to play the CD during each visit.

Quick Check

✔ *What does our parish do for people?* (Our parish helps many people.)

✔ *Whom does our parish help?* (Our parish helps those who are in need, such as the sick and poor.)

WE RESPOND   ___ minutes

Connect to Life Help the children to do the *We Respond* activity. Slowly read aloud each bulleted suggestion. Then invite volunteers to share the suggestions they circled. Ask them to explain the way they plan to carry out their choices.

Service Project Explain to the children a simple service project that you can work on together. Provide them with all the information about materials needed.

Pray Read the following prayer and ask the children to repeat the words: *Lord Jesus, help us to follow your example in our parish. We pray for all those who are in need. Amen.*

Plan Ahead for Day 5

Catechist Goal: To review chapter ideas and their relationship to our faith life

Preparation: Make copies of *Sharing Faith with My Family,* guide page 171E.

Catechist Goal

• To review the chapter ideas that are key to growing as disciples of Jesus Christ

Our Faith Response

• To decide on ways to grow as disciples by living out what we have learned

Show What *you* Know

Read the activity instructions. Ask the children to match the puzzle pieces. Explain that they can check their answers by making sure the puzzle pieces fit together.

Make *it* Happen

Ask a volunteer to read the instructions. Talk to the children about the people in the parish who help the children worship God, who teach the children about God, and who care for those in need. The children may answer the question generally, for example *my pastor*; or specifically, for example *Father Joe*. Children may write or draw their responses in the space provided. When they have finished, read the Disciple Challenge. Think of appropriate ways to thank these people as a class.

Reality Check

Remind the children that this activity is a checklist. Read the activity question. Invite the children to check one, some, or all of the ways.

Take Home

Read the activity aloud. Encourage the children to continue the discussion with their families. Encourage them to work together to help people who are hungry. Invite children to share any family experiences with the class.

Discuss and send home copies of *Sharing Faith with My Family*, guide page 171E.

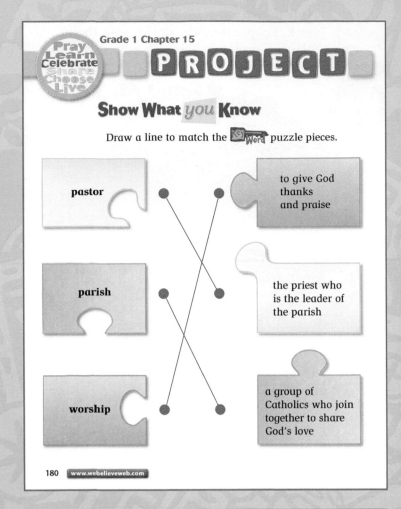

Grade 1 Chapter 15

PROJECT

Show What *you* Know

Draw a line to match the Key Word puzzle pieces.

pastor — to give God thanks and praise

parish — the priest who is the leader of the parish

worship — a group of Catholics who join together to share God's love

180 www.webelieveweb.com

DISCIPLE

Make *it* Happen
Think about the people in your parish. Answer each question.

Who helps you worship God?

Who teaches you about God?

Who cares for those who need help?

 DISCIPLE CHALLENGE Thank these people for the special work they do.

Reality Check

How is your parish like a family?

☑ We belong together.

☑ We help each other.

☑ We share God's love.

☑ We pray together.

Take Home

Some people do not have homes or jobs. These people need food. Many parish families join together to help people who are hungry. Some cook and serve meals to people who come to eat at a soup kitchen. Some collect food for the hungry. How can your family help people who are hungry?

181

Circle the correct answer.

1. Do the people in a parish pray, celebrate, and work together?

   (Yes)   No

2. Is a parish church a holy place?

   (Yes)   No

3. Is the president the priest who leads the parish?

   Yes   (No)

4. Do the people in a parish help many people?

   (Yes)   No

5. Do we forget about God when we worship him?

   Yes   (No)

What do the people in your parish do together? Possible responses: worship God; share God's love with others; learn how to be followers of Jesus; work together to help people

182

CHAPTER TEST

Read each test item aloud and allow time for the children to mark an answer. Decide whether the *Talk About It* activity will be a small group or whole class discussion. After you have finished, check the answers. Clarify any misconceptions.

Alternative Assessment

You may want the students to complete the following alternative-assessment activity.

Make a poster to welcome others to your parish. Show some of the ways your parish is like a family.

Additional Testing

• Chapter 15 Test in *Assessment Book*, pages 31–32

• CD-ROM *Test Generator and Resource*: Use Chapter 15 Test or customize your own.

Review

Review the definitions as they are presented in the chapter's *Key Word* boxes:

• parish (page 173)

• worship (page 175)

• pastor (page 176).

We Believe Statements

Review the four statements.

• Our parish is like a family.

• We gather together to worship.

• We work together as a parish.

• Our parish helps many people.

To use the Chapter 15 Study Guide, visit

www.webelieveweb.com

Overview

In Chapter 15 the children learned about the parish community and its activities. In this chapter the children will learn that we celebrate God's love in the sacraments.

Doctrinal Content	For Adult Reading and Reflection *Catechism of the Catholic Church*
The children will learn:	Paragraph
• Jesus celebrated God's love.	583
• We celebrate God's love.	1083
• Jesus gave us the sacraments.	1084
• The Church celebrates Seven Sacraments.	1113

sacrament (p. 189)

Catechist Background

Go to **www.webelieveweb.com**, Catechist/ Teacher, We Believe Correlations for this chapter's correlation to the Six Tasks of Catechesis.

What have been some of the important celebrations in your life?

Just as Jesus celebrated God's love in his life, so we, too, celebrate God's love. We do this when we celebrate the sacraments.

A sacrament is an effective sign given to us by Jesus Christ through which we share in God's life. "The seven sacraments touch all the stages and all the important moments of Christian life: they give birth and increase, healing and mission to the Christian's life of faith. There is thus a certain resemblance between the stages of natural life and the stages of the spiritual life." (CCC 1210)

We celebrate the Seven Sacraments. There are three Sacraments of Christian Initiation:

Baptism, Confirmation, and Eucharist. There are two Sacraments of Healing: Penance and Reconciliation, and Anointing of the Sick. There are two Sacraments at the Service of Communion: Holy Orders and Matrimony. Through the Seven Sacraments we celebrate God's love with us in Christ, our Lord and Savior.

How has the celebration of the sacraments brought you closer to God?

Lesson Planning Guide

Lesson Focus	Presentation	Materials

Day 1

page 183
✝ **We Gather in Prayer**

pages 184–185
Jesus celebrated God's love.

📖 *Psalm 100:1–2*

🎵 Celebrate God's love for us in song.
- Share responses for **We Gather**.
- Read the **We Believe** text about the special times Jesus celebrated.
- Read the psalm of praise to God.

🏃 Do the **We Respond** activity.
- Reflect on the question.

For the prayer space: a picture or statue of Jesus, photographs of sacrament celebrations

🎵 "We Celebrate with Joy," Carey Landry, #18, Grade 1 CD
- percussion instruments (option)

Day 2

pages 186–187
We celebrate God's love.

🏃 Act out responses for **We Gather**.
- Discuss the **We Believe** text about worshiping to celebrate God's love.

🏃 Do the coloring activity.
- Discuss responses for **We Respond**.

🏃 Do the drawing activity.
- Pray together.

- crayons or colored pencils
- Grade 1 CD (option)
- copies of reproducible master *What's the Word?*, guide page 183F

Day 3

pages 188–189
Jesus gave us the sacraments.

- Discuss the **We Gather** question.
- Present the **We Believe** text about sharing in God's life through the sacraments.

🏃 Complete the **We Respond** prayer.

- colored pencils or crayons
- copies of Reproducible Master 16, guide page 183G

Day 4

pages 190–191
The Church celebrates Seven Sacraments.

🎵 Sing the **We Gather** song.
- Present the **We Believe** text about the Seven Sacraments.

🏃 Do the **We Respond** picture-study activity and respond to the question.
- Read and discuss the *As Catholics* text.

🎵 "Celebrate God," Carey Landry, #19, Grade 1 CD

Day 5

pages 192–193
Project Disciple

page 194
Chapter 16 Test

- Complete the **Project Disciple** activities.
- Explain the *Take Home* activity.
- Discuss/send home **Sharing Faith with My Family**, guide page 183E.
- Complete **Chapter 16 Test**.
- Work on *Alternative Assessment* activity.

- pencils
- crayons or colored pencils
- copies of **Sharing Faith with My Family** reproducible master, guide page 183E

Enrichment Ideas

Chapter Story

Hi! My name is Adam. I'm watching my little sister while my parents are getting dressed. We're all going to Cousin Stephanie's wedding. I hope this wedding celebration is as much fun as Cousin Louis's was last year. My grandparents, aunts, uncles, and cousins were all there. Most of us sat together at church and at the celebration at the hall.

Everyone sang in church. We watched as Cousin Louis and his bride put rings on each other's fingers. We listened as they promised to love and care for each other always. Then we went to the hall for a big party. There was a lot of delicious food and there was music and dancing.

After the bride and groom left, and the party was over in the hall, we went to Uncle Leo and Aunt Imelda's house. There we listened to Nonna tell stories about other family weddings. We listened to my uncle and aunt tell stories about themselves when they were growing up.

We had a lot of fun on Cousin Louis's wedding day. I think Cousin Stephanie's celebration will be as great because all the same people in my family will be there.

▶ *Why is Adam looking forward to going to his cousin's wedding?*

FAITH and MEDIA

▶ On Day 1, as you discuss songs of praise, and on Day 5, as you consider the *Our Catholic Life* text about songs of praise and love, remind the children that songs, which we use to tell stories and send messages, are examples of media. When we sing songs to praise God and show our love for him, and when songwriters write new songs to praise God, both singers and songwriters are using the medium of song to do God's work in the world.

CHAPTER PROJECT: SIGNS OF GOD'S LOVE

Each day this week ask the children to name signs of God's love that they experienced that day. You may want to name your own signs to encourage the children's sharing. For example, *I heard a bird singing this morning. Someone held a door open for me this morning.* Each day give a child an index card. Have him or her draw a picture to illustrate a favorite sign of love. Collect the cards each day. Keep the cards on the prayer table during the week. On Day 5, describe the picture on each card. After each description, ask the children to say: *Thank you, God, for signs of your love.*

PROJECT DISCIPLE

Additional Activities

What's the Word?

(Use on Day 2.)

Materials needed: copies of reproducible master, guide page 183F, colored pencils or crayons

Distribute copies of the Scripture reproducible master. Ask a volunteer to be the Reader. Remind the children that they will read the part of All. Invite the children to draw a picture as instructed. Share the drawings as a class.

Celebrate!

Materials needed: sentence strips

Distribute a sentence strip to each child. Provide the following prompt: *God, I will celebrate your love this week by*. Invite each child to complete the sentence by writing on the sentence strip. You may want to display the prompt and responses in the classroom as a reminder of the ways the children can share God's love.

Show What you Know

Help children to make connections by encouraging a class discussion about celebrations. Ask the children about celebrations they have experienced, about ways they celebrate, and about their feelings during and after celebrations. You may include family, holiday or other seasonal celebrations and celebrations about good news. Segue from this discussion into the chapter's lessons.

More to Explore

Invite the children to use the words of praise they have learned throughout the chapter and the year to write a song or cheer. Divide the children into small groups and allow each group time to brainstorm and then practice their cheer or song. Provide help and input as needed. Make time for each group to perform their final cheer or song for the class. Consider using a camera to record each group's performance for a series of "music videos" praising God.

Meeting Individual Needs
Children Who Are Bodily-Kinesthetic Learners

Structure your lesson so children have ample opportunities for movement and a change of pace. Encourage their participation in role-playing activities.

We Believe Resources

- Grade 1 *Review & Resource Book*, pages 37–39
- Grade 1 *Family Book*, pages 46–48
- Grade 1 *Assessment Book*, pages 33–34
- Grade 1 CD-ROM *Test Generator and Resource*: Use Chapter 16 Test or customize your own.
- **www.webelieveweb.com**

Sharing What I Learned

Look at the pictures below. Use each picture to tell your family what you learned in this chapter.

Jesus Is with Us

Get your family together. Cut out this picture of Jesus. Glue it to a piece of cardboard or stiff paper. Stand this picture on your prayer table. Talk with your family about Jesus and the sacraments he gave us. Remember they are ways to celebrate God's love.

Pray Together

Jesus, thank you for the special times we share together.

Visit Sadlier's
www.WeBelieveweb.com

Connect to the Catechism
For adult background and reflection, see paragraphs 583, 1083, 1084, and 1113.

PROJECT DISCIPLE

Pray
Learn
Celebrate
Share
Choose
Live

Name _____

What's *the* Word?

Reader: We worship God at Mass with our parish on Sunday. We praise God with some of the same words the people used to praise Jesus. They welcomed Jesus with the following words.

All: "Hosanna!
Blessed is he who comes in name of the Lord."
(John 12:13)

Draw a picture to show you and your parish praying these words at Mass.

Circle each way you can show people your love.

I can help them clean.

I can tell them, "I love you."

I can make a special treat.

I can give them a gift.

I can share a story with them.

I can put my things away.

We Celebrate the Sacraments

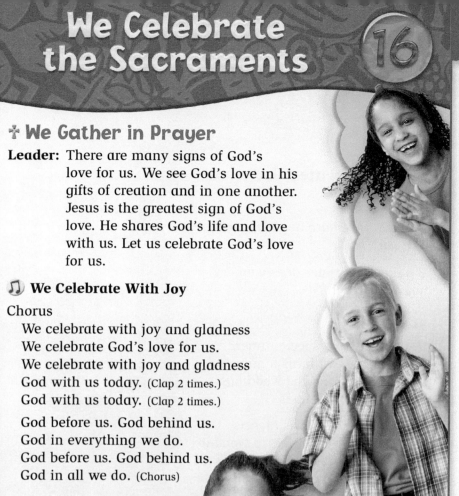

✝ We Gather in Prayer

Leader: There are many signs of God's love for us. We see God's love in his gifts of creation and in one another. Jesus is the greatest sign of God's love. He shares God's life and love with us. Let us celebrate God's love for us.

🎵 We Celebrate With Joy

Chorus

We celebrate with joy and gladness
We celebrate God's love for us.
We celebrate with joy and gladness
God with us today. (Clap 2 times.)
God with us today. (Clap 2 times.)

God before us. God behind us.
God in everything we do.
God before us. God behind us.
God in all we do. (Chorus)

183

PREPARING TO PRAY

The children will celebrate God's love for us in word and song.

• Play "We Celebrate with Joy," #18 on the Grade 1 CD. Have the children practice singing and clapping at the appropriate times.

• Have percussion instruments available. Give them to a few children to play during the song. (option)

The Prayer Space

• Display the following items: a picture or statue of Jesus to remind us that Jesus is the greatest sign of God's love for us; photographs of sacrament celebrations: a wedding Mass, a Baptism, a First Holy Communion Mass.

📖 **This Week's Liturgy**
Visit **www.webelieveweb.com** for this week's liturgical readings and other seasonal material.

Lesson Plan

We Gather in Prayer ___ minutes

✝ Pray

• Gather the children in the prayer space. Pray the Sign of the Cross together.

• Begin reading the words of the prayer leader.

• Invite the children to sing "We Celebrate With Joy."

Family Connection Update

Invite the children to share their family discussions about helping people who are hungry.

Catechist Goal

- To explain that Jesus' words and actions celebrated God's love

Our Faith Response

- To celebrate God's love by our words and actions

Lesson Materials

- Grade 1 CD

Teaching Tip

Sensitivity to Family Experiences

Be aware that all the children's families may have different celebratory experiences. For this chapter, do not require that all the children share responses to the *We Gather* questions. Only ask volunteers to share responses.

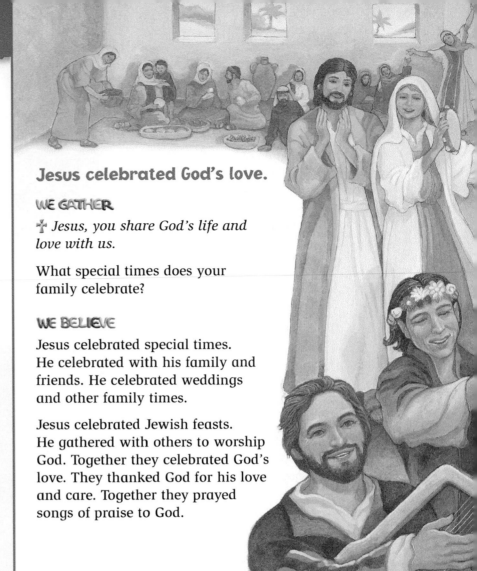

Jesus celebrated God's love.

WE GATHER

✝ *Jesus, you share God's life and love with us.*

What special times does your family celebrate?

WE BELIEVE

Jesus celebrated special times. He celebrated with his family and friends. He celebrated weddings and other family times.

Jesus celebrated Jewish feasts. He gathered with others to worship God. Together they celebrated God's love. They thanked God for his love and care. Together they prayed songs of praise to God.

184

Lesson Plan

WE GATHER _____ minutes

✝ **Pray** Pray the Sign of the Cross and the *We Gather* prayer.

Focus on Life Read aloud the *We Gather* question. Pause briefly to allow all the children time to reflect. Then invite volunteers to tell about their special family celebrations. Share the *Chapter Story*, guide page 183C. Tell the children that in this lesson they will learn how Jesus celebrated God's love.

WE BELIEVE _____ minutes

Jesus Celebrates Read the *We Believe* statement together. Ask: *How do you think Jesus celebrated God's*

love? Invite the children to look at the picture of Jesus as you read the first two *We Believe* paragraphs. Then explain: *The picture shows Jesus with his mother and family at a wedding celebration.* Ask: *How are the people celebrating?*

Rejoice About God's Love Pause briefly after you read each line of Psalm 100. Ask the children to repeat each line. Repeat the verses with them several times. Ask the children whether they have ever heard these verses before. Point out: *You may have heard them when you worshiped God with the parish.*

Here is one of these songs of praise to God.

"Shout joyfully to the LORD, all you lands;
worship the LORD with cries of gladness;
come before him with joyful song."
Psalm 100:1–2

We can pray these words of praise.
Sometimes we pray them when we
worship God as a parish.

WE RESPOND

Pray together the song of praise
above. Make up actions for the prayer.

How else will you celebrate
God's love today?

185

ACTIVITY BANK

Curriculum Connection
Social Studies

Have the children look at the picture on these pages. Then have the children close their eyes and think about a family celebration today. Draw a two-column chart on the board or on chart paper. Ask: *How are the celebrations in Jesus' time and celebrations today the same?* List responses in the first column. Then ask: *How are the celebrations different?* List responses in the second column.

SAME	DIFFERENT
People are happy.	Musicians play different instruments.

Quick Check

✔ *With whom did Jesus celebrate God's love?* (Jesus celebrated God's love with his family and friends.)

✔ *In what ways did Jesus worship God with others?* (Jesus joined others in thanking God for his love and care. He prayed songs of praise.)

WE RESPOND   ___ minutes

Connect to Life Invite the children to suggest prayerful actions for the psalm verse. Help the group choose one action for each line. Then pray the psalm in word and actions.

Discuss the *We Respond* question with the group.

Pray Invite the children to stand and sing the chorus of "We Celebrate with Joy," #18 on the Grade 1 CD.

Plan Ahead for Day 2

Catechist Goal: To introduce some of the ways we celebrate God's love

Preparation: Make copies of *What's the Word?*, guide page 183F.

Catechist Goal

• To introduce some of the ways we celebrate God's love

Our Faith Response

• To be grateful for God's love

Lesson Materials

• crayons or colored pencils
• copies of reproducible master *What's the Word?*, guide page 183F

Teaching Note

Memorization of the Sacraments

The purpose of the material presented in this chapter is to introduce the sacraments as signs of God's love. Stress this concept with the children. On Day 4 the children will look at the name of each sacrament and a photo of a celebration of this sacrament. It is not recommended that you require the children to memorize the names of the sacraments at this time. The children will learn more about Baptism, Eucharist, and Penance in chapters that follow.

We celebrate God's love.

WE GATHER

✝ *God, we praise you for your love.*

🧍 Pretend that someone your family loves is coming to your home. How will you celebrate this visit? Act out what you will say and do.

WE BELIEVE

We gather with our parish family to celebrate God's love. We gather to worship together.

When we worship, we thank God for sending his Son. We remember the things that Jesus said and did. We ask the Holy Spirit to help us.

When we worship, we use special words and actions.

🧍 Color in the letters of these special words we pray.

Alleluia
Amen

186

Lesson Plan

WE GATHER ___ minutes

✝ **Pray** Help the children recall what they learned in the previous day's lesson. Then invite them to pray the Sign of the Cross and the *We Gather* prayer.

Focus on Life Read the directions for the *We Gather* activity. Tell the children that you are going to pretend together that a relative is coming to visit. Let a volunteer name a relative, real or pretend. Let all of the children suggest ways the family can celebrate the guest's visit. Have volunteers act out the celebration. Tell the children that in this lesson they will learn ways in which we celebrate God's love.

WE BELIEVE ___ minutes

Celebrate God's Love Read aloud the first three *We Believe* paragraphs. On the board have drawn a circle with the label *Our Parish Celebrates*. Draw lines from the circle. Ask the children what the parish does together on Sunday. As the children respond, write their responses on the lines. (Possible responses: pray, participate at Mass, sing, see friends, and talk to our priest.) Tell the children that these are all ways in which we celebrate God's love together.

Color Words of Praise Read the directions for the *We Believe* activity and the words of praise. Encourage the children to use bright colors to color the words. Ask the children to say the two words joyfully and prayerfully. Then read the last *We Believe* paragraph.

When we worship God together, we do different things. We ask God to be with us. We pray using words, songs, and actions. We listen to God's Word.

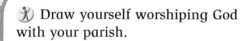

What are some ways you pray and thank God?

Stand and pray.

Alleluia. God, we praise you.
God, we thank you.
God, we love you. Amen.

👤 Draw yourself worshiping God with your parish.

187

ACTIVITY BANK

Multiple Intelligences
Verbal-Linguistic
Activity Materials: large sheet of poster board or chart paper

Help the children use the word *worship* to complete an acrostic activity. Write the letters of the word as shown below. Have them use the letters to write phrases or sentences about worshiping God.

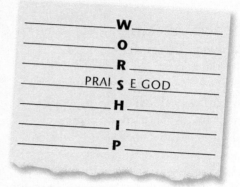

Scripture
Interpersonal, Spatial
For a Scripture activity, see *What's the Word?*, guide page 183F.

Talk About Worship Let the children talk about their favorite ways of worship. Prompt them to think of the special times when they have celebrated God's love—Easter, Christmas, weddings, Sunday Mass.

Quick Check

✔ *Why do we gather with our parish family to worship?* (We celebrate God's love.)

✔ *What is one important thing we do when we worship God?* (Possible responses: We thank God for sending his Son; we remember the things that Jesus did; we ask the Holy Spirit to help us.)

WE RESPOND _____ minutes

Connect to Life Read the *We Respond* question aloud. Ask volunteers to share their responses. Then read the *We Respond* activity directions. Give the children time to draw and share their drawings. As the children are working, play "We Celebrate with Joy," #18 on the Grade 1 CD.

Pray Read the prayer words. Have the children suggest an action for each sentence. Invite the children to gather in the prayer space. Then pray together the *We Respond* prayer.

Plan Ahead for Day 3

Catechist Goal: To emphasize that Jesus gave us the sacraments

Preparation: Make copies of Reproducible Master 16, guide page 183G.

187

Catechist Goal

• To emphasize that Jesus gave us the sacraments

Our Faith Response

• To recognize the sacraments as signs of God's love

 **sacrament**

Lesson Materials

• copies of Reproducible Master 16

Teaching Tip

Making Choices Activity

   The activity on Reproducible Master 16 involves children choosing what they can do to show people their love. There are no incorrect choices. Accept that some children may circle all the sentences. Some may circle a few. When the children have finished the circling activity, reread the sentences. Ask the children to think about which choice is the easiest for them to do. Then have them draw a heart beside their favorite way.

188

Jesus gave us the sacraments.

WE GATHER

✝ *Jesus, thank you for giving us signs of God's love.*

Think about the people you love. How can you show them your love?

WE BELIEVE

God loves us very much. He loves us so much he sent his Son to us. Jesus, the Son of God, shares God's life and love with us.

Jesus wants each of us to share in God's life. So he gave us seven special signs of God's life and love. The seven special signs Jesus gave us are called sacraments. A **sacrament** is a special sign given to us by Jesus.

We gather with our parish family to celebrate the sacraments. Jesus is with us each time we celebrate.

Lesson Plan

WE GATHER ___ minutes

✝ **Pray** Remind the children that Jesus gives us his love each and every day. Then invite them to pray with you the *We Gather* prayer of thanksgiving.

Focus on Life Invite the children to close their eyes and picture the people whom they love. Then have them open their eyes. Ask: *How can we show our love for these people?* Distribute copies of Reproducible Master 16. Read each of the sentences. Have the children circle each way that tells how they can show people their love. Encourage the children to take the activity sheet home to show their families.

WE BELIEVE ___ minutes

Learn About the Sacraments Read aloud the *We Believe* paragraphs. Emphasize the following points.

• *Jesus gave us special signs of God's life and love.*

• *We call these special signs of God's life and love the sacraments.*

• *We celebrate the sacraments with our parish family.*

• *Jesus is with us in a special way when we celebrate the sacraments.*

ACTIVITY BANK

Multiple Intelligences
Spatial
Activity Materials: modeling clay of various colors, ledger-size paper

Remind the children that Jesus gave us the sacraments as special signs of God's love for us. Give modeling clay of different colors and a ledger-sized sheet of paper to groups of three or four children. Let the children form the numeral 7 and the letters of the word *sacraments* in clay on the paper. Let the children share their clay creations with other groups.

WE RESPOND

Trace over the words in this prayer.

Jesus, thank you for the

_____

sacraments.

Thank you for the

_____

signs of God's life and love.

Key Word
sacrament a special sign given to us by Jesus

189

Quick Check

✔ *What is a sacrament?* (A sacrament is a sign of God's life and love.)

✔ *Who gave us the sacraments?* (Jesus gave us the sacraments.)

WE RESPOND ___ minutes

Connect to Life Read the directions for the *We Respond* activity. Ask the children to read the prayer together. Then let the children state how many sacraments there are (seven) and what the sacraments are signs of (God's life and love).

Pray Invite the children to pray the *We Respond* prayer.

Plan Ahead for Day 4

Catechist Goal: To describe each of the Seven Sacraments

Preparation: Have available the Grade 1 CD.

Catechist Goal

• To describe each of the Seven Sacraments

Our Faith Response

• To associate the name of each sacrament with a picture of the sacrament's celebration

Lesson Materials

• Grade 1 CD

The Church celebrates Seven Sacraments.

WE GATHER

✝ *Jesus, you are with us always.*

🎵 **Celebrate God**

Celebrate God with your hands.
Celebrate God with your voice.
Celebrate God in all that you do.
And God will be with you.

WE BELIEVE

The Church celebrates Seven Sacraments. We receive the sacraments at different times in our lives. But Jesus shares God's life with us in each of the sacraments. Each sacrament helps us to grow closer to God.

Look at the pictures. Each one shows a sacrament that is being celebrated.

190

Lesson Plan

WE GATHER

_____ minutes

✝ **Pray** Pray the Sign of the Cross and the *We Gather* prayer.

Focus on Life Tell the children that they have a lot to celebrate: *God gave us Jesus; Jesus gave us signs of God's love, the sacraments.* Play the song "Celebrate God," #19 on the Grade 1 CD. Ask the children to read the words. Then sing the song together.

WE BELIEVE

_____ minutes

Preview Read aloud the *We Believe* statement. Ask the children to recall what they know about the sacraments.

Learn More About the Sacraments Ask a volunteer to read aloud the first *We Believe* paragraph. Then talk about the photos; focus on one photo at a time, name the sacrament, and then read the appropriate description in the following list.

• *In Baptism we receive God's life and love and become members of the Church.*

• *In Confirmation God's life and love within us is made stronger.*

• *In the Eucharist we receive Jesus Christ himself.*

• *In Penance and Reconciliation we tell God we are sorry. We receive God's forgiveness.*

• *Anointing of the Sick is for people who are sick.*

• *In Holy Orders a man is made a priest or a deacon.*

• *In Matrimony a man and woman become husband and wife.*

Penance and Reconciliation

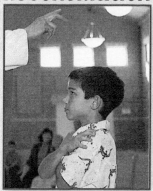

Anointing of the Sick

Matrimony

Holy Orders

WE RESPOND

Talk about what is happening in each picture on these pages. Do these pictures remind you of things you have seen in your parish?

As Catholics...

We use the gifts of God's creation during the celebration of the sacraments. For example, water and oils are used to bless us. Light from candles reminds us that Jesus is with us. Bread made from wheat and wine made from grapes are used, too.

With your family, thank God for all he has given us.

191

ACTIVITY BANK

Family and Parish
Talk About Celebrations

Have volunteers talk about sacrament celebrations in which they have participated. Ask the volunteers to describe what happened in church and how their families celebrated at home.

Quick Check

✔ *How many sacraments does the Church celebrate?* (The Church celebrates Seven Sacraments.)

✔ *Name one of the sacraments.* (Accept the name of any of the Seven Sacraments.)

WE RESPOND   ___ minutes

Connect to Life Direct attention once again to each photo. Read the name of the sacrament being celebrated. Have the children repeat it. Then discuss the *We Respond* question.

Pray Conclude by inviting the children to pray: *Jesus, thank you for giving us the sacraments.*

Plan Ahead for Day 5

Catechist Goal: To review chapter ideas and their relationship to our faith life

Preparation: Make copies of *Sharing Faith with My Family,* guide page 183E.

Catechist Goal

• To review the chapter ideas that are key to growing as disciples of Jesus Christ

Our Faith Response

• To decide on ways to grow as disciples by living out what we have learned

Show What *you* Know

Read the activity instructions. Model making the square around the *Key Word*. Invite the children to find the *Key Word* in their chapter.

Picture This

Read the activity instructions. Allow the children time to look at the photos. Refer them to pages 190–191 to review the sacrament names and photos.

Question Corner

Ask a volunteer to read the activity instructions. Explain that the children will be taking a survey. Model making a mark in the chart. Allow time for the children to walk around the room and ask several friends to answer the question. Ask volunteers to share their results. Remind the children that the most popular action would have received the most marks.

Fast Facts

Note that in the picture a parish is gathered for Mass. Ask a volunteer to read the fact. Remind the children that going to Mass is an important way to celebrate God's love.

Take Home

Ask the children to share some of their favorite songs from Mass. Share your favorite. Read the activity. Encourage the children to sing songs of praise with their families, at home and at Mass.

Discuss and send home copies of *Sharing Faith with My Family*, guide page 183E.

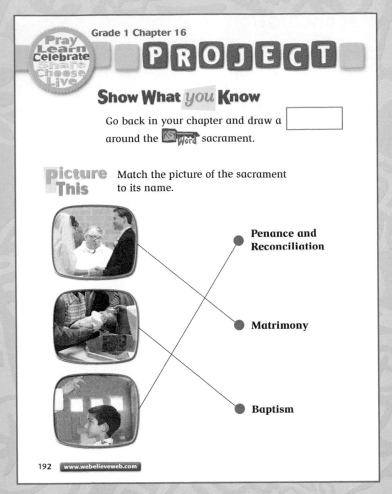

Pray Learn Celebrate Share Choose Live

Grade 1 Chapter 16

PROJECT

Show What *you* Know

Go back in your chapter and draw a [ ] around the [Key Word] sacrament.

Picture This

Match the picture of the sacrament to its name.

• **Penance and Reconciliation**

• **Matrimony**

• **Baptism**

DISCIPLE

Pray Learn Celebrate Share Choose Live

Question Corner

Show this chart to friends and family members. Ask each person, "Which is your favorite way to celebrate God's love?" Each time someone names one of the actions, put a mark in the space below it.

sing	pray	listen	gather

↳ **DISCIPLE CHALLENGE** Count up the marks in each box. Which action is the most popular?

Fast Facts

You can celebrate God's love at Mass every week.

Take Home

Some people use their talent to write songs of praise and thanks to God. We sing some of these songs when our parish family gathers to worship God. We sing these songs when we celebrate the sacraments. The next time you are at Mass, listen for these songs of praise and thanks to God. Join in the singing!

CHAPTER TEST

Circle the correct answer.

1. Jesus shares God's life with us in _____ of the sacraments.

   (each)   some

2. _____ gave us the sacraments.

   Peter   (Jesus)

3. The Church celebrates _____ Sacraments.

   (Seven)   Ten

4. _____ is a special word we use when we worship God.

   Hello   (Alleluia)

5. Jesus _____ gather with others to worship God.

   (did)   did not

What are some of the special words and actions we use to worship God? Possible responses: Alleluia; Amen; stand and pray

194

CHAPTER TEST

Read each test item aloud and allow time for the children to mark an answer. Decide whether the *Talk About It* activity will be a small group or whole class discussion. After you have finished, check the answers. Clarify any misconceptions.

Alternative Assessment

You may want the students to complete the following alternative-assessment activity.

Make a banner that shows how we celebrate God's love.

Additional Testing

• Chapter 16 Test in *Assessment Book*, pages 33–34

• CD-ROM *Test Generator and Resource*: Use Chapter 16 Test or customize your own.

Review

Review the definition as it is presented in the chapter's *Key Word* box:

• sacrament (page 189).

We Believe Statements

Review the four statements.

• Jesus celebrated God's love.

• We celebrate God's love.

• Jesus gave us the sacraments.

• The Church celebrates Seven Sacraments.

To use the Chapter 16 Study Guide, visit

www.webelieveweb.com

The Church Welcomes New Members

Overview

In Chapter 16 the children learned about the Seven Sacraments of the Catholic Church. In this chapter the children will learn about the Sacrament of Baptism.

Doctrinal Content	For Adult Reading and Reflection *Catechism of the Catholic Church*
The children will learn:	Paragraph
• The Church welcomes new members at Baptism.	1267
• At Baptism we receive God's life.	1265
• We say and do special things to celebrate Baptism.	1234
• In Baptism we are joined to Jesus and one another.	1271

Key Words

Baptism (p. 196)
grace (p. 199)

Catechist Background

How can being a part of a community of faith help you to live as a Christian?

Go to **www.webelieveweb.com**, Catechist/Teacher, We Believe Correlations for this chapter's correlation to:
• Six Tasks of Catechesis
• Catholic Social Teaching.

God created us out of love to live in relationship with him and others. Things did not, however, turn out as God planned. Through the story of Adam and Eve in Genesis, we learn that our ancestors chose by their own free will to disobey God, and thus sin entered the world. We believe that every person is born with and is affected by this sin that is called "Original Sin."

But the story does not end with sin. God loves us so much that he continues to call us back to that state of original grace. We are given the chance to live free from sin in the Sacrament of Baptism. Baptism washes away sin, restoring us as children of God. In Baptism we first receive grace, the gift of God's life within us. Baptism also initiates us into the faith community and the sacramental life of the Church, which aid us in living the life God intended for us.

The Rite of Baptism is rich with symbolic words and actions. The sign of the cross is traced on our foreheads to show to whom we now belong. We are immersed or water is poured on us three times, while being baptized "in the name of the Father, and of the Son, and of the Holy Spirit." We are anointed with oil. We receive a new white garment, clothing ourselves in Christ. We receive a white candle, the light of Christ, which is to be kept burning in our hearts and lives.

In Baptism, we die to sin and death to rise to new life in Christ. With the community at our side, we begin our journey to life everlasting.

Which symbol of Baptism means the most to you? Why?

Lesson Planning Guide

Lesson Focus	Presentation	Materials

Day 1

page 195
We Gather in Prayer

pages 196–197
The Church welcomes new members at Baptism.

- Pray a prayer to the Blessed Trinity.
- Respond to the **We Gather** question.
- Read the **We Believe** text about becoming members of the Church at Baptism.
- Discuss the **We Respond** question.
- 🎵 Sing a song about being a member of the Church.
- Read and discuss the *As Catholics* text.

See note about the prayer space on guide page 195

- copies of reproducible master *What's the Word?*, guide page 195F
- poster board
- highlighters or crayon
- 🎵 "We Are the Church," Christopher Walker, #20, Grade 1 CD

Day 2

pages 198–199
At Baptism we receive God's life.

- 🏃 Do the **We Gather** activity.
- Read and discuss the **We Believe** text about the gift of God's grace.
- Discuss responses in **We Respond**.
- Allow time for quiet reflective prayer.

- crayons or colored pencils

Day 3

pages 200–201
We say and do special things to celebrate Baptism.

Rite of Baptism

- Share responses to the **We Gather** questions.
- Present the **We Believe** text about the special things that happen during the celebration of Baptism.
- Share responses for **We Respond**.

- bowl of holy water

Day 4

pages 202–203
In Baptism we are joined to Jesus and one another.

- Review the beginning of the celebration of Baptism in **We Gather**.
- Present the **We Believe** text about the Sacrament of Baptism.
- Share responses for **We Respond**.
- 🏃 Decorate the candle.

- crayons or colored pencils
- copies of Reproducible Master 17, guide page 195G
- scissors, paste
- battery-operated candle

Day 5

pages 204–205
Project Disciple

page 206
Chapter 17 Test

- Complete the **Project Disciple** activities.
- Explain the *Take Home* activity.
- Discuss/send home **Sharing Faith with My Family**, guide page 195E.
- Complete **Chapter 17 Test**.
- Work on *Alternative Assessment* activity.

- pencils
- crayons or colored pencils
- copies of **Sharing Faith with My Family** reproducible master, guide page 195E

For additional ideas, activities, and opportunities: Visit Sadlier's **www.WE BELIEVE web.com**

195B

Enrichment Ideas

Chapter Story

One Saturday night Marissa's family was getting ready for church the next day. Marissa was in her room, but she could still hear the sound of her baby brother crying loudly. Her family had just adopted a baby boy. They named him Carlos. Marissa was not sure she liked having a baby brother because she thought everyone had forgotten about her.

Marissa's mom and dad came into her room. Marissa's mom gave her a gift box. When Marissa opened it, she saw a shirt that said, "I'm a big sister." Then her dad said, "Tomorrow is a special day. We're taking Carlos to church to be baptized. We know we haven't been able to spend a lot of time with you, Marissa. But when you were a baby, we gave you a lot of special attention. The day of your Baptism was a special day for the whole family. We want tomorrow to be a special one for Carlos."

The next morning when Marissa's family got to church, Father Messina met them outside. Marissa watched Father as he spoke and then looked at Carlos. But Carlos did not look at Father. The baby looked at Marissa and smiled. Marissa thought, "He is cute." She put her hand on his. She said, "Well, Baby Brother, welcome to the family. We're going to make this a very special day. And I'll be able to tell you all about what happened when you are as old as me."

▶ *Did Marissa do the right thing at church? Tell why or why not?*

FAITH and MEDIA

▶ On Day 3, if you show the children a video of an actual Baptism as suggested in the *Activity Bank*, remind the class that you are using one of the many media you have discussed during this school year—in this case, the medium of video—to help spread the Good News of Jesus.

▶ On this week's *Sharing Faith with My Family* page (Day 5) the children are asked to talk with family members about Baptism celebrations and to look at pictures and videos of these celebrations. Remind the children that using media to record important milestones in the faith life of individual families (and of the parish family) is a wonderful way to preserve our memories of these special events and to share the experiences with others.

CHAPTER PROJECT: MEMBERSHIP BADGES

Help the children make Church membership badges. Give each child a 6-inch by 4-inch sheet of yellow or white construction paper. Ask the children to draw blue wavy lines along the bottom of their papers. Explain that the lines stand for water. At the top of the paper have the children write their name in big letters. Following their name, have the children write: *is a member of the Church.* Help the children to punch two holes at the top of the paper. Cut a piece of yarn long enough for each child to wear as a neck chain. Thread the yarn through both holes. Tie the ends of yarn together. Allow the children to wear their badges during the week.

PROJECT DISCIPLE

Pray
Learn
Celebrate
Share
Choose
Live

Additional Activities

What's *the* Word?

(Use on Day 1.)

Materials needed: copies of reproducible master, guide page 195F

Distribute copies of the Scripture reproducible master. Explain that the children will listen to a story about the Apostle Philip. Explain that this is a story about a Baptism. Ask volunteers to read the parts of Philip and Readers 1–5. Invite the children to listen carefully as the story is read.

Picture This

Materials needed: drawing paper, crayons or colored pencils

Invite the children to complete a picture story of the Sacrament of Baptism. Provide guidelines for the important events that should be included but allow the children freedom to add details. They may choose to write a picture story of their own Baptism, a family member's Baptism, or the Baptism of a fictional character. Invite the children to share their picture stories with their classmates.

Make *it* Happen

Materials needed: writing paper, envelopes, pencils

Invite the children to write a letter to welcome a member of the Church who has just been baptized. Provide writing paper and pencils. Remind children that the recipient of their letters may either be a baby, a child, or an adult. Help the children to craft letters using what they have learned about the Sacrament of Baptism. When the children are finished, give the letters to a person in the parish who can distribute them to those who have just been baptized. Be sure the children do not include identifying or personal information.

Celebrate!

Invite the children to bring in photos of their own Baptisms or those of other children in their families if they are able and willing. Display the photos in the classroom on a "guess who" bulletin board. Affix the photos (with removable adhesive) to a folded sheet of paper so the children can peek under the photos to reveal the name of the person in the photo.

Meeting Individual Needs
Children with Auditory Needs

It is important to use many visual aids for the children with auditory needs. When playing a video of a Baptism celebration, stop the video after each part. Ask the children to look at you as you clearly enunciate the words of your explanation.

We Believe Resources

- Grade 1 *Review & Resource Book*, pages 40–42
- Grade 1 *Family Book*, pages 49–51
- Grade 1 *Assessment Book*, pages 35–36
- Grade 1 CD-ROM *Test Generator and Resource*: Use Chapter 17 Test or customize your own.
- **www.webelieveweb.com**

Sharing What I Learned

Look at the pictures below. Use each picture to tell your family what you learned in this chapter.

Remembering Baptism

Help your family remember what happens at Baptism.

Pour water into a glass bowl or clear container. Put the bowl on the table that you use for family meals. Remember together that water is an important sign of Baptism.

Before meals this week, ask family members to dip their fingers into the water. Then pray the Sign of the Cross.

Talk about your family's Baptism celebrations. Look at pictures and videos of these celebrations.

Visit Sadlier's

www.WeBelieveweb.com

Connect to the Catechism
For adult background and reflection, see paragraphs 1267, 1265, 1234, and 1271.

PROJECT DISCIPLE

Name _____

What's *the* Word?

Reader 1: The Apostles of Jesus went to different lands. They told people about Jesus. They baptized many people.

Reader 2: One day the Apostle Philip was walking. He saw a man riding in a chariot. The man was reading God's Word.

Philip: "Do you understand what you are reading?"
(Acts 8:30)

Reader 3: The man said he did not understand. He invited Philip to ride in the chariot. He wanted Philip to teach him.

Reader 4: The men rode on. They saw a body of water in front of them. The man wanted to be baptized.

Reader 5: Philip baptized the man. Then Philip went to other towns. He taught people about Jesus. He baptized many of the people he met.

Cut out the pictures. Complete each sentence. Paste or tape the correct picture in the box.

An important sign of Baptism is

[ ].

It is a sign of grace, God's life and love.

At Baptism a [ ] was placed on us. The priest prayed that we would live as a follower of Jesus.

A [ ] was given to our family. The priest prayed that we would always walk in the light of Christ.

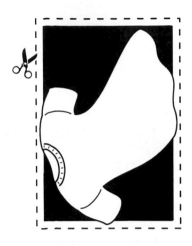
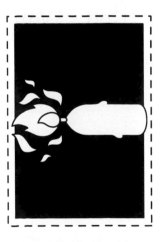

The Church Welcomes New Members

✝ **We Gather in Prayer**

Leader: God the Father,
All: We praise you.

Leader: Jesus, Son of God,
All: Show us how to live.

Leader: God the Holy Spirit,
All: Help us each day.

195

PREPARING TO PRAY

The children will pray to the Blessed Trinity.

• Have a container of holy water available. Show the children how to dip their finger tips into the holy water and then make the sign of the cross. Explain that each child will do this during the prayer.

• Make a large "Welcome" poster. Explain that the Church welcomes us at Baptism. Ask two volunteers to hold the sign during the prayer.

The Prayer Space

• Place a white tablecloth on the prayer table. Place on the table the following: a clear container of holy water, to represent new life with God; a white handkerchief for a white garment which represents that we are to live as followers of Jesus; a battery-operated candle or an unlit candle to represent Jesus, the Light of the World.

📖 **This Week's Liturgy**

Visit **www.webelieveweb.com** for this week's liturgical readings and other seasonal material.

Lesson Plan

We Gather in Prayer ___ minutes

✝ Pray

• Ask the children to name the Three Persons of the Blessed Trinity.

• Ask the children to open their books to page 195. Have them look at the illustration on the page. Explain that water is a sign of life. Invite the children to gather in the prayer space.

• Remind the children that the Sign of the Cross is a prayer to the Blessed Trinity. Ask the children to take turns dipping their finger tips in the holy water and then making the Sign of the Cross.

• Lead the children in prayer.

Family Connection Update

Invite the children to share their experiences of singing with their families at Mass.

Catechist Goal

• To present that the Church welcomes new members at Baptism

Our Faith Response

• To recognize the importance of Baptism

 **Baptism**

Lesson Materials

• highlighters or crayons
• Grade 1 CD
• copies of reproducible master *What's the Word?*, guide page 195F

As Catholics...

When We Celebrate Baptism

After you have presented the lesson, read the *As Catholics* paragraph. Ask the children to share how old they were when they were baptized. Ask if they know someone who was baptized when he or she was an older child or an adult.

The Church welcomes new members at Baptism.

WE GATHER

✝ *God, we are your children.*

Look at the picture of the Stanik family. What do you think Father Marcos is saying to them?

WE BELIEVE

Father Marcos and the whole parish are welcoming the Stanik family. They are bringing their baby to celebrate the Sacrament of Baptism. The baby's name is Leo.

In Baptism, Leo will become a child of God. He will become a member of the Church.

Baptism is the sacrament in which we become children of God and members of the Church. Baptism is the first sacrament we receive.

 Baptism the sacrament in which we become children of God and members of the Church

196

Lesson Plan

WE GATHER ___ minutes

✝ **Pray** Remind the children that we are children of God and followers of Jesus. Then pray together the Sign of the Cross and the *We Gather* prayer.

Focus on Life Have the children look at the picture on pages 196 and 197. Ask them what they think the priest might be saying to the Stanik family. Help the children conclude that Father is welcoming the family. Invite volunteers to act out the situation. Then share the *Chapter Story* on guide page 195C. Tell the children that in this lesson they will learn that at Baptism we become children of God and members of the Church.

WE BELIEVE ___ minutes

Learn About the Church's Welcome Review what the sacraments are. On the board write the words *Baptism* and *baptized*. Explain: *Baptism is the name of the sacrament. When we receive the sacrament, we say that we are baptized.*

Read aloud the *We Believe* paragraphs. Emphasize the following points:

• *In Baptism, we become children of God and members of the Church.*
• *Baptism is the first sacrament we receive.*
• *We celebrate Baptism with our parish family.*

Have the children highlight or underline the third *We Believe* paragraph.

When we were baptized, we became children of God. We became members of the Church, too. We celebrated Baptism with our parish family. They welcomed us into the Catholic Church.

As Catholics...

We receive the Sacrament of Baptism once. Some people are baptized when they are babies. Others are baptized when they are older. Older children, teenagers, or adults are usually baptized at a celebration on the night before Easter Sunday.

How old were you when you were baptized?

WE RESPOND

Why do you think Baptism is so important?

🎵 **We Are the Church**

We are the Church,
happy to be
the children in God's family.
(Repeat)

197

ACTIVITY BANK

Parish
Welcome Cards
Activity Materials: drawing paper, list of names of children to be baptized, crayons or colored pencils

Inquire in your parish office for the names of the families who are scheduled to have a child baptized in the upcoming weeks. Have the children make a welcome card for each child. You might want to write a special welcoming message as a class. Record the children's ideas on chart paper. Then have the children copy the message in their cards. Invite them to decorate the front of the cards. Deliver these cards to the parish office for distribution at the Baptism celebrations.

Scripture
Interpersonal, Linguistic
For a Scripture activity, see *What's the Word?*, guide page 195E.

Quick Check

✔ *What is Baptism?* (Baptism is the sacrament in which we become children of God and members of the Church.)

✔ *With whom do we celebrate the Sacrament of Baptism?* (We celebrate Baptism with our parish family.)

WE RESPOND ____ minutes

Connect to Life Encourage the children to think about what they have learned in the lesson. Then read aloud the *We Respond* question. Invite volunteers to share their responses. Help all to understand that Baptism is important because in this sacrament we

become children of God and members of the Church. Ask volunteers to share why they are happy to be children in God's family. Play the song "We Are the Church," #20 on the Grade 1 CD. Have the children read the words together and then practice singing.

Pray Lead the children as you sing together "We Are the Church."

Plan Ahead for Day 2

Catechist Goal: To highlight that we receive God's life at Baptism

Preparation: Arrange a time for the priest to talk to the children and show them the baptismal pool or font in the parish church.

Catechist Goal

• To highlight that we receive God's life at Baptism

Our Faith Response

• To express thanks to God for his gift of grace

 **grace**

Lesson Materials

• crayons or colored pencils

Teaching Note

The We Believe *Program*

The purpose of this chapter is to introduce the children to the Sacrament of Baptism. These concepts are more fully developed in Chapter 4 of the Grade 2 *We Believe* text. It is recommended that you keep to the simple explanations of grace and the celebration of the sacrament presented in the first grade text.

At Baptism we receive God's life.

WE GATHER

✝ *God, we want to grow in your love.*

🧑 Look at the picture. What does the plant need so it can grow? Add to the picture what the plant needs.

Why is water important?

WE BELIEVE

Water is an important sign of Baptism. During the sacrament we are placed in water, or water is poured on us.

This happens in a special place in our parish church. This place is called the baptismal pool or font.

198

Lesson Plan

WE GATHER ___ minutes

✝ **Pray** Explain to the children that they will pray the *We Gather* prayer on page 198 as a choir. Assign the children to three groups. Invite one group to pray the prayer aloud. Then ask the second group to join in the prayer. Finally invite all the groups to pray the words together.

Focus on Life Have the children look at the picture of the plant. Invite them to complete the picture by drawing what the plant needs to grow. Ask volunteers to share their finished pictures with the entire group. Help the children understand that plants need water and light to grow. Ask: *Why is water so important to plants, animals, and people?* Tell the children that in this lesson they will learn that water is an important sign at Baptism.

WE BELIEVE ___ minutes

Learn About a Sign of Baptism Invite a volunteer to read aloud the *We Believe* statement. Draw wavy lines on the board to represent waves of water. On the waves print *Baptism*. Then direct attention to the picture of the baptismal pool. Tell the children that the priest blesses the water in the pool during the celebration of the sacrament. (If possible, take the children to see the church's baptismal pool or font.)

Learn About Grace Read aloud the *We Believe* paragraphs. Explain: *At Baptism God gives us a share in his life.* Print the word *grace* on the wave you have drawn on the board.

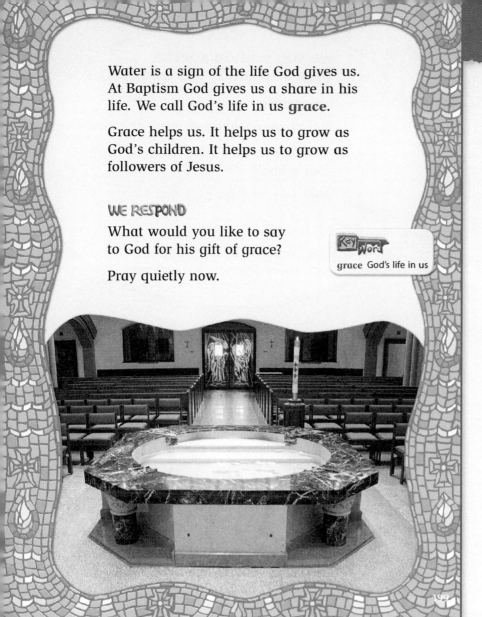

Water is a sign of the life God gives us. At Baptism God gives us a share in his life. We call God's life in us **grace**.

Grace helps us. It helps us to grow as God's children. It helps us to grow as followers of Jesus.

WE RESPOND

What would you like to say to God for his gift of grace?

Pray quietly now.

Key Word

grace God's life in us

ACTIVITY BANK

Multiple Intelligences

Intrapersonal and Interpersonal
Activity Materials: a large tub of water, rectangular-shaped sponges (one for each child)

Fill a large tub or bin with water. Put the tub in the prayer space. Give each child a sponge. Help him or her cut out the first letter of his or her first name. When the children are finished, invite them to gather around the container of water with their sponge letters. Tell the children that their sponge letters stand for them. Remind the group: *Water is the sign of grace, God's life in us.* Have the children place their sponge letters in the water. Pray together: *Jesus, help us grow as God's children. Help us to grow as your followers.* During the week keep the container of water with the sponges in the prayer space. On Day 5 dry the sponge letters and give them to the children to take home.

Explain: *Water helps our bodies to grow. Grace, God's life in us, helps us to grow as God's children. It also helps us to grow as followers of Jesus.*

Sing a Song About Grace Explain: *Grace helps us to live the way God wants us to live.* Invite the children to celebrate the gift of grace by singing a song to the tune of "Mary Had a Little Lamb."

Grace is G—od's life in us,
life in us, life in us.
Grace is G—od's life in us.
We are children of God.

Quick Check

✔ *What is grace?* (Grace is God's life in us.)

✔ *What is an important sign of Baptism?* (Water is an important sign of Baptism.)

WE RESPOND   ___ minutes

Connect to Life Read the *We Respond* question. Offer your own response to the question.

Pray Ask the children to pray to God silently.

Plan Ahead for Day 3

Catechist Goal: To teach what is said and done during the celebration of Baptism

Preparation: Prepare to explain the steps of the celebration of Baptism.

Chapter 17 • Day 3

Catechist Goal

- To teach what is said and done during the celebration of Baptism

Our Faith Response

- To reflect on our own Baptism

Lesson Materials

- a bowl of water (holy water if possible)

Teaching Note

Role of Godparents

In today's lesson the children will be learning about the celebration of Baptism. When they talk about their own celebrations of Baptism, they may mention their godparents. Use this opportunity to explain the role of godparents. Explain: *The Church asks godparents to help us live as followers of Jesus.* Encourage the children to talk to their parents about the role of their godparents. Elicit from the children some ways in which their godparents help them. In the closing prayer you may wish to thank God for the gift of godparents.

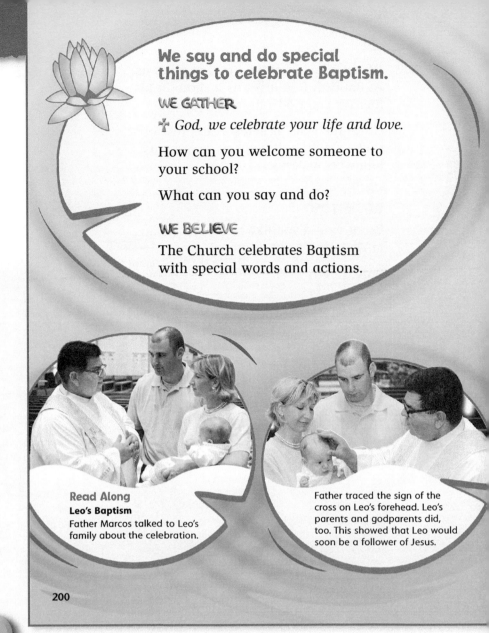

We say and do special things to celebrate Baptism.

WE GATHER

✝ *God, we celebrate your life and love.*

How can you welcome someone to your school?

What can you say and do?

WE BELIEVE

The Church celebrates Baptism with special words and actions.

Read Along
Leo's Baptism
Father Marcos talked to Leo's family about the celebration.

Father traced the sign of the cross on Leo's forehead. Leo's parents and godparents did, too. This showed that Leo would soon be a follower of Jesus.

200

Lesson Plan

WE GATHER

___ minutes

✝ **Pray** Pray together the Sign of the Cross and the *We Gather* prayer.

Focus on Life Read aloud the *We Gather* questions. Invite the children to act out ways of welcoming others. Help the children to conclude that we use words and actions to welcome people. Tell the children that in this lesson they will learn about the celebration of Baptism.

WE BELIEVE

___ minutes

Learn About the Celebration Read aloud the *We Believe* statement. Explain: *The Church uses special words and actions to celebrate the Sacrament of Baptism.* Invite the children to look at the pictures as you read the text and captions. Stress: *We are all baptized with special words and actions.*

Explain that in some churches the baby is placed in the baptismal pool. In other churches (one with baptismal fonts) water is poured on the baby's head.

Act Out the Celebration Ask volunteers to be the Stanik family and members of the parish. Use a doll as the baby. Trace the sign of the cross on the doll's forehead. Say the words of Baptism as you pour water on the doll's forehead.

Look at the Pictures Review the pictures as you encourage discussion about each one.

- For the picture on the far left, ask: *What do you think Father Marcos is saying to Leo's family?*

Father placed Leo in the water of the baptismal pool three times. He said the words of Baptism:

Leo, I baptize you in the name
of the Father,
and of the Son,
and of the Holy Spirit.

Each of us was baptized with water and these words, too.

WE RESPOND

What would you like to ask your family about the celebration of your Baptism?

ACTIVITY BANK

Faith and Media
View a Baptism Celebration
Activity Materials: video of a celebration of the Sacrament of Baptism

After presenting the lesson, watch a video of a celebration of the Sacrament of Baptism. Pause at certain points of the video to help the children relate what is happening to what they learned in the text. If the video shows people's faces, ask the children to talk about the feelings of the Church members as they participate in the Baptism.

• For the picture on the right on page 200, ask: *Why did Father Marcos and Leo's parents and godparents trace the sign of the cross on Leo's forehead?*

Quick Check

✔ *How does the Church celebrate Baptism?* (The Church celebrates Baptism with special words and actions.)

✔ *What happened after Father Marcos placed Leo in the water?* (He baptized him in the name of the Father, and of the Son, and of the Holy Spirit.)

WE RESPOND ___ minutes

Connect to Life Read the *We Respond* question. Invite volunteers to share questions about Baptism that they would like to ask their families. Write each question on the board or on chart paper. Encourage the children to ask their families some of these questions.

Pray Place a bowl of water (holy water if possible) on the prayer table. Invite the children to gather at the prayer table. Have them take turns dipping the fingers of their right hands into the water and praying the Sign of the Cross. Then lead the children in a prayer. For example, you might pray: *God, thank you for welcoming us as your children at Baptism.*

Plan Ahead for Day 4

Catechist Goal: To explain that at Baptism we are joined to Jesus and one another

Preparation: Make copies of Reproducible Master 17, guide page 195G.

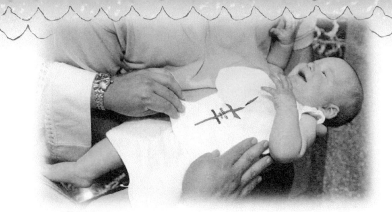

Catechist Goal

• To explain that at Baptism we are joined to Jesus and one another

Our Faith Response

• To help one another live as baptized followers of Jesus

Lesson Materials

• copies of Reproducible Master 17

• crayons, scissors, paste

• battery-operated candle

Teaching Tip

Cooperative Groups

In today's lesson the children will work in cooperative groups to complete an activity. When assigning children to their groups, consider that the students in each group have a range of ability levels and learning styles. Before beginning the activity, clearly explain your expectations that the children should be considerate of one another and follow classroom rules. As they work, monitor their progress.

In Baptism we are joined to Jesus and one another.

WE GATHER

✝ *In the name of the Father, and of the Son, and of the Holy Spirit. Amen.*

Talk about what happened at the beginning of Leo's Baptism.

WE BELIEVE

These words and actions were also a part of Leo's Baptism.

Read Along

A white garment was put on Leo. Father prayed that Leo would always live as a follower of Jesus.

A candle was given to Leo's family. Someone from the family lit the candle. Father prayed that Leo would always walk in the light of Christ.

Everyone prayed the Lord's Prayer.

202

Lesson Plan

WE GATHER

_____ minutes

✝ **Pray** Invite the children to begin the lesson by entering into prayer. Pray together the Sign of the Cross and the *We Gather* prayer.

Focus on Life Encourage discussion about the beginning of the celebration of Leo's Baptism. If necessary, review the text and photos of Day 3's lesson. Tell the children that in this lesson they will learn more about the words and actions with which we celebrate Baptism.

WE BELIEVE

_____ minutes

Look at the Pictures Ask the children to look at each picture on these pages as you read the text.

Invite them to talk about the pictures by asking them the following questions:

• *What did Father Marcos pray as he placed a white garment on Leo?* (He prayed that Leo would live as a follower of Jesus.)

• *What did Father pray as someone lit the candle?* (He prayed that Leo would always walk in the light of Christ.)

• *What prayer did everyone pray together?* (Everyone prayed the Lord's Prayer.)

Work in Groups Distribute copies of Reproducible Master 17. Organize the class into groups of three or four children. Give each group scissors and paste or tape. Encourage the children in each group to help one another complete the activity on the sheet. Read the

These same words and actions were part of the celebration of our Baptism.

As baptized members of the Church, we help one another to follow Jesus. We share in God's life together. We share our beliefs.

WE RESPOND

What will you do to live as a follower of Jesus?

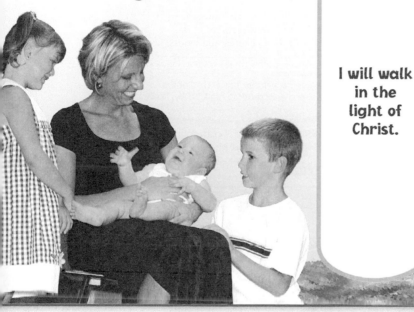 Decorate this candle.

I will walk in the light of Christ.

ACTIVITY BANK

Catholic Social Teaching

Call to Family, Community, and Participation

In class remind the children that our godparents help us to live as followers of Jesus. Send a note home to the parents and ask them to allow the children to call or send an e-mail message to their godparents. Encourage the children to tell their godparents what they are learning about the Blessed Trinity, the Church, and the Church's celebration of the sacraments. Have the children act out their phone conversations or write some things they could include in their e-mail messages.

---

directions and the activity sentences. When the groups have finished, share the correct answers with them. (1. water; 2. white garment; 3. candle)

Quick Check

✔ *What do baptized members of the Church help each other do?* (We help each other to be followers of Jesus.)

✔ *What do baptized members of the Church share?* (We share in God's life together, and we share beliefs.)

WE RESPOND ___ minutes

Connect to Life Read aloud the *We Respond* question. Have volunteers share their responses. List the

responses on the board or on chart paper. Then read the words *I will walk in the light of Christ.* Provide time for the children to decorate the candle.

Pray Invite the children to gather at the prayer table. Turn on a battery-operated candle you have placed there. Lead the children in the following prayer: *Jesus, we are your followers. We want to walk in your light always. Amen.*

Plan Ahead for Day 5

Catechist Goal: To review chapter ideas and their relationship to our faith life

Preparation: Make copies of *Sharing Faith with My Family,* guide page 195E.

Catechist Goal

• To review the chapter ideas that are key to growing as disciples of Jesus Christ

Our Faith Response

• To decide on ways to grow as disciples by living out what we have learned

Show What *you* Know

Complete the activity together. Project or recreate the puzzle on the board. Begin by asking the children the clue for 1 across: *What is God's life in us?* Model writing *grace* in the 1 across space in the puzzle. Repeat for *Baptism*.

Celebrate!

Encourage the children to remember what they have learned about Baptism. Complete a graphic organizer to help the children focus their ideas. Allow them to decorate the banner in the activity with words and pictures. Read the Disciple Challenge. Encourage the children to ask family members about their Baptisms.

Picture This

Help the children to sequence the photos from Leo's Baptism. Note that the 1 beside the picture means it happened first. Help them label the other pictures 2, 3, and 4. If the children need to review what happened at Leo's Baptism, refer them to pages 200–202 of their texts.

Take Home

Read the activity. Point out the picture to the left and talk about containers for holy water. Challenge the children to tell their families about holy water and to find it in their parish churches.

Discuss and send home copies of *Sharing Faith with My Family*, guide page 195E.

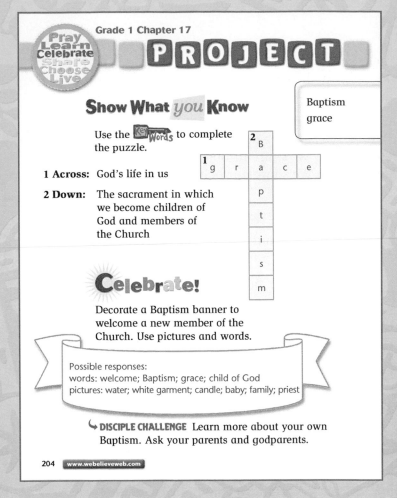

Grade 1 Chapter 17

PROJECT

Show What *you* Know

Use the Key Words to complete the puzzle.

Baptism
grace

1 Across: God's life in us

2 Down: The sacrament in which we become children of God and members of the Church

```
            2
            B
  1
  g  r  a  c  e
            p
            t
            i
            s
            m
```

Celebrate!

Decorate a Baptism banner to welcome a new member of the Church. Use pictures and words.

Possible responses:
words: welcome; Baptism; grace; child of God
pictures: water; white garment; candle; baby; family; priest

↳ **DISCIPLE CHALLENGE** Learn more about your own Baptism. Ask your parents and godparents.

204   www.webelieveweb.com

DISCIPLE

Picture This

Number the pictures of Leo's Baptism to put them in order.

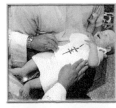 3
 2
 1
 4

Take Home

Holy water is water that has been blessed by a priest. The priest traces a cross over the water with his hand. He says a special prayer. Holy water is kept in a special container in church. With your family, find the holy water in your parish church.

205

CHAPTER TEST

Chapter 17 • Day 5

Circle the correct answer.

1. Is Baptism the third sacrament we receive?

   Yes   (**No**)

2. Is water an important sign of Baptism?

   (**Yes**)   **No**

3. Do we become members of the Church in Baptism?

   (**Yes**)   **No**

4. Is grace God's life in us?

   (**Yes**)   **No**

5. Does the Church celebrate Baptism with special words and actions?

   (**Yes**)   **No**

Why are we given a white garment and a candle at Baptism? So that we will always live as followers of Jesus and always walk in the light of Christ

206

CHAPTER TEST

Read each test item aloud and allow time for the children to mark an answer. Decide whether the *Talk About It* activity will be a small group or whole class discussion. After you have finished, check the answers. Clarify any misconceptions.

Alternative Assessment

You may want the students to complete the following alternative-assessment activity.

> *Make a card for someone who is going to be baptized. Tell why Baptism is a happy celebration.*

Additional Testing

• Chapter 17 Test in *Assessment Book*, pages 35–36

• CD-ROM *Test Generator and Resource*: Use Chapter 17 Test or customize your own.

Review

Review the definitions as they are presented in the chapter's *Key Word* boxes:

• Baptism (page 196)

• grace (page 199).

We Believe Statements

Review the four statements.

• The Church welcomes new members at Baptism.

• At Baptism we receive God's life.

• We say and do special things to celebrate Baptism.

• In Baptism we are joined to Jesus and one another.

To use the Chapter 17 Study Guide, visit

www.webelieveweb.com

Overview

In Chapter 17 the children learned that the Church welcomes new members in Baptism. In this chapter they will learn ways members of the Church follow Jesus and share the light of his love.

Doctrinal Content	For Adult Reading and Reflection *Catechism of the Catholic Church*
The children will learn:	Paragraph
• Jesus is the Light of the World.	748
• We receive the light of Christ.	1216
• Jesus asks us to share his peace.	2304
• We can make choices as children of God.	1730

peacemaker (p. 213)

Catechist Background

What parts of your life are hidden in darkness?

Go to **www.webelieveweb.com**, Catechist/Teacher, We Believe Correlations for this chapter's correlation to:
- Six Tasks of Catechesis
- Catholic Social Teaching
- *Catechetical Formation in Chaste Living.*

The Son of God came into the world to free us from sin and to show us what God's love is like. Through Jesus' words and actions, we see God's love at work. In the Gospel of John, Jesus tells his followers, "I am the light of the world. Whoever follows me will not walk in darkness, but will have the light of life" (John 8:12).

At our Baptism we received a candle lit from the Paschal candle, which symbolized the light of Christ. We were told to keep this light burning and to walk always as children of the light. We receive the light of Christ both as a gift of light in our own life and as a symbol of who we are to become. As followers of Christ, our words and actions are meant to give witness to the one light of the world, Jesus Christ.

One important way we become light for the world is as peacemakers. In a world torn by violence, hatred, and despair, we try to live in peace and justice. Each week in our celebration of the Eucharist, we offer a powerful prayer to our neighbors when we turn and say, "Peace be with you." And each week we face choices to either love and bring peace, or to ignore and tear down. The grace of Baptism and the other sacraments gives us the strength to choose love and peace. We become light for the world when all that we do brings wisdom and warmth to those around us.

"You are the light of the world. . . . Just so, your light must shine before others, that they may see your good deeds and glorify your heavenly Father." (Matthew 5:14, 16)

How have you been light to your family, your friends, and the children you teach?

Lesson Planning Guide

Lesson Focus	Presentation	Materials

Day 1

page 207
✝ **We Gather in Prayer**

pages 208–209
Jesus is the Light of the World.

📖 *John 8:12*

- Read the Scripture passage.
- 🎵 Respond to the reading in song.
- Share responses for **We Gather**.
- Read the Scripture in **We Believe** about Jesus, the Light of the World.
- Discuss the **We Respond** question.
- 🏃 Draw Jesus, the Light of the World.

For the prayer space: pictures of light sources, a picture or statue of Jesus, two flashlights, and yellow or orange tablecloth

🎵 "Walk in the Light," Carey Landry, #21, Grade 1 CD
- crayons or colored pencils

Day 2

pages 210–211
We receive the light of Christ.

- Discuss the **We Gather** questions.
- Read the **We Believe** text about ways to show others the light of Christ.
- Discuss the **We Respond** question.
- 🎵 Sing a song to respond.

🎵 "Walk in the Light," Carey Landry, #22, Grade 1 CD
- a few flashlights

Day 3

pages 212–213
Jesus asks us to share his peace.

📖 *Matthew 5:1, 9*

- Share responses for **We Gather**.
- Discuss the **We Believe** text about ways we can share Jesus' peace.
- Read the Scripture story.
- Share responses for **We Respond**.
- 🏃 Role-play being peacemakers.
- Read and discuss the *As Catholics* text.

- copies of reproducible master *What's the Word?*, guide page 207F

Day 4

pages 214–215
We can make choices as children of God.

- Share responses for **We Gather**.
- Present the **We Believe** text about making choices.
- 🏃 Do the picture-story activity.
- Discuss the **We Respond** questions.
- Pray to the Holy Spirit for help.

- copies of Reproducible Master 18, guide page 207G
- crayons or colored pencils

Day 5

pages 216–217
Project Disciple

page 218
Chapter 18 Test

- Complete the **Project Disciple** activities.
- Explain the *Take Home* activity.
- Discuss/send home **Sharing Faith with My Family**, guide page 207E.
- Complete **Chapter 18 Test**.
- Work on *Alternative Assessment* activity.

- pencils
- copies of **Sharing Faith with My Family** reproducible master, guide page 207E

For additional ideas, activities, and opportunities: Visit Sadlier's  www.WeBelieveweb.com

Chapter Story

One night Sean was sitting outside waiting for his grandparents. They were going to take a walk on the beach. Sean's grandparents had just moved to a seacoast town in the South. Sean was visiting them for the first time. That afternoon the sun was shining brightly. Sean had enjoyed playing by the water.

Sean jumped up when his grandmother came outside. She told him, "Grandpop is going to rest. You tired him out today. So you and I will just walk a little way."

Sean said, "Look, Grandmom. The moon is full. It's making a path on the water."

Sean and his grandmother walked a little farther on the beach. Sean saw a tower. "What's that building, Grandmom?" he asked.

Sean's grandmother answered, "That's a lighthouse. Long ago light would shine from the tower. The light guided the fishing boats at night. That helped them not to crash into the rocks."

"How did the light shine?" Sean asked.

"I'm not sure but we can take a tour tomorrow. We can climb up almost to the top. Would you like to do that?" Grandmom asked.

▶ *What do you think Sean answered?*

FAITH and MEDIA

▶ On Day 1, after the children have drawn their pictures showing Jesus as the Light of the World (*We Respond* activity), you might go online to show them William Holman Hunt's famous painting "The Light of the World." The children might be interested to learn that in the year 1905, in a time before the invention of television, the Internet, or most of the media we take for granted today, this painting was sent from England on ships and trains on a tour around the world. Many hundreds of people in places as far away from England as Canada, Australia, and New Zealand traveled miles to see it. Today we can see the same painting instantly on the Internet and can also post our own pictures of Jesus as the Light of the World on the Internet for millions of people to see, all at the same time and within seconds of the pictures being posted.

CHAPTER PROJECT: A CLASS CANDLE

Make a large candle by rolling a large sheet of poster board into a cylinder. Tape or staple both ends together securely. Glue a large sheet of yellow tissue paper along the inside rim of the candle to make a flame. Stand the candle in the prayer space.

Throughout the week, have the children find pictures in magazines and newspapers of people spreading the light of Christ. Tape or paste the pictures to the candle.

PROJECT DISCIPLE

Pray
Learn
Celebrate
Share
Choose
Live

Additional Activities

What's *the* Word?

(Use on Day 3.)

Materials needed: copies of reproducible master, guide page 207F

Distribute copies of the Scripture reproducible master. Explain that the children will listen to a story about the forgiveness. Ask volunteers to read the parts of Peter, Jesus, and Reader. Invite the children to listen carefully as the story is read.

Picture This

Materials needed: poster board with image of Jesus in the center, magazines, drawing paper, colored pencils or crayons, glue, scissors

Prepare a poster board by affixing an image of Jesus to the center. Distribute magazines and drawing paper and allow time for the children to look through the magazines for or draw an image of something that gives us light. Allow the children to cut out the images or drawings and affix them onto the poster. Talk about all the images the children have found and affixed. Display the poster in the classroom.

Make *it* Happen

Materials needed: outdoor play space, ball

Bring the children to an outdoor play area where there is plenty of room for movement. Bring a soft gym ball. Invite the children to gather around. The game rules are a variation on the popular children's game "spud." One child begins by throwing the ball into the air and calling out: *[Child's name] is a follower of Jesus!* The child whose name has been called catches or retrieves the ball. Once the ball is in-hand, the child calls out for all the children to freeze. The child makes five steps in one direction, each step spelling out a letter of Jesus' name. The child may then lightly throw the ball towards another child. If tagged by the ball, then it is this child's turn to throw the ball into the air and call Jesus' next "follower." Repeat until all the children have had a turn or time allows.

More *to* Explore

As the children learn more about making choices, be sure to provide choices in the classroom. When you do so, discuss the options. Remind the children that this is a situation in which they are able to make a choice.

Meeting Individual Needs
Children with Visual Needs

Whenever you put something in writing for your class, you can help your visually challenged children to understand by providing audio helps. To do so, read aloud what you have written, and then have the children read it with you. You can also provide the children descriptions of any graphic displays you use, such as charts, bulletin boards, or graphic organizers.

We Believe Resources

- Grade 1 *Review & Resource Book*, pages 43–45
- Grade 1 *Family Book*, pages 52–54
- Grade 1 *Assessment Book*, pages 37–38
- Grade 1 CD-ROM *Test Generator and Resource*: Use Chapter 18 Test or customize your own.
- **www.webelieveweb.com**

SHARING FAITH
with My Family

Sharing What I Learned
Look at the pictures below. Use each picture to tell your family what you learned in this chapter.

Sharing Jesus' Gifts

Look at the candle. Color a section of the candle beside each thing your family can do to share Jesus' gifts of peace and light. Write your own ideas for other things you can do.

Pray together. Jesus, help us to share your light.

- Share what we have with others.
- Care about the way others feel.
- Say and do kind things.
- Try to get along with everyone.
- _____
- _____

Visit Sadlier's
www.WeBelieveweb.com

Connect to the Catechism
For adult background and reflection, see paragraphs 748, 1216, 2304, and 1730.

PROJECT DISCIPLE

Pray
Learn
Celebrate
Share
Choose
Live

Name _____

What's *the* Word?

Reader: One day Jesus was teaching. Peter asked him a question.

Peter: "Lord, if my brother sins against me, how often must I forgive him? As many as seven times?"
(Matthew 18:21)

Jesus: "I say to you, not seven times but seventy-seven times." (Matthew 18:22)

Reader: Jesus was telling Peter that he always wants us to forgive others. Jesus wants us to forgive others and to share God's peace with them.

Name _____

Look at each picture story. Circle the picture
that shows the child making a loving choice.

✞ We Gather in Prayer

Leader: Let us listen to the Word of God.

📖 John 8:12

Read Along

One day Jesus was talking to a crowd. He said to them, "I am the light of the world. Whoever follows me will not walk in darkness, but will have the light of life."

🎵 Walk in the Light

Jesus is the Light for all:
Walk, walk in the light!
We follow him as we hear
  his call.
Walk, walk in the light!

Walk, walk in the light!
(Sing 3 times.)

Walk in the light
  of the Lord!

207

PREPARING TO PRAY

The children will listen to a Scripture story and respond by singing.

• Read the words of the song "Walk in the Light." Have children repeat each line. Then play the song, #21 on the Grade 1 CD. Have the children practice singing.

• Give two children flashlights. Explain that during the prayer they are to shine the light on the picture or statue of Jesus on the prayer table.

The Prayer Space

• Display pictures of different natural and manufactured sources of light, especially a lighthouse.

• On the prayer table drape a yellow or orange tablecloth.

• Place a picture or statue of Jesus on the table.

📖 **This Week's Liturgy**
Visit **www.webelieveweb.com** for this week's liturgical readings and other seasonal material.

Lesson Plan

We Gather in Prayer ___ minutes

✞ Pray

• Invite the children to gather in the prayer space with the words, *We gather in prayer.*

• Make the Sign of the Cross together. And then read aloud the Scripture reading.

• Pause briefly. Then ask the children who are holding the flashlights to shine the lights on the picture or statue of Jesus.

• Have the children sing "Walk in the Light."

Family Connection Update

Invite the children to share their experiences of finding holy water in their parish churches.

Catechist Goal

• To explain that Jesus called himself the Light of the World

Our Faith Response

• To recognize that Jesus is the Light of the World

Lesson Materials

• crayons or colored pencils

Teaching Tip

Using a Timer

Using a kitchen timer can help your children stay focused when working independently or in groups. Explain that you will set the timer for a specific amount of time, such as ten minutes. When the timer rings, the activity is over. If the children are not finished their work, assure them that they can complete the work at a later time in class or at home. Consider using a timer for today's *We Respond* activities.

Jesus is the Light of the World.

WE GATHER

✝ *Jesus, we want to follow you.*

Think about things that give light.
How does the light of the sun help us?
How does a flashlight help us?
How do the lights in our homes help us?

WE BELIEVE

📖 John 8:12

Read Along

One day Jesus was talking to a crowd. He said to them, "I am the light of the world. Whoever follows me will not walk in darkness, but will have the light of life." (John 8:12)

We believe that Jesus is the Light of the World. He helps us to see what God's love is like. He shares God's life with us.

Jesus wants us to follow him. If we follow him, we will have life with God.

208

Lesson Plan

WE GATHER ___ minutes

✝ **Pray** Ask the children to close their eyes and think about Jesus. Then pray together the Sign of the Cross and the *We Gather* prayer.

Focus on Life Read the *We Gather* questions. Pause after each question to let the children respond. (They may say that the sun gives us light and makes us warm; a flashlight helps us find our way in the dark; lights in our homes help us see or read.) If you have time, share the *Chapter Story* on guide page 207C. Tell the children that in this lesson they will learn that Jesus is the Light of the World.

WE BELIEVE ___ minutes

Jesus Our Light Write the *We Believe* statement on the board. Read the statement aloud with the children. Ask: *Why do you think Jesus is called the Light of the World?* Encourage them to share their responses.

Tell the children that the Bible reading is from the Gospel of John. If possible, show the children where the story is in the Bible. Then read John 8:12 to the children.

Stand for the Truth Have volunteers read the *We Believe* paragraphs. Then explain to the children that you want them to stand after you read each sentence that is true. Read the following sentences.

WE RESPOND

What are some ways you can follow Jesus?

🏃 Draw a picture to show that Jesus is the Light of the World.

209

Multiple Intelligences
Spatial
Activity Materials: newspapers, paintbrushes, wax crayons, black or dark blue poster paint, drawing paper, craft sticks

Set up workstations. Line the surfaces with newspaper. Give each child a sheet of drawing paper. Have the children use brightly colored crayons to color over the sheet. Then have them paint over the colored sheet with the poster paint. Allow the sheets to dry. Then have the children use craft sticks to etch the name *Jesus* on the sheet. They may also want to etch stars, beams of light, or light streaks. Display the children's work in the prayer space.

• *We believe that Jesus is just what he said he was, the Light of the World.* (true)

• *We believe that Jesus wants us to share God's life with us.* (true)

• *We believe that Jesus wants us to follow him.* (true)

Quick Check

✔ *Who is the Light of the World?* (Jesus is the Light of the World.)

✔ *In what ways is Jesus the Light of the World?* (He helps us to see what God's love is like. He shares God's life with us.)

WE RESPOND ___ minutes

Connect to Life Discuss the *We Respond* question. Then invite the children to complete the drawing activity. Encourage the children to share and talk about their pictures.

Pray Invite the children to pray with you: *Jesus, you are the Light of the World.*

Plan Ahead for Day 2

Catechist Goal: To examine what it means to receive the light of Christ

Preparation: Plan your own response to the *We Respond* question. Have available the Grade 1 CD.

Catechist Goal

• To examine what it means to receive the light of Christ

Our Faith Response

• To share the light of Christ with others

Lesson Materials

• Grade 1 CD

• a few flashlights

Teaching Tip

Questioning Techniques

As you ask the daily *Quick Check* and other questions, you may wish to employ the following questioning techniques:

• After asking a question, try to make eye contact with as many of the children as possible. This will show that you think that each of them is capable of answering correctly.

• For yes-or-no questions, allow all of the children to answer simultaneously by using a thumbs-up or thumbs-down gesture.

We receive the light of Christ.

WE GATHER

✝ *Jesus, help us to share your light.*

Think about someone who was kind to you.
What did the person do or say?
How did this make you feel?

WE BELIEVE

When we are baptized, we receive the light of Christ. We are told to "walk always as children of the light."

As children of the light, we are followers of Jesus. We:

• believe in Jesus

• act as Jesus wants us to

• love one another.

210

Lesson Plan

WE GATHER ___ minutes

✝ **Pray** Remind the children that Jesus is the Light of the World. Pray the Sign of the Cross and then ask the children to extend their arms and stretch out their hands in front of them. Pray together the *We Gather* prayer.

Focus on Life Read aloud the *We Gather* questions. Pause briefly to allow the children to reflect on their answers. Ask volunteers to share their responses. Encourage them to discuss how acts of kindness can make us feel. (Possible responses: special, thankful, surprised) Tell the children that in this lesson they will learn about sharing the light of Christ with others.

WE BELIEVE ___ minutes

Receive Christ's Light Ask the children to tell what it means to receive. Invite a volunteer to read aloud the *We Believe* statement. Read the first *We Believe* paragraph.

Read About the Light Tell the children that they will read the text for *We Believe* together. Say that if they feel you tap their shoulder, they should read aloud the next sentence. Circulate among the children as they read, signaling whose turn it is to read by tapping a child on the shoulder.

Discuss Ways of Sharing Direct the children's attention to the photographs on these two pages. For each photo ask: *How are these people showing others the light of Christ?*

We show others the light of Christ when we:
- help our family and friends
- share what we have with others
- care about the way others feel.

WE RESPOND

How can you show others that you have received the light of Christ?

🎵 **Walk in the Light**

We walk together in Jesus' light:
Walk, walk in the light!
And let our own light shine so bright.
Walk, walk in the light!

Walk, walk in the light! (Sing 3 times.)
Walk in the light of the Lord!

211

ACTIVITY BANK

Multiple Intelligences
Interpersonal

Engage the children in an imaginative activity. Tell the children that today they will be sharing the light of Christ. Pantomime lighting a candle and passing it on to a child. As you do, say, *Let's share the light of Christ.* Coach the children to pass the candle, each one saying to the next, *Let's share the light of Christ.* When the candle comes back to you, ask the children to think of one way they will share the light of Christ this week. Then pray, *May we all share the light of Christ. Amen.*

Quick Check

✔ *When do we receive the light of Christ?* (When we are baptized, we receive the light of Christ.)

✔ *When do we show others the light of Christ?* (We show the light of Christ when we help others, share what we have, and care about other's feelings.)

WE RESPOND ____ minutes

Connect to Life Encourage the children to recognize that people are also sharing the light of Christ with them. Help them to give examples. (The children may cite their parents hugging them, a big sister helping them do their chores, and so on.)

Read the *We Respond* question. As children share their responses, write them on chart paper. Allow a few quiet moments for children to choose from the list one or two things that they will do this week.

Pray Give a few children flashlights. Have them turn the lights on and walk ahead of the others as the children process around the room. Play the song, "Walk in the Light," #22 on the Grade 1 CD. As the children walk, have them sing along with the recording.

Plan Ahead for Day 3

Catechist Goal: To describe what it means to be a peacemaker

Preparation: Make copies of *What's the Word?*, guide page 207F.

Catechist Goal

• To describe what it means to be a peacemaker

Our Faith Response

• To be peacemakers as Jesus wants us to be

 **peacemaker**

Lesson Materials

• copies of reproducible master *What's the Word?*, guide page 207F

As Catholics...

Pope Pius X

After you have presented the lesson, read the *As Catholics* text. Ask: *How was Pope Saint Pius X a peacemaker?* (He tried to keep countries from going to war.) Ask the children to share their responses to the question. Help them to understand that the leaders of many countries and many Church leaders work for world peace.

Jesus asks us to share his peace.

WE GATHER

✝ *Jesus, we want to share your peace.*

Have you ever heard someone talk about peace? When?

WE BELIEVE

Jesus wanted his followers to be at peace. He wanted them to live in God's love. He wanted them to get along with one another. He wanted them to show love for one another.

📖 Matthew 5:1, 9

Read Along

One day Jesus went up a mountain. There he spoke to many people. He told them how to live as God's children. He said,
"Blessed are the peacemakers,
    for they will be called the children of God."
(Matthew 5:9)

212

Lesson Plan

WE GATHER ___ minutes

✝ **Pray** Invite the children to close their eyes and imagine that they are sitting outside in a peaceful place. Then pray together the *We Gather* prayer.

Focus on Life Invite the children to share their responses to the *We Gather* question. Help the children to understand that sometimes they will hear their parents or other adults talk about peace. Help them understand that whenever anyone talks about being kind or about considering someone else's feelings, that person is talking about peace. Tell the children that in this lesson they will learn that Jesus wants us to be peacemakers.

WE BELIEVE ___ minutes

Learn About the Key Word Print the word *peacemaker* on the board. Ask two volunteers to circle the two words that are part of this word. Tell the children that *peacemaker* is an important word in today's lesson.

Read the Text Have a volunteer read the first *We Believe* paragraph. Then ask: *What did Jesus want his followers to do?*

Listen to Jesus' Words Ask the children to sit quietly and look at the picture of Jesus teaching the crowd. Point out to the group that they are being

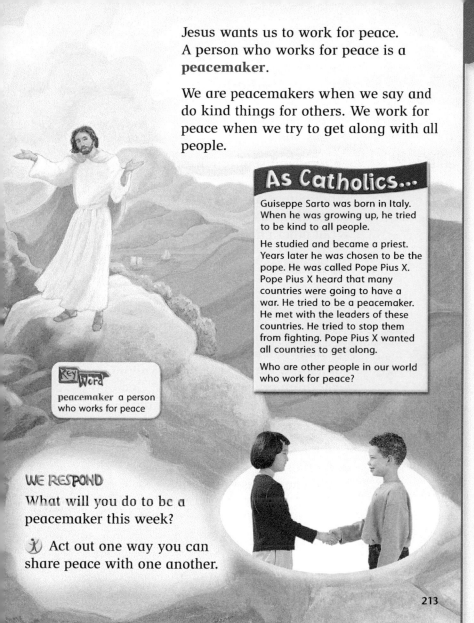

Jesus wants us to work for peace. A person who works for peace is a **peacemaker**.

We are peacemakers when we say and do kind things for others. We work for peace when we try to get along with all people.

As Catholics...

Guiseppe Sarto was born in Italy. When he was growing up, he tried to be kind to all people.

He studied and became a priest. Years later he was chosen to be the pope. He was called Pope Pius X. Pope Pius X heard that many countries were going to have a war. He tried to be a peacemaker. He met with the leaders of these countries. He tried to stop them from fighting. Pope Pius X wanted all countries to get along.

Who are other people in our world who work for peace?

Key Word

peacemaker a person who works for peace

WE RESPOND

What will you do to be a peacemaker this week?

X Act out one way you can share peace with one another.

213

ACTIVITY BANK

Multiple Intelligences

Interpersonal and Intrapersonal
Activity Materials: paper plates, crayons or markers

Form small groups. Ask the children in each group to decide on three things they can do to help them get along with other children. Then invite each group to share ideas with the class. Write on the board: *I am a peacemaker.* Give each child a paper plate. Help the children write the sentence that is on the board onto one side of the paper plate. On the other side, have the children draw a picture of themselves getting along with others. Encourage the children to share what they have drawn. Urge them to take the plates home to remind them that Jesus wants us to be peacemakers.

Scripture

Linguistic, Interpersonal

For a Scripture activity, see *What's the Word?*, guide page 207F.

---

peaceful. Ask them to be as peaceful as they can be as they listen to the words of Jesus. Then read aloud the Scripture passage.

Have volunteers read the last two *We Believe* paragraphs. Help the children to understand that when we do kind things for others, we are being peacemakers.

Quick Check

✔ *What is a peacemaker?* (A peacemaker is someone who works for peace.)

✔ *How can we be peacemakers?* (We can be peacemakers by doing kind things for others and getting along with other people.)

WE RESPOND ___ minutes

Connect to Life Read the *We Respond* question together. Have volunteers act out some things that they can do this week to be peacemakers.

Pray Invite the children to gather in the prayer space. Pray together: *Jesus, help us to be peacemakers.*

Then ask the children to shake hands as a sign that they want to do as Jesus asked.

Plan Ahead for Day 4

Catechist Goal: To emphasize that our choices can show our love for God

Preparation: Make copies of Reproducible Master 18, guide page 207G.

Catechist Goal

• To emphasize that our choices can show our love for God

Our Faith Response

• To show our love for God in our choices

Lesson Materials

• copies of Reproducible Master 18
• crayons or colored pencils

Teaching Tip

Faith and Media

Be aware and try to watch the television programs that are popular with the children. Mention specific examples of the actions of major characters. Discuss the ways followers of Jesus act. Try to clear up misconceptions the children may have about characters' negative behavior.

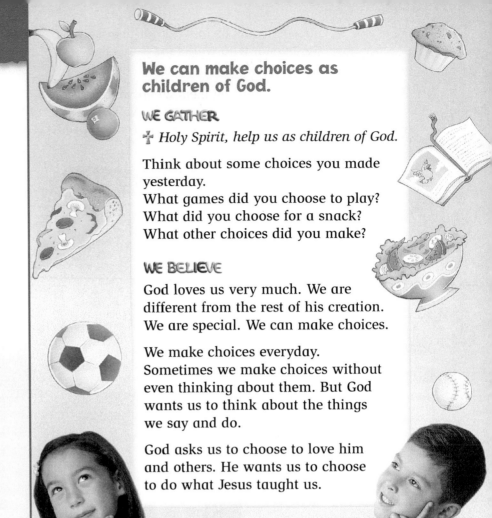

We can make choices as children of God.

WE GATHER

✝ *Holy Spirit, help us as children of God.*

Think about some choices you made yesterday.
What games did you choose to play?
What did you choose for a snack?
What other choices did you make?

WE BELIEVE

God loves us very much. We are different from the rest of his creation. We are special. We can make choices.

We make choices everyday. Sometimes we make choices without even thinking about them. But God wants us to think about the things we say and do.

God asks us to choose to love him and others. He wants us to choose to do what Jesus taught us.

214

Lesson Plan

WE GATHER ___ minutes

✝ **Pray** Invite the children to pray the Sign of the Cross and the *We Gather* prayer on page 214 together.

Focus on Life Ask the children to think about the choices that they made yesterday. Then read the *We Gather* questions. Invite the children to share their responses with a partner. Then explain that there are other kinds of choices we make. Read the following examples:

• *We can choose to listen in school.*
• *We can choose to help out at home.*

Tell the children that in this lesson they will learn that God helps them to make choices.

WE BELIEVE ___ minutes

Learn About Choices Read aloud the *We Believe* paragraphs. Stress the following points:

• *God wants us to think about the things we say and do.*
• *God wants us to choose to do what Jesus taught us.*
• *God wants us to choose to love him and others.*

Do the Activity Ask a volunteer to read the directions for the *We Believe* activity. Encourage the children to discuss what they see in each picture. Ask them to discuss the choices Tomás has. Ask: *Which choice is a loving one?*

✖ Here is a picture story. Circle the picture showing Tomás making a loving choice.

| Tomás wants to use his 🖤 sister's. | Tomás can choose to just take the ball. **OR** | Tomás can choose to ask his sister. |

WE RESPOND

Do you think it is always easy to make choices that show love for God and others? Tell why or why not.

Pray together now.

Holy Spirit, help us to make loving choices.
Help us to do what Jesus taught us.
Help us to live as children of God.
Help us to walk always as children of the light.

215

Multiple Intelligences
Bodily-Kinesthetic
Activity Materials: props
   Remind the children that every day we can make choices to do what Jesus taught us. Have the children work in groups to act out the following choice situations:

• A child has lost his lunch. How should his friend respond?
• Two children both want the same toy. How should they solve the problem?
• A child is being made fun of. How should the other children respond?

   After the children act out the situations, have the rest of the class tell whether they think the actors made loving or unloving choices.

Make a Choice Distribute copies of Reproducible Master 18. Read the activity directions. Have volunteers explain what is happening in each picture. Give the children a few minutes to circle the pictures. Then discuss each loving choice (top: brother sharing sandwich; bottom: child helping mother with laundry).

Quick Check

✔ *How are we different from the rest of God's creation?* (We are special because we can make choices.)

✔ *What does God want us to choose to do?* (God wants us to love him and others. He wants us to do what Jesus taught us.)

WE RESPOND   __ minutes

Connect to Life Invite the children to share their responses to the *We Respond* question. Tell them: *We can ask the Holy Spirit to help us to make loving choices.*

Pray Close the lesson by praying together the prayer to the Holy Spirit.

Plan Ahead for Day 5

Catechist Goal: To review chapter ideas and their relationship to our faith life

Preparation: Make copies of *Sharing Faith with My Family*, guide page 207E.

Catechist Goal

• To review the chapter ideas that are key to growing as disciples of Jesus Christ

Our Faith Response

• To decide on ways to grow as disciples by living out what we have learned

Show What *you* Know

Read the question. Give children time to write the *Key Word*.

Picture This

Review some ways that children can share the light of Christ: help others to follow Jesus; share in God's life together; share our beliefs. Allow time for the children to write ideas in the candle.

What Would *you* do?

Read the paragraph. Ask the children what they can discern from the children's facial expressions in the picture. Instruct the children to draw themselves in the picture as a peacemaker. Ask each child to tell what he or she is doing to be a peacemaker.

More *to* Explore

Read the activity instructions. Encourage the children to write the name of a peacemaker or to draw a picture of the person in the heart. Remind them it could be a member of their school, family, or parish.

Take Home

Read aloud the paragraph. Remind the children that they prayed with light in the chapter's opening prayer. Ask the children to try praying with candlelight as a family.

Discuss and send home copies of *Sharing Faith with My Family*, guide page 207E.

Grade 1 Chapter 18

PROJECT

Show What *you* Know

Who is a person who works for peace?

_____

peacemaker

Possible responses: help family members and friends;

share with others; care about others' feelings

Picture This

On the candle write three ways that you can share the light of Christ.

216 www.webelieveweb.com

DISCIPLE

What Would *you* do?

William and Rebecca are arguing in the playground. What could you do as a peacemaker? Add yourself to the picture.

Possible drawings: child may draw him- or herself intervening; encouraging William and Rebecca not to argue; alerting a teacher

More *to* Explore

Work with a friend. Who is a peacemaker in the world today? Write the person's name or draw a picture of the person in the heart.

Take Home

People all over the world gather to share Jesus' light by praying together. Sometimes people hold candles or other kinds of lights as they pray. Try this with your family. Gather together to pray. Use candles or other lights. As you pray, remember that Jesus is the Light of the World.

217

CHAPTER TEST

Circle the correct answer.

1. Is Jesus the Light of the World?

(Yes)   No

2. Do we show others the light of Christ when we tell lies?

Yes   (No)

3. Are we peacemakers when we fight?

Yes   (No)

4. Can we make choices to love God and others?

(Yes)   No

5. Do we receive the light of Christ at Baptism?

(Yes)   No

 Talk about ways we can work for peace at home, in school, and in our neighborhoods.
Possible responses: say and do kind things for others; try to get along with all people

218

CHAPTER TEST

Read each test item aloud and allow time for the children to mark an answer. Decide whether the *Talk About It* activity will be a small group or whole class discussion. After you have finished, check the answers. Clarify any misconceptions.

Alternative Assessment

You may want the students to complete the following alternative-assessment activity.

Make a booklet. On each page draw a picture of someone sharing the light of Christ. Write what the person is doing.

Additional Testing

• Chapter 18 Test in *Assessment Book*, pages 37–38

• CD-ROM *Test Generator and Resource*: Use Chapter 18 Test or customize your own.

Review

Review the definition as it is presented in the chapter's *Key Word* box:

• peacemaker (page 213).

We Believe Statements

Review the four statements.

• Jesus is the Light of the World.

• We receive the light of Christ.

• Jesus asks us to share his peace.

• We can make choices as children of God.

To use the Chapter 18 Study Guide, visit

www.webelieveweb.com

218

Overview

In Chapter 18 the children learned ways members of the Church follow Jesus. In this chapter they will learn about God's forgiveness.

Doctrinal Content	For Adult Reading and Reflection *Catechism of the Catholic Church*
The children will learn:	Paragraph
• Jesus told us about God's forgiveness.	1421
• God is always ready to forgive us.	1431
• We celebrate God's forgiveness.	1440
• Jesus asks us to forgive others.	2840

Penance and Reconciliation (p. 225)

Catechist Background

Think of a time when you hurt someone and were forgiven. How did you feel?

Go to **www.webelieveweb.com**, Catechist/ Teacher, We Believe Correlations for this chapter's correlation to:
- Six Tasks of Catechesis
- Catholic Social Teaching
- *Catechetical Formation in Chaste Living.*

In Baptism our sins were forgiven, and we were given the freedom to live as children of God. But we do not always use that freedom to choose love. Often we make choices that hurt others and ourselves, and like the prodigal son in Scripture, we distance ourselves from God.

The Good News, however, is that we do not have to be a slave to sin. Jesus showed us, in his actions and in the stories he told, a God who loves us deeply; a God we can dare to call "Abba," or "Daddy." When we celebrate the Sacrament of Penance and Reconciliation, we celebrate God's abiding and merciful love.

The purpose of this chapter is to communicate this forgiving love of God to the children as we introduce to them the Sacrament of Penance and Reconciliation. Our part in the sacrament is to be

truly sorry for our sins, to confess them to a priest, and to "repair" the breach our sins have caused through a work of reparation, or penance. In our Act of Contrition, we also promise not to sin again.

The Sacrament of Penance helps to maintain the bond of love that ties us to God and to one another in the human and Church community. In Baptism, we were given God's life. Sin weakens that life within us. In Penance, we are given a "second chance" to open ourselves again to God's life and love, and to share that divine life and love through our forgiveness of others.

For what do you need to ask forgiveness? To whom do you need to give forgiveness?

Lesson Planning Guide

Lesson Focus	Presentation	Materials

Day 1

page 219
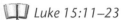
We Gather in Prayer

pages 220–221
Jesus told us about God's forgiveness.

 Luke 15:11–23

- Reflect on ways that we have followed Jesus.
- Share responses for We Gather.
- Read the Scripture story in We Believe about the forgiving father.
- Do the activity.
- Discuss the We Respond question.

See Preparing to Pray, guide page 219.

- copies of reproducible master *What's the Word?*, guide page 219F

Day 2

pages 222–223
God is always ready to forgive us.

- Do the We Gather role-playing activity.
- Read and discuss the We Believe text about God's forgiveness.
- Discuss responses for We Respond.
- Sing a song about being a child of God.

- "Children of God," Christopher Walker, #23, Grade 1 CD
- copies of Reproducible Master 19, guide page 219G
- construction paper, scissors, glue

Day 3

pages 224–225
We celebrate God's forgiveness.

- Share responses for We Gather.
- Present the We Believe text about the ways we celebrate the Sacrament of Penance.
- Share responses to the We Respond question and read the directive.
- Read and discuss the *As Catholics* text.

Day 4

pages 226–227
Jesus asks us to forgive others.

- Do the We Gather activity and act out the events in the pictures.
- Present the We Believe text about the importance of forgiving others.
- Do the We Respond activity.
- Pray to the Holy Spirit for help to love and forgive others.

- crayons or colored pencils

Day 5

pages 228–229
Project Disciple

page 230
Chapter 19 Test

- Complete the Project Disciple activities.
- Explain the *Take Home* activity.
- Discuss/send home Sharing Faith with My Family, guide page 219E.
- Complete Chapter 19 Test.
- Work on *Alternative Assessment* activity.

- pencils
- crayons or colored pencils
- copies of Sharing Faith with My Family reproducible master, guide page 219E

Enrichment Ideas

Chapter Story

Tasha shared a room with her sister, Kara. One day Tasha's mother came into the room where Tasha was watching television. She said, "Tasha, your side of your room is a mess. Your sister and I would like you to go clean it now."

Tasha was watching her favorite show. She just kept watching the TV until her mother turned it off. Tasha's mom said, "Go to your room, Tasha."

Tasha stomped her feet when she was going to her room. Her sister was not there. Tasha wanted to sit down but she had a hard time finding a spot. She said to herself, "I guess my part of the room is messy. Mom and Kara were right."

Tasha started to clean her room. She put her toys and clothes away. She thought, "I should have gone to my room when Mom told me to. I'm really sorry I didn't listen to her. I'm going to tell Mom I'm sorry. Then I'll show her my room."

Tasha found her mother in the kitchen. Her mom still looked hurt. Tasha said, "I'm sorry for not listening to you, Mom. Please come and see my room."

Tasha's mom was surprised at the great job Tasha did. She hugged Tasha and said, "Tasha, I'm glad you told me that you were sorry. Thanks for showing me by cleaning your room. I forgive you. Now let's go find Kara. The three of us can share a special snack."

▶ *How do you think Tasha's mom felt when Tasha said she was sorry? How do you think Tasha felt when her mom forgave her?*

FAITH and MEDIA

▶ If you decide to discuss books and movies that tell stories, you might consider including online books and video. There are a variety of Web sites that offer popular and original books in eBook format. Streaming video abounds on the Internet. Whenever you use the Internet as a classroom tool, preview any sites and content before allowing children to view it. Use only child safe search engines and monitor student use of the computer or Internet.

CHAPTER PROJECT: PUPPET PLAYS

Have the children work in small groups to make puppets to dramatize the Scripture story of the forgiving father. Provide the groups with small paper sacks, yarn, fabric pieces, and other materials needed to make puppets and scenery. Then ask each group to prepare a dramatization of the story.

Provide time during the week for the children to present their dramatizations. You may want to invite the principal and other classes to your room for the presentations. Then share a special snack to celebrate God's forgiveness.

PROJECT DISCIPLE

Pray
Learn
Celebrate
Share
Choose
Live

Additional Activities

What's *the* Word?

(Use on Day 1.)

Materials needed: copies of reproducible master, guide page 219F

Distribute copies of the Scripture reproducible master. Explain that the children will sing a song to remember the story of the forgiving father and his son. Read the directions aloud. Invite the children to sing the verses after you. Once the children are familiar with the words and the tune, sing the song through together.

What Would *you do*?

Materials needed: index cards with various scenarios written on them, basket or container

Prepare a set of index cards with various scenarios written on them that will require resolution. For example: *Jillian is angry because her sister made a mess of her toys.* Invite the children to sit in a circle and take turns drawing an index card from the container and reading it aloud. Allow the children to propose several possible solutions in which forgiveness is achieved. Discuss each one.

More *to* Explore

Explain to the children that stories can be found in books and movies and that many stories teach us the same lessons that Jesus taught us. Ask the children if they can offer an example of such a book or movie. Choose an appropriate story to read aloud to the children. Have a class discussion about the ways the story teaches us one of the lessons that Jesus taught.

Pray Today

Allow each child to write his or her own prayer to God to thank him for his forgiveness and love. Invite each child to write the words of the prayer down and to take it out to pray during a few moments each day. Encourage the children, at the end of the week, to remember and to continue to pray this prayer.

Meeting Individual Needs

Children with Attention Deficit Hyperactivity Disorder

For many kinesthetic activities, children may have difficulty staying on task. Before you engage the children in act-out activities, for example, meet with the children with attention deficit hyperactivity disorder. Establish a signal that reminds the children to slow down or stay on task. Flash this sign as needed during the activity.

We Believe Resources

- Grade 1 *Review & Resource Book*, pages 46–48
- Grade 1 *Family Book*, pages 55–57
- Grade 1 *Assessment Book*, pages 39–40
- Grade 1 CD-ROM *Test Generator and Resource*: Use Chapter 19 Test or customize your own.
- **www.webelieveweb.com**

Sharing What I Learned

Look at the pictures below. Use each picture to tell your family what you learned in this chapter.

A Peace Plan

Talk about why it is important to make up with others when we have hurt them. How can each of these actions help?

- Say we are sorry.
- Talk over what we have done.
- Ask for forgiveness.
- Forgive others.

A Prayer for Forgiveness

God, we know that you always forgive us when we are sorry. Thank you for your love and forgiveness.

- For the times we did not listen to each other,
  please forgive us.
- For the times we have said things that hurt others,
  please forgive us.
- For the times we were not kind or caring,
  please forgive us.

Visit Sadlier's

www.WeBelieveweb.com

 Connect to the Catechism
For adult background and reflection, see paragraphs 1421, 1431, 1440, and 2840.

219E

PROJECT DISCIPLE

Pray
Learn
Celebrate
Share
Choose
Live

Name _____

What's *the* Word?

Remember the story of the father and son. They were both happy when the son came home. Sing this song about that time.

🎵 **Father, Forgive Me** ("The Wheels of the Bus")

Son
Father, I'm sorry
for what I've done,
   what I've done,
   what I've done.
Father, I'm sorry
for what I've done.
Please, forgive me.

Father
Son, I forgive you.
I'm glad you're home,
   glad you're home,
   glad you're home.
Son, I forgive you.
I'm glad you're home.
Come celebrate.

219F

Name _____

Find an important message. Cut out the
puzzle pieces. On a sheet of construction
paper, put the puzzle pieces together.
Glue the pieces to the construction paper.
Then read the message.

to forgive.

God is

always

ready

We Celebrate God's Forgiveness

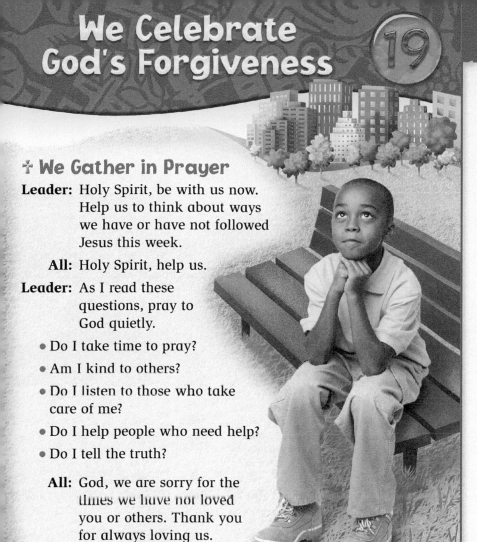

✝ We Gather in Prayer

Leader: Holy Spirit, be with us now. Help us to think about ways we have or have not followed Jesus this week.

All: Holy Spirit, help us.

Leader: As I read these questions, pray to God quietly.

- Do I take time to pray?
- Am I kind to others?
- Do I listen to those who take care of me?
- Do I help people who need help?
- Do I tell the truth?

All: God, we are sorry for the times we have not loved you or others. Thank you for always loving us. We want to keep growing in your love.

219

PREPARING TO PRAY

The children will reflect on ways they have followed or not followed Jesus.

• Help the children to make a "We Celebrate God's Forgiveness" poster. Print the words on a sheet of poster board. Give the children small purple construction paper circles. Have them print their initials on the circles. Then tape or paste the circles to the poster.

The Prayer Space

• Display the poster in the prayer space.

• On the prayer table place the Bible opened to the story of the forgiving father (Luke 15:23).

📖 **This Week's Liturgy**
Visit **www.webelieveweb.com** for this week's liturgical readings and other seasonal material.

Lesson Plan

We Gather in Prayer ___ minutes

✝ Pray

• Ask the children to gather in the prayer space.

• Invite the children to pray the Sign of the Cross with you. Then lead the children in prayer.

• After you read each question, pause and count to seven to allow the children time to reflect.

• Then have the children pray the response together.

Family Connection Update

Invite the children to share family prayer experiences using candles or other lights.

Catechist Goal

• To present Jesus' teaching about God's forgiveness

Our Faith Response

• To try to love and forgive as Jesus did

Lesson Materials

• copies of reproducible master *What's the Word?*, guide page 219F

Teaching Note

Reconciliation and the We Believe *Program*

   The purpose of this chapter is to stress God's forgiveness and to introduce the Sacrament of Penance. In the *We Believe* Grade 2 text the sacrament is presented in greater detail.

Jesus told us about God's forgiveness.

WE GATHER

✝ *Jesus, thank you for teaching us about God's love.*

What is your favorite story?
Who is in the story?
What is the story about?
What happens at the end of the story?

WE BELIEVE

Jesus told stories to teach us about God's love and forgiveness. Here is one story he told.

📖 Luke 15:11–23

Read Along

A loving father had two sons. One day, the younger son asked his father for money. The son took the money and left home. He spent the money having fun.

Soon all the money was gone. The young man had nowhere to live and nothing to eat. He knew that what he had done had hurt his father. He wanted to go home and tell his father how sorry he was.

When the young man was near his home, his father ran out to meet him. He gave him a big hug. He was so glad to see his son again. The son told his father he was sorry. The father said, "Let us celebrate with a feast!" (Luke 15:23)

220

Lesson Plan

WE GATHER ____ minutes

✝ **Pray** Remind the children that Jesus loves them. Then pray together the Sign of the Cross and the *We Gather* prayer.

Focus on Life Ask the children to think about and share their answers to the *We Gather* questions. Share with the children a favorite story of your own. Help the children to see that there are many different kinds of stories to enjoy. Tell the children that in this lesson they will hear a story that Jesus told to teach us about love and forgiveness.

WE BELIEVE ____ minutes

Share a Scripture Story Invite a volunteer to read the *We Believe* statement. Explain to the children that

Jesus told stories about God's forgiveness. Explain: *Jesus told these stories because he knew it was very important for us to learn about God's love and forgiveness.* Read aloud the story about the father and his younger son. When you have finished, ask: *How would you feel if you were the father in the story? How would you feel if you were the son?*

Do the Activity Invite volunteers to read the three parts of the story as they are summarized on page 221. Then help the children to number the events in the correct sequential order. If the children have made a mistake, help them to understand the correct order of events.

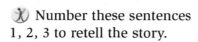

👤 Number these sentences 1, 2, 3 to retell the story.

_____3_____ When the son was near home, his father came to meet him. He hugged him. They celebrated with a feast.

_____1_____ The son asked his father for money. The son left home. He spent all the money.

_____2_____ The son knew that what he had done had hurt his father. He went home to tell his father he was sorry.

Jesus told this story to teach us that God always loves us. God is like the forgiving father in this story.

WE RESPOND

Why were love and forgiveness important in this story?

221

ACTIVITY BANK

Multiple Intelligences
Bodily-Kinesthetic
Activity Materials: costumes and props

Have the children imagine what the celebration of the father and his son was like after his son returned home. Have volunteers act out what people said and did.

Curriculum Connection
Language Arts
Activity Materials: chart paper

Help the children make up a forgiveness story. Print the word *Forgiveness* as a title on chart paper. Begin the story by writing *One day.* Print volunteer contributions on the chart. Reread the story to the children. Invite the children to conclude the story with some forgiving words and actions.

Scripture
Musical

For a Scripture activity, see *What's the Word?*, guide page 219F.

Act Out the Story Call on volunteers to take the parts of the father and the son and act out the Bible story. Encourage the rest of the children to watch and listen carefully. Then let other volunteers also act out the story. Emphasize the reasons Jesus told this story: *He wanted to teach us:*

• *God always loves us.*

• *God is like the forgiving father in the story.*

Quick Check

✔ *What did Jesus' story teach us about?* (Jesus' story taught us about God's love and forgiveness.)

✔ *Why did the father give his son a hug?* (The father loved his son and wanted to show that he forgave him.)

WE RESPOND   _____ minutes

Connect to Life Read the *We Respond* question. Invite volunteers to share their responses. Remind the children that both the father and son were happier when they got back together. Ask: *How do you feel when someone forgives you?*

Pray *Thank you, God, for being our forgiving Father.*

Plan Ahead for Day 2

Catechist Goal: To emphasize that God is always ready to forgive us

Preparation: Make copies of Reproducible Master 19, guide page 219G.

Catechist Goal

• To emphasize that God is always ready to forgive us

Our Faith Response

• To know that God always forgives us

Lesson Materials

• copies of Reproducible Master 19
• Grade 1 CD
• construction paper (one sheet for each child)
• scissors and glue

Teaching Tip

Singing Together

When the children are singing a song that is on the Grade 1 CD, play the recording at a low volume. This will help the children keep to the correct tempo. Have the children stand. Encourage all the children to sing. Point out: *God wants to hear everyone's voice.*

God is always ready to forgive us.

WE GATHER

✝ *God, you are our loving Father.*

Ⓧ Read the story about Tony. Act out what he should do next.

Tony's mom asked him to help his little sister tie her shoes. Tony said, "I don't feel like it." Then Tony thought about what he had said.

WE BELIEVE

We try to do things that show love for God and others. We try to follow God's laws. Jesus followed God's laws. He wants us to follow God's laws, too.

Sometimes we choose not to follow God's laws. We do things that do not show love for God and others.

Jesus taught us to ask God to forgive us. God always forgives us if we are sorry.

222

Lesson Plan

WE GATHER ___ minutes

✝ **Pray** Ask the children to stand. Ask them to hold their right hands over their hearts as they pray the *We Gather* prayer together.

Focus on Life Read aloud the activity directions. Help the children to conclude that Tony has a choice about what he does next. Allow several volunteers to act out what they think Tony should do next. Invite volunteers to share a time when they said something without thinking. Then ask what they did about it. You may want to share the *Chapter Story* on guide page 219C. Tell the children that in this lesson they will learn about God's forgiveness.

WE BELIEVE ___ minutes

Respond to the Message Remind the children that God loves us always. Then ask the children to read the *We Believe* statement together.

If you have shared the *Chapter Story*, ask: *What did Tasha do that did not show love for God or her mother?* (At first she did not do what her mother wanted her to do.)

Ask volunteers to read the *We Believe* paragraphs. Then ask the children to highlight or underline the last *We Believe* paragraph.

Find an Important Message Give each child a copy of Reproducible Master 19 and a sheet of

WE RESPOND

God is always ready to forgive you.
How does that make you feel?

🎵 **Children of God**

Chorus
    Children of God in one family,
    loved by God in one family.
    And no matter what we do
    God loves me and God loves you.

    Jesus teaches us to love.
    Sometimes we get it wrong.
    But God forgives us ev'ry time
        for we belong to the (Chorus).

    Jesus wants us to
        be sorry.
    Sometimes we get
        it wrong.
    But God forgives us
        ev'ry time
        for we belong to the
        (Chorus).

223

ACTIVITY BANK

Faith and Media
Sharing a Prayer
Activity Materials: voice recorder or video camera
    Have the children work in groups. Ask each group to write a prayer to thank God for always being ready to forgive us. Record the groups reading their prayers and singing "Children of God." Share the recording with other classes.

construction paper. Help the children to complete the puzzle. Tell the children that they will see an important message. (God is always ready to forgive us.) Suggest that the children take their puzzle message home and put it in a place where they will see it often.

Quick Check

✔ *When does God forgive us?* (God always forgives us when we say we are sorry.)

✔ *How can we follow God's laws?* (We can follow God's laws by showing love for God and others.)

WE RESPOND ____ minutes

Connect to Life Read aloud the *We Respond* text and question. Ask the children to brainstorm with you

the words that relate how that makes them feel. Print their words on a chart. Invite the children to read with you the words on their list. Then ask the children to stand and show without speaking how they feel.

Teach the Song Play the song "Children of God," #23 on the Grade 1 CD. Have the children practice singing.

Pray Sing "Children of God" prayerfully.

Plan Ahead for Day 3

Catechist Goal: To explain the Sacrament of Penance

Preparation: Plan a visit to the church to see the reconciliation room.

Catechist Goal

• To explain the Sacrament of Penance

Our Faith Response

• To identify ways to tell God that we are sorry

 **Penance and Reconciliation**

As Catholics...

The Reconciliation Room

After you have presented the lesson, read the *As Catholics* text. If possible, take the children to see the reconciliation room in the church. While in church pray together to thank God for his forgiveness.

We celebrate God's forgiveness.

WE GATHER

✝ *God, thank you for your forgiveness.*

What are some ways to show others that you are sorry?

WE BELIEVE

When we make up with someone, we come back together again. This is called reconciliation.

We can always come back to God and ask for forgiveness. Jesus gave us a way to do this. It is the Sacrament of **Penance and Reconciliation**. We can call this sacrament the Sacrament of Penance.

224

Lesson Plan

WE GATHER
_____ minutes

✝ **Pray** Explain to the children that we should feel happy about receiving God's forgiveness. Then pray together the *We Gather* prayer.

Focus on Life Read aloud the *We Gather* question and have the children brainstorm ways that they can show others that they are sorry. Explain that they can say they are sorry through both words and actions. Tell the children that in this lesson they will learn about a way we celebrate God's forgiveness.

WE BELIEVE
_____ minutes

Review the Scripture Story Have volunteers use their own words to retell the Scripture story on page 220. Emphasize that after the son said he was sorry and his father forgave him, they had a celebration.

Learn About the Sacrament Print the word *Penance* on the board. Explain that Penance is the sacrament in which we receive and celebrate God's forgiveness. Read the first two *We Believe* paragraphs. Then read about the different things we do during the celebration of the sacrament.

Relate the Photos to the Text Ask the children to look at the photographs on these pages. Explain that:

• Photo on the left: *The priest is welcoming the child.*

• Photo in the middle: *The priest and the child are talking.*

• Photo on the right: *The priest is sharing God's forgiveness with the child.*

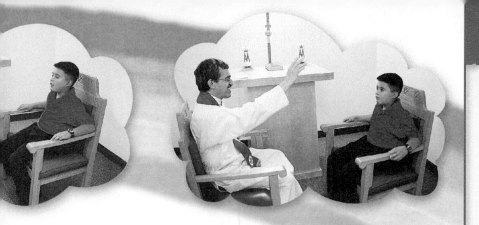

In this sacrament we receive and celebrate God's forgiveness. We do these things.

- We think about what we have said and done. We are sorry for the times we have not loved God and others.
- We meet with the priest.
- We listen to a story from the Bible about God's forgiveness.
- We talk to the priest about what we have done. We tell God we are sorry.
- The priest shares God's forgiveness with us.

WE RESPOND

How can we tell God we are sorry? Talk to your family about God's love and forgiveness.

Key Word

Penance and Reconciliation the sacrament in which we receive and celebrate God's forgiveness

As Catholics...

We usually celebrate the Sacrament of Penance in our parish church. There is a special place in church where we meet with the priest. Here we can talk with the priest face-to-face, or we can talk from behind a screen.

Where is the Sacrament of Penance celebrated in your parish church?

225

ACTIVITY BANK

Parish
Guest Speaker

Invite one of the priests of the parish to talk to the children about God's forgiveness and the Sacrament of Penance. Show the lesson of the children's text to the priest. Ask him to keep his explanation as simple as possible. Also ask your guest to show the children the stole he wears to celebrate the sacrament. You may want to plan a simple celebration with the priest to thank God for his forgiveness.

Quick Check

✔ *When can we ask God for forgiveness?* (We can always ask God for forgiveness.)

✔ *What is the sacrament of Penance?* (Penance is the sacrament in which we receive and celebrate God's forgiveness.)

WE RESPOND ___ minutes

Connect to Life Read the *We Respond* question. Explain: *It will be a while before you celebrate the Sacrament of Penance for the first time. But you can always tell God you are sorry.* Encourage the children to talk with their families about God's love and forgiveness.

Pray Invite the children to pray to God silently about something they might have said or done for which they are sorry. Then conclude by praying together the Lord's Prayer.

Plan Ahead for Day 4

Catechist Goal: To emphasize the importance of forgiving others

Preparation: Think about TV programs or movies that show someone forgiving another person.

Catechist Goal

• To emphasize the importance of forgiving others

Our Faith Response

• To try to be forgiving of others

Teaching Note

Being Forgiving

In your normal interactions with the children become conscious of opportunities to display a forgiving nature. Encourage the children to apologize to you when they do something wrong. Tell the children you forgive them. Also ask the children to apologize to others when they hurt them. Encourage all to share forgiveness and God's peace.

Jesus asks us to forgive others.

WE GATHER

✝ Holy Spirit, help us to share God's peace.

🧍 Look at the pictures.
Act out what you think is happening.

WE BELIEVE

When we celebrate the Sacrament of Penance, we receive God's forgiveness. We receive God's peace.

Jesus told his followers that it is important to forgive others. Jesus asks all of us to be forgiving. He wants us to share God's peace.

226

Lesson Plan

WE GATHER
___ minutes

✝ **Pray** Help the children to recall what they have learned about God's forgiveness of others. Then together pray the *We Gather* prayer.

Focus on Life Ask the children to look at the photos on page 226. Let two volunteers act out what the friends might be saying. Give other pairs an opportunity to present other ideas. Lead the children to understand that the exact words the friends say may be different, but the important thing that is happening is that the two are making up. If you have time, discuss TV programs or movies that showed someone forgiving another person. Tell the children that in this lesson they will learn that it is important to forgive others.

WE BELIEVE
___ minutes

Learn About Forgiving Others Read together the *We Believe* statement. Stress: *Jesus forgave others. He wants his followers to do the same.* Then invite volunteers to read the *We Believe* paragraphs.

On the board write the following verse of the Lord's Prayer:

Forgive us our trespasses
As we forgive those who trespass against us.

Tell the children that when they pray these words, they should remember that we are to ask God for forgiveness, and Jesus wants us to forgive others. Explain: *It is not always easy to forgive people who have hurt us. At these times the Holy Spirit will help us.*

WE RESPOND

Ask the Holy Spirit to help you to be loving and forgiving.

(✘) Read the story.

Fran's little brother left her favorite book outside. It started raining. All the pages got wet.

Then Fran's brother said, "I am sorry, Fran. Please forgive me."

What would Fran say to be forgiving? Circle the words.

- "I am going to break one of your toys."
- ⟨"I loved that book, but I forgive you."⟩
- "Go away. I do not want to talk to you."

227

Catholic Social Teaching
Call to Family, Community, and Participation

Activity Materials: a hat, slips of paper with one child's name on each

Place all of the children's names inside a hat, and have each child draw someone else's name. They should then draw a picture or write a letter to that child in which they share God's peace. For example, a child might draw a picture of two people laughing together. The picture or letter should show the other child love and kindness. They should be labeled "to" and "from" appropriately. When the children complete their letters, deliver them. Then ask the children to move around the room so that they can shake hands with and thank the child who sent them a sign of God's peace.

Quick Check

✔ *What do we receive in the Sacrament of Penance?* (We receive God's forgiveness and God's peace.)

✔ *How can we share God's peace with others?* (We can share God's peace by being loving and forgiving.)

WE RESPOND ___ minutes

Connect to Life Explain to the children that they are going to listen to a story and answer a question about it. Read the *We Respond* story. Then give the children time to read and circle the response that they think is the best. Discuss all three options, and help the children to see that the second choice is the loving and forgiving one. Ask the children to name some other ways they can share God's forgiveness and love with others.

Pray Pray these words:

Holy Spirit, please help us to do what Jesus asks. Please help us to be loving and forgiving. Amen.

Plan Ahead for Day 5

Catechist Goal: To review chapter ideas and their relationship to our faith life

Preparation: Make copies of *Sharing Faith with My Family*, guide page 219E.

Catechist Goal

• To review the chapter ideas that are key to growing as disciples of Jesus Christ

Our Faith Response

• To decide on ways to grow as disciples by living out what we have learned

Show What *you* Know

Read the instructions and the message. Invite the children to write the missing letters into the empty spaces. Read the completed message.

Reality Check

Read the instructions. Note that each child may have a different choice. Once children have made a selection, read the Disciple Challenge. Talk about why it is important to tell God and others when one is sorry.

Make *it* Happen

Read the instructions. Help the children to divide a simple story into three parts: beginning, middle, and end. Help them to identify a problem (beginning); include a turning point (middle); and propose a solution (end). Invite the children to share their picture stories with those sitting nearest to them.

Take Home

Remind the children that sometimes family members have disagreements. Invite the children to be peacemakers at school and at home. Read the activity. Encourage the children to make forgiveness charts to promote peace in the home.

Discuss and send home copies of *Sharing Faith with My Family,* guide page 219F.

Grade 1 Chapter 19

PROJECT

Show What *you* Know

Fill in the missing letters to read an important message.

I can receive and celebrate God's forgiveness in the Sacrament of

P e n a n c e a n d
R e c o n c i l i a t i o n.

Reality Check

Check your favorite way to tell someone you are sorry.

❏ Please forgive me.

❏ I am sorry.

❏ I apologize for what I did.

↳ **DISCIPLE CHALLENGE** Remember to tell God and others when you are sorry.

228 www.webelieveweb.com

DISCIPLE

Make *it* Happen

Write a forgiveness picture story in the space below. Be sure to include a beginning, a middle, and an end to your story.

beginning	middle	end

Take Home

Invite your family to make a chart at home that tallies the number of times family members forgive each other. When someone forgives, he or she puts a checkmark on the chart.

229

CHAPTER TEST

Circle the correct answer.

1. Jesus told stories about God's love and _____.

   forgetting   (forgiveness)

2. In one of Jesus' stories God is like the _____.

   son   (forgiving father)

3. God is _____ ready to forgive us.

   (always)   sometimes

4. In the Sacrament of Penance, we _____ and celebrate God's forgiveness.

   (receive)   return

5. It is _____ to forgive others.

   not important   (important)

TALK ABOUT IT

What are some things we do when we celebrate the Sacrament of Penance? Accept bulleted list on page 225.

230

CHAPTER TEST

Read each test item aloud and allow time for the children to mark an answer. Decide whether the *Talk About It* activity will be a small group or whole class discussion. After you have finished, check the answers. Clarify any misconceptions.

Alternative Assessment

You may want the students to complete the following alternative-assessment activity.

Find a picture to show how people share God's forgiveness. Tell what you think is happening in the picture.

Additional Testing

• Chapter 19 Test in *Assessment Book*, pages 39–40

• CD-ROM *Test Generator and Resource*: Use Chapter 19 Test or customize your own.

Review

Review the definition as it is presented in the chapter's *Key Word* box:

• Penance and Reconciliation (page 225).

We Believe Statements

Review the four statements.

• Jesus told us about God's forgiveness.
• God is always ready to forgive us.
• We celebrate God's forgiveness.
• Jesus asks us to forgive others.

To use the Chapter 19 Study Guide, visit

www.webelieveweb.com

Lent

Lent is a preparation for the celebration of Easter. For the Lenten liturgy disposes both catechumens and the faithful to celebrate the Paschal Mystery: catechumens, through the several stages of Christian initiation; the faithful, through reminders of their own baptism and through penitential practices.

(Norms Governing Liturgical Calendars, 27)

Overview

In this chapter the children will learn that Lent is the time when the Church gets ready to celebrate Jesus' Death and Resurrection.

For Adult Reading and Reflection
You may want to refer to paragraph 540 of the *Catechism of the Catholic Church*.

Catechist Background

Go to www.webelieveweb.com, Catechist/ Teacher, We Believe Correlations for this chapter's correlation to Six Tasks of Catechesis.

How have you observed Lent in the past?

Lent is the season of preparation for the celebration of Easter, the greatest feast of the Church year. For catechumens (those preparing for Baptism) and for all the faithful, it is a time to focus on Sacraments of Christian Initiation, the first of which is Baptism, the sacrament through which we die to sin and rise to new life in Christ. We remember that:

"The God of power and Father of our Lord
    Jesus Christ
has freed [us] from sin
and brought [us] to new life
through water and the Holy Spirit."
(Rite of Baptism, 62)

Lent is a penitential season, a time for ongoing conversion, not only for catechumens but also for all the baptized. We gradually turn our hearts more towards God and towards the needs of others. For forty days, from Ash Wednesday until the Evening Mass of the Lord's Supper on Holy Thursday, we pray, fast, and give alms to those in need. The forty days of this season remind us of the forty days Jesus spent in the desert, alone in prayer, totally dependent upon his God and Father.

We enter Lent knowing our need for a deeper turning, a deeper conversion, as disciples of the risen Lord. We enter Lent needing God's guidance amid myriad choices of modern life. We enter Lent with the mark of ashes on our foreheads. This ancient ritual of repentance helps us to "Remember how brief is my life," (Psalm 89:48) and challenges us to proclaim the Gospel, in the time we have been given, with our lives.

How will you observe Lent this year? How will you help the children to celebrate the season?

Lesson Planning Guide

Lesson Focus	Presentation	Materials
Day 1		
Guide page 231C **Guide and Text page 231** **Introduce the Season**	• Read the *Chapter Story*. • Introduce the season of Lent. • Listen to a Scripture verse.	
Day 2		
Guide and Text pages 232–233 **We Gather** **We Believe**	• Share responses to the We Gather questions. • Present the We Believe text about ways to grow closer to Jesus during Lent. ✖ Do the picture study.	• purple crayon
Day 3		
Guide and Text page 234 **We Respond**	✖ Explain the We Respond directions to be completed during Lent.	• crayons or colored pencils
Day 4		
Text page 235 **Guide page 235–236** **We Respond in Prayer**	• Pray to God for his trust and love. • Pray the Our Father.	🎵 "People Worry," Paule Freeburg and Christopher Walker, #4, Grade 1 CD • prayer space items: purple table cloth, Bible, cross, bowl of water
Day 5		
Text page 236 **Guide pages 235–236, 236A** **Project Disciple**	• Complete the Project Disciple activities. Discuss the *Take Home* activity. • Complete the Reproducible Master 20 activity. See guide pages 231C and 236A. • Discuss/send home Sharing Faith with My Family, guide page 236B.	• pencils • crayons or colored pencils • copies of Reproducible Master 20, guide page 236A • copies of Sharing Faith with My Family reproducible master, guide page 236B

For additional ideas, activities, and opportunities: Visit Sadlier's **www.WeBelieve.web.com**

Chapter Story

Caroline's birthday was coming up. Caroline was excited. Her Aunt Faith was coming for dinner. Caroline thought, "Maybe she'll bring my present. Aunt Faith always gives me something special."

When Aunt Faith arrived, Caroline ran to greet her. Caroline was disappointed when she saw that her aunt was not carrying a gift box or bag. After everyone finished dinner, Dad said, "Caroline, why don't you and Aunt Faith go in to the living room while I get dessert ready."

Caroline and her aunt sat on the couch. Aunt Faith pulled a small wrapped box from her purse and gave it to Caroline. Caroline opened the box to find a gold cross and chain. When Caroline put on the cross, Aunt Faith said, "Now that you are seven I think you'll take care of this special gift. Your grandmother gave it to me on my seventh birthday. She said, 'When you wear this cross, remember that you are a follower of Jesus. Remember all he did for us. Remember that he taught us to be loving and kind.'"

Caroline hugged her aunt. "Oh, thank you, Aunt Faith. I will take care of this special gift. I'll remember what you said. When I get older, I can give it to my goddaughter or daughter."

What was special about Aunt Faith's gift to Caroline?

PROJECT DISCIPLE
Additional Activities

Celebrate!

Explain to the children that during Lent we can grow closer to Jesus by helping people who are sick, lonely, or sad. Distribute Reproducible Master 20, guide page 236A, and a sheet of white construction paper to each child. Invite the children to color the activity sheet before helping them glue it to construction paper and fold it in half horizontally to make a card. The message should be on the inside of the card. Allow the children to decorate the outside of the card. Collect the finished cards and give them to parish members who minister to the sick. Ask them to deliver the cards to people who would appreciate the message.

Make it Happen

Explain to the children that some people give up treats or special snacks during Lent. Then they give the money they would have spent to the poor. Keep a jar or container on your desk for coins. Tell the children that they can put money they save in the container. Explain: *We will use the money we save to buy books about Jesus to send to children who are too poor to buy them.* Find out a group to whom you could send the books.

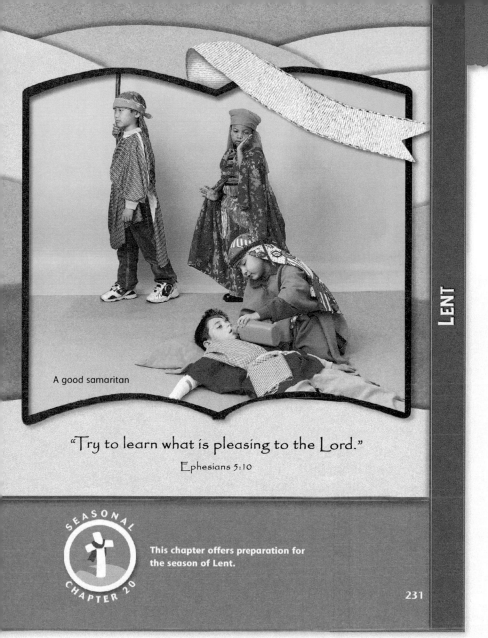

A good samaritan

"Try to learn what is pleasing to the Lord."

Ephesians 5:10

SEASONAL

This chapter offers preparation for the season of Lent.

CHAPTER 20

231

Catechist Goal

• To present Lent as the special time when the Church gets ready to celebrate Jesus' Death and Resurrection

Our Faith Response

• To think of ways to help us grow closer to Jesus

Whole Community Catechesis

An Online Resource

Celebrate **Lent** *as a class, school, and/or a parish community.* Gather In My Name *events comes complete with detailed leader's guide, preparation charts, handouts, promotional ideas, organizational materials, and much more. Go to:*

www.webelieveweb.com

Lesson Plan

Introduce the Season ___ minutes

• **Pray:** *Jesus, every day may I grow closer to you.*

• **Direct** attention to the photo on page 231. Ask: *What does the photo show?* (The children are acting out Jesus' story of the good Samaritan.)

• **Tell** the children that they are going to learn about Lent, which is a time when the Church gets ready to celebrate Jesus' Death and his rising to new life.

• **Read** aloud the verse from Ephesians. Explain the meaning of the words: *When we learn what Jesus taught his followers, we are learning what is pleasing to him. We are learning what he wants us to do.* At this time you may want to read the *Chapter Story* on page 231C.

Chapter 20 • Lent

Lesson Materials

- copies of Reproducible Master 20
- purple crayon
- Grade 1 CD
- drawing paper and crayons
- scissors
- glue

Teaching Note

Time to Present the Chapter

Present this lesson during the first week of Lent. Each week of the season remind the children that Lent is a special time to grow closer to Jesus. Explain: *Praying, doing kind acts, and listening to stories about Jesus help us to get ready to celebrate Jesus' Death and Resurrection at Easter time.*

The Church gets ready to celebrate Jesus' Death and Resurrection.

WE GATHER

When do you remember what your family has done for you? When do you remember what God has done for you?

WE BELIEVE

Lent is a special time in the Church. We remember all that Jesus has done for us. We get ready for the Church's great celebration of Jesus' Death and Resurrection.

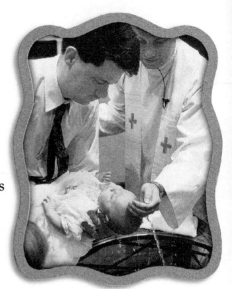

Lent is a time to remember our Baptism. In Baptism we first received grace, the gift of God's life. During Lent we praise Jesus for sharing his life with us.

We were baptized in the name of the Father, and of the Son, and of the Holy Spirit. Praying the Sign of the Cross reminds us of our Baptism.

Talk about the special things that happened at your Baptism.

Lesson Plan

WE GATHER ___ minutes

Focus on Life Read the first *We Gather* question. Ask volunteers to share their responses. (Possible responses include: family celebrations, when we are saying our nighttime prayers, sometimes when we are spending quiet time alone.) Read the second question and have volunteers share their responses. Point out that their responses to the second question may be the same as they were to the first question.

WE BELIEVE ___ minutes

- **Read** the *We Believe* statement. Write the word *Resurrection* on the board. Explain: *We use this word when we are talking about Jesus' rising to new life.*

- **Remind** the children about what they learned about Baptism in Chapter 17. Read the *We Believe* text on page 232. Stress that at Baptism we became children of God and received the gift of God's love.

- **Ask** the children to stand and pray the Sign of the Cross together.

Close your eyes. Thank Jesus for sharing his life with you. Now pray together the Sign of the Cross.

During Lent we try to grow closer to Jesus. We pray and follow his example. We thank God for his great love. We celebrate God's forgiveness. We help people who are sick, hungry, and lonely.

Followers of Jesus Christ should always do these things. However, they have special meaning when we do them during Lent.

LENT

 Look at the pictures on this page. Act out what the people in the pictures are doing and saying.

233

ACTIVITY BANK

Multiple Intelligences

Spatial

Activity Materials: drawing paper, crayons

Give each child a sheet of drawing paper. Have the children fold the papers in half and then open them out flat again. Explain: *Draw a picture on each side of the paper to show something you can do during Lent to grow closer to Jesus.* When the children are finished, ask them to share their pictures with the group. Display the pictures in the prayer space.

• **Read** what the Church does during Lent on page 233. Have the children use a purple crayon to underline the second paragraph.

Read the activity directions. Have volunteers act out what the people in each picture on page 233 are saying and doing.

• **Point out** to the children that the Church uses the color purple for Lent. Tell them: *The priest wears purple when we gather to celebrate Mass.*

Quick Check

✔ *What do we get ready for in Lent?* (We get ready to celebrate Jesus' Death and Resurrection.)

✔ *What do we remember in Lent?* (We remember all that Jesus has done for us. We remember our Baptism.)

CONNECTION

To Catholic Social Teaching

Option for the Poor and Vulnerable

One of the Church's traditional practices during Lent is to give money to people who are poor and hungry. Explain to the children the custom of "giving up" or "not having" special food treats or not buying a game or book. Tell them: *You can then give your money to a collection for people who are poor or hungry.* If you take up a collection in class, you may want to consider donating the money to the local Saint Vincent de Paul Society. This society is in many parishes and its members are always helping people who are in need.

WE RESPOND

Each time you do something to grow closer to Jesus during Lent, color one of the spaces in this cross.

234

Lesson Plan

WE RESPOND
_____ minutes

Connect to Life Show the children stained-glass works of Jesus and his followers. Explain: *A very, very long time ago there were not many books printed. Many people did not know how to read. So artists made stained-glass windows for people to look at in church. Looking at the scenes in the window helped people learn about Jesus and his teaching.*

Read the activity directions. Tell the children that they should keep their stained-glass cross in a place where they will see it often. Explain: *There are forty days in Lent. Each day you do something to grow closer to Jesus, color in one of the spaces.*

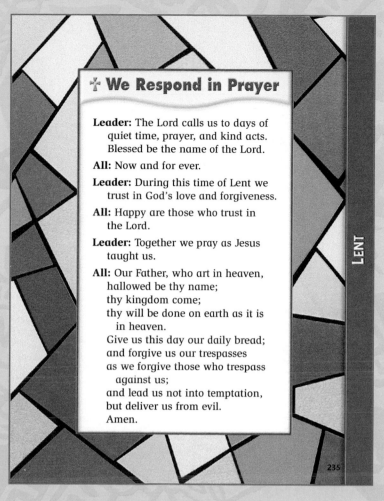

✝ We Respond in Prayer

Leader: The Lord calls us to days of quiet time, prayer, and kind acts. Blessed be the name of the Lord.

All: Now and for ever.

Leader: During this time of Lent we trust in God's love and forgiveness.

All: Happy are those who trust in the Lord.

Leader: Together we pray as Jesus taught us.

All: Our Father, who art in heaven, hallowed be thy name; thy kingdom come; thy will be done on earth as it is in heaven. Give us this day our daily bread; and forgive us our trespasses as we forgive those who trespass against us; and lead us not into temptation, but deliver us from evil. Amen.

LENT

235

Pray Learn Celebrate Share Choose Live

Grade 1 Lent

PROJECT DISCIPLE

Celebrate! Draw yourself doing something that brings you closer to Jesus during Lent.

Possible drawings: pray to Jesus; follow Jesus' example; celebrate God's forgiveness; help people who are sick, hungry, or lonely

Pray Today Finish this prayer.

Jesus, thank you for sharing your

Possible responses: love; life; light
.

Thank you for giving me

Possible responses: love; friendship; the Good News
.

Amen.

Take Home

Talk about ways your family can grow closer to Jesus during Lent.

Plan to make one of these ways happen.

236　www.webelieveweb.com

We Respond in Prayer (p. 235)

Prepare the prayer space by placing a Bible, a cross, and a bowl of water on a purple cloth. Ask the children to think about all Jesus has done for us. Invite them into the prayer space. Sprinkle water on them. Pray the Sign of the Cross before joining hands to pray the Our Father. As the children return to their seats, invite them to sing "People Worry," #4 on the Grade 1 CD.

 This Week's Liturgy
Visit www.webelieveweb.com for this week's liturgical readings and other seasonal material.

Project Disciple (p. 236)

Celebrate!

Read the activity instructions. Review the information from page 233 of the student text. Invite the children to draw a way they can grow closer to Jesus during Lent. Encourage the children to remember these ways during Lent.

Pray Today

Read the instructions. Prompt the children to complete the sentences of the prayer. Encourage the children to pray and share the prayer during Lent.

Take Home

Remind the children that their families can grow closer to Jesus during Lent. Invite the children to make a plan to do something together.

Discuss and send home copies of *Sharing Faith with My Family*, guide page 236B.

Project Disciple Additional Activities See the activities suggested on page 231C of the guide.

Name _____

Make a card to send someone who is sick, lonely, or sad.

Do not worry Jesus is with you.

SHARING FAITH
with My Family

Sharing What I Learned

Look at the pictures below. Use each picture to tell your family what you learned in this chapter.

Growing Closer to Jesus

Lent is a time to grow closer to Jesus. Talk with your family about ways you can do this. Write one way on each leaf of this vine. Put your vine in a place where your family will see it often. Try to do some of these things during Lent.

Visit Sadlier's

www.WeBelieveweb.com

Connect to the Catechism
For adult background and reflection, see paragraph 540.

The Three Days

Christ redeemed us all and gave perfect glory to God principally through his paschal mystery: dying he destroyed our death and rising he restored our life. Therefore the Easter Triduum of the passion and resurrection of Christ is the culmination of the entire liturgical year.

(Norms Governing Liturgical Calendars, 18)

Overview

In this chapter the children will learn that during the Three Days we celebrate Jesus' dying and rising to new life.

For Adult Reading and Reflection
You may want to refer to paragraph 617 of the *Catechism of the Catholic Church*.

Go to **www.webelieveweb.com**, Catechist/Teacher, We Believe Correlations for this chapter's correlation to:
- Six Tasks of Catechesis
- *Catechetical Formation in Chaste Living.*

Catechist Background

What do you consider to be the most important three days of the liturgical year?

The Church's celebration of the Triduum, the Three Days, begins on Holy Thursday and ends on Easter Sunday evening. Each liturgical celebration from the Mass of the Lord's Supper on Holy Thursday to Evening Prayer on Easter Sunday is part of the celebration of the Paschal Mystery, Christ's Passion, Death, and Resurrection from the dead. If we sincerely participate in these celebrations, we may sense that our ordinary lives are truly lived in Christ, with him, and through him in sorrow and joy.

Within the Triduum, the Easter Vigil is the high point, because this is the celebration of the night when Christ passed from death to life, the night when hope and joy are once again restored to us. Celebrating our belief in Christ crucified, buried,

and risen—and thus handing on our faith in him—is a baptismal ministry shared by all believers.

During the Triduum, as we enter deeply into the "hour" of Christ's Passover, we are asked to join him. We are asked to leave sin and death behind, and walk with Jesus into new life, love, peace, and forgiveness. Jesus Christ whom we follow has conquered death and sin. "You too must think of yourselves as [being] dead to sin and living for God in Christ Jesus" (Romans 6:11).

How will you participate in the Church's celebration of the Triduum, the Three Days?

Lesson Planning Guide

Lesson Focus	Presentation	Materials
Day 1		
Guide page 237C **Guide and Text page 237** **Introduce the Season**	• Introduce the Three Days. • Read the *Chapter Story*. • Proclaim words on the banner.	
Day 2		
Guide and Text **pages 238–239** **We Gather** **We Believe**	• Share responses to the We Gather question. • Present the We Believe text about the Church celebrating the Death and Resurrection of Jesus. • Complete the activity by drawing one way to celebrate the Three Days.	• crayons or colored pencils
Day 3		
Guide and Text page 240 **We Believe** **We Respond**	• Present the We Believe text. ♪ Sing the We Respond song.	♪ "Awake! Arise, and Rejoice," Marie-Jo Thum, #24, Grade 1 CD
Day 4		
Text page 241 **Guide page 241–242** **We Respond in Prayer**	• Praise God together. ♪ Respond in song.	♪ "Shout from the Mountains," Marie-Jo Thum, #25, Grade 1 CD • prayer space: white tablecloth, cross, basket of bread and grapes, bowl of water, battery-operated candle
Day 5		
Text page 242 **Guide pages 241–242, 242A** **Project Disciple**	• Complete the Project Disciple activities. Discuss the *Take Home* activity. • Complete the Reproducible Master 21 activity. See guide pages 237C and 242A. • Discuss/send home Sharing Faith with My Family, guide page 242B.	• pencils • copies of Reproducible Master 21, guide page 242A • copies of Sharing Faith with My Family reproducible master, guide page 242B

For additional ideas, activities, and opportunities: Visit Sadlier's **www.WeBelieveweb.com**

Chapter Story

On the way home from Mass on the Sunday before Easter, Joseph's family stopped at his grandparent's house. Joseph's grandmother had made a palm cross to give to his parents. Joseph had learned the story of how people welcomed Jesus to Jerusalem on the Sunday before he died and rose to new life.

Joseph talked to his grandfather while he was waiting for his parents. Joseph's grandfather said, "Joseph, a very important celebration of the Church will be this week. The family will be gathering with the parish on Holy Thursday night, Good Friday, and Holy Saturday night."

Joseph answered, "I know Grandpop. Mrs. Pichardo told us we were going to learn about the celebration this week. We already learned about Lent. Mom, Dad, and I have been getting ready to celebrate Jesus' Death and Resurrection."

Joseph's grandfather said, "I'm glad you're learning about the Church's celebration. I'll see you on Holy Thursday night after Mass. You can tell me about the Three Days."

"That's a great idea, Grandpop," Joseph answered.

Do you think Joseph liked to learn about the Church's special times of celebration? Why do you like to learn about these special times?

PROJECT DISCIPLE
Additional Activities

Pray Today

Help the children write a prayer to say during the Three Days. Make copies for the children and invite them to take the prayer home and put it in a place where they will see and pray it often.

Celebrate!

Distribute copies of Reproducible Master 21, guide page 242A. Explain to the children that they will make Three Days mobiles. Allow the children to color and cut out the circles. Help them punch a hole at the top of each circle and to use string or yarn to attach each circle to a hanger. Explain the order: the bread and grapes circle should be on the left; the cross circle should be in the middle; and the candle and water circle should be on the right. Encourage the children to take the mobiles home to share them with their families.

Lord, through your cross you brought joy to the world.

SEASONAL
CHAPTER 21

This chapter includes the three days from Holy Thursday evening until Easter Sunday.

237

Chapter 21 • Three Days

Catechist Goal

• To present the Church's celebration of the Three Days

Our Faith Response

• To celebrate in prayer and song Jesus' dying and rising to new life

Gather In My Name

Whole Community Catechesis

An Online Resource

For the **Triduum** *season use the Easter GIMN event or the Eucharist GIMN event to highlight the season. Gather In My Name events come complete with a detailed leader's guide, preparation charts, handouts, promotional ideas, organizational materials, and much more. Go to:*

www.webelieveweb.com

Lesson Plan

Introduce the Season ___ minutes

• **Pray:** *Jesus, we believe in you. We thank you for your love.*

• **Ask:** *During Lent, what have we been getting ready to celebrate?* (Jesus' Death and Resurrection) Discuss with the children what they have been doing to get ready.

• **Have** the children open their texts to page 237. Direct attention to the photo on the page. Point out that the children in the photo have gathered to pray to Jesus. Ask: *What do you think the children are saying?* Have volunteers share their responses.

• **Share** the *Chapter Story* on page 237C. Tell the children that in this chapter they will learn about the Church's celebration of the Three Days.

• **Pray** together the prayer on the banner.

237

The Church celebrates that Jesus died and rose to new life.

WE GATHER

Think about the crosses that you see. How are they different?

WE BELIEVE

Lent is a time that gets us ready for the Church's greatest celebration. Lent gets us ready for the great Three Days. These Three Days celebrate Jesus' dying and rising to new life.

During the Three Days, we gather with our parish. We celebrate at night and during the day.

We do the things Jesus asked us to do. We remember that Jesus gave himself to us at the Last Supper. We remember the ways Jesus loved and served others.

We listen to readings from the Bible. We pray before the cross. The cross reminds us of Jesus' dying and rising to new life.

238

Lesson Materials

- copies of Reproducible Master 21
- Grade 1 CD
- crayons
- white construction paper
- scissors and glue
- hole puncher
- lengths of string or yarn

Teaching Note
Presenting the Chapter

If you meet with the children during Holy Week, present the chapter at this time. If you do not meet during Holy Week, present the chapter the week before Holy Week.

Lesson Plan

WE GATHER _____ minutes

Focus on Life Read the *We Gather* section. Ask the children to share how the crosses that they see are different.

Write the word *crucifix* on the board. Pronounce the word for the children and have them repeat it. Explain that a crucifix is a cross that has the body of Jesus on it.

WE BELIEVE _____ minutes

• **Ask** the children to read the *We Believe* statement at the top of page 238.

• **Pause** to allow the children time to think about the *Chapter Story*. Then read the *We Believe* paragraphs on page 238.

🧑 Draw a picture here to show one way you will celebrate the Three Days with your parish.

THE THREE DAYS

ACTIVITY BANK

Multiple Intelligences

Intrapersonal

Activity Materials: writing paper

Give each child a sheet of writing paper. Ask the children to write a letter to Jesus to thank him for dying and rising to new life. Tell the children that they can use their books to help them with spelling.

• **Point out** the photos on pages 238 and 239. Explain: *On Holy Thursday we celebrate that Jesus gave us the gift of himself in the Eucharist. On Good Friday we remember that Jesus died on the cross. On Holy Saturday night, we remember that Jesus rose to new life. We remember that at Baptism we became children of God and followers of Jesus.*

🧑 **Read** the activity directions and allow the children time to complete their drawings.

Quick Check

✔ *What does the Church celebrate during the Three Days?* (The Church celebrates Jesus' dying and rising to new life.)

✔ *When we pray before the cross, what does the cross remind us of?* (The cross reminds us of Jesus' dying and rising to new life.)

CONNECTION

To Liturgy

Each year at the beginning of Easter Vigil, the Church celebrates the service of light. The priest lights a fire outside of church, blesses the fire, and then lights the Easter candle with this fire. Then the deacon or priest lifts the candle and sings, "Christ our Light." Everyone sings in response, "Thanks be to God." The priest or deacon sings these words three times and we respond each time. When the procession enters the church, we light the small candles from the light of the Easter candle. When the procession reaches the altar, all the lights in the church are turned on and the priest or deacon sings a special Easter proclamation. Take the children to church to see the Easter candle.

We sing with joy to celebrate that Jesus rose from the dead. We remember our Baptism in a special way. We welcome new members into the Church. We celebrate with songs of joy and praise.

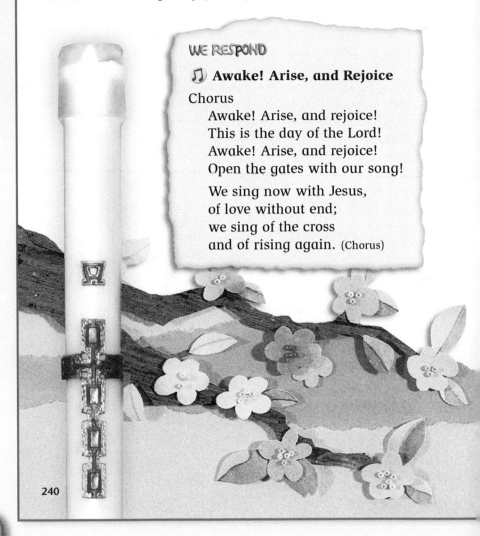

WE RESPOND

♫ **Awake! Arise, and Rejoice**

Chorus
Awake! Arise, and rejoice!
This is the day of the Lord!
Awake! Arise, and rejoice!
Open the gates with our song!

We sing now with Jesus,
of love without end;
we sing of the cross
and of rising again. (Chorus)

240

Lesson Plan

WE BELIEVE (continued)

• **Read** aloud the paragraph at the top of page 240. Point out the photo of the candle. Say: *This is the Easter candle that is lit during the celebration on Holy Saturday night.* If possible, take the children to church to show them the Easter candle.

WE RESPOND ___ minutes

• **Play** "Awake! Arise, and Rejoice," #24 on the Grade 1 CD. Have the children practice singing.

• **Invite** the children to gather in the prayer space. Have them sing, "Awake! Arise, and Rejoice."

✝ We Respond in Prayer

Leader: Lord, through your cross you brought joy to the world.

All: Lord, through your cross you brought joy to the world.

Leader: Holy is God!

All: Holy is God!

Leader: Holy and strong!

All: Holy and strong!

♫ **Shout from the Mountains**

And we sing:
Holy, holy,
holy is God!
Holy, holy,
holy and strong!

241

THE THREE DAYS

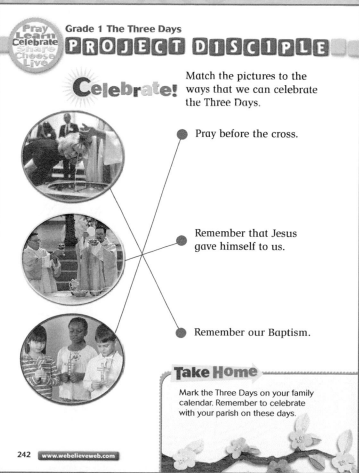

Grade 1 The Three Days

PROJECT DISCIPLE

Celebrate!

Match the pictures to the ways that we can celebrate the Three Days.

● Pray before the cross.

● Remember that Jesus gave himself to us.

● Remember our Baptism.

Take Home

Mark the Three Days on your family calendar. Remember to celebrate with your parish on these days.

We Respond in Prayer (p. 241)

Prepare the prayer space by placing a Bible, a cross, a basket of bread and grapes, a bowl of water, and a battery operated candle on a white cloth.

Turn off the overhead lights and ask the children to reflect that:
• *Jesus gave himself to us at the Last Supper.*
• *Jesus died for us on the cross.*
• *Jesus rose to new life.*

Light the candle and gather in the prayer space. Pray the Sign of the Cross and the prayer. Explain: *Because Jesus died on a cross for us and rose to new life, we can have new life.* Sing "Shout from the Mountains," #25 on the Grade 1 CD.

📖 This Week's Liturgy

Visit **www.webelieveweb.com** for this week's liturgical readings and other seasonal material.

Project Disciple (p. 242)

Celebrate!

Read the instructions. Ask the children to match the pictures to the sentences. Encourage the children to celebrate the Three Days in all three ways.

Take Home

Mark the Three Days on a classroom calendar. Encourage the children to do the same at home. Encourage the children to celebrate the Three Days with their families and the parish.

Discuss and send home copies of *Sharing Faith with My Family*, guide page 242B.

Project Disciple Additional Activities See the activities suggested on page 237C of the guide.

Name _____

Use these circles to make a Three Days mobile.

Sharing What I Learned

Look at the pictures below. Use each picture to tell your family what you learned in this chapter.

The Three Days

The Church's celebration of the great Three Days begins on Holy Thursday evening and ends on Easter Sunday evening. Mark these days on your family calendar. Talk together about ways your parish celebrates on these days.

Visit Sadlier's

www.WEBELIEVEweb.com

Connect to the Catechism
For adult background and reflection, see paragraph 617.

ASSESSMENT

Unit 3 Test

Read aloud each set of test directions. You may also choose to read aloud each test item. Wait for a minute for the children to indicate their responses in writing before proceeding to the next item or set of directions.

Alternative Assessment

You may want the children to complete the following alternative-assessment activity.

Draw a picture of a way to worship God.

Additional Testing

• Unit 3 Test in Grade 1 *Assessment Book*, pages 41–42

• Unit 3 Alternative Assessment in Grade 1 *Assessment Book*, page 55

• CD-ROM *Test Generator and Resource*: Use Unit 3 Test or customize your own.

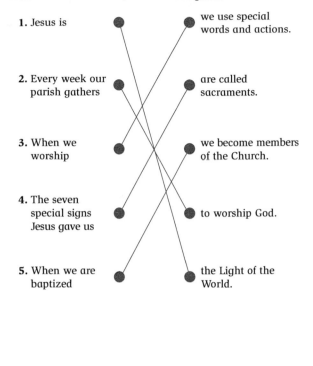

Grade 1 Unit 3

UNIT TEST

Draw a line to match the sentence parts.

1. Jesus is — the Light of the World.

2. Every week our parish gathers — to worship God.

3. When we worship — we use special words and actions.

4. The seven special signs Jesus gave us — are called sacraments.

5. When we are baptized — we become members of the Church.

continued on next page   243

Grade 1 Unit 3

Read the sentences below.
Use a ⟨ blue ⟩ to circle the ones about Baptism.
Use a ⟨ purple ⟩ to circle the ones about Penance.

6. We are welcomed to the Church. blue

7. We tell God we are sorry. purple

8. We are invited to walk in the light of Christ. blue

9. Water is a sign of the life God gives us. blue

10. The priest shares God's forgiveness with us. purple

244

We Celebrate and Live Our Faith

UNIT 4

Chapter 22 Jesus Gives Us the Eucharist 247

Chapter 23 We Celebrate the Mass 259

Chapter 24 We Share God's Love 271

Chapter 25 We Honor Mary and the Saints 283

Chapter 26 We Care for the Gifts of God's Creation 295

Seasonal Chapter

Chapter 27 Easter

245

PROJECT DISCIPLE

DEAR FAMILY

In Unit 4 your child will grow as a disciple of Jesus by:

- appreciating that at Mass we celebrate what Jesus did at the Last Supper
- gathering with the parish family for the celebration of the Mass
- sharing God's love by loving and serving our family and others
- honoring Mary and all the saints by asking them to pray for us and by following their example
- caring for all of God's creation, and respecting all people as Jesus taught us to do.

Saint Stories

Introduce your child to Saint Jerome who is the Patron of Scripture Scholars. As a young student, he learned Latin and Greek and later translated the Bible into Latin. He said, "Now we must translate the words of Scripture into deeds, and instead of speaking holy words, we must do them." What words of Scripture can you do today? Pray to Saint Jerome before the Liturgy of the Word at Mass this Sunday.

Celebrate!

In Chapter 22, your child is reminded of the Third Commandment, "Remember to keep holy the Lord's Day." Participating in the Sunday celebration of the Mass is the first way we keep the Lord's Day holy. We can also spend time together as a family and do something for those in need. Plan to make this Sunday holy by doing all of these!

Reality Check

"Parents should initiate their children at an early age into the mysteries of the faith of which they are the 'first heralds' for their children."

(Catechism of the Catholic Church, 2225)

picture This

Chapter 23 has many photos of what happens at Mass. Look at the pictures together, and ask your child about what is happening in each one. How are the photos like what happens at your parish? How are they different?

Show That You Care

At the end of Mass, we often hear these words: "Go in peace." What are some ways in which your family shows love for the Lord and serves him? Choose one special way you will love and serve the Lord this week.

Take Home

Each chapter in your child's *We Believe* Grade 1 text offers a "Take Home" activity that invites your family to support your child's journey to more fully become a disciple of Christ.

Be ready for this unit's Take Home:

Chapter 22: Listing people who help us worship at Mass

Chapter 23: Praying for parishioners who are sick

Chapter 24: Sharing God's love as a family

Chapter 25: Making a family tree

Chapter 26: Caring for God's creation

246

CLASS CONNECTION

Read aloud the unit title and the chapter titles. Ask the children: *What do you think you will be learning in this unit?* Invite a few volunteers to respond. Then explain to the children that they will be learning about celebrating the Mass and sharing God's love with others.

HOME CONNECTION

Project Disciple Dear Family

Sadlier *We Believe* calls on families to become involved in:

- learning the faith
- prayer and worship
- living their faith.

Highlighting of these unit family pages and the opportunities they offer will strengthen the partnership of the Church and the home.

For additional information and activities, encourage families to visit Sadlier's

www.WeBelieveweb.com

Chapter 22 · Jesus Gives Us the Eucharist

Overview

In Chapter 19 the children learned about God's forgiveness. In this chapter the children will learn that in the Sacrament of the Eucharist, bread and wine become the Body and Blood of Jesus Christ.

Doctrinal Content	For Adult Reading and Reflection *Catechism of the Catholic Church*	
The children will learn:		Paragraph
• Jesus shared a special meal with his followers.		1339
• We celebrate what Jesus said and did at the Last Supper.		1341
• We celebrate the Sacrament of the Eucharist.		1346
• We join with our parish for the celebration of Mass.		2178

Key Words

Eucharist (p. 250)
Mass (p. 252)

Catechist Background

What are some ways you remember a loved one who has died?

Before Jesus died on the cross, he shared a special meal with his disciples. It was the time of the Jewish feast of Passover, when the events of God's great work in freeing the people from slavery in Egypt are recalled in the midst of a sacred meal. Jesus gathered with his disciples. During the meal, he offered the bread and the wine as his Body and Blood. We call this meal the "Last Supper," because it was the last meal Jesus was to share with his disciples before his Death. He also gave his disciples this command: "do this in memory of me" (Luke 22:19).

After the Death and Resurrection of Jesus, the Church began to gather and obey Jesus' command. They would share a meal, and in the midst of the meal, they would offer thanks and praise to God and share the Eucharist, the bread and wine that had become the Body and Blood of Christ. This ritual action, combined with the reading of Scripture in the community, became the celebration of the Eucharist.

Today we gather weekly to celebrate the Mass. "Sunday, the 'Lord's Day,' is the principal day for the celebration of the Eucharist because it is the day of the Resurrection." (CCC 1193) For Christians, the Lord's Day is from sundown on Saturday to sundown on Sunday. Many parishes begin their weekly celebration of Mass with a Saturday evening Mass that anticipates the Sunday celebration. When we gather to celebrate the Eucharist, we obey the Third Commandment to keep holy the Lord's Day and we obey Christ's command to "do this in memory of me" (Luke 22:19).

How does participating in the Mass help you to remember Jesus?

Go to **www.webelieveweb.com**, Catechist/Teacher, We Believe Correlations for this chapter's correlation to the Six Tasks of Catechesis.

Lesson Planning Guide

Lesson Focus	Presentation	Materials
Day 1		
page 247  **We Gather in Prayer** **pages 248–249** *Jesus shared a special meal with his followers.* 📖 *Matthew 26:26–28*	• Praise God together in prayer. 🧍 Share responses to the We Gather incomplete sentences. • Read the Scripture story about the Last Supper in We Believe. • Discuss the We Respond questions.	For the prayer space: fabric table-cloth, Bible, basket of bread and grapes • highlighter or crayon • copies of reproducible master *What's the Word?*, guide page 247F
Day 2		
pages 250–251 *We celebrate what Jesus said and did at the Last Supper.* 📖 *Luke 22:19*	• Read the We Gather text about ways to remember special times. • Present the We Believe text about celebrating the Eucharist. 🧍 Complete the We Respond prayer and pray it quietly.	
Day 3		
pages 252–253 *We celebrate the Sacrament of the Eucharist.*	• Share responses to the We Gather questions. • Present the We Believe text about ways Jesus is with us at Mass. 🎵 Sing the We Respond song to celebrate Jesus with us in the Eucharist.	• copies of Reproducible Master 22, guide page 247G 🎵 "We Come to Share God's Special Gift," Christopher Walker, #26, Grade 1 CD
Day 4		
pages 254–255 *We join with our parish for the celebration of Mass.*	🧍 Act out the We Gather activity. • Present the We Believe text about joining our parish for Mass. 🧍 Do the We Respond puzzle activity. • Read and discuss the *As Catholics* text.	
Day 5		
pages 256–257 **Project Disciple** **page 258** **Chapter 22 Test**	• Complete the Project Disciple activities. • Explain the *Take Home* activity. • Discuss/send home Sharing Faith with My Family, guide page 247E. • Complete Chapter 22 Test. • Work on *Alternative Assessment* activity.	• pencils • crayons or colored pencils • copies of Sharing Faith with My Family reproducible master, guide page 247E

For additional ideas, activities, and opportunities: Visit Sadlier's **www.WeBelieveweb.com**

247B

Enrichment Ideas

Chapter Story

When Augusto came home from soccer practice, his parents were busy in the kitchen. They had all the mixing bowls out on the countertop.

Augusto asked, "What are you doing?"

Augusto's father answered, "We're making a special meal for your sister's birthday. Aunt Beatrice and Uncle César are joining us and so are Emilia's two best friends, Chris and Lizbeth. We are making homemade pizza, so we'll need to make enough for everyone."

"May I help?" asked Augusto.

"Why, of course. Give me that big spoon over there," said Mom, sounding like a chef in a restaurant.

Augusto watched his mother pour tomato sauce into a pot. She let him stir the sauce before she put it on the stove. Then he watched his dad make balls of pizza dough. Augusto helped to flatten the dough. His mom and dad cut vegetables and cheese for the pizza toppings.

How surprised Emilia would be when she realized that her favorite people would be together for her birthday. She would also be surprised that her favorite meal would be shared.

Later that afternoon Augusto greeted the guests. He watched out the window, waiting for his sister to get home from the park. He opened the door for her and everyone yelled, "Surprise!"

The family and friends sat down at the table. The pizza looked and smelled delicious. Before everyone began to enjoy the meal, Augusto's mom asked him to say a prayer. He prayed, "Dear God, thank you for this special meal. We are happy for Emilia on her birthday. And we are happy she likes homemade pizza!"

▶ *What made Emilia's birthday a special celebration?*

FAITH and MEDIA

▶ If you have the children do the "Gift Window" *Chapter Project,* you might also tell them about stained-glass windows as a medium of mass communication. In the Middle Ages, when most people did not know how to read and books were very rare and very expensive, even the very poorest and the very youngest members of the community could "read" stories from the Bible and lessons of the faith in the beautiful stained-glass windows of churches and cathedrals. These light- and color-filled places of worship came to be called "Bibles in stone and glass."

▶ If you bring art books to class show the children paintings of the Last Supper. Remind the children that paintings and drawings are examples of media.

CHAPTER PROJECT: GIFT WINDOW

After you have presented the Day 2 lesson, remind the children that the word *eucharist* means "to give thanks." Brainstorm with the children gifts for which they are thankful (some examples might be family, home, and food). Write all responses on the board. Then have the children work in small groups. Give each group a large piece of poster board with sections cut out to look like a frame for a stained-glass window. Distribute other smaller pieces of poster board that have been cut into different shapes and that can be attached to the window sections. Have the children draw and color one of the gifts listed on each of the small pieces. Then have the children tape or glue the drawings onto the "windows." Display the windows around the classroom as a reminder of the many gifts God has given us.

PROJECT DISCIPLE

Pray
Learn
Celebrate
Share
Choose
Live

Additional Activities

What's the Word?

(Use on Day 1.)

Materials needed: copies of reproducible master, guide page 247F

Explain to the children that they will be doing an activity to remember the story of the Last Supper. Distribute copies of the Scripture reproducible master. Choose four volunteers to read the parts of Reader 1, Reader 2, Andrew, and John. Ask the other children to follow along as the story is read.

Make it Happen

Materials needed: empty cartons, construction paper, glue, scissors, and markers

Remind the children that some people do not have enough to eat. Tell them Jesus wants everyone to have enough food. Explain that you are going to organize a food drive. You will collect non-perishable food items to donate to a few families. Have the children work in small groups. Give each group an empty carton and materials to decorate the carton. Send notes home to inform families about the food collection. Once the food has been collected and the cartons are filled, donate it to a local food bank or pantry.

Show What you Know

Materials needed: copies of a sheet of paper with the word *MASS* written vertically and write-on lines before and after each letter

Invite the children to write acrostic poems using the word *Mass*. Model writing an acrostic poem by writing the letters *M-A-S-S* vertically on the board. Help the children to use the letters in the word *Mass* to write phrases about worshiping God and the celebration of Mass. Encourage them to finish their poems individually or in small groups. Collect and display the completed poems.

Picture This

Exposing children to fine art is a wonderful way to help them make connections. Explain that because the Last Supper was so important, many artists have depicted the event in their artwork. Display Leonardo da Vinci's iconic painting of the Last Supper in your classroom. If you have an interactive whiteboard, zoom in on the faces of Jesus and the Apostles. Ask the children to describe what is happening in the painting based on what they have learned about the Last Supper.

Meeting Individual Needs
English Language Learners

For children who are learning English, provide visual symbols to help the children to understand chapter ideas and *Key Words*. Whenever possible, show pictures of what is being discussed in the lesson. For example, when explaining the words *Eucharist* and *Mass*, show photographs of the celebration. Ask the children to share with the class some of the prayers of the Mass in their own languages.

We Believe Resources

- Grade 1 *Review & Resource Book*, pages 49–51
- Grade 1 *Family Book*, pages 62–64
- Grade 1 *Assessment Book*, pages 43–44
- Grade 1 CD-ROM *Test Generator and Resource*: Use Chapter 22 Test or customize your own.
- **www.webelieveweb.com**

Sharing What I Learned

Look at the pictures below. Use each picture to tell your family what you learned in this chapter.

We Give Thanks

When we celebrate the Eucharist, we give thanks to God. We thank Jesus for all he has done for us.

Gather your family together. Use the letters in the word *eucharist*. Name gifts you would like to thank God for. You can add more, too!

Pray and thank God for his gifts together.

_____ E	ACH OTHER _____
_____ U	_____
_____ C	_____
_____ H	_____
_____ A	_____
_____ GR	ANDPARENTS
_____ I	_____
_____ S	_____
_____ T	_____

Connect to the Catechism
For adult background and reflection, see paragraphs 1339, 1341, 1346 and 2178.

PROJECT DISCIPLE

Pray
Learn
Celebrate
Share
Choose
Live

Name _____

What's *the* Word?

Reader 1: Imagine you are walking down the street in Jerusalem. Listen as the followers of Jesus, John and Andrew, speak to each other.

Reader 2: They are talking about what Jesus did on the night before he died.

Andrew: John, do you remember what Jesus did while we were eating our special meal?

John: Yes, Andrew, I do. Jesus picked up the bread. He said a special blessing, and then he broke the bread and gave it to us.

Andrew: Jesus said, "Take and eat; this is my body." (Matthew 26:26)

John: And then Jesus took the cup of wine. He gave thanks, and then gave us the cup.

Andrew: That's right, John. Jesus said, "Drink from it, all of you, for this is my blood." (Matthew 26:27–28)

John: Jesus told us to remember what he did for us. He gave us the gift of himself.

Look at the first four sentences. Each sentence is a clue. Each clue will help you find one letter of a special word.

1. This letter is in MAT but not in CAT. _____

2. This letter is in PAT but not in PET. _____

3. This letter is in SAT but not in BAT. _____

4. This letter is in SEE but not in BEE. _____

Use the special word to finish this sentence.

The Church's greatest
    celebration is the ___ ___ ___ ___.

Jesus Gives Us the Eucharist

22

✝ **We Gather in Prayer**

Leader: Let us join hands and form a circle of friends.

Reader 1: O God, we gather now to pray.
All: We praise you together.

Reader 2: We listen to your Word.
All: We praise you together.

Reader 3: We lift up our hearts.
All: We praise you together.

Reader 4: We share your love with everyone.
All: We praise you together.

247

PREPARING TO PRAY

The children will gather to praise God.

• Remind the children: *A circle has no beginning or end. This is why a circle can remind us of God's never-ending love.* Explain to the children that they will stand in a circle for the gathering prayer.

• Ask four volunteers to be readers. Give the children a few minutes to prepare.

The Prayer Space
• Cover the prayer table with a fabric tablecloth.

• On the table place an opened Bible and a basket of bread and grapes.

 This Week's Liturgy
Visit **www.webelieveweb.com** for this week's liturgical readings and other seasonal material.

Lesson Plan

We Gather in Prayer ___ minutes

✝ **Pray**

• Pray the Sign of the Cross. Then invite the children to gather in the prayer space and join hands to form a prayer circle.

• Cue Reader 1 to read the prayer. After the children respond, pause briefly. Then cue the next reader to begin.

Family Connection Update
Invite the children to share their families' discussions about forgiveness.

Catechist Goal

• To introduce what Jesus said and did at the Last Supper

Our Faith Response

• To appreciate Jesus' Last Supper as a special meal

Lesson Materials

• highlighter or crayon
• copies of reproducible master *What's the Word?*, guide page 247F

Teaching Note

The We Believe *Program and the Sacrament of the Eucharist*

The purpose of this chapter is to introduce the children to the Church's celebration of the Sacrament of the Eucharist. The chapter's concepts are more fully developed in the Grade 2 text, particularly Chapters 15 and 16.

Jesus shared a special meal with his followers.

WE GATHER

✝ *God, let us share in your life.*

🏃 Think about a holiday celebration. Here are some things you do to celebrate. Finish the sentences using these words.

| friends   meal   God   family |

Gather your __f__ __a__ __m__ __i__ __l__ __y__.

Invite __f__ __r__ __i__ __e__ __n__ __d__ __s__.

Have a __m__ __e__ __a__ __l__ together.

Thank __G__ __o__ __d__ for this special time.

WE BELIEVE

On the night before he died, Jesus was with his followers in Jerusalem. They had gathered for a Jewish holiday. They were celebrating with a special meal. Jesus told them that he loved them.

248

Lesson Plan

WE GATHER   ___ minutes

✝ **Pray** Invite the children to pray the Sign of the Cross and the *We Gather* prayer.

Focus on Life Encourage the children to recall the special days they celebrate with their families. For example, a birthday, an anniversary, or a holiday is a special time we share with our loved ones. Ask: *How does your family celebrate a special day?* Read aloud the *We Gather* paragraph and the activity directions. Then read the words in the word box aloud together. Ask the children to complete each sentence with one of the words. When most of the children have finished, have them take turns reading their completed sentences. Share the *Chapter Story* on guide page 247C.

WE BELIEVE   ___ minutes

Learn About Jesus Read aloud the *We Believe* statement. Explain: *In the Bible we read about different times Jesus shared meals with his followers and friends. We will now learn about the last time Jesus ate and celebrated with them.* Read aloud the first *We Believe* paragraph.

Read Scripture Ask the children to look at the picture of Jesus and his followers. Read the story of the Last Supper from the Gospel of Matthew.

Explain: *We call the meal Jesus shared that night the Last Supper. It was the last meal Jesus shared with his followers before he died.*

Here is what Jesus said and did.

📖 Matthew 26:26–28

Read Along

While they were eating, Jesus picked up the bread. He blessed it and broke it. He gave it to his friends. He said, "Take and eat; this is my body." (Matthew 26:26)

Then Jesus took a cup of wine. He gave God thanks. He passed the cup to his friends and said, "Drink from it, all of you, for this is my blood." (Matthew 26:27–28)

We call this last meal Jesus shared with his followers the Last Supper. Jesus gave his followers the gift of himself. The bread and wine became the Body and Blood of Jesus.

WE RESPOND

Imagine you are at the Last Supper.
How do you think Jesus' followers feel?
How do you think Jesus feels?
How do you feel?

249

ACTIVITY BANK

Multiple Intelligences

Bodily-Kinesthetic

Activity Materials: costumes and props

Have the children work in small groups. Invite each group to act out the story of the Last Supper. Allow time for each group to present its dramatization for the other groups.

Scripture

Linguistic, Interpersonal

For a Scripture activity, see *What's the Word?*, guide page 247F.

Ask: *Why was the Last Supper a very special meal?* Emphasize that it was very special because Jesus gave us the gift of himself. Read aloud the last *We Believe* paragraph. Ask the children to highlight or underline the last two sentences.

Quick Check

✔ *What is the last meal Jesus shared with his followers called?* (The last meal Jesus shared is the Last Supper.)

✔ *What did Jesus give to his followers at the Last Supper?* (Jesus gave the gift of himself.)

WE RESPOND   ___ minutes

Connect to Life Invite the children to look at the picture of Jesus with his followers on these pages. Ask

them to imagine themselves in the room with Jesus and his followers. Then ask the children to listen as you read the *We Respond* questions. Invite volunteers to share their responses. Help the children to conclude that Jesus would be happy to share a meal with his friends, just as his followers would be happy that Jesus was with them. Jesus might have felt sad because he knew that the meal was the last he would share with his followers.

Pray Invite the children to pray a silent prayer to thank Jesus for giving himself to us in a special way.

Plan Ahead for Day 2

Catechist Goal: To present the connection between the Last Supper and the Eucharist

Preparation: Reflect on Jesus' gift of himself in the Eucharist.

Catechist Goal

• To present the connection between the Last Supper and the Eucharist

Our Faith Response

• To give thanks to Jesus for the gift of the Eucharist

 **Eucharist**

Teaching Tip

Brainstorming Rules

You may wish to discuss the following rules of brainstorming to help the activity run more smoothly.

• Begin by having everyone in the group think of ideas and say them aloud.
• Write down all the ideas.
• Do not judge or reject any idea when it is first spoken.
• Once all the ideas have been written down, have the group go through them, one by one, to decide which ideas are appropriate.

We celebrate what Jesus said and did at the Last Supper.

WE GATHER

✝ *Jesus, we remember what you have done for us.*

Here are some ways to remember special times.

• Talk about them with friends and family.
• Take pictures or videos and look at them later.
• Celebrate them again and again.

WE BELIEVE

Jesus told his followers to remember what he said and did at the Last Supper.

The Church does this at the celebration of the Eucharist. Together we celebrate what Jesus said and did at the Last Supper.

The **Eucharist** is the sacrament of the Body and Blood of Jesus Christ. In this sacrament, the bread and wine become the Body and Blood of Jesus Christ.

 Eucharist the sacrament of the Body and Blood of Jesus Christ

250

Lesson Plan

WE GATHER _____ minutes

✝ **Pray** Remind the children that Jesus gave us the gift of himself at the Last Supper. Then pray the *We Gather* prayer together.

Focus on Life Have the children brainstorm ways they can remember special celebrations. (photographs, e-mails, home videos, and so on). Print the children's responses on the board. Then read the *We Gather* paragraph. Tell the children that in this lesson they will learn about a way we remember what Jesus said and did at the Last Supper.

WE BELIEVE _____ minutes

Think About Jesus' Words and Actions Invite a volunteer to read aloud the first two *We Believe* para-

graphs. Explain that Jesus told his followers to remember his words and actions. Then read aloud again the Scripture story of the Last Supper. Ask: *What did Jesus do at the Last Supper?* (He blessed bread, broke it, and gave it to his followers; he took a cup of wine, gave God thanks, and gave the wine to his friends.) Then ask: *What did Jesus say?* ("Take and eat; this is my body" [Matthew 26:26]. "Drink from it, all of you, for this is my blood" [Matthew 26:27–28].) Tell the children that we remember Jesus' words and actions during the celebration of the Eucharist.

Learn About the Eucharist Print the word *Eucharist* on the board. Emphasize that we do what Jesus said and did at the Last Supper when we celebrate the Sacrament of the Eucharist.

ACTIVITY BANK

Curriculum Connection
Science and Social Studies
Activity Materials: photographs or
pictures of wheat and bread, flour,
water

Explain: *Bread is a very important
kind of food. People of all countries
eat bread because it helps our bodies
to grow and become strong.*

Give a simple explanation of how
bread is made. Show the children
wheat stalks. Explain that the kernels
are ground up to make flour. Show
the children flour and tell them that
water and a few other ingredients are
added. Flat cakes, rolls or loaves are
formed. Then the rolls are placed in
the oven to make bread.

The word *eucharist* means "to give
thanks." At the celebration of the
Eucharist, we thank God for his many
gifts. We thank Jesus for all he has
done for us.

WE RESPOND

Pray quietly. Think of all the things
Jesus has done for us.

✗ Finish this prayer.

Thank you, Jesus, for

_____

_____

_____

251

Read the third *We Believe* paragraph. Ask the children
to look at the pictures on these two pages. Explain that
the Eucharist is the sacrament of the Body and Blood of
Christ. Then read aloud the last *We Believe* paragraph.

Remember the Key Word Ask the children to
review the meaning of *Eucharist*. Have each child work
with a partner to use the word in a sentence. Ask volunteers to share their responses.

Quick Check

✔ *At the Last Supper, what did Jesus tell his followers to
do?* (He told them to "do this in memory of me."
[Luke 22:19])

✔ *What is the Eucharist?* (The Eucharist is the sacrament of the Body and Blood of Christ.)

WE RESPOND ___ minutes

Connect to Life Discuss with the children all the
things Jesus has done for us. Invite volunteers to share
responses. (Responses might include: Jesus gave us the
gift of himself; Jesus takes care of us; and so on.)

Pray Ask the children to thank Jesus for all the things
he has done for them.

Plan Ahead for Day 3

Catechist Goal: To explain that we worship
God when we pray at Mass

Preparation: Make copies of Reproducible
Master 22, guide page 247G.

Catechist Goal

• To explain that we worship God when we pray at Mass

Our Faith Response

• To worship God in prayer and at Mass

 **Mass**

Lesson Materials

• copies of Reproducible Master 22
• Grade 1 CD

Teaching Tip

Celebrating Throughout the World
   Show the children a globe or world map. Point out that people in parishes throughout the world gather on Sunday for Mass. Explain that people pray and sing the prayers of the Mass in their own languages.

We celebrate the Sacrament of the Eucharist.

WE GATHER

✝ *Jesus, thank you for the gift of yourself in the Eucharist.*

When do we worship God? What are some ways we praise and thank him?

WE BELIEVE

The **Mass** is another name for the celebration of the Eucharist. The Mass is the Church's greatest celebration.

At Mass we worship God together. We praise the Father for his love. We celebrate the life of his Son, Jesus. We ask the Holy Spirit to help us celebrate.

Mass another name for the celebration of the Eucharist

252

Lesson Plan

WE GATHER ___ minutes

✝ **Pray** Invite the children to pray aloud the Sign of the Cross and the *We Gather* prayer.

Focus on Life Help the children to answer the *We Gather* questions. Encourage the children to name possible ways that we praise and thank God. Tell the children that in this lesson they will learn that we worship God together when we celebrate Mass.

WE BELIEVE ___ minutes

Learn About the Mass Ask the children what the Eucharist is. Read aloud the *We Believe* statement. Read the four *We Believe* paragraphs, pausing after each one to ask the following questions:

• After the first, ask: *What is the Mass?* (The Mass is another name for the celebration of the Eucharist.)

• After the second, ask: *What do we do at Mass?* (We praise the Father; we celebrate the life of his Son; we ask the Holy Spirit to help us celebrate.)

• After the third and fourth, ask: *How is Jesus with us at Mass?* (The different ways are listed in the paragraph.)

Participating in the Mass Direct attention to the photographs. Ask the children: *What do the pictures show?* (They show the parish participating at Mass.) Have the children close their eyes and imagine that they are at the Mass. Have the children continue to do this as you read the last *We Believe* paragraph aloud again.

Review the Key Word Ask the children to recall the meaning of the word *Mass*. Then invite them to

Jesus is with us in a special way at Mass. He is with us when we gather together. He is with us when we listen to God's Word.

Jesus is with us when we remember what he said and did at the Last Supper. He is with us when we share his Body and Blood.

WE RESPOND

Jesus is with us always. He is with us in a special way when we celebrate the Eucharist.

🎵 **We Come to Share God's Special Gift**

We come to share God's
    special gift:
Jesus here in Eucharist
    for you, for me,
    for all God's family;
    for me, for you
God's love is always true!

253

ACTIVITY BANK

Parish
Mass Greeters
    Find out from the pastor or the parish liturgical committee whether the first graders and their parents might be given an opportunity to participate in the ministry of hospitality at one Sunday liturgy. Enlist the help of a few parents or older siblings. Explain to the children how important it is to welcome people to Mass. Also have the children practice distributing parish bulletins or other handouts.

---

use the word correctly in a sentence. (Examples: Every Sunday we participate at Mass; we remember Jesus at Mass.)

Complete the Reproducible Master Distribute copies of Reproducible Master 22. Read aloud the directions and make sure the children understand what they are to do. Have the children work in pairs. When the children have finished writing, read aloud the correct responses. (M, A, S, S; Mass)

Quick Check

✔ *What do we do at Mass?* (We worship God and give thanks for the gift of Christ's Body and Blood.)

✔ *What do we remember at Mass?* (We remember what Jesus said and did at the Last Supper.)

WE RESPOND ___ minutes

Connect to Life Have a child read aloud the *We Respond* paragraph. Tell the children that Jesus is with them when they are sleeping, eating, and playing. Remind them that he is with all of us in a special way during Mass. Read the words of the song "We Come to Share God's Special Gift" with the children. Then play the song, #26 on the Grade 1 CD. Pray by singing the song together.

Plan Ahead for Day 4

Catechist Goal: To describe what we do at Mass

Preparation: Reflect on the importance of your participation during Mass.

Catechist Goal

• To describe what we do at Mass

Our Faith Response

• To name ways we can participate at Mass

As Catholics...

Our Sunday Celebration

After the children have completed the *We Respond* section, read aloud the *As Catholics* text. Have the children highlight or underline the second paragraph. Then invite volunteers to share their responses to the question. Ask the children to name ways they can keep Sunday holy. (Possible responses: After Mass they can spend time with their family or visit someone who is lonely.)

We join with our parish for the celebration of Mass.

WE GATHER

✝ *Jesus, we celebrate your love for us.*

👤 What are some school celebrations you enjoy? Act out ways you take part in one celebration.

WE BELIEVE

Every Sunday we gather as a parish to celebrate Mass. A priest leads us in this celebration.

We take part in the celebration of the Mass. We praise God by singing and praying. We listen to God's Word.

We offer our prayers to God. The priest does what Jesus did at the Last Supper.

We are sent out to share God's love with others.

254

Lesson Plan

WE GATHER ___ minutes

✝ **Pray** Invite the children to pray the *We Gather* prayer.

Focus on Life Read aloud the *We Gather* questions. Invite the children to name some school celebrations they enjoy. Ask: *Who joins you in celebrating?* Ask volunteers to act out ways they participate in the celebrations they named. Tell the children that in this lesson they will learn that we take part in the Mass with the other members of our parish.

WE BELIEVE ___ minutes

Learn About the Celebration Ask the children to recall what a parish is. Read aloud the *We Believe*

statement. Ask: *Whom do you see when you participate at Mass on Sunday?* Help the children to conclude that we see the priest, other families, singers, musicians, readers, and other helpers. Explain that all these people help us to participate. Also explain that the priest leads us in the celebration.

Then ask: *What are some of the ways we take part in the celebration?* (Answers might include: We praise God; we sing and pray; we listen to God's Word.) Emphasize that it is important that every person takes part.

Finally, ask: *What are your favorite songs that we sing during Mass? What are some prayers that we pray during Mass?* After the children have shared their responses, explain that in the next chapter they will learn more about the prayers of the Mass.

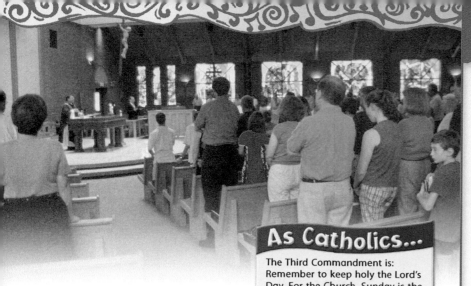

WE RESPOND

What can you do to take part in the celebration of Mass?

Three things you can do are hidden in the puzzle. Find and circle them.

As Catholics...

The Third Commandment is: Remember to keep holy the Lord's Day. For the Church, Sunday is the Lord's Day. This is because Jesus rose to new life on a Sunday.

The Lord's Day begins on Saturday evening and ends on Sunday evening. During this time we gather with our parish to celebrate Mass. This celebration is the greatest way we can keep the Lord's Day holy.

What are some other ways you can keep Sunday holy?

At Mass this Sunday, do these things to praise God and remember his great love for us.

255

ACTIVITY BANK

Liturgy
Celebrating in Song
Activity Materials: parish songbooks
Invite a parish song leader or musician to talk to the children about the work involved in preparing music for Mass. The song leader or musician should emphasize the ways music helps us celebrate together as God's family.

Quick Check

✔ *Who leads the celebration of the Mass?* (A priest leads the celebration.)

✔ *How do we praise God during Mass?* (We praise God by singing and praying.)

WE RESPOND
___ minutes

Connect to Life Invite a volunteer to read aloud the *We Respond* question and the activity directions. Before the children begin to work, draw a sample word search on the board. You may want to use the following:

B C W O R D T R

Have a volunteer find the word *word* on the board and circle it. Then invite the children to find the three words hidden in the puzzle. When most of the children have finished the puzzle, read the three words aloud. Then read the last *We Respond* paragraph. Encourage the children to pray, sing, and listen at Mass on Sunday.

Pray Pray together: *God, we want to join with our parish for the celebration of the Mass.*

Plan Ahead for Day 5

Catechist Goal: To review chapter ideas and their relationship to our faith life

Preparation: Make copies of *Sharing Faith with My Family*, guide page 247E.

Catechist Goal

- To review the chapter ideas that are key to growing as disciples of Jesus Christ

Our Faith Response

- To decide on ways to grow as disciples by living out what we have learned

Show What you Know

Review the meaning of the *Key Words*. Allow time for children to write a sentence. Ask volunteers to share their sentences.

Question Corner Read the instructions. Clarify that the frowning face means the statement makes the children feel sad and the smiling face makes them feel happy. Read each statement. Ask the children to draw a frown or smile in the respective circles. Note that *Remember me* might make the children feel sad or happy. Discuss the children's responses.

What's the Word?

Read the activity. Review the words of Scripture. Invite the children to underline them in the passages and to circle the bread and wine in the Last Supper art.

Reality Check

Read the question and choices. Instruct the children to check all appropriate boxes. Invite the children to write in their own response.

Take Home

Encourage the children to pay special attention as they attend Mass with their family members and to talk about who helps them celebrate.

Discuss and send home copies of *Sharing Faith with My Family*, guide page 247E.

Grade 1 Chapter 22

PROJECT

Show What you Know

Write the two in one sentence.

> Mass
> Eucharist

The Mass is another name for the celebration of

the Eucharist.

Question Corner Pretend that you are with Jesus at the Last Supper. How does each statement make you feel?

Draw 😊 or ☹️.	
This is my last meal with you.	☹️
I give you the gift of myself.	😊
Remember me.	☹️
I love you.	😊

DISCIPLE

What's the Word?

Remember what Jesus said at the Last Supper.

"Take and eat; this is my body."
(Matthew 26:26)

"Drink from it, all of you, for this is my blood." (Matthew 26:27–28)

Thank Jesus for all he has done for us.

Reality Check

When is Jesus with you?

❑ When I am at Mass
❑ When I celebrate Jesus' life
❑ When I pray with my parish
❑ Always
❑ Another time:

Answers will vary.

Take Home

The most important thing our parish does is celebrate Mass together on Sunday. People of the parish give their time to help us celebrate. Talk with your family about who is at Mass to help celebrate the Eucharist. Make a list together.

CHAPTER TEST

Use the words in the box to complete the sentences.

> parish
>
> Eucharist
>
> Mass
>
> meal
>
> priest

1. The Last Supper is the special

   _____meal_____ that Jesus shared before he died.

2. The _____Eucharist_____ is the sacrament of the Body and Blood of Jesus Christ.

3. The _____Mass_____ is another name for the celebration of the Eucharist.

4. A _____priest_____ leads us in the celebration of the Mass.

5. We join with our _____parish_____ for the celebration of Mass.

 In what ways is Jesus with us during the celebration of Mass? In the Sacrament of the Eucharist the bread and wine become the Body and Blood of Jesus Christ.

258

CHAPTER TEST

Read each test item aloud and allow time for the children to mark an answer. Decide whether the *Talk About It* activity will be a small group or whole class discussion. After you have finished, check the answers. Clarify any misconceptions.

Alternative Assessment

You may want the students to complete the following alternative-assessment activity.

> *Send a card to a friend. Use words and pictures to tell about the ways we remember what Jesus said and did at the Last Supper.*

Additional Testing

• Chapter 22 Test in *Assessment Book*, pages 43–44

• CD-ROM *Test Generator and Resource*: Use Chapter 22 Test or customize your own.

Review

Review the definitions as they are presented in the chapter's *Key Word* boxes:

• Eucharist (page 250)

• Mass (page 252).

We Believe Statements

Review the four statements.

• Jesus shared a special meal with his followers.

• We celebrate what Jesus said and did at the Last Supper.

• We celebrate the Sacrament of the Eucharist.

• We join with our parish for the celebration of Mass.

To use the Chapter 22 Study Guide, visit

www.webelieveweb.com

Overview

In Chapter 22 the children learned that Jesus gave us the Eucharist. In this chapter they will learn more about what we say and do at Mass.

Doctrinal Content	For Adult Reading and Reflection *Catechism of the Catholic Church*
The children will learn:	Paragraph
• We gather to worship God.	1348
• We listen to God's Word.	1349
• Our gifts of bread and wine become the Body and Blood of Christ.	1353
• We grow closer to Jesus and one another.	1396

Key Words

Gospel (p. 263)
altar (p. 265)

Catechist Background

Which part of the Mass most moves you?

Go to **www.webelieveweb.com**, Catechist/Teacher, We Believe Correlations for this chapter's correlation to:
- Six Tasks of Catechesis
- Catholic Social Teaching.

We come together for Mass each week to give praise and thanks to God. The Mass has two major parts: the Liturgy of the Word and the Liturgy of the Eucharist.

At the beginning of Mass we gather to praise God and ask God and one another for forgiveness. During the Liturgy of the Word, we listen to three readings from the Bible. The first reading is usually from the Old Testament; the second reading is from the New Testament. The third reading is the Gospel reading, taken from one of the four Gospels in the New Testament. We then hear the homily given by the priest or deacon to help us apply God's Word to our lives. We pray the Creed, and conclude the Liturgy of the Word with prayers of intercession for the Church and the world.

The Liturgy of the Eucharist begins as we prepare ourselves, the altar, and the gifts for the Eucharist. After the preparation of the gifts, the Eucharistic Prayer is led by the priest. During the Eucharistic Prayer the bread and wine become the Body and Blood of Christ. Before we can receive Jesus present in the Eucharist, we make sure our relationships with one another are right. We pray the Our Father, we offer one another peace, and we pray for forgiveness and peace in our own life. We then receive Holy Communion, the great gift of Jesus' own Body and Blood. At the conclusion of Mass, we are blessed and sent forth.

How might you participate more fully in the Mass?

Lesson Planning Guide

Lesson Focus	Presentation	Materials
Day 1		
page 259 **We Gather in Prayer** **pages 260–261** *We gather to worship God.* *The Roman Missal*	• Praise God together in prayer. 🧍 Act out responses to the **We Gather** question. • Present the **We Believe** text and begin to learn Mass responses. 🧍 Do the activity. • Discuss the **We Respond** questions.	For the prayer space: praise poster, Bible, basket or plate filled with grapes and bread • drawing paper • crayons
Day 2		
pages 262–263 *We listen to God's Word.* *The Roman Missal*	🧍 Complete the **We Gather** activity. • Read and discuss the **We Believe** text about listening to God's Word at Mass. • Discuss the **We Respond** question. • Read and discuss the *As Catholics* text.	
Day 3		
pages 264–265 *Our gifts of bread and wine become the Body and Blood of Christ.* *The Roman Missal*	• Share responses for **We Gather**. • Present the **We Believe** text. • Read the **We Respond** directives and allow time for quiet prayer.	• copies of reproducible master *What's the Word?*, guide page 259F
Day 4		
pages 266–267 *We grow closer to Jesus and one another.* *The Roman Missal*	• Respond to the **We Gather** questions. • Present the **We Believe** text about receiving the Eucharist. • Share responses to the **We Respond** question. 🎵 Respond in song.	• copies of Reproducible Master 23, guide page 259G 🎵 "We Come to Share God's Special Gift," Christopher Walker, #27, Grade 1 CD
Day 5		
pages 268–269 **Project Disciple** **page 270** **Chapter 23 Test**	• Complete the **Project Disciple** activities. • Explain the *Take Home* activity. • Discuss/send home **Sharing Faith with My Family**, guide page 259E. • Complete **Chapter 23 Test**. • Work on *Alternative Assessment* activity.	• pencils • crayons or colored pencils • copies of **Sharing Faith with My Family** reproducible master, guide page 259E

For additional ideas, activities, and opportunities: Visit Sadlier's **www.WeBelieveweb.com**

Chapter Story

Mia woke up early on Sunday morning. Today was a very special Sunday. Mia's family was going to bring the gifts to the priest during Mass.

On Wednesday Mrs. Sanchez had called Mia's parents to ask them to bring the gifts of bread and wine to the priest during the Sunday Mass. Mia's dad told the family at dinner that night. He said that he had told Mrs. Sanchez, "Yes, it will be an honor."

Mia began to practice that night after dinner. She practiced walking and carrying a plate. On Sunday morning Mia was the first one ready for Mass. She was usually the last person ready.

When Mia's family went into church, they talked with Mr. Nelson. He was one of the ushers. Mr. Nelson showed the family the small table with the gifts.

Then Mass began. Mia sang, prayed, and listened to the readings. After the prayers for the Church, Mr. Nelson walked with the family to the gift table. Mia's brother carried the gift of wine and Mia's mother walked beside him. Mia carried the gift of bread. She was glad that her father walked beside her. He helped her not to feel nervous.

After Mass Father Raul thanked Mia's family. They all smiled when Mia asked Father, "Can we carry the gifts again at next Sunday's Mass?"

▶ *Why do you think it was an honor for Mia's family to be chosen to bring the gifts to the priest?*

FAITH and MEDIA

▶ On Day 2, as you discuss the Bible as the book of God's Word, remind the children that books are examples of media, and that the Bible is the greatest book—and the greatest medium of mass communication—ever given to us.

▶ Also on Day 2, after you have presented the *As Catholics* text, remind the children that when we pass along news, either directly or through media (via e-mail and letters and in stories on TV, on the radio, on the Internet, and in newspapers), we must be careful to tell the news correctly. First, we must listen carefully to make sure that we have heard the news correctly and that we understand it. Then we must tell it with care to the next person, making sure that he or she hears the news correctly and understands it.

CHAPTER PROJECT: OUR MASS RESPONSES

After presenting the lessons each day this week, have the children look at their texts, and highlight or underline in one color the words of the priest. Then have them highlight or underline our responses in another color. Also have the children look at the Mass booklet on pages 321–324. Emphasize that it is important for each of us to sing and pray the responses when we gather at Mass.

PROJECT DISCIPLE

Pray
Learn
Celebrate
Share
Choose
Live

Additional Activities

What's the Word?

(Use on Day 3.)

Materials needed: copies of reproducible master, guide page 259F

Distribute copies of the Scripture reproducible master. Choose eight volunteers to read the parts of Readers 1–8. Ask the other children to follow along as the story is read. After Reader 8 finishes, ask: *How did the men know it was Jesus who had been with them?* Then discuss with the children the importance of listening to God's Word and receiving Jesus in Holy Communion at Mass.

Make it Happen

Remind the children that we present gifts to God during Mass. Help them understand that part of the money collected from parishioners as offerings to God is used to serve the community and for the general upkeep of the parish. The money may be used to help people who are poor or do not have jobs. It also helps families without homes, or those who cannot afford school supplies. Encourage the children to set aside a bit of allowance, if possible, for the collection basket.

More to Explore

Arrange a time for the children to visit the sanctuary at the parish. Prepare by talking about the *My Parish Church* diagram on pages 318–319 of the student texts. Take the children to church for a close-up look at the altar, vestments, unconsecrated bread and wine, chalice and paten, and other things used during the celebration of the Mass. Explain the significance of each object. Remind the children that they should be quiet, reverent, and respectful while in church.

Pray Today

Reserve some wall space in your classroom. Distribute a sentence strip to each child. Read aloud the following prompt: *Jesus, at Mass I . . . .* Instruct each child to write a descriptive word or phrase to complete the sentence. Display the prompt on the wall along with the children's responses. You may want to include your own response.

Meeting Individual Needs
Children with Auditory Needs

For the children with auditory needs you may wish to record the Mass prayers and responses presented in this chapter. Allow the children to listen to the recording during their free time. Explain that they can adjust the volume to best hear the prayers clearly.

We Believe Resources

- Grade 1 *Review & Resource Book*, pages 52–54
- Grade 1 *Family Book*, pages 65–67
- Grade 1 *Assessment Book*, pages 45–46
- Grade 1 CD-ROM *Test Generator and Resource*: Use Chapter 23 Test or customize your own.
- **www.webelieveweb.com**

Sharing What I Learned

Look at the pictures below. Use each picture to tell your family what you learned in this chapter.

Celebration of Mass

Talk with your family about the special ways you each take part in the celebration of the Mass. Ask each family member to draw his or her picture taking part in Mass. Show your pictures to each other.

Pray or sing this song together as a family.

🎵 **We Come to Share God's Special Gift**

We come to share God's
  special gift:
Jesus here in Eucharist
For you, for me, for all God's
  family;
For me, for you God's love is
  always true.

Visit Sadlier's

www.WeBelieveweb.com

Connect to the Catechism
For adult background and reflection, see paragraphs 1348, 1349, 1353 and 1396.

PROJECT DISCIPLE

Name _____

What's *the* Word?

Reader 1: You may hear this Gospel story at Mass.

Reader 2: Two followers of Jesus were walking on the road to a town near Jerusalem.

Reader 3: They were talking. That morning, Jesus had risen from the dead.

Reader 4: A man joined them. They did not know that the man was Jesus.

Reader 5: As they walked, Jesus explained some of God's Word to them. But the followers still did not know it was Jesus.

Reader 6: The sun began to set. The followers asked Jesus to stay with them.

Reader 7: When the men sat down at the table, Jesus "took bread, said the blessing, broke it, and gave it to them." (Luke 24:30)

Reader 8: As soon as he did this, the followers knew that the man was Jesus!

Name _____

Tell the order in which we do things when
we celebrate Mass. Use the numbers 1 to 5.

_____ People bring gifts of bread
and wine to the priest.

_____ We praise God with the words,
"Glory to God in the highest."

_____ We share a sign of peace.

_____ We listen to readings from
the Bible.

_____ People receive the Body and
Blood of Christ.

We Celebrate the Mass

23

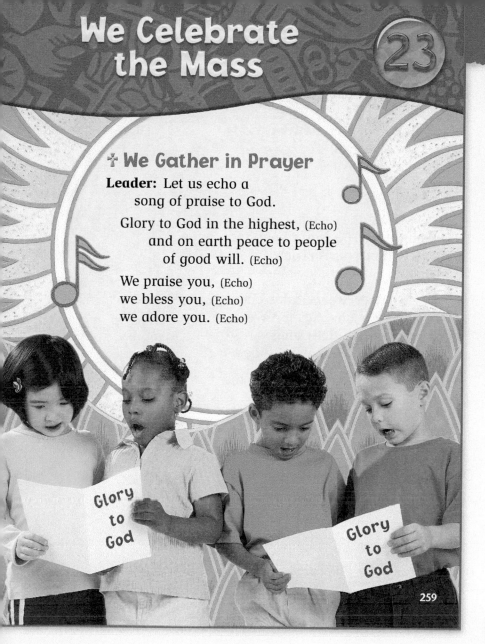

✝ We Gather in Prayer

Leader: Let us echo a song of praise to God.

Glory to God in the highest, (Echo) and on earth peace to people of good will. (Echo)

We praise you, (Echo) we bless you, (Echo) we adore you. (Echo)

Glory to God

Glory to God

259

PREPARING TO PRAY

The children will praise God by praying a prayer we pray at Mass.

• Give each child a sheet of drawing paper. Have the children draw pictures of themselves worshiping God at Mass. Then glue or tape the pictures to a sheet of poster board. On the poster board write: *We praise you, God.*

The Prayer Space

• Display the praise poster.

• On the prayer table place an opened Bible and a basket or plate filled with grapes and bread.

 **This Week's Liturgy**

Visit **www.webelieveweb.com** for this week's liturgical readings and other seasonal material.

Lesson Plan

We Gather in Prayer ___ minutes

✝ Pray

• Invite the children to the prayer space.

• Pray the Sign of the Cross together. Then lead the children in the prayer. Ask them to raise their arms in the air as you praise God together.

Family Connection Update

Invite the children to share their families' discussions about the people of the parish.

Catechist Goal

• To explain that parishioners gather to worship God at Mass

Our Faith Response

• To identify ways we can participate in the beginning of the Mass

Teaching Note

An Instructional Mass

One of the most helpful ways to clarify what the Mass is about is to plan an instructional Mass for the children. Consult with a priest of your parish about the possibility of his celebrating such a Mass with the class. If he is able to do so, the priest will pause before celebrating each major part of the Mass to explain to the children what is about to happen. After the Mass be sure to have the children thank the priest for explaining each part of the Mass to them.

We gather to worship God.

WE GATHER

✝ God, we worship you. We give you thanks.

🧎 What are some ways we welcome people?
Act out some ways.

WE BELIEVE

The Mass is the Church's greatest celebration. The most important time that our parish comes together is for Sunday Mass.

As we gather, we welcome one another. We join together. We stand and sing. This shows we are happy to celebrate together.

The priest welcomes us. With the priest, we pray the Sign of the Cross. The priest says,
"The Lord be with you."

We answer together,
"And with your spirit."

These words remind us that Jesus is with us at Mass.

Then we ask God and one another for forgiveness.

260

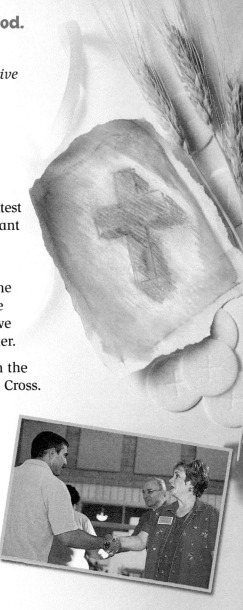

Lesson Plan

WE GATHER   ___ minutes

✝ **Pray** Ask the children to pray together the Sign of the Cross and the *We Gather* prayer.

Focus on Life Read aloud the *We Gather* question. Ask the children to name different times that we welcome people. Invite volunteers to act out ways of welcoming. Then ask the children to share what makes them feel welcome. Tell the children that in this lesson they will learn how the members of the parish welcome one another and join together to celebrate Mass.

WE BELIEVE   ___ minutes

Learn How the Mass Begins Read together the *We Believe* statement. Ask volunteers to share their ideas of what it means to worship. Explain to the children that when we worship, we sing and pray to God to show our love. Then read aloud the first and second *We Believe* paragraphs.

Celebrate Our Faith Read the third *We Believe* paragraph. Ask the children to stand and pray the Sign of the Cross. Pray: *The Lord be with you.* Ask the children to pray the appropriate response: *And with your spirit.*

Review Hand Signs Talk about the ways we use our hands to express our faith at Mass. Review making the Sign of the Cross. Then invite the children to share other hand motions used at Mass such as the priest lifting hands in praise and people shaking hands to share a sign of peace.

We praise God by singing or praying aloud.
Our prayer begins:

"Glory to God

in the highest,
and on earth peace to people of good will."

🧍 Color the words that begin our
prayer of praise.

WE RESPOND

What are some ways the members of
your parish welcome one another as
the Mass begins?

Next Sunday, what
can you do to
take part in
the beginning
of Mass?

261

ACTIVITY BANK

Parish
Welcome Pennants
Activity Materials: markers, pennant-shaped pieces of poster board or felt, construction paper, scissors, felt scraps, glue

Have the children work in small groups to make "welcome" pennants to greet parishioners as they enter the church to celebrate Mass. Tell the children to print the word *Welcome* on their pennants. Then ask them to decorate their pennants with pictures of items that invite parishioners to feel welcomed to participate at Mass together. These items might include a Bible, musical notes, bread and wine, a cross, a handshake, or smiling faces. Ask the pastor if you may display the pennants in the vestibule of the church for the next few Sundays.

Do the Activity Read the directions for the *We Believe* activity. Tell the children to use colors that remind them of being happy.

Quick Check

✔ *When is the most important time the parish comes together?* (The most important time we gather is for Sunday Mass.)

✔ *What do we do as we gather at Mass?* (We welcome one another; we join together; we stand and sing; we pray.)

WE RESPOND _____ minutes

Connect to Life Read aloud the first *We Respond* question. (Possible responses: smiling and saying hello;

moving over to make room for other people to sit; standing to sing the welcome song at the beginning of Mass.)

Read the second *We Respond* question. Print the children's responses on chart paper. Remind them that it is important that each person join in singing and praying.

Pray Pray together three times: *Glory to God!*

Plan Ahead for Day 2

Catechist Goal: To teach that the readings at Mass are the Word of God

Preparation: Be prepared to explain to the children the role the deacon plays at Mass.

Catechist Goal

• To teach that the readings at Mass are the Word of God

Our Faith Response

• To listen and respond to God's Word

 **Gospel**

We listen to God's Word.

WE GATHER

✠ God, we praise you for your glory.

🧍 When do you listen to stories from the Bible? Write who or what your favorite story is about.

_____

_____

_____

WE BELIEVE

The Bible is the book of God's Word. At Sunday Mass we listen to three readings from the Bible. We listen carefully so that we may grow in God's love.

The first reading is about God's people who lived before Jesus Christ was born. The second reading is about the teachings of the Apostles. It is also about the beginning of the Church.

After each of these readings, the reader says, "The word of the Lord."

We answer, "Thanks be to God."

262

As Catholics...

The Good News of Jesus

After you have presented the lesson, read the *As Catholics* text. Invite volunteers to share their responses to the *As Catholics* question.

Lesson Plan

WE GATHER — minutes

✠ **Pray** Invite the children to pray the Sign of the Cross. Explain to them that the word *glory* means "greatness." Then ask them to pray together the *We Gather* prayer on page 262.

Focus on Life Encourage the children to describe what it means to be a good listener. Ask the children to share their answers to the first *We Gather* question. Then invite them to write who or what their favorite Bible stories are and what they are about. Ask volunteers to share the important points of their favorite stories with the class. Ask each volunteer to talk about why he or she liked the story and what he or she learned from it. You may also wish to share your favorite Bible story.

WE BELIEVE — minutes

Learn About the Readings at Mass Read the first two *We Believe* paragraphs. Then ask:

• *What is the first reading about?* (God's People who lived before Jesus Christ was born)

• *What is the second reading about?* (the teaching of the Apostles and the beginning of the Church)

Learn About the Gospel Read aloud the first paragraph on page 263. Stress that the Gospel is the Good News about Jesus Christ and his teachings.

Review our response after the first and second readings and our response after the Gospel.

Next we stand and sing Alleluia or other words of praise. This shows we are ready to listen to the reading of the Gospel. The **Gospel** is the Good News about Jesus Christ and his teachings.

The priest or deacon reads the Gospel to us. Then he says, "The Gospel of the Lord."

We answer, "Praise to you, Lord Jesus Christ."

The priest or deacon talks to us about all the readings. We listen. We learn how we can grow as followers of Jesus. We learn how to be members of the Church.

After the priest's talk, we stand. We say aloud what we believe as Catholics.

Then we pray for the Church and all people. After each prayer, we say, "Lord, hear our prayer."

WE RESPOND

At Mass next Sunday listen carefully to the readings. How can you show others you have heard God's Word?

Gospel the Good News about Jesus Christ and his teachings

As Catholics...

The word *Gospel* means the "Good News of Jesus Christ." The Good News is that Jesus is the Son of God, who told us of God the Father's love.

Jesus taught us how to live. He died and rose to new life for us. This is the Good News we celebrate.

What can you tell someone about the Good News of Jesus Christ?

263

ACTIVITY BANK

Multiple Intelligences
Interpersonal

Have the children work in pairs. Ask the children to tell their partners something that they know about Jesus. Then ask the partners to share this information with the rest of the class. Explain to the children that if they are listening carefully, they should be able to learn from the information and repeat it correctly. Remind them that they must listen carefully in order to learn more about God and to share God's Word with others.

Curriculum Connection
Geography
Activity Materials: world map, globe, or map of Israel

Point out the countries of Israel and Egypt on a world map. Tell the children that many of the Bible stories they listen to are about what happened in these countries. Ask them to recall the names of towns, cities, and other places in Israel they have learned about: Nazareth, Bethlehem, Jerusalem, Sea of Galilee. Help the children locate these places on the map.

Explain the Deacon's Role Explain that sometimes a deacon takes part in the celebration of the Mass. When a deacon takes part, he reads the Gospel, gives the talk after the Gospel, prays some special prayers, and helps the priest at the altar. If possible, invite a deacon from the parish to visit and to talk with the children.

Quick Check

✔ *Why should we listen carefully to God's Word?* (We listen to God's Word so we can grow in God's love.)

✔ *What is the Gospel?* (The Gospel is the Good News about Jesus Christ and his teachings.)

WE RESPOND
__ minutes

Connect to Life Read aloud the *We Respond* text on page 263. Invite the children to respond to the question. Point out that if we live out in our everyday lives what we have learned, we can show that we have heard God's Word.

Pray Stand and pray together: *Praise to you, Lord Jesus Christ.*

Plan Ahead for Day 3

Catechist Goal: To emphasize that the bread and wine become the Body and Blood of Christ

Preparation: Make copies of *What's the Word?*, guide page 259F.

Catechist Goal

• To emphasize that the bread and wine become the Body and Blood of Christ

Our Faith Response

• To recognize that the bread and wine become the Body and Blood of Christ

 **altar**

Lesson Materials

• copies of reproducible master *What's the Word?*, guide page 259F

Teaching Note

The We Believe *Program and the Mass*

In Chapter 17 of the Grade 2 *We Believe* text, the children will learn about the Liturgy of the Word. In Chapter 18, they will learn about the Liturgy of the Eucharist. Please note that it is not necessary for the first graders to know the names of the two main parts of the Mass.

Our gifts of bread and wine become the Body and Blood of Christ.

WE GATHER

✝ *God, we offer ourselves to you.*

Think about the ways your family gets ready for special meals. How do you get the table ready?

WE BELIEVE

The **altar** is the table of the Lord. The priest prepares the altar for the celebration of the Eucharist.

Everything we have is a gift from God. At the Eucharist we offer these gifts back to God. We offer ourselves, too.

People bring gifts of bread and wine to the priest. The priest prepares the gifts of bread and wine. We pray, "Blessed be God for ever."

264

Lesson Plan

WE GATHER ___ minutes

✝ **Pray** Explain to the children: *To offer ourselves means "to give God our love and thanks."* Invite the children to pray together the *We Gather* prayer.

Focus on Life Read aloud the *We Gather* question and invite the children's responses. (Possible responses: We put a special tablecloth and dishes on the table. Sometimes we put flowers or candles there.) Share the *Chapter Story* on guide page 259C.

WE BELIEVE ___ minutes

Learn More About the Mass Read aloud the first *We Believe* paragraph. Ask volunteers to explain what the altar looks like during Mass. Then point out the photo of people bringing the gifts to the priest (Chapter 22, page 252). Ask: *Would you like to do this sometime? Why or why not?* Invite volunteers to share their responses.

Read the second and third *We Believe* paragraphs. Ask the children to say aloud the words we pray while the priest prepares the gifts of bread and wine.

Ask: *What did Jesus say and do at the Last Supper?* Invite volunteers to respond. Then read the last four *We Believe* paragraphs. Explain that this is the most special time of the celebration of Mass. Stress: *Jesus Christ is really present in the Eucharist. When we pray, "Amen," we are saying that we believe that Jesus Christ is really present in the Eucharist.*

Then we remember what Jesus said and did at the Last Supper. The priest takes the bread. He says,
"TAKE THIS, ALL OF YOU, AND EAT OF IT, FOR THIS IS MY BODY, WHICH WILL BE GIVEN UP FOR YOU."

Then the priest takes the cup of wine. He says,
"TAKE THIS, ALL OF YOU, AND DRINK FROM IT, FOR THIS IS THE CHALICE OF MY BLOOD . . ."

The bread and wine become the Body and Blood of Christ. This is done by the power of the Holy Spirit and through the words and actions of the priest. Jesus Christ is really present in the Eucharist.

We sing or pray, "Amen."
We are saying, "Yes, I believe."

WE RESPOND

Pray quietly. Thank Jesus for being with us in the Eucharist.
Then together sing or say "Amen."

altar the table of the Lord

ACTIVITY BANK

Parish
Prayer Cards
Activity Materials: poster board, crayons, colored pencils, or markers

Ask your parish director of religious education for the number of groups of children who are preparing to receive first Holy Communion. Help the children make a card for each group. Have the children decorate each card and write a message promising to pray for the children as they prepare for the special celebration. Have the children in your group sign their names on the back of each card.

Scripture
Linguistic, Interpersonal
For a Scripture activity, see *What's the Word?*, guide page 259F.

265

Quick Check

✔ *What is the altar?* (The altar is the table of the Lord.)

✔ *What do we pray when the priest prepares the gifts?* (We pray, "Blessed be God for ever.")

WE RESPOND ___ minutes

Connect to Life If possible, visit the parish church. Ask the children to gather around the altar. Ask a parish priest to show the children a chalice, paten, and a large and small communion hosts.

Pray Allow the children time to pray silently, thanking Jesus for the gifts he has given us. Then lead the children in singing an "Amen" that you often pray during Mass.

Plan Ahead for Day 4

Catechist Goal: To explore the ways that we grow closer to Jesus and one another at Mass

Preparation: Make copies of Reproducible Master 23, guide page 259G.

Catechist Goal

• To explore the ways that we grow closer to Jesus and one another at Mass

Our Faith Response

• To choose ways we will grow closer to Jesus and one another

Lesson Materials

• copies of Reproducible Master 23

• Grade 1 CD

Teaching Tip

Song Lyrics

This lesson includes a song about sharing the Eucharist. It will be helpful to the children if you project the lyrics or print them on chart paper. Point to the words as the children read the verses a few times. Explain any words or concepts that the children do not understand. Then ask the children to sing the song together. Understanding the words of this song will help the children grasp the idea of how special it is to celebrate the Eucharist.

We grow closer to Jesus and one another.

WE GATHER

✝ *Jesus, we believe you are present in the Eucharist.*

What is the prayer that Jesus taught us? When do you pray this prayer?

WE BELIEVE

After the bread and wine have become the Body and Blood of Christ, we get ready to receive Jesus. Together we pray or sing the Our Father.

Then we turn to the people who are near us. We share a sign of peace. We say a prayer to ask Jesus for forgiveness and peace.

Then the priest invites us to share in the Eucharist. The people who have received first Holy Communion come forward to receive the Body and Blood of Christ. They answer, "Amen."

While this is happening, we sing a song of thanks. This shows that we are joined with Jesus and all the members of the Church. We grow closer to him and one another.

266

Lesson Plan

WE GATHER
___ minutes

✝ **Pray** Pray together the *We Gather* prayer.

Focus on Life Read aloud the *We Gather* questions. Remind the children that the prayer that Jesus taught us is the Lord's Prayer. Ask: *What is another name for the Lord's Prayer?* (the Our Father) Discuss with the children the times they pray this prayer.

WE BELIEVE
___ minutes

Learn More About the Eucharist Read aloud the *We Believe* text. Stress our prayer responses.

Share a Sign of Peace Reread the second *We Believe* paragraph. Ask: *How do people in your parish share a sign of peace?* (Possible responses: shaking hands, giving a hug, saying "Peace" to one another.)

Do an Ordering Activity Distribute copies of Reproducible Master 23. Read the sentences and help the children put them in the correct order. (3, 1, 4, 2, 5)

Then there is some quiet time. We thank Jesus for giving himself to us in the Eucharist. After this the priest blesses us.
The priest or deacon may say, "Go in peace."
We say, "Thanks be to God."

We are sent to share with others the Good News of Jesus. We go out to live as Jesus' followers.

WE RESPOND

What are some ways you can grow closer to Jesus?

🎵 **We Come to Share God's Special Gift**

We come to share God's special gift:
Jesus here in Eucharist
For you, for me, for all God's family;
For me, for you God's love is always true!

267

ACTIVITY BANK

Liturgy and Music
Illustrate Lyrics
Activity Materials: drawing paper, crayons or markers, Grade 1 CD

Have the children reread the words for the song "We Come to Share God's Special Gift." Give each child a sheet of drawing paper. Have the children illustrate the lyrics of the song. Play the recording of the song, #27 on the Grade 1 CD as the children are working. When the children are finished, display the illustrations in the prayer space.

Quick Check

✔ *How do we prepare ourselves to receive Jesus?* (We pray the Our Father; we share a sign of peace; we ask Jesus for forgiveness and peace.)

✔ *What do we show when we sing a song of thanks while people are receiving the Body and Blood of Christ?* (We show that we are joined with Jesus and all the members of the Church.)

WE RESPOND ___ minutes

Connect to Life Invite the children to read and discuss the *We Respond* question. Ask them to share ways they can grow closer to Jesus. Encourage the children to consider ways that they can live as Jesus' followers at home and at school.

You may want to have the children make their Mass booklets, pages 321–324. Review the Mass by going over each page. Pray the prayers of the Mass together. Encourage the children to use these booklets at Mass.

Pray Play the song "We Come to Share God's Special Gift," #27 on the Grade 1 CD. Then invite the children to sing the song together.

Plan Ahead for Day 5

Catechist Goal: To review chapter ideas and their relationship to our faith life

Preparation: Make copies of *Sharing Faith with My Family,* guide page 259E.

Catechist Goal

• To review the chapter ideas that are key to growing as disciples of Jesus Christ

Our Faith Response

• To decide on ways to grow as disciples by living out what we have learned

Show What *you* Know

Read the clues and allow time for the children to write the answers. Encourage children to share the riddles.

Pray Today

Read the activity. Invite volunteers to read the prayers the children are saying. Have the children repeat the prayers. Encourage the children to pass on these prayers by praying them with a friend.

What Would *you* do?

Invite the children to look at the picture as you read the activity instructions. Brainstorm a list of possible responses. Invite the children to write their favorite response in the speech bubble.

Make *it* Happen

Read the activity instructions. Discuss ways the children can participate. Possible responses are attending, singing, praying, and listening.

Take Home

Read the paragraph. Explain that one way to help people who are sick is by praying for them. Encourage the children to pray with their families for people who are sick.

Discuss and send home copies of *Sharing Faith with My Family*, guide page 259E.

Grade 1 Chapter 23

PROJECT

Show What *you* Know

> Gospel
> altar

Guess the Key Word for each riddle.

> The priest prepares me for the celebration of the Eucharist. I am the table of the Lord.

I am the _____ altar _____.

> To show you are ready to listen to me, you stand and sing words of praise. I am the Good News about Jesus Christ and his teachings.

I am the _____ Gospel _____.

Pray Today

The prayers that the children are saying are from Sunday Mass.

Now, pass it on!

Lord, hear our prayer.

Thanks be to God.

DISCIPLE

What Would *you* do?

Imagine your friend asks you, "What is the Good News about Jesus Christ?"
Possible responses:

> Jesus is the Son of God, who told us of God the Father's love. Jesus taught us how to live. He died and rose to new life for us.

What would you say to him or her? Write it in the speech bubble.

Make *it* Happen

Do your best to participate at Mass this Sunday!

Take Home

After Mass priests, deacons, or extraordinary ministers of Holy Communion take the Eucharist to people who cannot attend Mass because they are sick. As a family, pray for all those who are sick.

CHAPTER TEST

Circle the correct answer.

1. The altar is the _____ of the Lord.

   (table)   home

2. The _____ is the Good News about Jesus Christ and his teachings.

   (Gospel)   first reading

3. When we pray "Amen," we are saying, _____.

   ("Yes, I believe")   "Forgive me"

4. When people receive the Body and Blood of Christ, they say _____.

   "Thank you"   ("Amen")

5. We get ready to receive Jesus in Holy Communion by praying the _____.

   (Our Father)   Hail Mary

 What are some things we do at the beginning of Mass? See pages 260–261.

270

CHAPTER TEST

Read each test item aloud and allow time for the children to mark an answer. Decide whether the *Talk About It* activity will be a small group or whole class discussion. After you have finished, check the answers. Clarify any misconceptions.

Alternative Assessment

You may want the students to complete the following alternative-assessment activity.

> *Tell what happens during Mass. Draw a picture or write sentences.*

Additional Testing

• Chapter 23 Test in *Assessment Book*, pages 45–46

• CD-ROM *Test Generator and Resource*: Use Chapter 23 Test or customize your own.

Review

Review the definitions as they are presented in the chapter's *Key Word* boxes:

• Gospel (page 263)

• altar (page 265).

We Believe Statements

Review the four statements.

• We gather to worship God.

• We listen to God's Word.

• Our gifts of bread and wine become the Body and Blood of Christ.

• We grow closer to Jesus and one another.

To use the Chapter 23 Study Guide, visit

www.webelieveweb.com

Chapter 24 We Share God's Love

Overview

In Chapter 23 the children learned about the celebration of the Mass. In this chapter the children will learn how we can share God's love.

Doctrinal Content	For Adult Reading and Reflection *Catechism of the Catholic Church*
The children will learn:	Paragraph
• Jesus shows us how to love and serve.	2196
• When we pray, we show God that we love him.	2558
• We share God's love with our families.	2217
• We share God's love with others.	1825

Go to **www.webelieveweb.com**, Catechist/Teacher, We Believe Correlations for this chapter's correlation to:
- Six Tasks of Catechesis
- Catholic Social Teaching.

Catechist Background

Who taught you how to love?

Love is the path and the goal of the Christian life. As Saint John tells us, "God is love, and whoever remains in love remains in God and God in him" (1 John 4:16).

An important part of our love relationship with God is prayer. Prayer can be talking to God, or listening; it can involve thoughts or simply our presence. Prayer can take many forms, including private prayer or communal prayer, personal prayer, or prayer for others. When we pray, we may use our own words, the words of the Church, the words of Scripture, or the words of hymns. Prayer is the foundation of our experience and expression of love for God.

God's love is first discovered and shared in the family. The family is called the "domestic church," because parents "are the first heralds of the faith with regard to their children" (*Dogmatic Constitution on the Church*, 11). It is within the family that uncondi-

tional love is first experienced, virtues are practiced, and prayer is taught. Parents foster the Christian vocation of their children, and children, in turn, should obey and respect their parents.

The love of God that is experienced and shared in the family is then extended to the larger Church family and the world. As Christians, we follow the example of Jesus, who shows us how to love and serve. Out of love for us, Jesus suffered, died, and rose from the dead. His commandment to us is simple: ". . . love one another. As I have loved you, so you should love one another" (John 13:34). Grounded in the Christian training we received in the home and rooted in prayer, we share God's love with others and follow in the footsteps of Jesus Christ.

How do you share God's love with others?

Lesson Planning Guide

Lesson Focus	Presentation	Materials

Day 1

page 271
✝ **We Gather in Prayer**

pages 272–273
Jesus shows us how to love and serve.

📖 *John 13:34; 20:19, 21*

📖 Listen to Scripture and pray together for love and peace.
- Discuss the We Gather question.
- Present the We Believe text about loving and serving God.
- Share responses for We Respond.

For the prayer space: Bible, pictures of people sharing love and peace

- index cards
- copies of reproducible master *What's the Word?*, guide page 271F

Day 2

pages 274–275
When we pray, we show God that we love him.

- Share responses for We Gather.
- Read and discuss the We Believe text about praying to God.
- 🏃 Do the We Respond prayer writing activity.
- Read and discuss the *As Catholics* text.

Day 3

pages 276–277
We share God's love with our families.

- Share responses for We Gather.
- Present the We Believe text about sharing God's love with family members.
- 🏃 Do the role-playing activity.
- Read the We Respond directive and question.

Day 4

pages 278–279
We share God's love with others.

- Respond to the We Gather questions.
- Present the We Believe text about sharing God's love with others.
- Discuss the pictures.
- 🏃 Do the We Respond activity about serving others.
- 🎵 Respond in song.

- parish bulletin
- copies of Reproducible Master 24, guide page 271G
- 🎵 "Walk in Love," Jack Miffleton, #28, Grade 1 CD

Day 5

pages 280–281
Project Disciple

page 282
Chapter 24 Test

- Complete the Project Disciple activities.
- Explain the *Take Home* activity.
- Discuss/send home Sharing Faith with My Family, guide page 271E.
- Complete Chapter 24 Test.
- Work on *Alternative Assessment* activity.

- pencils
- crayons or colored pencils
- copies of Sharing Faith with My Family reproducible master, guide page 271E

Chapter Story

After Mass last Sunday, there was a lot of excitement at Ginny Ruiz's house. It was Ginny's grandfather's birthday. All of Ginny's aunts, uncles, and cousins were coming over that afternoon for a big party.

Ginny's baby brother, Sammy, started to cry when the family walked into the house. The phone kept ringing until Ginny's mom answered it. It was Ginny's Uncle Felix. Ginny heard her mom tell him, "I don't know how I am going to be ready. There is so much to do, and I have to take care of the baby at the same time."

Uncle Felix said, "Put Ginny on the phone for a minute." When Ginny said hello, her uncle said, "Ginny, I'm going to send your older cousin, Tony, to help. Can you help him take care of your baby brother?"

Ginny said, "Sure, Uncle Felix. We'll watch Sammy together."

Ginny and Tony did a great job. They fed Sammy. They played with him until all of the guests arrived for the party.

The party was the best party that Ginny had ever seen. Her grandfather was so happy. Everyone cheered when he blew out all the candles on his cake.

That night Ginny's mother said, "Ginny, I am so proud of you. You were wonderful helping your cousin with Sammy today. I don't know what I would have done without your help."

▶ *Why was Ginny's mom proud of her?*

FAITH and MEDIA

▶ If you plan on doing the second activity of the Day 2 *Activity Bank,* offer the children the opportunity to complete their drawings electronically with *Kid Pix* or some other drawing program.

▶ If a parish Web site exists, have the children find out more about what the parish community is doing to help others.

CHAPTER PROJECT: LOVING AND SERVING GOD

Invite the children to make up skits that they will perform for the class. Explain that the skits need to show situations in which they are sharing God's love with others. You might want to brainstorm some ideas with the children and then have them work in groups to make up their skits. Remind the children that when they share love with others they are also serving God. To help enhance the children's performance, have available costumes and props for the children to use. Be prepared to offer assistance wherever needed.

PROJECT DISCIPLE

Pray
Learn
Celebrate
Share
Choose
Live

Additional Activities

What's *the* Word?

(Use on Day 1.)

Materials needed: copies of reproducible master, guide page 271F

Distribute copies of the Scripture reproducible master. Choose four volunteers to read the parts of Readers 1–4. Ask the other children to follow along as the story is read. When Reader 4 has finished, invite the children to write their responses to the prompt. Invite volunteers to share their responses with their classmates. Explain that the children can say this in prayer to Jesus.

Pray Today

Allow time each day of the week for the children to pray the prayer they wrote on Day 2 quietly. Allow them to open their books to page 275 to read the prayer silently. You might play quiet instrumental music in the classroom for a soothing, peaceful setting. Pray with the children to model a prayerful posture and attitude. Encourage the children to take time to pray every day.

More *to* Explore

Materials needed: different examples of liturgical music

Talk to the children about ways that music lifts our spirits and helps us worship God, especially when we sing at Mass. Throughout the week, take time to play liturgical music quietly while the children work. Allow them to listen to the different examples you provide and sing along if they are familiar with the music.

Picture This

Materials needed: colored pencils

Make a class picture book. Run off a copy of a blank page with the title: *A picture of a way we share God's love with our families*. Distribute a copy to each child. Invite the children to illustrate a way they share God's love with their family members. Bind the book and add it to the classroom library for the children to enjoy.

Meeting Individual Needs
Children Who Are Interpersonal Learners

Children who are interpersonal learners enjoy socializing and discussing things with peers. Children who are intrapersonal learners prefer working alone and like reflective activity. When assigning children group work or discussion, try to keep a balance of both types of learners in each group. After group discussion or activities, set aside time for all the children to reflect on what they have just said or done.

We Believe Resources

- Grade 1 *Review & Resource Book*, pages 55–57
- Grade 1 *Family Book*, pages 68–70
- Grade 1 *Assessment Book*, pages 47–48
- Grade 1 CD-ROM *Test Generator and Resource*: Use Chapter 24 Test or customize your own.
- **www.webelieveweb.com**

SHARING FAITH
with My Family

Sharing What I Learned

Look at the pictures below. Use each picture to tell your family what you learned in this chapter.

Planning to Share God's Love

Get together with your family. Think of simple ways you can share God's love with the people on this list.

Keep the list in a place where everyone can see it. Then pray together. Ask the Holy Spirit to help you share God's love with all people.

Our Family
_____

People at Work or School
_____

People in Our Neighborhood
_____

People in Our Parish
_____

People of the World
_____

Visit Sadlier's

www.WeBelieveweb.com

Connect to the Catechism
For adult background and reflection, see paragraphs 2196, 2558, 2217, and 1825.

PROJECT DISCIPLE

Pray
Learn
Celebrate
Share
Choose
Live

Name _____

What's *the* Word?

Reader 1: On the night before Jesus died, he talked about many things. He did this after he gave them the gift of his Body and Blood.

Reader 2: He told his followers, "As the Father loves me, so I also love you." (John 15:9)

Reader 3: Jesus also said, "This is my commandment: love one another as I love you." (John 15:12)

Reader 4: Then Jesus said to his followers, "You are my friends if you do what I command you." (John 15:14)

Imagine you were with Jesus and his followers that night. Write what you would have said to Jesus.

_____

_____

_____

On each flower petal, write something you can do to share God's love with others.

John 13:34

Jesus said, "As I have loved you, so you also should love one another."

We Share God's Love (24)

✝ We Gather in Prayer

Leader: After Jesus rose to new life, he visited his followers. Let us listen to Jesus' words when he first visited them.

📖 John 20:19, 21

Reader: Jesus came and stood near them. He said, "Peace be with you." (John 20:21)

All: Jesus, you gave us your gifts of peace and love.

Leader: Jesus told his followers that he wanted them to share God's love with everyone. We are followers of Jesus. He wants us to share God's love, too.

All: Jesus, help us to share your gifts of love and peace with everyone.

271

PREPARING TO PRAY

The children will listen to a Scripture reading and respond in prayer.

• Choose volunteers to be the prayer leader and reader. Give the children time to prepare what they will read.

• Use index cards to prepare a gift card to give each child. On the card write the child's name and the message: *Jesus gives you love and peace.*

The Prayer Space

• Display photos of people sharing Jesus' gifts of love and peace with others.

• On the prayer table place an open Bible and the gift cards that you have prepared.

📖 **This Week's Liturgy**
Visit **www.webelieveweb.com** for this week's liturgical readings and other seasonal material.

Lesson Plan

We Gather in Prayer ___ minutes

✝ Pray

• Ask the children to open their books to page 271. Invite the children to the prayer space by saying: *We gather in prayer.* Have the children bring their open books with them.

• Ask the prayer leader to begin praying.

• Pause briefly after the reader is finished reading the Scripture passage.

• Then have children continue praying.

• Give the children their gift cards before they return to their seats.

Family Connection Update
Invite the children to share their family experiences of praying for the sick.

271

Catechist Goal

• To explain that we can love and serve others

Our Faith Response

• To follow Jesus' example by loving and serving others

Lesson Materials

• copies of reproducible master *What's the Word?*, guide page 271F

Teaching Tip

Picture-Discussion Activities

There are two picture-discussion activities in this chapter. Help the children who have visual needs by assigning them partners who are visual learners.

Jesus shows us how to love and serve.

WE GATHER

✝ *Jesus, help us to follow you each day.*

Think of a time someone trusted you to do something important.
How did you feel after you did what they asked?

WE BELIEVE

Jesus trusted God his Father. He did the things his Father asked him to do. Jesus told everyone about God. He shared God's love with all people.

Jesus told his followers, "As I have loved you, so you also should love one another." (John 13:34) Jesus showed us how to love and serve God and one another, too.

We love and serve God by learning the ways he wants us to live. We try to do the things he wants us to do. We tell others about God and share his great love.

272

Lesson Plan

WE GATHER   ___ minutes

✝ **Pray** Invite the children to begin the lesson by praying the Sign of the Cross. Then pray together the *We Gather* prayer.

Focus on Life Help start the discussion of the *We Gather* question by sharing a personal experience. As the children share their experiences and feelings, ask them why, in each case, people trusted them. Help the children understand that people trust us when we show that we want to serve others, to help, and to be generous. Tell the children that in this lesson they will learn that Jesus showed us how to love and serve.

WE BELIEVE   ___ minutes

Read the Text Ask volunteers to read aloud the *We Believe* paragraphs. Emphasize the following points:

• *Jesus trusted God his Father.*

• *Jesus showed us how to love and serve others.*

• *We love and serve God by doing what Jesus wants us to do.*

Talk About the Picture Ask the children to describe what they see in the picture on pages 272 and 273. Invite them to explain how the people in the picture are loving and serving God by helping others. When the children are finished sharing, point out:

• *A child is helping a woman on the steps.*

Look at the picture. Tell how the people are loving and serving God.

WE RESPOND

What is one thing you will do to share God's love today?

273

Catholic Social Teaching

Call to Family, Community, and Participation

Read the following situations. Invite the children to show what loving things they can do in each situation:

• *You are learning how to ride a bicycle. An older brother or sister offers to help you. What do you say?*

• *When it comes to computer games, you feel you are really good. A friend thinks she can help you get better at it. What do you tell her?*

• *You have lost your way in a school hallway. An older student senses that you are lost and offers to help you find your way. You look at her and say . . .*

Help the children to conclude that we can love and serve God by accepting help from others.

Scripture

Linguistic, Interpersonal

For a Scripture activity, see *What's the Word?*, guide page 271F.

• *Children are picking up litter on the lawn.*

• *Many people have stopped to talk to other people in the parish, including the priest.*

• *In the upper right, other members of the family are waiting for the grandfather to get in the car.*

Encourage the children to share times when they served others in some of these ways.

Quick Check

✔ *Why did Jesus do whatever God asked him to do?* (Jesus loved and trusted God.)

✔ *What did Jesus tell us about loving others?* (Jesus said, "As I have loved you, so you also should love one another." [John 13:34])

WE RESPOND _____ minutes

Connect to Life Invite the children to answer the *We Respond* question. Encourage them to see that they can always ask God for help to do what he wants us to do.

Pray Gather the children in a circle. Invite the children to extend the sign of peace to each other as a reminder of God's love. Then invite the children to pray together: *God, help us to share your peace with others. Amen.*

Plan Ahead for Day 2

Catechist Goal: To introduce prayer as a way to show our love for God

Preparation: Prepare examples of the different kinds of prayer described in *As Catholics.*

Catechist Goal

• To introduce prayer as a way to show our love for God

Our Faith Response

• To express our love for God in prayer

Forms of Prayer

After you have presented the lesson, read aloud the *As Catholics* text. The children have been learning that we grow closer to God when we pray. Remind them that we pray by talking and by listening. Provide an example of each type of prayer described in the paragraph.

274

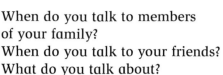

When we pray, we show God that we love him.

WE GATHER

✝ *God, we want to be close to you.*

When do you talk to members of your family?
When do you talk to your friends?
What do you talk about?

WE BELIEVE

We spend a lot of time with the people we love. We talk and listen to them. We share what is important to us. We grow closer to each other.

We show God we love him when we pray. Prayer is listening to and talking to God. We grow closer to God when we pray.

Jesus taught us that God is his Father. He prayed to his Father often. He wants us to pray often, too. We pray to the Blessed Trinity: God the Father, God the Son, and God the Holy Spirit.

Lesson Plan

WE GATHER _____ minutes

✝ **Pray** Invite the children to pray the *We Gather* prayer.

Focus on Life Read the *We Gather* questions. Invite volunteers to share their responses. Help the children to conclude that family and friends grow closer by talking with and listening to one another. Tell the children that in this lesson they will learn how we grow closer to God by talking to him in prayer.

WE BELIEVE _____ minutes

Learn More About Prayer Ask the children to share what they have learned about prayer. Then invite the children to read aloud the *We Believe* statement.

Ask volunteers to read aloud the first three *We Believe* paragraphs. Then ask the following questions:

• *What prayers to the Blessed Trinity have you learned this year?* (Sign of the Cross, Glory to the Father)

• *What is the prayer Jesus taught us?* (the Lord's Prayer)

We can pray by ourselves. We can pray with our families, with our friends, and with our parish. We can use our own words to pray. We can pray the prayers of the Church.

As Catholics...

There are many ways to pray. We can praise God. We can tell God we are sorry for something we have done wrong. We can thank God for his loving care. We can ask God for what we need. We can pray for other people.

Try to pray in one or more of these ways today.

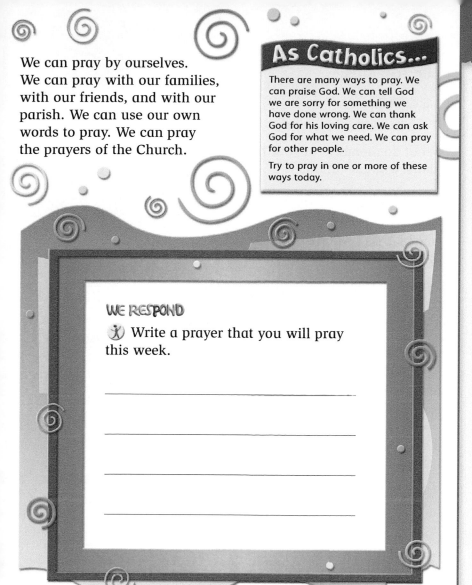

WE RESPOND

Write a prayer that you will pray this week.

_____

_____

_____

_____

275

Catechist Goal

• To describe how we can share God's love with our families

Our Faith Response

• To share God's love with our families

Teaching Tip

Maintaining a Balanced Discussion

Some of the children in your group may be enthusiastic in discussing and sharing about their families. Affirm what the children are saying but try to help them realize when they are sharing too much personal information. Some children in difficult situations may not want to share in discussions. Be aware of these children. Tell them that they can discuss families in general. Assure all the children that God loves all families and is with them always.

We share God's love with our families.

WE GATHER

✝ Thank you, God, for our families.

What do members of your family share with one another?

WE BELIEVE

God wants us to love and serve him. We do this when we share God's love with our families.

We share God's love with our families in these ways.

• We are kind and helpful.
• We obey our parents and all those who care for us.
• We take care of the things that belong to our family.
• We show our love for all family members.
• We say we are sorry and forgive one another.

276

Lesson Plan

WE GATHER ___ minutes

✝ **Pray** Ask the children to close their eyes and imagine that they are with their families. Then pray aloud the *We Gather* prayer.

Focus on Life Read the *We Gather* question. Explain that, often without realizing it, families share many things. Invite volunteers to share their responses. (Possible responses: space, things in the house, meals, special times, love and friendship) Then read the *Chapter Story* on guide page 271C. Tell the children that in this lesson they will learn that God wants us to share his love with our families.

WE BELIEVE ___ minutes

Learn Ways to Share with Families Read aloud the *We Believe* paragraphs. Have the children form five groups. To each group assign one of the ways that families share God's love listed on page 276. Ask each group to think of specific things to do to share God's love in that way. Make sure the groups understand what they are to do. Have someone from each group share the group's example with the class.

Do the Activity Invite the children to study and discuss the pictures on pages 276 and 277. Then ask volunteers to act out what the family members are doing and saying in each picture. Encourage the children to describe the way the people in each picture show a way we can serve God.

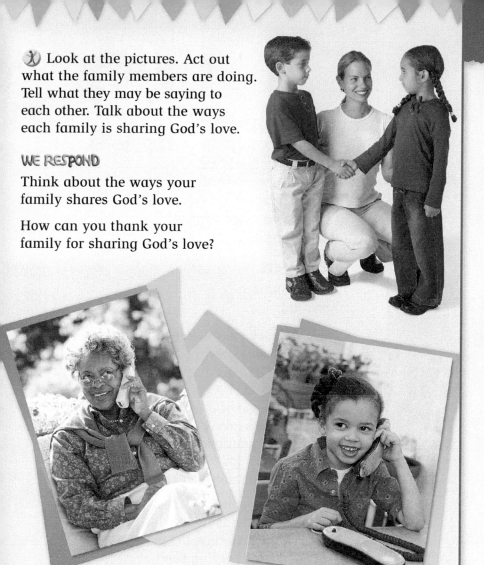

👤 Look at the pictures. Act out what the family members are doing. Tell what they may be saying to each other. Talk about the ways each family is sharing God's love.

WE RESPOND

Think about the ways your family shares God's love.

How can you thank your family for sharing God's love?

ACTIVITY BANK

Catholic Social Teaching

Call to Family, Community, and Participation

Activity Materials: index cards (five for each child), crayons or colored pencils

Give each child five index cards. Explain to the children that they are going to use the cards to make coupons. On each coupon the children should draw a picture of something that they can do to help their families. For example on one coupon they can draw plates, forks, or spoons, to show that they will help set the table or wash the dishes. Ask volunteers to share other ideas. Allow the children time to complete their coupons. Encourage them to take the coupons home. Explain that they should give a coupon to their families when they will help in the way shown in the picture on the coupon.

Quick Check

✔ *What do we do when we share God's love with our families?* (We love and serve God.)

✔ *How do we share God's love with our families?* (Accept the ways listed on page 276.)

WE RESPOND ___ minutes

Connect to Life Read aloud the *We Respond* question. On the board or chart paper, list the children's responses. Encourage the children to choose one way they will share God's love in their families. Have them choose one way to thank their families for sharing God's love.

Pray Invite the children to gather in the prayer space. Ask them to pray after you:

I love my family, and my family loves me.
Thank you, God, for my special family.

Plan Ahead for Day 4

Catechist Goal: To teach that we share God's love with others

Preparation: Have the Grade 1 CD available. Make copies of Reproducible Master 24, guide page 271G.

Catechist Goal

• To teach that we share God's love with others

Our Faith Response

• To work with our family and the parish community to serve others

Lesson Materials

• parish bulletin
• copies of Reproducible Master 24
• Grade 1 CD

Teaching Tip

Being Safe While Helping Others

As catechists we encourage the children to be helpful and loving. Nevertheless, we also want them to be safe. Remind the children to always ask a parent or caregiver whether it is all right to help another person. Caution the children to be sure to have a responsible adult or older brother or sister accompany them whenever they visit or help others.

We share God's love with others.

WE GATHER

✝ *Holy Spirit, help us to live as Jesus did.*

Have you helped someone this week? How did you help?

WE BELIEVE

God made each of us. He made us to share God's love with everyone. We can join with our own families to share God's love. We can join with members of our parish to do this, too.

Look at the pictures on these pages. Talk about what is happening in each picture. Tell how the people are loving and serving God.

278

WE GATHER ___ minutes

✝ **Pray** Pray aloud together the *We Gather* prayer.

Focus on Life Read the *We Gather* questions. Provide quiet time for the children to reflect on what they have done to help others. Then invite volunteers to share their responses.

WE BELIEVE ___ minutes

Share God's Love Read aloud together the *We Believe* statement. Tell the children that they will now learn ways we can share the love of God.

Read the Text Ask a volunteer to read aloud the *We Believe* text. Emphasize the following points:

• *God made us to share his love with everyone.*
• *We can share God's love with our families.*
• *We can share God's love with the members of our parish.*

Do the Activity Have the children work in pairs. Have the partners discuss how the people in each picture are sharing God's love.

Distribute copies of Reproducible Master 24. Explain to the children that they are to decide on ways they can share God's love with others. Then they are to write one way on each flower petal. Encourage the children to display their signs at home.

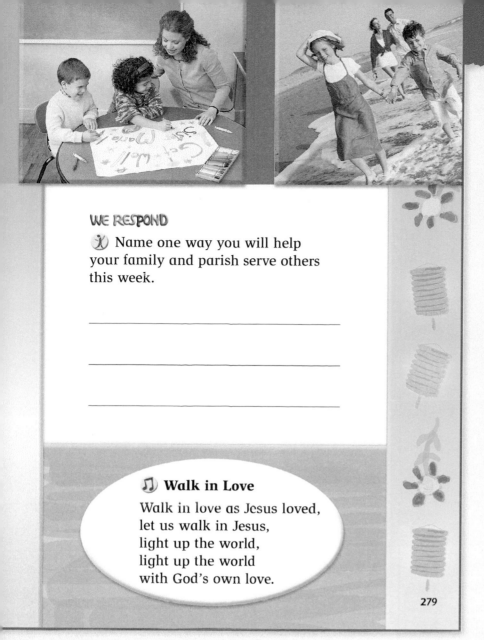

WE RESPOND

Name one way you will help your family and parish serve others this week.

_____

_____

_____

🎵 **Walk in Love**

Walk in love as Jesus loved,
let us walk in Jesus,
light up the world,
light up the world
with God's own love.

ACTIVITY BANK

Parish

Message Piñatas

Activity Materials: paper bags (one for each group), yarn, party streamers, sentence strips (20 per group)

Help the children to make piñatas to give to other groups of children in the parish. Have the children work in groups. Give each group a paper bag, yarn, and party streamers. Have the children use the streamers to decorate the outside of the bag. Give the group about 20 sentence strips. Have the children draw a heart on each strip and write the message: *Jesus loves you.* Put the message strips inside the piñata bags. Then tie the open ends of the bags with yarn or string. Also attach a length of string or yarn which can be used to hang their piñatas. Give the piñatas to the preschool or kindergarten teachers to use with their groups.

279

Quick Check

✔ *Why did God make us?* (God made us to share his love with everyone.)

✔ *Who can we join with to share God's love?* (We can join with our families and the members of our parish.)

WE RESPOND   ___ minutes

Connect to Life Read the directions for the *We Respond* activity. Talk about specific ways the children can help their families and parish serve others this week. If you have a parish bulletin, you might read aloud ways the children and their families can volunteer to help the parish. Write these ways on the board or on chart paper. Then have the children complete the activity.

Pray Invite the children to gather in the prayer space. Remind them of God's love for them and of ways they can share that love with others. As a closing prayer ask the children to join you in singing "Walk in Love," #28 on the Grade 1 CD.

Plan Ahead for Day 5

Catechist Goal: To review chapter ideas and their relationship to our faith life

Preparation: Make copies of *Sharing Faith with My Family,* guide page 271E.

Catechist Goal

• To review the chapter ideas that are key to growing as disciples of Jesus Christ

Our Faith Response

• To decide on ways to grow as disciples by living out what we have learned

Show What *you* Know

Read the instructions and sentences, pausing to indicate the missing word. Encourage the children to refer back to the *We Believe* statements to find and write the missing word. Read the finished sentences. Ask children to say the word *love* each time it appears.

Make *it* Happen

Read the paragraph. Fold a large sheet of poster board in half to make an oversized greeting card. On the front, write *Thank You.* Allow small groups of children to decorate portions of the card with pictures and messages and to sign their names. Present the card to the parish priest.

Picture This

Read the instructions. Allow children time to complete the chart. Ask them to compare the ways they have depicted.

Take Home

Ask the children to name ways families can share God's love. Review the bulleted list. Invite the children to initial beside a way they can share God's love. Ask them to invite their family members to do the same.

Discuss and send home copies of *Sharing Faith with My Family,* guide page 271E.

Grade 1 Chapter 24

PROJECT

Show What *you* Know

There is an important word missing from these statements. Write it in.

Jesus shows us how to ___love___ and serve.

When we pray, we show God that we ___love___ him.

We share God's ___love___ with our families.

We share God's ___love___ with others.

Make *it* Happen

Parish priests lead us in the celebration of the Eucharist. They help us prepare to celebrate the other sacraments. They visit people who are sick. They help people learn more about the Bible and the Church. As a class, write a card to your parish priest to thank him for serving God and others.

280 www.webelieveweb.com

DISCIPLE

Picture This

Draw a picture of:

a way that you show your family members you love them	a way that you show God you love him
Accept drawings of bulleted list of ways on page 276.	Possible drawings: pray; learn the ways God wants us to live; tell others about God; share God's love with our families and others

↳ DISCIPLE CHALLENGE How are these ways alike? How are they different?

Take Home

Invite each member of your family to complete the following. Write your initials beside one thing you will do to share God's love with your family this week.

• I will be kind and helpful.
• I will obey my parents.
• I will take care of things that belong to my family.
• I will forgive others.

281

CHAPTER TEST

Circle the correct answer.

1. Do we serve God when we show others his love?

    (Yes)   No

2. Do we share God's love with our family members when we take things that belong to them?

    Yes   (No)

3. Do we share God's love when we forgive one another?

    (Yes)   No

4. Did Jesus tell everyone about God?

    (Yes)   No

5. Is there only one way to pray?

    Yes   (No)

TALK ABOUT IT

How do we share God's love with our families? Accept bulleted list of ways on page 276.

282

CHAPTER TEST

Read each test item aloud and allow time for the children to mark an answer. Decide whether the *Talk About It* activity will be a small group or whole class discussion. After you have finished, check the answers. Clarify any misconceptions.

Alternative Assessment

You may want the students to complete the following alternative-assessment activity.

Make a poster titled "Loving and Serving God." Use pictures from newspapers or magazines or draw your own pictures.

Additional Testing

• Chapter 24 Test in *Assessment Book*, pages 47–48

• CD-ROM *Test Generator and Resource*: Use Chapter 24 Test or customize your own.

Review

We Believe Statements

Review the four statements.

• Jesus shows us how to love and serve.

• When we pray, we show God that we love him.

• We share God's love with our families.

• We share God's love with others.

To use the Chapter 24 Study Guide, visit

www.webelieveweb.com

Chapter 25 We Honor Mary and the Saints

Overview

In Chapter 24 the children learned that they can love and serve God by sharing his love with their families and others. In this chapter the children will learn about Mary and the ways in which we honor her and the saints.

Doctrinal Content	For Adult Reading and Reflection *Catechism of the Catholic Church*
The children will learn:	Paragraph
• Mary is the mother of Jesus.	964
• The Church honors Mary.	963
• The saints are close to God.	954
• We honor all the saints of the Church.	956

saints (p. 289)

Catechist Background

Who are some people our society honors? Why?

As Catholics we believe in the Communion of Saints. When we profess this belief, we acknowledge that the Church is more than simply the people we see at Mass on Sunday. It is even more than the people worldwide, who gather each week to celebrate the Mass in parishes throughout the world. The Church is also made up of those who have gone before us; those who are no longer living on earth, but have life everlasting with God in Heaven. These are the saints, the followers of Jesus who have died and now live forever with God. We honor the saints because they are our ancestors in faith.

The Church honors in a most special way the first of all saints, Mary, the mother of Jesus. We honor Mary because by her saying "yes" to God, she made our salvation possible. We honor Mary as the perfect disciple because she was Jesus' mother, first teacher, and first disciple. For these reasons we address Mary with special titles and say special prayers in her name.

Throughout the year we acknowledge different aspects of Mary's life by celebrating special feast days. We also celebrate feast days of different saints, usually on the day of their death. On November 1 we honor all saints, known or unknown, who have died and now live with God forever. "By keeping the memorials of the saints— first of all the holy Mother of God, then the apostles, the martyrs, and other saints—on fixed days of the liturgical year, the Church on earth shows that she is united with the liturgy of heaven." (CCC 1195)

Go to **www.webelieveweb.com**, Catechist/ Teacher, We Believe Correlations for this chapter's correlation to the Six Tasks of Catechesis.

What saint has inspired you in your faith life?

Lesson Planning Guide

Lesson Focus	Presentation	Materials
Day 1		
page 283 ✚ **We Gather in Prayer** **pages 284–285** *Mary is the mother of Jesus.* 📖 *Luke 1:26–28, 35*	• Listen to Scripture. 🎵 Respond to Scripture in song. 🧍 Act out responses for **We Gather**. • Present the **We Believe** text about Mary, the mother of Jesus. • Share responses for **We Respond**.	For the prayer space: pictures or statues of Mary and the saints 🎵 "Joseph Was a Good Man," #29, Grade 1 CD • copies of reproducible master *What's the Word?*, guide page 283F
Day 2		
pages 286–287 *The Church honors Mary.*	• Share responses for **We Gather**. • Read and discuss the **We Believe** text about ways we honor Mary. 🧍 Do the unscramble activity. • Discuss the **We Respond** directive. • Pray the Hail Mary. • Read and discuss the *As Catholics* text.	• crayons or colored pencils
Day 3		
pages 288–289 *The saints are close to God.*	• Respond to the **We Gather** questions • Present the **We Believe** text about saints. 🧍 Do the picture-study activity to learn about some of the saints of the Church. • Respond to the **We Respond** question.	• world map or globe • yellow crayons or markers
Day 4		
pages 290–291 *We honor all the saints of the Church.*	• Share responses for **We Gather**. • Present the **We Believe** text about honoring the saints. • Share responses for **We Respond**. 🎵 Celebrate in song.	• copies of Reproducible Master 25, guide page 283G • crayons • glue, glitter, and drinking straws 🎵 "When the Saints Go Marching In," #30, Grade 1 CD
Day 5		
pages 292–293 **Project Disciple** **page 294** **Chapter 25 Test**	• Complete the **Project Disciple** activities. • Explain the *Take Home* activity. • Discuss/send home **Sharing Faith with My Family**, guide page 283E. • Complete **Chapter 25 Test**. • Work on *Alternative Assessment* activity.	• pencils • copies of **Sharing Faith with My Family** reproducible master, guide page 283E

For additional ideas, activities, and opportunities: Visit Sadlier's **www.WEBELIEVEweb.com**

Enrichment Ideas

Chapter Story

One day last week Andy helped his mom clean her closet. He found a large box filled with photographs. Andy's mom saw him looking in the box. She said, "When we're finished cleaning, we'll take a look at the photos."

When Andy started looking through the box, he did not recognize people in some of the black and white photos. One picture was from a newspaper. It showed a woman folding a lot of blankets. Andy's mom said, "That is your Great Grandmom Elizabeth. She always tried to help care for others. The picture shows a time when she helped the parish pack blankets to send to a shelter for people whose homes were damaged by a storm."

Andy said, "Wow, it must have been great to see someone from our family in the newspaper."

Andy's mom answered, "Well, I guess it was, but your great grandmother did things for others because she was kind and caring. It did not matter to her that other people knew what she was doing."

Then Andy's mom told him of some of the other ways Great Grandmom Elizabeth helped people. When his mom was finished, Andy asked, "May I bring this photo to school? I want to tell my class about what a "great" great grandmom I have."

▶ *Do you know anyone like Andy's great grandmother? Tell about one way that this person helped others.*

FAITH and MEDIA

▶ On Day 3, as you discuss the saints pictured on pages 288 and 289, you might remind the children that they can go to various media—books, videos, and the Internet—to find out more about these saints.

▶ If you bring in art books showing paintings of Mary or share pictures from the Internet (*Connections: To the Arts*), remind the children that looking at pictures of Mary in books and on the Internet is another example of the ways we can use media every day to help us learn more about our faith.

CHAPTER PROJECT: A BIG BOOK OF SAINTS

Remind the children of the stories of the saints they have learned about in Kindergarten and Grade 1. Have the children work in pairs. Give each pair a sheet of poster board. Assign one of the saints to each pair. Ask each pair to make a storyboard about the saint on the poster board. When the children have completed their storyboards, collect them and put them together in one big book. Keep the book in your prayer space.

PROJECT DISCIPLE

Pray
Learn
Celebrate
Share
Choose
Live

Additional Activities

What's the Word?

(Use on Day 1.)

Materials needed: copies of reproducible master, guide page 283F

Distribute copies of the Scripture reproducible master. Explain to the children that in Jesus' time, parents brought their children to the Temple in Jerusalem. Explain that the children would receive a special blessing there. Choose volunteers to read the parts of Readers 1–7. After Reader 7 has finished, ask the children to discuss what happened in the Temple.

Picture This

Collect images of Mary from many cultures. Compile these into a slideshow or an album and show it to the children. Tell them that all these images are of the same person, and invite them to guess that it is Mary, the mother of Jesus. Include a copy of the familiar image of Mary from their textbooks. Ask the children: *Why do you think Mary looks different in all of these pictures?* Explain that different groups of people depict Mary in different ways just like we honor her in different ways. Invite children to bring a copy of a picture of Mary that they look at in their families to incorporate into the album or slideshow.

More to Explore

Materials needed: classroom computer and projector or interactive whiteboard

As the children learn more about the saints, visit *Lives of the Saints* on **www.webelieveweb.com**. Choose one of the featured saints from the current page or the saints archive. Invite the children to look at the saint's picture and to listen as you read some of the information provided. Download the primary activity and invite the children to work on it in class or at home with their families. Tell the children they can learn about saints any time by visiting this Web site.

Question Corner

As children learn about saints in this chapter, encourage them to interview family members about saints for whom they are named. Prepare a chart of common saints' names and leave dot stickers beside it. Display it in the classroom and allow children to place a sticker beside the name of a saint for whom they or family members are named. Leave additional space for children to write in a name of a saint who is not included on the list. Discuss as a class the popular or interesting saints for which people are named.

Meeting Individual Needs
English Language Learners

Call on the children who are learning to speak English to share with their classmates the names of Mary in their native languages. Also ask these children to share ways that Mary and the saints are honored in their countries.

We Believe Resources

- Grade 1 *Review & Resource Book*, pages 58–60
- Grade 1 *Family Book*, pages 71–73
- Grade 1 *Assessment Book*, pages 49–50
- Grade 1 CD-ROM *Test Generator and Resource*: Use Chapter 25 Test or customize your own.
- **www.webelieveweb.com**

Sharing What I Learned

Look at the pictures below. Use each picture to tell your family what you learned in this chapter.

For All to See and Pray

Pray the Hail Mary often with your family.

Hail Mary, full of grace,
the Lord is with you!
Blessed are you among women,
and blessed is the fruit of
        your womb, Jesus.
Holy Mary, Mother of God,
pray for us sinners,
now and at the hour
        of our death.
Amen.

Visit Sadlier's

www.WeBelieveweb.com

 Connect to the Catechism
For adult background and reflection, see paragraphs 964, 963, 954, and 956.

PROJECT DISCIPLE

Pray
Learn
Celebrate
Share
Choose
Live

Name _____

What's *the* Word?

Reader 1: When Jesus was a baby, Mary and Joseph took him to the Temple. They took Jesus there for a special blessing.

Reader 2: There was a holy man in the Temple. He was waiting to see Jesus. He was waiting to see the person God had promised to send.

Reader 3: The holy man took Jesus in his arms. He blessed God and thanked him for letting him see Jesus. He called Jesus a light.

Reader 4: Mary and Joseph were surprised with what the holy man said about Jesus.

Reader 5: There was also a holy woman in the Temple. She, too, was waiting to see Jesus.

Reader 6: When the woman saw Jesus, she told everyone that Jesus was the person God had promised to send.

Reader 7: Then Mary and Joseph left the Temple. They returned to the town of Nazareth. "The child grew and became strong." (Luke 2:40)

283F

Name _____

Make a "saints sparkler." Color the sparkle burst. Cut along the dashed lines. Sprinkle glitter on top of the sparkler.

Punch a hole in the center of the sparkler. Put a drinking straw through the hole. Twirl or wave your sparkler to honor the saints.

We Honor Mary and the Saints

✝ We Gather in Prayer

Leader: God chose Mary to be the Mother of his own Son, Jesus. Listen to God's Word.

📖 Luke 1:26–28, 35

Read Along

Before Jesus was born, God sent an angel to Mary. The angel said to Mary, "Hail, favored one! The Lord is with you." (Luke 1:28) The angel told Mary that she was going to have a son. The angel told her, "The child to be born will be called holy, the Son of God." (Luke 1:35)

Leader: Joseph was Mary's husband. He loved and cared for Mary and Jesus.

🎵 **Joseph Was a Good Man**

Joseph was a good man,
a good man, a good man,
Joseph was a good man,
chosen by the Lord.
And Joseph loved a lady,
Joseph loved a lady,
Joseph loved a lady,
chosen by the Lord.

283

PREPARING TO PRAY

The children will listen to a story from Scripture and sing a song about Saint Joseph.

• Read together the words of the song, "Joseph Was a Good Man." Play the song, #29 on the Grade 1 CD. Have the children practice singing.

The Prayer Space

• Display pictures or statues of Mary and the saints.

• Place a tablecloth on the prayer table. Also place a Bible and figures of Mary and Joseph from a Christmas crèche.

📖 **This Week's Liturgy**
Visit www.webelieveweb.com for this week's liturgical readings and other seasonal material.

Lesson Plan

We Gather in Prayer ___ minutes

✝ Pray

• Have the children open their books to the opening prayer on page 283. Ask the children to look at the picture of the Holy Family.

• Invite the children to gather in the prayer space. Pray the Sign of the Cross together.

• Read aloud the Bible story. Say: *The Word of God,* and invite the children to join you in saying, *Amen.*

• Sing together "Joseph Was a Good Man."

Family Connection Update

Invite the children to share their experiences of sharing God's love with their families.

Catechist Goal

• To present Mary's role as the mother of Jesus

Our Faith Response

• To express our love for Mary

Lesson Materials

• copies of reproducible master *What's the Word?*, guide page 283F

Teaching Tip

Review

Before you present the *We Believe* text, refer the children to Chapter 3 of their books. Ask the children to look at the pictures on pages 45, 46, 48, 49, and 51 of their text. Have volunteers share what the children have learned about Mary and the Holy Family.

Mary is the mother of Jesus.

WE GATHER

✝ *God, you give us people who care for us.*

🏃 How do mothers care for and help their children? Act out some ways.

WE BELIEVE

God asked Mary to be the Mother of his Son. Mary said "yes" to God. Mary gave birth to God's only Son, Jesus.

Mary loved Jesus. Mary cared for him. She helped him learn many things.

284

Lesson Plan

WE GATHER ___ minutes

✝ **Pray** Invite the children to think about the people who care for them. Then pray the Sign of the Cross and the *We Gather* prayer.

Focus on Life Ask the children to share their answers to the *We Gather* question. Encourage them to complete the activity, acting out the roles of loving, caring mothers. Tell the children that in this lesson they will learn about Mary's love for Jesus.

WE BELIEVE ___ minutes

Read the Text Ask a volunteer to read aloud the *We Believe* statement. Explain that Mary showed great love

for Jesus. Ask volunteers to read the *We Believe* text. Emphasize the following points.

• *Mary is the mother of Jesus.*

• *Mary loved and cared for Jesus as mothers love and care for their children today.*

• *Jesus loved his mother and wants us to love and care for her, too.*

• *Mary shows us how to live as Jesus asks us to.*

Reflect and Share Have the children work in pairs. Explain that you are going to ask a question and that each pair should think about the answer together. Then, when each pair has agreed on an answer, the whole class will share their answers. Ask: *We just read that Mary helped Jesus learn many things. What do you think Mary helped Jesus learn?*

All through his life, Mary saw the wonderful things that Jesus did. Mary listened to Jesus teach. She watched him heal the sick. She celebrated special times with him.

Jesus always loved his mother. He wanted his followers to love and care for her, too. Mary shows us how to live as Jesus asks us to.

WE RESPOND

Jesus wants us to love his mother. How can we show our love for Mary?

285

ACTIVITY BANK

Curriculum Connection
Language Arts and Art
Activity Materials: crayons or markers, drawing paper

Help the children make a storyboard about Mary. Ask the children to draw three squares in a row on a piece of paper. Explain that they will draw a picture of Mary in each square. For example, in the first square the children might draw a picture of the angel visiting Mary. In the second they might draw Mary and Jesus doing something together. In the third they might draw the Holy Family. Ask the children to print a sentence about each picture below it.

Scripture
Linguistic

For a Scripture activity, see *What's the Word?*, guide page 283F.

Discuss the Pictures Invite the children to look at the pictures of Mary and Jesus on these pages. Ask volunteers to describe what Mary and Jesus are saying and doing in each picture. Discuss other things that Mary and Jesus did together.

Quick Check

✔ *Who is the mother of Jesus?* (Mary is the mother of Jesus.)

✔ *What does Mary show us?* (Mary shows us how to live as Jesus asks us to.)

WE RESPOND ___ minutes

Connect to Life Read the *We Respond* question. Pause briefly for reflection. Then ask volunteers to share

their responses. (Possible responses: Pray to her; talk about her with others; act as Jesus did by sharing God's love with others.)

Pray Invite the children to pray together: *God, thank you for giving us Mary to love and care for us.*

Plan Ahead for Day 2

Catechist Goal: To describe ways the Church honors Mary

Preparation: Find out different ways that your parish honors Mary.

Catechist Goal

- To describe ways the Church honors Mary

Our Faith Response

- To honor Mary by learning the Hail Mary

Lesson Materials

- crayons or colored pencils

As Catholics...

Honoring Mary

After you have presented the lesson, read the *As Catholics* text to the children. Ask them to think of ways your parish honors Mary on special days. Help them to recall songs and prayers that are used in your parish. Explain that throughout the world Catholics honor Mary in many different ways.

The Church honors Mary.

WE GATHER

✝ *Holy Mary, pray for us.*

When we honor people, we show them how special they are to us.

Name someone you would like to honor. Tell why.

WE BELIEVE

The Church honors Mary. We honor her because she is the mother of Jesus. To show our love for Mary, we sometimes call her "Our Lady" and "The Blessed Mother."

✴ Unscramble the words to complete the sentence.

R M O E T H   U R C H C H

We also honor Mary as the

<u>M</u> <u>O</u> <u>T</u> <u>H</u> <u>E</u> <u>R</u> of the <u>C</u> <u>H</u> <u>U</u> <u>R</u> <u>C</u> <u>H</u>.

286

Lesson Plan

WE GATHER   __ minutes

✝ **Pray** Pray the Sign of the Cross and the *We Gather* prayer.

Focus on Life Invite a volunteer to read the *We Gather* text aloud. Ask the children to name people whom they would like to honor and tell why. Begin the discussion by sharing your own reflections. Then discuss ways we can honor the people we have named. (Possible responses: Give the person a gift; do something nice for the person; tell others about the person.) Tell the children that in this lesson they will learn some ways the Church honors Mary.

WE BELIEVE   __ minutes

Learn Ways to Honor Mary Read the *We Believe* statement together. Explain: *The Church shows its love for Mary in many different ways.* Ask a volunteer to read aloud the first *We Believe* paragraph. Ask the children to use yellow crayons or pencils to highlight the titles *Our Lady* and the *Blessed Mother.*

Complete the Activity Invite the children to work in pairs to complete the activity. Allow about five minutes for the partners to unscramble the letters. Read the completed sentence together. Have the children use yellow crayons or pencils to highlight this title of Mary.

We honor Mary in different ways. One way is to celebrate her feast days. On these days, we remember special times in the lives of Mary and Jesus.

The Church also has prayers to honor Mary. We can say these prayers often. One special prayer that we say is the Hail Mary.

Hail Mary, full of grace,
the Lord is with you!
Blessed are you among women,
and blessed is the fruit of
   your womb, Jesus.
Holy Mary, Mother of God,
pray for us sinners,
now and at the hour of our death.
Amen.

WE RESPOND

Talk with a friend about ways you can honor Mary this week. Then choose one you will do.

Pray together the Hail Mary.

As Catholics...

We honor Mary in a special way on certain days of the year. On some of these days, parishes gather together for processions. On these special prayer walks, the people sing songs to Mary and pray special prayers. They put flowers in front of a statue of Mary. In this way they honor Mary.

Find out ways your parish honors Mary.

ACTIVITY BANK

Multicultural Connection
Our Lady of Guadalupe

Point out that the picture on page 286 is of Our Lady of Guadalupe. Explain that we celebrate the feast of Our Lady of Guadalupe every year on December 12. Tell the children that many Hispanic communities have processions to honor Mary on that day. Have the children look at the photo of a procession on page 287. Invite any child who has taken part in a procession in honor of Mary to tell the class about the experience.

Pray the Hail Mary Continue reading the *We Believe* text with the children. Ask the children to read silently as you read the Hail Mary aloud. Have the children use one color to underline the first part of the Hail Mary—from the word *Hail* to the word *Jesus*. Have the children use another color to underline the second part of the prayer. Help the children read aloud the words of each part.

Quick Check

✔ *Why does the Church honor Mary?* (Mary is the mother of Jesus.)

✔ *What is one special prayer that we say to honor Mary?* (We pray the Hail Mary.)

WE RESPOND _____ minutes

Connect to Life Have the children discuss in pairs ways they will honor Mary this week. After the partners have brainstormed together what they will do, encourage them to honor Mary in at least one of the ways the pair has discussed.

Pray Have the children walk prayerfully to the prayer space. Then pray together the Hail Mary.

Plan Ahead for Day 3

Catechist Goal: To explain that the saints were special followers of Jesus

Preparation: Have available a world map or globe.

Catechist Goal

• To explain that the saints were special followers of Jesus

Our Faith Response

• To follow the example of the saints

 **saints**

Lesson Materials

• world map or globe
• yellow crayons or markers

Teaching Note

The We Believe *Program and Saints*

In the Kindergarten *We Believe* text, the children learned about the following saints: Rose of Lima, Joseph, Francis of Assisi, Patrick, Peter, Thérèse of Lisieux, Frances of Rome, Martin de Porres, Katharine Drexel, and John Bosco. Before you present the *We Believe* text, you may want to have volunteers share what they remember about these saints.

The saints are close to God.

WE GATHER

✝ *God, keep us close to you.*

When you listen to stories about your family, how do you feel? What are some things you learn?

WE BELIEVE

The Church shares stories about many of Jesus' followers. Some of these stories are about the saints.

The **saints** are followers of Jesus who have died and now live forever with God.

The saints tried to live the way Jesus asked. They loved God very much. They tried to share God's love with others. They prayed to God often.

Saint Katharine Drexel began schools for Native American and African American children.

Saint Andrew Kim Taegon was the first priest and pastor in Korea.

Saint Francis Xavier taught the people of India to know God.

288

Lesson Plan

WE GATHER

_____ minutes

✝ **Pray** Ask the children what it means to be close to someone. Pray together the Sign of the Cross and the *We Gather* prayer.

Focus on Life Read the *We Gather* questions. Invite volunteers to share their responses. Help the children conclude that when we listen to family stories, we hear about some caring things family members have done. Read the *Chapter Story* on page 283C. Tell the children that in this lesson they will learn that the saints are close to God and show us how to be followers of Jesus.

WE BELIEVE

_____ minutes

Learn About the Saints Ask a volunteer to read aloud the *We Believe* statement. Remind the children that

they have just been thinking about the things they can learn from stories about members of their families. Now they will learn from stories about members of the Church. Read the first *We Believe* paragraph aloud. Write the word *saints* on the board. Explain who the saints are by reading the second *We Believe* paragraph. Have the children read the third *We Believe* paragraph together.

Talk About the Pictures Invite the children to look at the pictures of the saints. Read aloud the caption under each picture.

Find the Saints Using a map of the world or a globe, help the children find the country in which each saint lived and worked. (These countries are not identified in the children's text: Saint Katharine Drexel, the United States; Saint Teresa of Avila, Spain; Saint John Vianney, France; Saint Anne, Israel.)

Look at the pictures on these pages. They show some saints of the Church. Read the sentence below each picture.

 Use a yellow crayon. Highlight each saint's name.

Talk about some people you know who do the things these saints did.

WE RESPOND

Which of these saints can you be like?

Key Word

saints followers of Jesus who have died and now live forever with God

Saint Anne was the mother of Mary and the grandmother of Jesus.

Saint Teresa of Avila wrote books and letters to help people love Jesus.

Saint John Vianney was a parish priest who served his people.

289

Chapter 25 • Day 3

ACTIVITY BANK

Multiple Intelligences
Musical, Bodily-Kinesthetic
Activity Materials: rhythm sticks, tambourine, or drum

Invite the children to honor each of the saints they learned about in the lesson. Have the children join hands to form a circle. Explain to the children that after you say a saint's name, they are to raise their arms and step toward the center of the circle. For example, you might say *Saint Anne, pray for us,* and the children will step forward. They then should return to their original positions. You may want some of the children to accompany the prayer movements with rhythm sticks, a tambourine, or a drum.

Complete the Activity Invite the children to use yellow crayons or markers to highlight the names of the saints in their books. Encourage an open discussion of people the children know who do the things these saints did.

Quick Check

✔ *Who are the saints?* (The saints are followers of Jesus who have died and now live forever with God.)

✔ *What did the saints do?* (Accept the actions that are listed in the third *We Believe* paragraph.)

WE RESPOND
_____ minutes

Connect to Life Review the six saints presented in the lesson. Then invite the children to share their answers to the *We Respond* question. As the children tell whom they can be like, encourage them to explain why.

Pray Invite the children to look again at the pictures of the saints. Explain that after you say each saint's name, the children should respond: *Thank you for showing us how to follow Jesus.* Then conclude by praying together: *God, help us to follow the saints.*

Plan Ahead for Day 4

Catechist Goal: To highlight ways the Church honors the saints

Preparation: Make copies of Reproducible Master 25, guide page 283G.

289

Catechist Goal

• To highlight ways the Church honors the saints

Our Faith Response

• To ask the saints to pray for us

Lesson Materials

• copies of Reproducible Master 25
• crayons or markers
• glue, glitter, and drinking straws

Teaching Note

Pictures and Statues of the Saints

Point out to the children that one way we honor Mary and the saints is by putting statues or pictures of them in our churches and homes. When we look at the pictures and statues, we remember the different things the saints did to show they were followers of Jesus. We can remember to ask the saints to help us grow close to God.

We honor all the saints of the Church.

WE GATHER

✝ *Holy Spirit, help us to become saints.*

Look at the picture. The children are dressed as their favorite saints. Who is your favorite saint? Tell why.

WE BELIEVE

There are many, many saints. We do not know all their names.

All the saints loved God very much. They put God first in their lives. They tried to be kind and fair. They shared God's peace with others.

Saint John Bosco

Saint Peter

Saint Mary Magdalen

290

Lesson Plan

WE GATHER

___ minutes

✝ **Pray** Invite the children to pray the Sign of the Cross and the *We Gather* prayer.

Focus on Life Invite the class to spend a few moments studying the picture of the children dressed as saints. Then encourage an open discussion of the children's favorite saints. Tell the children that in this lesson they will learn that we can honor the saints by trying to be more like them.

WE BELIEVE

___ minutes

Think About the Saints Tell the children that there are very many saints. Read the *We Believe* statement aloud together. Explain that we do not know the

names of all the saints, but we do know that all the saints tried to live as Jesus asks us to. Ask: *What else do we know about the saints?* (They live forever close to God.) Read the first *We Believe* paragraph aloud.

Discuss the Text Ask a volunteer to read the second *We Believe* paragraph aloud. Then invite the class to discuss what makes the saints special.

Learn About Honoring the Saints Open a calendar to November. Ask a volunteer to point to November 1. Explain that on this date every year we celebrate All Saints' Day. Say: *On this feast we gather with our parish to celebrate Mass.* Have volunteers read the third and fourth *We Believe* paragraphs aloud.

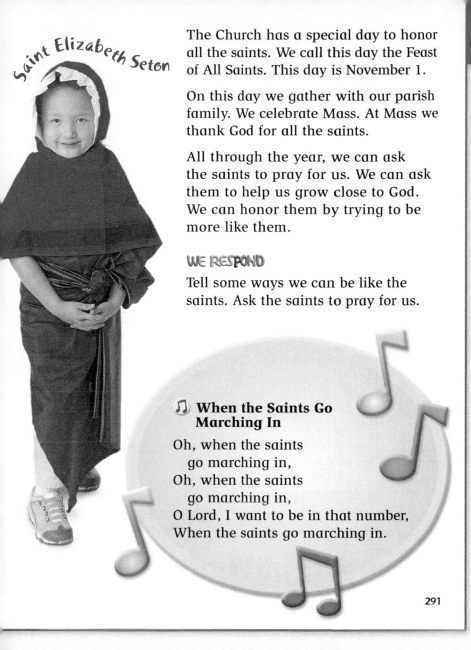

Saint Elizabeth Seton

The Church has a special day to honor all the saints. We call this day the Feast of All Saints. This day is November 1.

On this day we gather with our parish family. We celebrate Mass. At Mass we thank God for all the saints.

All through the year, we can ask the saints to pray for us. We can ask them to help us grow close to God. We can honor them by trying to be more like them.

WE RESPOND

Tell some ways we can be like the saints. Ask the saints to pray for us.

♫ **When the Saints Go Marching In**

Oh, when the saints
   go marching in,
Oh, when the saints
   go marching in,
O Lord, I want to be in that number,
When the saints go marching in.

291

ACTIVITY BANK

Multiple Intelligences
Spatial, Bodily-Kinesthetic
Activity Materials: costumes and props
Plan to have a procession to honor the saints. Invite the children to ask their families to help them find out more about their favorite saints. Invite each child to make a costume to wear and to find a prop that they could carry in the procession. (For example, a child dressed as Saint Joseph would carry a carpenter's tool.)

Faith and Media
Becoming Saints Collage
Activity Materials: Catholic and other appropriate magazines, scissors, glue, large sheet of paper
Have the children look through magazines to find pictures that show people following the example of the saints by doing something for others. Ask the children to cut out the pictures and glue them on a large sheet of paper to make a *Becoming Saints* collage.

Explain that we do not have to wait for this date to honor the saints. Ask a volunteer to read the final *We Believe* paragraph aloud.

Make Saint Sparklers Distribute copies of Reproducible Master 25. Read the directions for making "saint sparklers." Help the children with each step. While they are working, play "When the Saints Go Marching In," #30 on the Grade 1 CD.

Quick Check

✔ *On what special day do we honor all the saints?* (We honor the saints on All Saints' Day, November 1.)

✔ *How do we honor all the saints?* (We gather with our parish family; we take part in Mass; we thank God for all the saints; we try to be more like the saints.)

WE RESPOND ___ minutes

Connect to Life Discuss ways we can be like the saints. Play the recording of "When the Saints Go Marching In."

Pray Invite the children to carry and wave their saint sparklers as they walk around the room singing the song to honor the saints.

Plan Ahead for Day 5

Catechist Goal: To review chapter ideas and their relationship to our faith life

Preparation: Make copies of *Sharing Faith with My Family*, guide page 283E.

Catechist Goal

• To review the chapter ideas that are key to growing as disciples of Jesus Christ

Our Faith Response

• To decide on ways to grow as disciples by living out what we have learned

Show What *you* Know

Help the children to unscramble the word. Review the definition. Ask the children to name some saints.

Picture This

Invite the children to complete the chart. Clarify that in this activity Mary refers to the mother of Jesus. Ask volunteers to share their responses. Compare the ways.

Saint Stories

Read aloud the paragraph about Joseph. Ask the children to name ways they might celebrate the Feast of Saint Joseph the Worker. Possible responses include: saying a prayer, asking Joseph to help all the workers of the world, or going to Mass.

Make *it* Happen

Read the activity and invite the children to decorate the words.

More *to* Explore

Read the activity. Encourage the children to learn about a patron saint and share their knowledge with classmates. Visit *Lives of the Saints* at **www.webelieveweb.com** to see the list of online saints.

Take Home

Read the paragraph. Encourage the children to involve grandparents or other family members in making a family tree.

Discuss and send home copies of *Sharing Faith with My Family*, guide page 283E.

292 and **293**

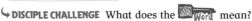

Grade 1 Chapter 25

PROJECT

Pray Learn Celebrate Share Choose Live

Show What *you* Know

Unscramble the 🔑 Word .

| t a s i n s | s a i n t s |

↳ **DISCIPLE CHALLENGE** What does the 🔑 Word mean?

followers of Jesus who have died and now live forever with God

Picture This

Draw a way you can honor your mother. Then, draw a way you can honor Mary.

| Possible drawings: hug her; say "I love you"; help her at home; make her a card or a gift; give her flowers; pray for her | Possible drawings: celebrate Mary's feast days; pray a special prayer to Mary; place flowers at a statue of Mary; gather for a procession |

How are these ways alike? How are they different?

DISCIPLE

Pray Learn Celebrate Choose Live

Saint Stories

Saint Joseph was the husband of Mary and foster father of Jesus. He cared for them. He worked as a carpenter. We can ask Saint Joseph to help all the workers of the world. We celebrate the Feast of Saint Joseph the Worker on May 1.

Hail Mary

Make *it* Happen

Jesus wants us to love his mother Mary. We can show our love by praying to her. Decorate the first words of this prayer.

More *to* Explore

Many people are named after a saint. Are you? Learn about this saint or another saint that interests you. Visit the library or *Lives of the Saints* at **www.webelieveweb.com**.

Take Home

Family was very important to Jesus. He and Mary and Joseph loved and cared for one another. Who loves and cares for you? Make a family tree. Include your family members. Talk about your family tree.

Circle the correct answer.

1. Mary is the _____ of Jesus.

   (mother)   sister

2. A special prayer we honor Mary with is the _____.

   Our Father   (Hail Mary)

3. _____ are followers of Jesus who have died and now live forever with God.

   (Saints)   Sacraments

4. There are _____ saints.

   (many)   just a few

5. The saints are _____ God.

   far away from   (close to)

What are some of the things we do to honor Mary? Possible responses: call her "Our Lady" and "The Blessed Mother"; celebrate her feast days; say special prayers; gather as a parish for a procession; pray the Hail Mary

294

CHAPTER TEST

Read each test item aloud and allow time for the children to mark an answer. Decide whether the *Talk About It* activity will be a small group or whole class discussion. After you have finished, check the answers. Clarify any misconceptions.

Alternative Assessment

You may want the students to complete the following alternative-assessment activity.

With a partner make up a prayer to honor Mary and the saints.

Additional Testing

• Chapter 25 Test in *Assessment Book*, pages 49–50

• CD-ROM *Test Generator and Resource*: Use Chapter 25 Test or customize your own.

Review

Review the definition as it is presented in the chapter's *Key Word* box:

• saints (page 289).

We Believe Statements

Review the four statements.

• Mary is the mother of Jesus.

• The Church honors Mary.

• The saints are close to God.

• We honor all the saints of the Church.

To use the Chapter 25 Study Guide, visit

www.webelieveweb.com

We Care for the Gifts of God's Creation

Overview

In Chapter 25 the children learned about Mary and the saints. In this chapter they will learn that we are to care for all of God's creation.

Doctrinal Content	For Adult Reading and Reflection *Catechism of the Catholic Church*
The children will learn:	Paragraph
• The world is God's gift to us.	2415
• Animals are part of God's creation.	2416
• We are all important to God.	356
• We care for and respect all people.	1825

Catechist Background

Go to **www.webelieveweb.com**, Catechist/ Teacher, We Believe Correlations for this chapter's correlation to:
• Six Tasks of Catechesis
• Catholic Social Teaching
• *Catechetical Formation in Chaste Living.*

How does being in nature draw you closer to God?

Many people feel close to God and drawn to prayer when they are in natural surroundings. Whether it is a majestic mountain, the vast sea, or a small, delicate flower, we are reminded that God is ever present with us. That is because, as we are told in Genesis, God created the natural world and saw that it was good.

The world is God's gift to us and we are to care for it as good stewards. We are meant to enjoy all of God's creation, but not exploit or abuse it. It is a free gift to us, but also ours to care for and tend.

As part of the natural world, animals are also God's creation. "*Animals* are God's creatures. He surrounds them with his providential care. By their mere existence they bless him and give him glory." (*CCC* 2416) It is our duty to care for the animals and show them kindness.

Of all God's creatures, human beings are made in God's image to know and to love God, thus sharing in God's own life. We are each created with unique gifts and talents, and by using those gifts and talents to love and serve God and others, we give glory to God. We are called to care for ourselves, honor our unique abilities, and use them for God's glory. We are also called to care for and respect all other people, for they, too, have been created with unique gifts and talents to serve God. We love one another when we see each other as a brother or sister in Christ and treat each other as we would want to be treated. Jesus summed this up in one command: "Do to others whatever you would have them do to you" (Matthew 7:12). By loving and respecting all God's gifts of the creation, we honor God our Creator.

In what ways to do you glorify God by caring for yourself, others, and the world?

Lesson Planning Guide

Lesson Focus	Presentation	Materials

Day 1

page 295
✝ **We Gather in Prayer**

pages 296–297
The world is God's gifts to us.

♪ Sing a song to praise God.
- Share responses for **We Gather**.
- Present the **We Believe** text about God's gifts of creation.
- Discuss the **We Respond** question.

🧍 Draw to complete a prayer.

For the prayer space: living plant, stuffed animals, a watering can, a rock, a class picture

♪ "Shout from the Mountains," Marie-Jo Thum, #31, Grade 1 CD
- picture books about nature (option)

Day 2

pages 298–299
Animals are part of God's creation.

📖 *Genesis 1:24–25*

- Share responses for **We Gather**.
- Read the **We Believe** text about ways we can care for God's gift of animals.
- Talk about the **We Respond** question.

🧍 Do the drawing activity.

- crayons or markers
- copies of Reproducible Master 26, guide page 295G

Day 3

pages 300–301
We are all important to God.

- Share with a partner the **We Gather** directives.
- Present the **We Believe** text about gifts and talents.
- Reflect on the **We Respond** questions.

♪ Thank God in song.

- Read and discuss the *As Catholics* text.

♪ "Malo! Malo! Thanks Be to God," Jesse Manibusan, #32, Grade 1 CD
- copies of reproducible master *What's the Word?*, guide page 295F

Day 4

pages 302–303
We care for and respect all people.

📖 *Matthew 7:12*

- Respond to the **We Gather** questions.
- Present the **We Believe** text about sharing God's love with others.

🧍 Make up a play about sharing God's love.

- Reflect on the **We Respond** question.

Day 5

pages 304–305
Project Disciple

page 306
Chapter 26 Test

- Complete the **Project Disciple** activities.
- Explain the *Take Home* activity.
- Discuss/send home **Sharing Faith with My Family**, guide page 295E.
- Complete **Chapter 26 Test**.
- Work on *Alternative Assessment* activity.

- pencils
- crayons or colored pencils
- copies of **Sharing Faith with My Family** reproducible master, guide page 295E

For additional ideas, activities, and opportunities: Visit Sadlier's **www.WeBelieveweb.com**

295B

Enrichment Ideas

Chapter Story

Sara's best friend David is in another first grade class. After school yesterday Sara told David, "Mrs. Ambrose is playing a game with us to teach us about different places in the world. We use our imaginations to travel. Then when we reach the place where we are traveling to, Mrs. Ambrose is our guide. She tells us about the different plants, animals, and people. She shows us pictures in books and videos."

David asked Sara, "Where did you go today?"

Sara answered, "Today we went to Australia. We learned about crocodiles, kangaroos, and koala bears. We learned that the koala bears eat leaves from eucalyptus trees. Mrs. Ambrose told us, 'They put eucalyptus in cough drops to help us when we have a cold.' We learned that many people live in cities. Some live and work on sheep ranches outside the cities."

David said to Sara, "You learned a lot about Australia! Where do you think you will travel tomorrow?"

Sara said, "I'm not sure but I'm sure we'll learn a lot about the people, animals, and plants there."

▶ *Where in the world would you like to travel? What do you already know about this place?*

FAITH and MEDIA

▶ As part of your discussion of our stewardship of God's creation, you might want to bookmark some suitable Web sites, such as that of the Catholic Conservation Center, to visit with the children. You might also want to bookmark and visit the Web sites of some of America's national parks, such as Yellowstone National Park, California's Muir Woods, and Arizona's Grand Canyon National Park, where you can see breathtaking photographs of the wonders of God's world.

▶ As suggested in *Connections: To the Arts*, if you plan to show the children some works of art that celebrate nature, you might bookmark some suitable Web sites in advance as well as bringing art books to class.

CHAPTER PROJECT: A BASKET OF GIFTS

Label a bushel basket *God's Creation* and place it in an area where the children will have access to it. Remind the children that they are learning about many gifts of God's creation and about their responsibility to take care of creation. Encourage the children to bring in symbols of creation to put in the basket. Examples might include pictures of mountains and other natural wonders, pine cones, seashells, flowers, stones, toy animals, and pictures of the children's own pets. Each day give the children an opportunity to display the items they have brought for the basket and explain how they can help care for the parts of creation that these symbols represent.

PROJECT DISCIPLE

Pray
Learn
Celebrate
Share
Choose
Live

Additional Activities

What's the Word?

(Use on Day 3.)

Materials needed: copies of reproducible master, guide page 295F

Distribute copies of the Scripture reproducible master. Choose volunteers to read the parts of Reader, Lisa, and Michael. Invite the other children to listen as the story is read. Then discuss the story. Ask the children to share ways they can take care of God's creation in their own neighborhoods.

Make it Happen

Have a week long talent show. Remind the children that each of us has unique gifts and talents. Assign each child a day of the week in which he or she will perform or present something that is special about him- or herself. If the children would like to share a gift or talent that is not conducive to the classroom, encourage them to bring in a video or artwork that demonstrates it instead. Limit each child to five minutes.

More to Explore

Materials needed: notebooks and pencils

Explain to the children that naturalists are people who enjoy observing, understanding, and recognizing patterns in nature. Take the children on a nature walk and invite them to bring a notebook or sketchbook and pencil. Invite them to walk around and observe the natural world. Allow them time to sketch in their notebooks some things they are noticing. Perhaps they see flowers or trees in bloom, notice an animal, or observe the sky. When the children return to the classroom, discuss what they have noticed and sketched. Follow the activity with a prayer thanking God for the diversity of creation.

Picture This

As the children learn about caring for the gifts of God's creation, show them works of art that celebrate nature, such as naturalist-artist John James Audubon's studies of the birds of America, Claude Monet's impressions of his gardens, or Vincent van Gogh's landscapes and his famous painting *The Starry Night*.

Meeting Individual Needs
Children Who Are Tactile Learners

Keep natural objects in the prayer space: pine cones, pine branch, seashells, pebbles, acorns, cactus plant, a container of sand. Have the tactile learners hold the objects in their hands and describe what the objects feel like.

We Believe Resources

- Grade 1 *Review & Resource Book*, pages 61–63
- Grade 1 *Family Book*, pages 74–76
- Grade 1 *Assessment Book*, pages 51–52
- Grade 1 CD-ROM *Test Generator and Resource*: Use Chapter 26 Test or customize your own.
- **www.webelieveweb.com**

Sharing What I Learned

Look at the pictures below. Use each picture to tell your family what you learned in this chapter.

Gifts to Share

Gather your family together. Everyone has gifts and talents. Name some that God has given to each of you. Write them on the gift box.

Talk together about ways you can use your gifts and talents to help others. Then place the gift box on your prayer table.

Name	Gifts and Talents
_____	_____
_____	_____
_____	_____
_____	_____

Pray together:
Thank you, God, for all your gifts.
May we use them respectfully.
May we keep finding ways
    to help your love grow.

Visit Sadlier's
www.WeBelieveweb.com

Connect to the Catechism
For adult background and reflection, see paragraphs 2415, 2416, 356, and 1825.

PROJECT DISCIPLE

Pray
Learn
Celebrate
Share
Choose
Live

Name _____

What's *the* Word?

Reader: Last week Lisa was talking to her older brother Michael after school.

Michael: Lisa, what did you learn today in religion class?

Lisa: We remembered that God created the world. Mrs. Perez said God wants us to watch over "the fish of the sea, the birds of the air, and all living things that move on the earth." (Genesis 1:28)

Michael: That's a big job God gave us!

Lisa: That's what I thought. Mrs. Perez said that God gave people and animals the green plants for food.

Michael: Taking care of trees and plants is part of our big job. This weekend let's help clean up the land where Mom and our neighbors are planting a vegetable garden. We'll be helping to grow healthy food.

Lisa: We'll also be doing what God wants, taking care of ourselves and others.

Name _____

Color the sign. Cut it out and put it in a
place where you will see it often.

Remember that God wants us to take
care of his gifts of creation.

We Care for the Gifts of God's Creation (26)

✝ We Gather in Prayer

Leader: Close your eyes and sit quietly. Think about all the gifts of God's creation. Now let us praise God for all these gifts.

🎵 Shout from the Mountains

Shout from the mountains,
Sing in the valleys,
Call from the waters,
Dance through the hills!
All of God's people,
All of God's creatures,
All of creation,
Join in the song!

And we sing:
Holy, holy, holy is God!
Holy, holy, holy and strong!

295

PREPARING TO PRAY

The children reflect on and celebrate God's gifts of creation.

• Play the song "Shout from the Mountains," #31 on the Grade 1 CD. Have the children practice singing the song.

• Have the children make up actions for the song.

The Prayer Space

• Display in the prayer space symbols of God's creation such as a living plant, stuffed animals, a watering can, a rock, a picture of the children in the class.

📖 **This Week's Liturgy**
Visit **www.webelieveweb.com** for this week's liturgical readings and other seasonal material.

Lesson Plan

We Gather in Prayer ___ minutes

✝ Pray

• Ask the children to close their eyes and reflect quietly about God's gifts of creation.

• Explain the symbolism of the prayer space items: *The plant and the animal figures remind us of the living things in this world; the water in the watering can and the rock remind us of other things in the world on which we depend; the picture of the children in the class reminds us that we are an important part of God's creation.*

• Invite the children to gather in the prayer space. Sing together "Shout from the Mountains."

Family Connection Update

Invite the children to share their family trees.

Catechist Goal

• To emphasize that all of creation is God's gift to us

Our Faith Response

• To care for God's creation

Lesson Materials

• picture books about nature (option)

Teaching Tip

Caring for Parts of Creation

Caring for God's world is a very big task for first graders. Help them to see they can make a difference by focusing on "parts" of God's world: their homes and yards, their neighborhood, their classroom, and their playground. One day they can focus on caring by cleaning up; on another day they can work on such improvements as planting flowers. As the children share their efforts with the class, they can begin to see that together we can care for all of God's creation.

The world is God's gift to us.

WE GATHER

✝ *Thank you, God, for all you have made.*

Close your eyes and picture yourself in your favorite outdoor place. Tell where you are. Tell what you see.

WE BELIEVE

God has given us all of creation to use and enjoy. The world is God's gift to us. It is full of beautiful places and wonderful plants and animals.

God asks us to take care of his creation. The gifts of creation are for all people. God wants people everywhere to be able to use these gifts. God wants us to share these gifts of creation.

Look at the pictures on these pages. Tell how the people are taking care of God's creation.

296

Lesson Plan

WE GATHER
_____ minutes

✝ **Pray** Pray together the Sign of the Cross and the *We Gather* prayer.

Focus on Life Read aloud the *We Gather* directions. Then invite the children to open their eyes and share the outdoor places they pictured and what they saw there. Read the *Chapter Story* on guide page 295C.

WE BELIEVE
_____ minutes

Learn About Creation Remind the children that God created all the wonderful gifts of creation. Ask volunteers to read aloud the first two *We Believe* paragraphs. Then tell the children that you are going to

read a few sentences. Explain: *Stand when I read a statement that is true.*

• *God gave us the world and everything in it as a gift.* (true)

• *God wants us to enjoy all of creation.* (true)

• *God does not care whether or not we take care of creation.* (not true)

• *Creation is meant to be for all people.* (true)

• *God wants people to share the gifts of creation.* (true)

Discuss the Photos Call attention to the photographs on page 296. Help the children understand the ways the people in each picture are helping God's creation. Point out: *When you are picking up litter as the people in the top photo are doing, you should wear gloves.*

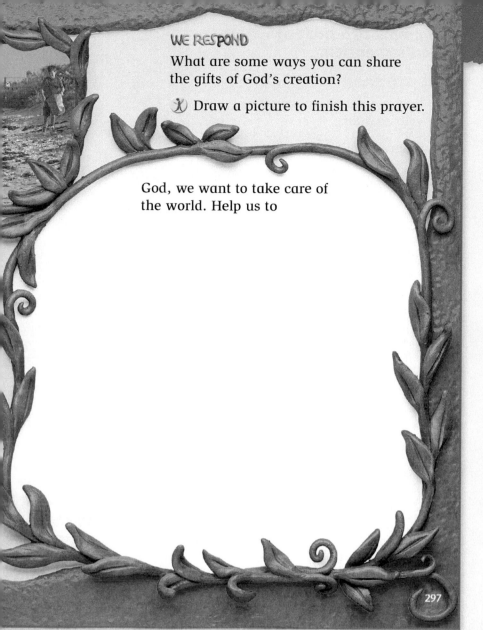

WE RESPOND

What are some ways you can share the gifts of God's creation?

Draw a picture to finish this prayer.

God, we want to take care of the world. Help us to

297

Multiple Intelligences
Bodily-Kinesthetic

Have the children work in groups. Let the children in each group choose gifts of God's creation they want to portray. One group of children might choose to be trees bending in the breeze, stars shining in the night sky, a school of fish swimming, birds flying, or deer leaping. Let each group whisper to you what part of God's creation it wants to portray. If necessary, suggest ways the group can act out its idea. When all groups are ready, let one group at a time prepare to perform while the other children close their eyes. Then, when the group says it is ready, the other children may open their eyes to watch the group perform. After each portrayal the other children may guess what part of God's creation the group is portraying.

Quick Check

✔ *Why did God give us all of creation?* (God gave us creation to use and enjoy.)

✔ *What does God want us to do with all of creation?* (God wants us to take care of it and share it.)

WE RESPOND _____ minutes

Connect to Life Read aloud the *We Respond* question. List the children's responses on the board. Read aloud the beginning of the prayer; then provide time for the children to complete their drawings. When all have finished, encourage volunteers to share their drawings with the class.

Pray Have the children hold up their books, opened to page 297. Explain: *You are offering your drawings as prayers to God.*

Plan Ahead for Day 2

Catechist Goal: To present that God wants us to care for animals

Preparation: Make copies of Reproducible Master 26, guide page 295G.

Catechist Goal

• To present that God wants us to care for animals

Our Faith Response

• To identify ways we can care for animals

Lesson Materials

• crayons or markers
• copies of Reproducible Master 26

Teaching Tip

Raising Awareness

In this lesson the children will learn that God wants us to care for animals as part of God's creation. In preparation, as you read newspapers and magazines, make note of features that promote positive ways of caring for animals. Tell the children that the ways we use water and land for recreation affect animals' sources of food and shelter. Talk with the children about the place of animals in our lives and about ways we can protect animals.

Animals are part of God's creation.

WE GATHER

✝ *God, help us share the gifts of your creation.*

Look at the animals on this page. Where can you find these animals?

WE BELIEVE

God created the world and filled it with animals. Animals are wonderful gifts from God.

📖 Genesis 1:24–25

Read Along

"Then God said, 'Let the earth bring forth all kinds of living creatures: cattle, creeping things, and wild animals of all kinds.' And so it happened: God made all kinds of wild animals, all kinds of cattle, and all kinds of creeping things of the earth. God saw how good it was." (Genesis 1:24–25)

When God created people, he told them to watch over the animals.

We care for the animals when we make sure they have food to eat and water to drink. We also make sure they have a place to live. We try to learn more about them and what they need.

 298

Lesson Plan

WE GATHER ___ minutes

✝ **Pray** Pray the Sign of the Cross and the *We Gather* prayer together.

Focus on Life Direct the children's attention to the photographs on these pages. Ask volunteers to identify the animals' habitats. Invite the children to name their favorite animals. List these on the board. Ask them to name these animals' habitats.

WE BELIEVE ___ minutes

Say What We Believe Read aloud the first *We Believe* paragraph and the Bible story. Ask volunteers to read aloud the last two *We Believe* paragraphs. Invite

the children to finish the following sentences as you read them aloud:

• *The animals are God's wonderful* (gifts).

• *God told people to take care of the* (animals).

• *People should make sure that animals have* (food, water, and a place to live).

Then ask: *How can we learn more about animals and what they need?* (Possible answers: Watch videos and TV programs about animals; study about them in school; read about them in books and magazines.)

WE RESPOND

What animals can you take care of?

👤 Who are some people in your town who take care of animals? Write or draw about what these people do.

299

ACTIVITY BANK

Curriculum Connection
Science
Activity Materials: index cards, string, tape, markers or crayons

Invite any children who exhibit a talent for categorizing animals to list the animals mentioned in class during this lesson. Then invite the children to make up different categories for the animals, such as places where these animals live or ways these animals move. Ask the children to use one color of marker or crayon to print the name of a category and the name of each animal that belongs in that category on separate index cards. Help the children to make an animal card mobile. Help the children to use tape and string to connect the category card at the top, to the cards for the animals in that category. Display the card mobiles in the prayer space. Thank God together for creating the animals.

Quick Check

✔ *What does God want people to do for animals?* (God wants us to take care of them.)

✔ *How can we care for animals?* (Accept what is described in the last *We Believe* paragraph.)

WE RESPOND ____ minutes

Connect to Life Read aloud the first *We Respond* question. Then invite the children to name animals they can take care of. Have a volunteer read aloud the activity directions. Encourage the children to think about people in the community who take care of animals. These might include farmers, animal rescue workers, and veterinarians. If possible, invite one of these caretakers to visit the class to share ways to take care of animals. Have the children write about or draw what these people do to care for animals. Encourage the children to include themselves in the drawings.

Do the Activity Distribute copies of Reproducible Master 26. Have the children make their signs.

Pray Have the children pray quietly, thanking God for his gift of animals.

Plan Ahead for Day 3

Catechist Goal: To teach that God made each of us special

Preparation: Make copies of *What's the Word?*, guide page 295F.

Catechist Goal

• To teach that God made each of us special

Our Faith Response

• To thank God for our individual gifts

Lesson Materials

• Grade 1 CD
• copies of reproducible master *What's the Word?*, guide page 295F

As Catholics...

Life: A Gift from God

   After presenting the lesson, read aloud the *As Catholics* text. Discuss the question at the end of the section. Emphasize that God wants us to do all we can to take good care of ourselves. Invite the children to suggest ways to thank God for the gift of life.

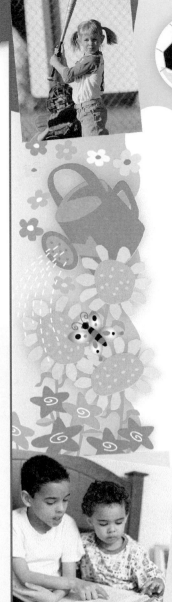

We are all important to God.

WE GATHER

✝ *We praise you, God.*

Find a partner. Tell some ways you two are alike. Name some ways you are different.

WE BELIEVE

God created each one of us. No two people in the world are exactly alike. We enjoy different things. We have different gifts and talents. We look different from one another.

God wants us to use our gifts and talents. We can use them to take care of creation and to care for one another.

Lesson Plan

WE GATHER   ___ minutes

✝ **Pray** Invite the children to pray a silent prayer of thanks for God's creation. Then ask them to pray the *We Gather* prayer.

Focus on Life Have the children work in pairs. Read the *We Gather* directions. Explain that the partners are to discuss the ways they are alike and the ways they are different. Then invite the partners to share with the class the similarities and differences they have discovered.

WE BELIEVE   ___ minutes

Stand If You Believe Help volunteers to read aloud the two *We Believe* paragraphs. Then explain that you are going to read a series of sentences. Explain to

the children that they are to stand if they hear something we believe and to sit or stay seated if they hear something that we do not believe.

• *God gives each person gifts and talents.* (stand)

• *Sometimes sisters are exactly the same in everything.* (sit)

• *God expects us to use the gifts he has given us.* (stand)

• *We should not use our gifts to help take care of creation.* (sit)

• *We can use our gifts to help take care of one another.* (stand)

Invite the children to look at the pictures on these pages. Ask: *Which of these activities do you like to do?* Ask volunteers to share their responses.

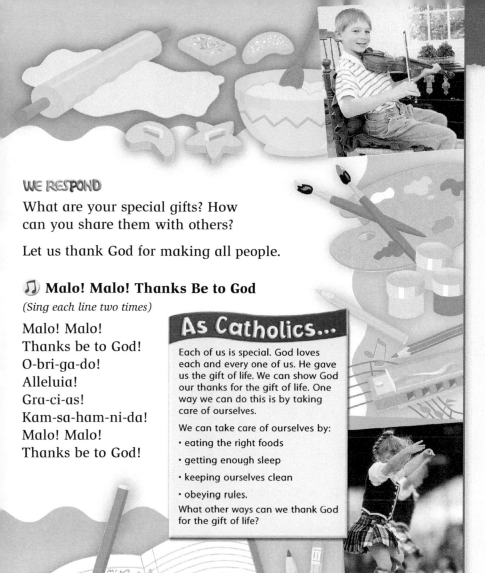

WE RESPOND

What are your special gifts? How can you share them with others?

Let us thank God for making all people.

♫ Malo! Malo! Thanks Be to God

(Sing each line two times)

Malo! Malo!
Thanks be to God!
O-bri-ga-do!
Alleluia!
Gra-ci-as!
Kam-sa-ham-ni-da!
Malo! Malo!
Thanks be to God!

As Catholics...

Each of us is special. God loves each and every one of us. He gave us the gift of life. We can show God our thanks for the gift of life. One way we can do this is by taking care of ourselves.

We can take care of ourselves by:
- eating the right foods
- getting enough sleep
- keeping ourselves clean
- obeying rules.

What other ways can we thank God for the gift of life?

ACTIVITY BANK

Faith and Media
Special Like Me
Activity Materials: colored index cards, poster board, markers, glue

To help the children recognize and celebrate how special each one is, have each child take a survey of five or six people. Those surveyed might be family members, friends, or teachers. The children should ask each person in his or her survey this question: *What is one thing that is special about me?* Have the children ask those being surveyed to print their answers to the question on colored index cards. When all have finished collecting their survey answers, have each child draw a self-portrait on a piece of poster board and glue all of his or her survey cards around the portrait. Then celebrate each child by reading aloud his or her cards. Thank God for each child's uniqueness.

Scripture
Linguistic, Interpersonal

For a Scripture activity, see *What's the Word?*, guide page 295F.

Quick Check

✔ *How has God blessed all of us?* (God has given all of us gifts and talents.)

✔ *How does God want us to use our gifts and talents?* (God wants us to use our gifts and talents to take care of creation and of each other.)

WE RESPOND ___ minutes

Connect to Life Read the *We Respond* questions. Give the children about two minutes of quiet time to reflect on their answers. Teach the children the song "Malo! Malo! Thanks Be to God," #32 on the Grade 1 CD. Explain: *When you sing this song, you are saying thank you to God in five different languages.* Teach the

children to pronounce each word for thank you; then tell them the language they are speaking:

- Mal-ō is *Tonganese.*
- Ōb-ri-ga-dō is *Portuguese.*
- Gra-see-as is *Spanish.*
- Kam-sa-ham-nee-da is *Korean.*

Pray Invite the children to return to the prayer space. Sing together "Malo! Malo! Thanks Be to God."

Plan Ahead for Day 4

Catechist Goal: To focus on ways to show care and respect to all people

Preparation: Be prepared to share one way in which you wish to be treated by others.

Catechist Goal

• To focus on ways to show care and respect to all people

Our Faith Response

• To name ways to show respect for one another

Teaching Tip

Reviewing

Help the children think about and discuss some of the important things they have learned this year. List the following topics on the board and invite volunteers to tell one thing they have learned: *God the Father, Jesus, the Holy Spirit, the Church, the sacraments, Mary and the saints.*

We care for and respect all people.

WE GATHER

✝ *Holy, holy, holy is God!*

Think about your:

• parents and grandparents

• brothers, sisters, or cousins

• neighbors

• classmates.

How do you talk to one another? How do you act toward one another?

WE BELIEVE

Jesus often talked about ways we should treat other people. This is what he told his followers one day.

📖 Matthew 7:12

Read Along
Jesus said, "Do to others whatever you would have them do to you." (Matthew 7:12)

Jesus meant that we should treat other people the way we want to be treated. We should show kindness and respect. We should share God's love with all people.

302

Lesson Plan

WE GATHER ___ minutes

✝ **Pray** Remind the children that each of them is special and unique. Pray together the Sign of the Cross and the *We Gather* prayer.

Focus on Life Have a volunteer read the *We Gather* section aloud. Give the children quiet time to think about their answers.

WE BELIEVE ___ minutes

Read About Respect Invite a volunteer to read aloud the *We Believe* statement. Ask: *What does it mean to respect someone?* Read aloud the first *We Believe* paragraph, the words of Jesus, and the second *We Believe* paragraph. Then together with the children read the list of ways to show respect on page 303.

Discuss Jesus' Words Invite the children to share their own experiences of respectful behavior. Encourage them to tell about times when they showed proper respect to others or were shown respect by others. Ask: *How did that make you feel?* As the children tell their stories, remind them that Jesus always wants us to share God's love with all people by treating everyone with love, care, and respect. Direct the children's attention to the pictures on these pages. Have volunteers tell the way the person or persons in each picture are putting Jesus' words into action.

Do the Activity Invite a volunteer to read the activity directions. Have the children work in pairs. Explain that each pair may choose one of the ways talked about or illustrated on these pages as the basis for a short play. Give the children time to develop

Here are some ways we can do this.

- Be polite. Say polite things like "Please" and "Thank you."

- Respect other people's belongings. Do not take anything without asking.

- Tell the truth. Do not tell lies.

- Ask for forgiveness if we have done something wrong. Say "I'm sorry."

- Forgive other people when they tell us they are sorry.

👥 Work with a partner. Choose one of the ideas above. Make up a play that shows people doing this. Then act it out.

WE RESPOND

Who can you show kindness and respect for this week?

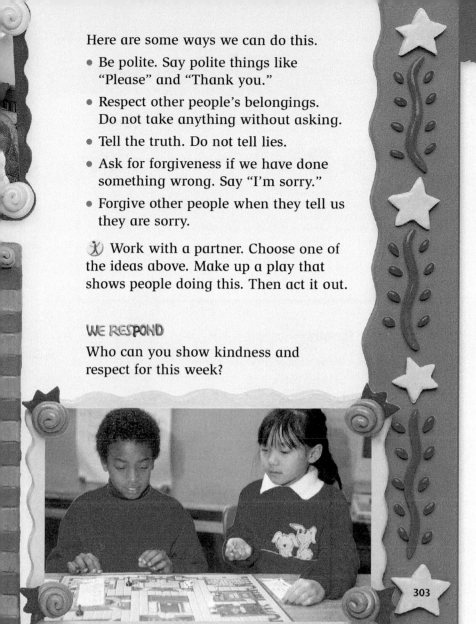

303

ACTIVITY BANK

Curriculum Connection
Language Arts
  Have the children think about books or movies about people who live in another country or are from different racial and ethnic backgrounds. Have each child prepare an oral presentation about the book or movie.
  You may want to ask the school or public librarian to recommend books about children of different cultures. Read the stories aloud during the coming week.

---

their ideas; then let each pair perform. Encourage the other children to applaud to show appreciation for each play.

Quick Check

✔ *In what way does Jesus want us to treat one another?* (Jesus wants us to treat others as we would want to be treated.)

✔ *What are some ways we can show our respect for others?* (Possible answers should include what is listed in *We Believe*.)

WE RESPOND _____ minutes

Connect to Life Read aloud the *We Respond* question. Allow a few moments of quiet time for the children to think about their responses. Then ask the children to pray quietly to ask God's help in being kind and respectful.

Pray Sing "Shout from the Mountains," #31 on the Grade 1 CD.

Plan Ahead for Day 5

Catechist Goal: To review chapter ideas and their relationship to our faith life

Preparation: Make copies of *Sharing Faith with My Family*, guide page 295E.

Catechist Goal

• To review the chapter ideas that are key to growing as disciples of Jesus Christ

Our Faith Response

• To decide on ways to grow as disciples by living out what we have learned

Show What *you* Know

Brainstorm a list of words that describe God's creation. Encourage the children to think of vivid words. Then read the activity instructions. Allow the children time to write or draw a description of God's creation. Together remember how wonderful God's creation is.

Reality Check

Read the incomplete message and the responses. Ask the children to check all the boxes that correctly complete the statement. Review the correct answers as a class. Talk together about why telling lies and taking others' belongings without asking are not ways to share God's love.

Question Corner Explain to the children that it is their turn to tell their stories. Read aloud the paragraph. Invite the children to draw their self portraits in the frame and to write a response to each question. Allow time for the children to interview each other by asking the questions and providing the responses they have written. Congratulate all the children on being disciples of Jesus.

Take Home

Remember together the ways to care for God's creation. Encourage the children to talk to their families about these ways.

Discuss and send home copies of *Sharing Faith with My Family*, guide page 295E.

Grade 1 Chapter 26

PROJECT

Show What *you* Know

Describe God's creation. Use words or pictures.

> Possible responses:
> words: gift; beautiful; wonderful; share; people; plants; animals; special
> pictures: variety of animals; people; places

Reality Check

Today I can share God's love by

☑ being polite.

❑ telling lies.

❑ taking others' belongings without asking.

☑ asking for forgiveness.

☑ forgiving others.

304   www.webelieveweb.com

DISCIPLE

Question Corner

Every person is special to God. You are special to God. Share your story. Draw a picture of yourself. Answer the questions below.

What makes you a disciple of Jesus?

_____

What is a special gift you have from God?

_____

How can you help take care of God's creation?

_____

_____

Take Home

Talk together about ways you can help care for God's creation as a family.

305

CHAPTER TEST

Use the words in the box to complete the sentences.

respect
treat
created
gift
animals

1. The world is God's

   _____gift_____ to all people.

2. God told people to watch over the

   _____animals_____ he created.

3. All people in the world are

   _____created_____ by God.

4. Jesus told us to _____treat_____ others the way we want to be treated.

5. Jesus wants us to treat all people with kindness

   and _____respect_____.

 TALK ABOUT IT

How can we share God's love with other people? Accept bulleted list of ways on page 303.

306

CHAPTER TEST

Read each test item aloud and allow time for the children to mark an answer. Decide whether the *Talk About It* activity will be a small group or whole class discussion. After you have finished, check the answers. Clarify any misconceptions.

Alternative Assessment

You may want the students to complete the following alternative-assessment activity.

> *Make a poster to thank God for all people and creation. Use pictures from magazines or draw your own.*

Additional Testing

• Chapter 26 Test in *Assessment Book*, pages 51–52

• CD-ROM *Test Generator and Resource*: Use Chapter 26 Test or customize your own.

Review

We Believe Statements

Review the four statements.

• The world is God's gift to us.

• Animals are part of God's creation.

• We are all important to God.

• We care for and respect all people.

To use the Chapter 26 Study Guide, visit

www.webelieveweb.com

Easter

The fifty days from Easter Sunday to Pentecost are celebrated in joyful exultation as one feast day . . . These above all others are the days for the singing of the Alleluia.

(Norms Governing Liturgical Calendars, 22)

Overview

In this chapter the children will learn that Easter is the time when the Church celebrates that Jesus rose to new life.

For Adult Reading and Reflection
You may want to refer to paragraph 641 of the *Catechism of the Catholic Church*.

Go to **www.webelieveweb.com**, Catechist/Teacher, We Believe Correlations for this chapter's correlation to the Six Tasks of Catechesis.

Catechist Background

What are some of the ways in which you celebrate Easter?

The Church celebrates the fifty days from Easter Sunday to Pentecost as one continuous feast day. They have been called "the Great Sunday" by Saint Athanasius because what Sundays are to the week, the Easter season is to the entire year. "Christ's Resurrection is the fulfillment of the promises of the Old Testament and of Jesus himself during his earthly life." (CCC 652) Jesus' divinity is confirmed by his Resurrection. When he died on the cross, Jesus Christ freed us from the shackles of sin. At his rising, he opened for us the path to new life.

The Resurrection was an historical event attested to by witnesses to the empty tomb and the disciples' encounters with the risen Lord. This transcendent event lies at the heart of our faith; it is the primary truth to which all Christ's followers testify. "If Christ has not been raised, then empty [too] is our preaching; empty, too, your faith." (1 Corinthians 15:14)

Our celebration of the Easter season encompasses the Ascension, the return of Jesus Christ to his Father in Heaven, and Pentecost itself. Ascension is celebrated on either the Thursday of the Sixth Week of Easter, or, in many dioceses, on the following Sunday. The Church rejoices that Jesus' post-Resurrection appearances culminate "with the irreversible entry of his humanity into divine glory" (CCC 659).

At Pentecost the Easter season concludes with the outpouring of the Holy Spirit, signaling the fulfillment of Christ's Passover. The promised Advocate has come to strengthen and unify the Church which was made manifest to the world at the first Pentecost.

How will you help others to experience Easter as a season of new life and joy?

Lesson Planning Guide

Lesson Focus	Presentation	Materials
Day 1		
Guide page 307C **Guide and Text page 307** **Introduce the Season**	• Introduce the Easter season. • Read the *Chapter Story*. • Proclaim Psalm 118:24.	
Day 2		
Guide and Text pages 308–309 **We Gather** **We Believe**	• Share responses to the We Gather question. • Read and act out the Scripture story about Jesus rising from the dead in We Believe.	• costumes for dramatization
Day 3		
Guide and Text page 310 **We Respond**	Draw signs of new life on the We Respond banner.	• crayons or colored pencils
Day 4		
Text page 311 **Guide page 311–312** **We Respond in Prayer**	• Rejoice in the risen Jesus in prayer. • Rejoice in song.	♫ "Alleluia No. 1," Donald Fishel, #33, Grade 1 CD • two-yard length of a pastel-colored party streamer (one for each child) • prayer space: spring flowers, pictures of signs of new life, white tablecloth, Bible, and bowl of holy water
Day 5		
Text page 312 **Guide pages 311–312, 312A** **Project Disciple**	• Complete the Project Disciple activities. Discuss the *Take Home* activity. • Complete the Reproducible Master 27 activity. See guide pages 307C and 312A. • Discuss/send home Sharing Faith with My Family, guide page 312B.	• pencils • copies of Reproducible Master 27, guide page 312A • copies of Sharing Faith with My Family reproducible master, guide page 312B

For additional ideas, activities, and opportunities: Visit Sadlier's **www.WeBelieve.web.com**

Chapter Story

It was Easter morning. During Mass Rosa was daydreaming about the chocolate bunny waiting for her at home. She could eat the bunny after Mass when her family went home for Easter breakfast.

After Mass Rosa's family wished Father Virgil a "Happy Easter." Then they began to walk home. Rosa tried to get everyone to walk faster, but it was a beautiful sunny day. Rosa's dad said they should take their time and enjoy the scenery along the way.

Rosa slowed down and looked around. In the green grass sprouting by the sidewalk, she spotted a golden dandelion. Rosa remembered that Father Virgil had talked about "new life." She smiled at the dandelion and said, "New life!"

A little further on, Rosa saw a woman pushing a baby carriage. The woman was wearing an Easter hat with flowers on it, and the baby was all dressed up in a colorful suit. Rosa smiled at them and said to herself, "New life!"

At the breakfast table, Mom thanked God for the food—including Rosa's chocolate bunny. Dad prayed, "Thank you, Jesus, for giving us new life." Rosa said, "Amen!" Then Rosa told the family all the signs of new life she had seen on the way home.

What signs of new life did Rosa see?

PROJECT DISCIPLE
Additional Activities

Celebrate!

Help the children make Easter dioramas. Ask each child to bring in a shoe box or the lid or base of a rectangular gift box. From construction paper, have the children cut out a large sun, butterflies, birds, grass, and flowers and glue the scenery into the box. Distribute copies of Reproducible Master 27, guide page 312A. Ask the children to color and cut out the figures and fold them on the solid lines. Invite the children to place the figures in the scene. Encourage the children to share the dioramas with their families and friends.

Make it Happen

Invite the children to share the joy of Easter by making seasonal cards for nursing home residents. If possible, have ready a list of names to whom the cards can be addressed. Have the children decorate the cards with signs of new life. Ask each child to write his or her own Easter message to an elderly person who needs to be reminded of God's love. Instruct the children not to include last names or any identifying information.

"This is the day the LORD has made; let us rejoice in it and be glad."

Psalm 118:24

SEASONAL CHAPTER 27

This chapter celebrates the entire Easter season.

Catechist Goal

• To explain that the Church celebrates that Jesus rose to new life during Easter time

Our Faith Response

• To recognize signs of new life and to celebrate the new life Jesus has given to us

Whole Community Catechesis

An Online Resource

Celebrate **Easter** *as a class, school, and/or a parish community. The event comes complete with detailed leader's guides, preparation charts, handouts, promotional ideas, organizational materials, and much more. Go to:*

www.webelieveweb.com

Lesson Plan

Introduce the Season ___ minutes

• **Pray** together: *Alleluia, Alleluia, Alleluia!*

• **Invite** the children to look at the photo on page 307. Ask: *What do you think the children are doing?* Help the children to conclude that the children are very happy to be celebrating Easter.

• **Point out** to the children that Easter is not just one day but it is a time that lasts for fifty days. Stress: *Easter is a very important time. We celebrate that Jesus rose to new life and that he shares new life with us.*

• **Read** the *Chapter Story* on guide page 307C. Discuss the signs of new life Rosa saw on her way home from church.

• **Invite** the children to stand and raise their arms in the air. Read each line of the psalm on page 307. Have the children repeat it.

Lesson Materials

- Grade 1 CD
- costumes for dramatization
- copies of Reproducible Master 27
- boxes for the Easter dioramas
- crayons, scissors, glue, construction paper

Teaching Note

Presenting the Chapter

Present this chapter as close to Easter Sunday as possible. All during the Easter season remind the children that you are celebrating that Jesus rose to new life.

The Church celebrates that Jesus rose to new life.

WE GATHER

What are some signs of new life? Share your ideas with one another.

WE BELIEVE

Easter is a time of great joy. The Three Days lead us to Easter Sunday. It is time to rejoice!

During Mass on Easter Sunday, we listen to the story of Jesus' rising from the dead. Here is what Saint Matthew tells us.

Matthew 28:1–10

Narrator: "After the sabbath, as the first day of the week was dawning, Mary Magdalene and the other Mary came to see the tomb. And behold, there was a great earthquake; for an angel of the Lord descended from heaven, approached, rolled back the stone, and sat upon it." (Matthew 28:1–2)

308

Lesson Plan

WE GATHER ___ minutes

Focus on Life Read the *We Gather* question. Ask: *What decorations do you see at Easter time?* (Possible responses include: baby chicks, bunnies, lambs, flowers, eggs, butterflies) Point out: *Easter time is during the beginning of spring when new grass and flowers start to bloom. Baby chicks and birds break out of their shells; bunnies and lambs are born; butterflies break out of their cocoons. All of these things in nature are signs of new life.*

WE BELIEVE ___ minutes

- **Read** aloud the first two *We Believe* paragraphs.

- **Direct** attention to the Scripture art on pages 308 and 309. Explain that it shows what happened early in the morning after Jesus had risen to new life.

- **Serve** as the narrator and select five children to serve as readers for a first reading of the Scripture story. Before beginning, explain:

    ◆ *Mary Magdalene and the other Mary were close friends and followers of Jesus.*

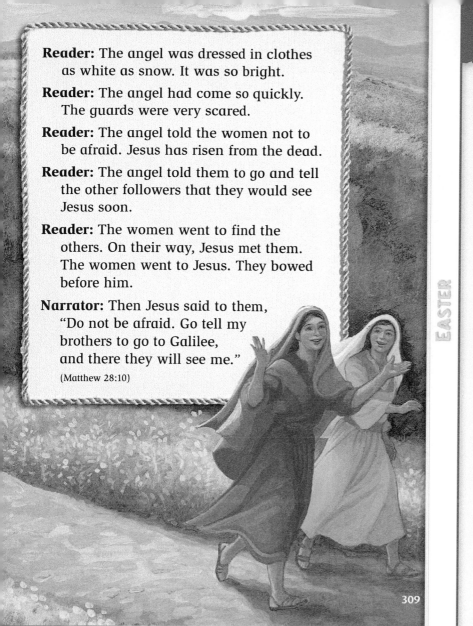

Reader: The angel was dressed in clothes as white as snow. It was so bright.

Reader: The angel had come so quickly. The guards were very scared.

Reader: The angel told the women not to be afraid. Jesus has risen from the dead.

Reader: The angel told them to go and tell the other followers that they would see Jesus soon.

Reader: The women went to find the others. On their way, Jesus met them. The women went to Jesus. They bowed before him.

Narrator: Then Jesus said to them, "Do not be afraid. Go tell my brothers to go to Galilee, and there they will see me."

(Matthew 28:10)

EASTER

309

ACTIVITY BANK

Faith and Media

Easter Posters

Activity Materials: poster board, crayons, construction paper, scissors, glue

Have the children work in groups. Give each group poster board on which to draw or glue paper-made signs of new life. Print on each poster: *Celebrate Easter. Celebrate the new life Jesus gives to us.* Display the posters in or near the parish church.

◆ *The tomb was a cave with a stone blocking the entrance.*

◆ *Galilee is the region where Jesus and many of his followers lived.*

Then have the readers stand with you facing the children and present a dramatic reading.

● **Enact** the story. Involve other children in acting out the Gospel story as Mary Magdalene, Mary, the angel, and Jesus. Distribute the improvised costumes. Invite a child to serve as the narrator. Have some children provide sound effects for dramatic emphasis.

Quick Check

✔ *What does the Church celebrate during Easter?* (We celebrate that Jesus rose to new life.)

✔ *What did the angel tell the women to do?* (He told them to go tell Jesus' other followers that they would see Jesus soon.)

CONNECTION

To Vocations

All Christians share the baptismal vocation of sharing the Good News of Jesus Christ with all people. Encourage the first graders to be attentive during the Easter season to sharing what they learn about Jesus with their families. Like the first witnesses to the Resurrection of the Lord, they can joyfully tell the Good News that Jesus has risen to new life. Also encourage the children to pray to the Holy Spirit for many more followers of Jesus who will give new life to the Church by becoming priests, religious sisters and brothers, lay missioners and missionaries.

WE RESPOND

During Easter we celebrate that Jesus rose to new life.

Decorate the Alleluia banner with signs of new life.

Alleluia!

310

Lesson Plan

WE RESPOND   ___ minutes

Connect to Life Point out the banner on page 310. Read the word *Alleluia.* Point out that we say or sing this word with great joy during Easter time.

Read the activity directions. Have the children decorate the banner with signs of new life. When the children have completed their work, ask them to show their banners to the entire group.

• **Take** the children to visit the parish church if you are presenting the chapter after Easter Sunday. Ask the children to note that white and gold are the colors the Church uses at this time. Point out the new Easter candle and the other decorations (banners, flowers, and so on).

• **Take** the children on a discovery walk around the neighborhood or in a nearby park. Ask the children to look for signs of new life. When you return to class, list on chart paper all the signs the children saw.

† **We Respond in Prayer**

Leader: Praised be the risen Jesus.
All: Let us rejoice and be glad, alleluia!

 Alleluia No. 1

Chorus
Alleluia, alleluia!
Give thanks to the risen
Lord.
Alleluia, alleluia!
Give praise to his name.

Spread the good news o'er
all the earth:
Jesus has died and has risen. (Chorus)

311

EASTER

We Respond in Prayer (p. 311)

Display a Bible, a bowl of holy water, spring flowers, and signs of new life on a white table cloth in the prayer space. Choose a prayer leader. Ask the children to imagine they are meeting Jesus after he rose to new life. Say: *Tell Jesus what is in your heart.* Invite the children into the prayer space with two-yard lengths of pastel-colored streamer paper. Sprinkle holy water on them. Pray the Sign of the Cross. Sing "Alleluia No. 1," #33 on the Grade 1 CD twice as the children wave their streamers.

This Week's Liturgy
Visit **www.webelieveweb.com** for this week's liturgical readings and other seasonal material.

Project Disciple (p. 312)

Celebrate!

Read the instructions. Help the children decode the words. Read the message together.

Fast Facts Read the fact. Ask the children to share experiences of decorating Easter eggs, eating chocolate eggs, or searching for hidden Easter eggs.

Take Home

Survey the children about family Easter traditions. Encourage the children to continue the discussion at home.

Discuss and send home copies of *Sharing Faith with My Family*, guide page 312B.

Project Disciple Additional Activities See the activities suggested on page 307C of the guide.

Pray
Learn
Celebrate
Share
Choose
Live

Grade 1 Easter
PROJECT DISCIPLE

Celebrate!
Use the code to discover an important message.

J	R	E	O	I	C	S	U	D	A	N	R	T	W	L	F
1	2	3	4	5	6	7	8	9	10	11	12	13	14	15	16

R E J O I C E ! J E S U S
2 3 1 4 5 6 3 — 1 3 7 8 7

D I E D A N D R O S E
9 5 3 9 — 10 11 9 — 2 4 7 3

T O N E W L I F E !
13 4 — 11 3 14 — 15 5 16 3

 **Fast Facts**

Eggs are a symbol of new life. So eggs are a symbol of Easter too! At Easter Jesus rose to new life.

Take Home

With your family list ways that you celebrate Easter together.

312 www.webelieveweb.com

Name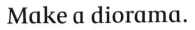

Make a diorama.

Color and cut out the figures below.

Your catechist will help you with the rest of the activity.

SHARING FAITH
with My Family

Sharing What I Learned

Look at the pictures below. Use each picture to tell your family what you learned in this chapter.

Blessing of the Home During Easter Time

Leader: God fills our hearts and homes with peace. Blessed be the name of the Lord.

All: Now and for ever.

Leader: Christ risen from the dead is our hope, joy, and comfort. May all who enter this home find Christ's light and love.

All: Alleluia, Alleluia, Alleluia.

Visit Sadlier's

www.WeBelieveweb.com

Connect to the Catechism
For adult background and reflection, see paragraph 641.

ASSESSMENT

Unit 4 Test

Read aloud each set of test directions. Also you may choose to read aloud each test item. Wait for a minute for the children to indicate their responses in writing.

Alternative Assessment

You may want the children to complete the following alternative-assessment activity.

Make a poster telling what you've learned about the Mass.

Additional Testing

• Unit 4 Test in Grade 1 *Assessment Book*, pages 53–54

• Unit 4 Alternative Assessment in Grade 1 *Assessment Book*, page 56

• Final Test (Units 1–4) in Grade 1 *Assessment Book*, pages 57–59

• CD-ROM *Test Generator and Resource*: Use Unit 4 Test or customize your own.

Grade 1 Unit 4

UNIT TEST

Circle the correct answer.

1. Is the Eucharist the sacrament of the Body and Blood of Jesus Christ? (Yes) No

2. Does Jesus want us to treat people unfairly? Yes (No)

3. Do we call the celebration of the Eucharist the Mass? (Yes) No

4. Did the saints put God last in their lives? Yes (No)

5. Does the Church honor Mary in different ways? (Yes) No

Write the correct word to finish each sentence.

6. The _____Mass_____ is the Church's greatest celebration.

7. The _____saints_____ are followers of Jesus who have died and now live forever with God.

8. The _____altar_____ is the table of the Lord.

> altar
> saints
> Mass

continued on next page   313

Grade 1 Unit 4

9. **Choose and circle one of the pictures. Write how the people are sharing God's love.**

Possible responses: The children are forgiving one another. The woman is a peacemaker.   Possible response: The child is helping to carry the groceries.

10. **Write sentences to tell a few ways you can share God's love.**

Possible responses: _____

We share God's love by telling others about God.

We share God's love when we are kind and helpful.

_____

_____

PROJECT DISCIPLE

Pray
Learn
Celebrate
Share
Choose
Live

RESOURCES

Family Survey 315B

Grade 1 Log 315

End-of-Year Prayer Service 317

My Parish Church 318

Grade 2 Sneak Peek 320

My Prayer for Discipleship Poster 320A

Family Blessing Poster 320B

My Mass Book 321

My Prayer Book 325

Sacraments 329

The Ten Commandments 329

Glossary 330

Index 334

Family Survey

Your child brought home three different kinds of family pages this year. Through these pages you shared faith together!

What was your favorite *Dear Family* activity?

_____

_____

What *Project Disciple Take Home* activity did your family enjoy the most?

_____

_____

_____

What *Sharing Faith with My Family* activity was your favorite? Why?

_____

_____

_____

Does your family have any special prayers or activities that you would like to share with other *We Believe* families? If so, tell us about them.

_____

_____

_____

Is there anything else you'd like to share?

_____

_____

_____

We'd like to hear from you!

Send us this survey at: *We Believe* Family Survey
C/O Sadlier, 9 Pine Street, New York, NY 10005
or at:

www.WE BELIEVE.web.com

Student Unit Opener Pages
PROJECT DISCIPLE DEAR FAMILY

Student Project Disciple Pages
TAKE HOME ACTIVITIES

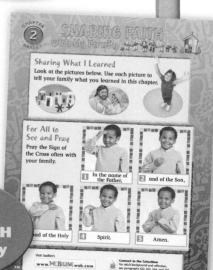

Teacher Guide
SHARING FAITH with My Family

CONGRATULATIONS
ON COMPLETING
YOUR YEAR AS
A GRADE 1 DISCIPLE!

Fold on this line.

**A RECORD OF MY JOURNEY
AS A GRADE 1 DISCIPLE**

_____

Name

Cut on this line.

Disciples of Jesus listen to and share God's Word.

My picture of my favorite story about Jesus

Disciples of Jesus pray every day.

A prayer I learned this year is

_____.

I pray this prayer

❏ by myself

❏ with my family

❏ with my classmates

❏ with my parish.

My prayer for summer is

_____.

4

5

Disciples of Jesus learn about their faith.

One thing I learned this year

• about following Jesus is

_____.

• about sharing my faith with others is

_____.

Disciples of Jesus live out their faith.

This summer I will live out my faith when I am

❑ with my family

❑ with my friends

❑ on vacation

❑ on day trips

❑ in my neighborhood

❑ in church

❑ _____.

Cut on this line.

Disciples of Jesus make loving choices.

This year I made a loving choice

• to care for God's world by

_____.

• to help my family by

_____.

This summer, I can show love for others by

_____.

Disciples of Jesus celebrate the Church year.

My favorite time of the Church year was

_____.

I celebrated with

_____.

We celebrated by

_____.

Pray
Learn
Celebrate
Share
Choose
Live

PROJECT DISCIPLE

End-of-Year Prayer Service

✝ We Gather in Prayer

Leader: We have learned many things about God this year.

Group 1: God is our loving Father.

Group 2: God sent his own Son, Jesus, to us.

Group 3: God shares his life and love with us.

Group 4: God wants us to share his love with others.

Leader: God, we want to remember all of these good things.

All: God, thank you for all your wonderful gifts. We believe that you are with us always. We want to share your love with others this summer.

🎵 We Celebrate With Joy

We celebrate with joy and gladness
We celebrate God's love for us.
We celebrate with joy and gladness
God with us today.
God with us today.

317

My Parish Church

CONNECTION

Multicultural Connection
To Parish

Help the children to realize that the parish church building is like a home to parishioners. Explain that everything in the church has significance for them—from the holy water fonts to the altar.

If possible, make arrangements for the class to tour the parish church and make a visit to the Most Blessed Sacrament. Point out the sanctuary lamp and the tabernacle. Invite a parish priest or deacon to talk to the children about the presence of Jesus in the Most Blessed Sacrament. Ask this person to show the children the inside of the tabernacle and explain that the priests and deacons take the Holy Communion Hosts to the parishioners who are sick or homebound.

Help the children locate the numbered items in the illustration of a parish church. Read the brief description for each item.

318

1 **sanctuary**—area in the church where the Mass is celebrated

2 **altar**—the table of the Lord where we celebrate the Sacrament of the Eucharist

3 **crucifix**—a cross with a figure of Christ crucified

4 **tabernacle**—the special place in the church in which the Blessed Sacrament is kept

5 **sanctuary lamp**—light or candle that is always lit near the tabernacle. It helps us to remember that Jesus is really present in the Blessed Sacrament.

6 **ambo (pulpit)**—place in the sanctuary where the Word of God is proclaimed

7 **chalice**—the special cup that holds the wine that will become the Blood of Christ

8 **paten**—a special plate that holds the bread that will become the Body of Christ

Find these things in your parish church:

1. sanctuary
2. altar
3. crucifix
4. tabernacle
5. sanctuary lamp
6. ambo (pulpit)
7. chalice

8. paten
9. cruets
10. presider's chair
11. processional cross
12. baptismal font or pool
13. Stations of the Cross
14. Reconciliation room or confessional

319

Multicultural Connection

To Prayer

Remind the children that when we visit Jesus in the Most Blessed Sacrament, we can speak to Jesus quietly. We can tell him of our love, our needs, our hopes, and our thanks.

Pause to allow the children to pray quietly. Then pray aloud the following prayer.

Jesus, thank you for the gift of yourself in the Eucharist. Thank you for strengthening me to be your disciple and to serve others. Help me to give thanks each day and to stay close to you always. Amen.

9 **cruets**—glass containers that hold the water and wine

10 **presider's chair**—chair on which the priest who is celebrating Mass sits

11 **processional cross**—cross with a figure of Christ crucified that is carried in the entrance procession, may also be carried during the presentation of the gifts, and during the recessional

12 **baptismal font or pool**—contains the water that is blessed and used during the Sacrament of Baptism

13 **Stations of the Cross**—fourteen pictures that help us to follow the footsteps of Jesus during his suffering and Death on the cross

14 **Reconciliation room or confessional**—a separate space for celebrating the Sacrament of Penance. This is a special space where you meet the priest for individual confession and absolution. You may sit and talk to him face-to-face or kneel behind a screen.

PROJECT DISCIPLE

You are learning and living out ways to be a disciple of Jesus Christ.

Look what awaits you in:

We Believe Grade 2: Jesus Shares God's Life.

You will learn about and live out that

- Jesus Christ is with us always.

- Jesus calls us to Penance and Reconciliation.

- Jesus gives himself in the Eucharist.

- We live our Catholic faith.

Until next year, pay attention each time you go to Mass. Look around you. Listen.

Here is one thing I know about the ways Jesus shares God's life with us.

_____

Here is one thing that I want to learn more about next year.

_____

We are blessed to share in God's life!

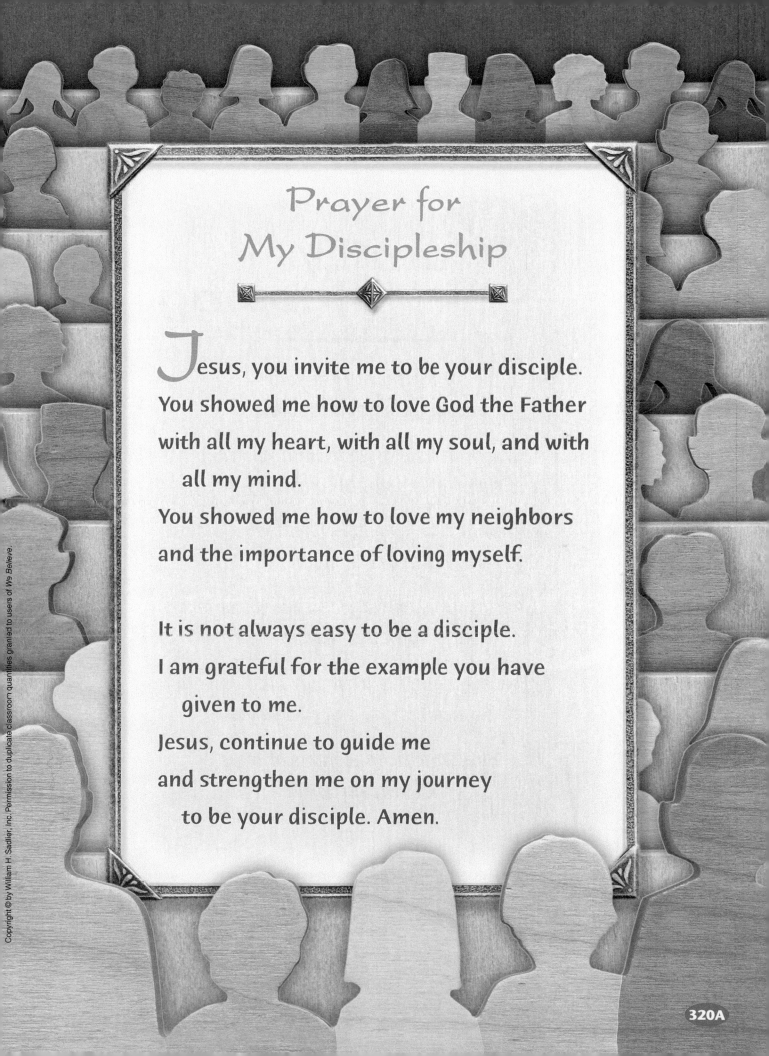

Prayer for My Discipleship

Jesus, you invite me to be your disciple.
You showed me how to love God the Father
with all my heart, with all my soul, and with
    all my mind.
You showed me how to love my neighbors
and the importance of loving myself.

It is not always easy to be a disciple.
I am grateful for the example you have
    given to me.
Jesus, continue to guide me
and strengthen me on my journey
    to be your disciple. Amen.

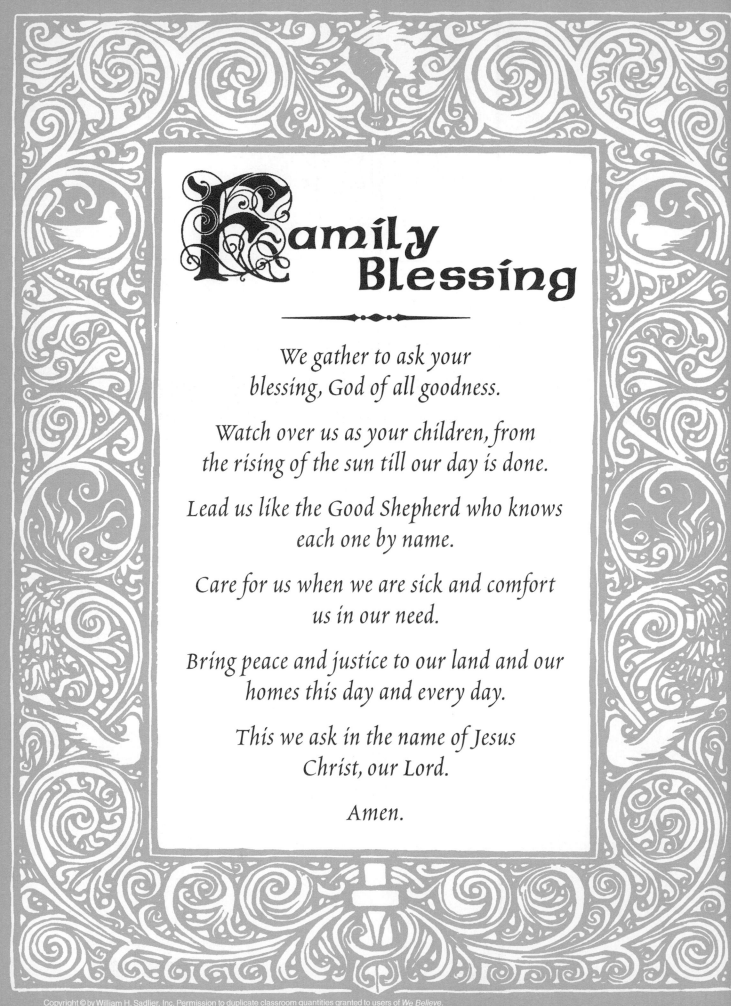

Family Blessing

We gather to ask your blessing, God of all goodness.

Watch over us as your children, from the rising of the sun till our day is done.

Lead us like the Good Shepherd who knows each one by name.

Care for us when we are sick and comfort us in our need.

Bring peace and justice to our land and our homes this day and every day.

This we ask in the name of Jesus Christ, our Lord.

Amen.

My Mass Book

Fold on this line.

Cut on this line.

The priest blesses us. The priest or deacon may say, "Go in peace."
We say,

"Thanks be to God."

We go out to live as Jesus' followers.

We welcome one another. We stand and sing. We pray the Sign of the Cross. The priest says, "The Lord be with you."
We answer,

"And with your spirit."

We gather with our parish. We remember and celebrate what Jesus said and did at the Last Supper.

Fold on this line.

Cut on this line.

We ask God and one another for forgiveness. We praise God as we sing,

"Glory to God in the highest, and on earth peace to people of good will."

Then the priest invites us to share in the Eucharist. As people receive the Body and Blood of Christ, they answer,

"Amen."

While this is happening, we sing a song of thanks.

We get ready to receive Jesus. Together we pray or sing the Our Father. Then we share a sign of peace. We say,

"Peace be with you."

Cut on this line.

Fold on this line.

We listen to two readings from the Bible. After each one, the reader says, "The word of the Lord." We answer,

"Thanks be to God."

Then the priest takes the cup of wine. He says, "TAKE THIS, ALL OF YOU, AND DRINK FROM IT, FOR THIS IS THE CHALICE OF MY BLOOD. . . ."

We stand to say aloud what we believe as Catholics. Then we pray for the Church and all people. After each prayer we say,

"Lord, hear our prayer."

We stand and sing **Alleluia.**

The priest or deacon reads the Gospel. Then he says, "The Gospel of the Lord." We answer,

"Praise to you, Lord Jesus Christ."

Cut on this line.

Fold on this line.

We sing or pray,

"Amen."

We believe Jesus Christ is really present in the Eucharist.

The priest prepares the altar. People bring gifts of bread and wine to the priest. The priest prepares these gifts. We pray,

"Blessed be God for ever."

Then we remember what Jesus said and did at the Last Supper. The priest takes the bread. He says, "TAKE THIS, ALL OF YOU, AND EAT OF IT, FOR THIS IS MY BODY, WHICH WILL BE GIVEN UP FOR YOU."

My Prayer Book

Find other versions of some of these prayers at www.webelieveweb.com

Fold on this line.

Cut on this line.

Angel of God

Angel of God,
my guardian dear,
to whom God's love commits
  me here,
ever this day be at my side,
to light and guard, to rule
  and guide.

Amen.

Glory Be to the Father

Glory be to the Father
and to the Son
and to the Holy Spirit
as it was in the beginning
is now, and ever shall be
world without end.

Amen.

Sign of the Cross

In the name of the Father,
and of the Son,
and of the Holy Spirit.

Amen.

Fold on this line.

Act of Contrition

Read Along
My God,
I am sorry for my sins with all my heart.
In choosing to do wrong
and failing to do good,
I have sinned against you
whom I should love above all things.
I firmly intend, with your help,
to do penance,
to sin no more,
and to avoid whatever leads me to sin.
Our Savior Jesus Christ
suffered and died for us.
In his name, my God, have mercy.

Our Father

Our Father, who art
    in heaven,
hallowed be thy name;
thy kingdom come;
thy will be done on earth
    as it is in heaven.

he ascended into heaven,
    and is seated at the right hand
    of God the Father almighty;
from there he will come to judge
    the living and the dead.

I believe in the Holy Spirit,
    the holy catholic Church,
    the communion of saints,
    the forgiveness of sins,
    the resurrection of the body,
    and life everlasting.

Amen.

The Apostles' Creed

Read Along

I believe in God the
Father almighty,
Creator of heaven and earth,

and in Jesus Christ,
his only Son, our Lord,
who was conceived by
the Holy Spirit,
born of the Virgin Mary,
suffered under Pontius Pilate,
was crucified, died and
was buried;
he descended into hell;
on the third day he rose again
from the dead;

Fold on this line.

Give us this day our
daily bread;
and forgive us our
trespasses
as we forgive those who
trespass against us;
and lead us not into
temptation,
but deliver us from evil.

Amen.

Cut on this line

Grace Before Meals

Bless us, O Lord, and these
your gifts
which we are about
to receive
from your goodness.
Through Christ our Lord.

Amen.

Holy Mary, Mother of God,
pray for us sinners,
now and at the hour of
our death.

Amen.

Hail Mary

Hail Mary, full of grace,
the Lord is with you!
Blessed are you among
    women,
and blessed is the fruit of
    your womb, Jesus.

Grace After Meals

We give you thanks
    almighty God
for these and all your gifts,
which we have received
    through
Christ our Lord.

Amen.

 Cut on this line.

Morning Offering

My God, I offer you today
all that I think and do
    and say,
uniting it with what
    was done
on earth, by Jesus Christ,
your Son.

Evening Prayer

Dear God, before I sleep
I want to thank you for
    this day
so full of your kindness
and your joy.
I close my eyes to rest
safe in your loving care.

The Seven Sacraments

The Sacraments of Christian Initiation
- Baptism
- Confirmation
- Eucharist

The Sacraments of Healing
- Penance and Reconciliation
- Anointing of the Sick

The Sacraments at the Service of Communion
- Holy Orders
- Matrimony

The Ten Commandments

1. I am the LORD your God: you shall not have strange gods before me.
2. You shall not take the name of the LORD your God in vain.
3. Remember to keep holy the LORD's Day.
4. Honor your father and your mother.
5. You shall not kill.
6. You shall not commit adultery.
7. You shall not steal.
8. You shall not bear false witness against your neighbor.
9. You shall not covet your neighbor's wife.
10. You shall not covet your neighbor's goods.

Glossary

altar (page 265)
the table of the Lord

Apostles (page 97)
the twelve men Jesus chose to
lead his followers

Baptism (page 196)
the sacrament in which we
become children of God and
members of the Church

Bible (page 21)
the book of God's Word

Blessed Trinity (page 36)
One God in the Three Persons:
God the Father, God the Son, and
God the Holy Spirit

Christmas (page 47)
the time when we celebrate the
birth of God's Son, Jesus

Church (page 133)
all the people who believe in Jesus
and follow his teachings

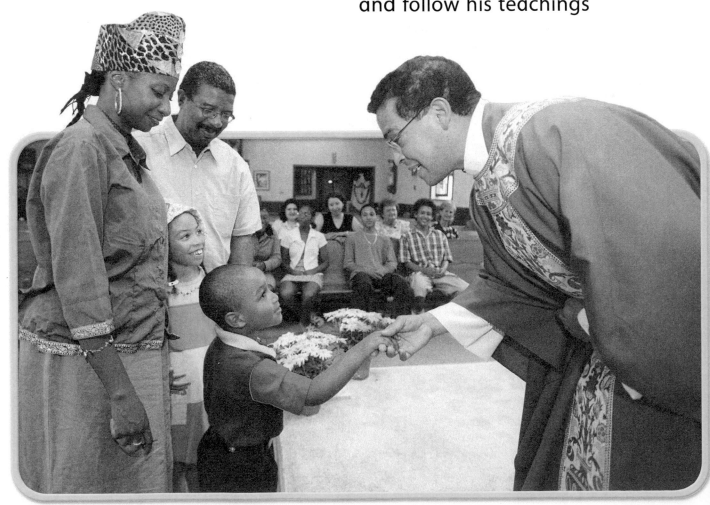

commandments (page 71)
laws or rules given to us
by God

creation (page 21)
everything God made

Easter Sunday (page 115)
the special day we celebrate
that Jesus Christ rose to
new life

Eucharist (page 250)
the sacrament of the Body
and Blood of Jesus Christ

Gospel (page 263)
the Good News about Jesus
Christ and his teachings

grace (page 199)
God's life in us

Holy Family (page 48)
the family of Jesus, Mary,
and Joseph

Lord's Prayer (page 101)
the prayer Jesus taught his followers

Mass (page 252)
another name for the celebration of the Eucharist

parish (page 173)
a group of Catholics who join together to share God's love

pastor (page 176)
the priest who is the leader of the parish

peacemaker (page 213)
a person who works for peace

Penance and Reconciliation (page 225) the sacrament in which we receive and celebrate God's forgiveness

Pentecost (page 125)
the day the Holy Spirit came to Jesus' followers

prayer (page 39)
listening to and talking to God

sacrament (page 189)
a special sign given to us by Jesus

saints (page 289)
followers of Jesus who have died
and now live forever with God

Sign of the Cross (page 39)
a prayer to the Blessed Trinity

Temple (page 113)
the holy place in Jerusalem where
the Jewish People prayed

trust (page 61)
to believe in someone's love for us

worship (page 175)
to give God thanks and praise

Index

The following is a list of topics that appear in the pupil's text.
Boldface indicates an entire chapter.

A

Advent, 81, 83, **155–160**
Advent wreath, 156–157
All Saints' Day, 88–89, 290–291
Altar, 264, 318–319
Andrew (Saint), 96
Andrew Kim Taegon (Saint), 288
Angels, 25, 32, 283, 308–309
Animals, 298–299
Anne (Saint), 289
Anointing of the Sick, Sacrament of, 191
Apostles, 97, 98, 144–145, 146, 262

B

Baptismal pool or font, 198, 201
Baptism, Sacrament of, 190, **195–206**, 210, 232,
    240
  celebration of, 200–203
  joining Jesus and each other in, 202–203
  receiving God's life at, 198–199
Bethlehem, 46, 47, 162
Bible, 21, 26, 38, 262–263
Bishops, 146–147, 149
Blessed Mother, 286
Blessed Trinity, **31–42**, 126, 274
  Sign of the Cross as prayer to, 38–39, 126, 274
Body and Blood of Jesus Christ, 249, 250–255,
    264–266

C

Catechists, 177
Catholics, 25, 37, 47, 61, 71, 101, 111, 125, 137,
    149, 177, 191, 197, 213, 225, 255, 263, 275,
    287, 301
Celebration of the Mass, 86, 252–255, **259–270**
Celebration of the sacraments, **183–194**
Choices, making, 214–215, 222
Christmas, 47, 81, 83, **161–165**
Church, **79–90**, 117, **131–142**, **143–154**, 155–160,
    161–165, 171–182, **183–194**, **195–206**, **219–230**,
    231–235, **237–241**, **247–258**, **259–270**, **271–282**,
    283–294
  began on Pentecost, 132–133
  bishops, 146–147
  Holy Spirit helps growth of, **131–142**
  honors Mary, 53, 286–287
  honors saints, 88–89, 290–291
  members of, 134–139, 141, 145, 147, 151, **171–182**,
    195–206, 240, 254, 257, 260–261, 263, 266, 269,
    315
  parish, **171–182**, 254
  serves, **143–154**
  shares God's love, **271–282**
  year, **79–89**

Commandments
Commandments, 70–71
Confirmation, Sacrament of, 190
Creation, 20–23, 24, 191, **295–306**
  caring for and sharing, 23–24, **295–306**
  gifts of, 20–25, 191, **295–306**
  of animals, 298–299
  of people, 22–25, 29, 298, 300–301
  of the world, 20–21, 296

D

Deacons, 263
Disciples. *See* Apostles, Followers of Jesus Christ.
Diocese, 147

E

Easter, 81, 83, 114–117, 240, **307–311**
Easter Sunday, 115, 197, 308
Eucharist, Sacrament of, 190, **247–258**, **259–270**
  Body and Blood of Jesus Christ, 249, 250–255,
    264–266
  celebration of, 190, 250–255, 264–267
  Jesus' gift of the, **247–258**
  Mass, 252–255, **259–270**

F

Family, **43–54**, 163, 164, 172–173, 186, 188, 276–277,
    291
  helping our, 49
  Jesus', **43–54**, 163
  parish, 172–179, 186, 188, 291
  prayer for, 49, 51
  sharing God's love with, 164, 276–277
Feasts, 88–89, 125, 287, 290–291
  of All Saints', 88–89, 290–291
  of Mary, 287
  of Pentecost, 125
Followers of Jesus Christ, 68–69, 88, **95–106**, 108–111,
    120–125, 132–133, 150, **207–218**, 248–249, 250,
    271, 309
Forgiveness, **219–230**, 303
Francis of Assisi (Saint), 29
Francis Xavier (Saint), 288

G

Glory, 127
God
  Blessed Trinity, 36–37, 41
  celebrating love of, **31–42**
  children of, **195–205**
  forgiveness of, **219–230**
  Jesus as greatest gift of, 32–35, 46–47
  laws of, 70–71, 74, 222
  our Father, **19–30**, 34
  praying to, 37, 38–39, 61, 100–103, 274–275

promises of, 26–27, 32–33
  sharing love of, **271–282**
  signs of God's love, **183–194**
  special gifts of, 24–25, 267, **295–306**
  trusting in, 61, 272–273
  Word of, 21, 262–263
  worshiping, 174–175, 186–187, 260–261
Good Samaritan, 74–75
Gospel, 263
Grace, 199
Great Commandment, 70–71, 74

H
Hail Mary, 287
Holy Communion, 266
Holy Family, **43–54**, 162–163
Holy Orders, Sacrament of, 191
Holy Spirit, 33, 36–39, **119–130**, **131–142**, 145, 149,
      186, 219, 227, 252, 265
  helping Church to grow, **131–142**
  Jesus sends, **119–130**
  coming at Pentecost, 132–133
Holy water, 205
Hosanna, 111

J
Jerusalem, 112, 124, 248
Jesus Christ
  birth and growth of, **43–54**
  Death and Resurrection of, **107–118**, 120–122, 232,
      238–241, **307–312**
  family of, **43–54**
  followers of, 68–69, 88, **95–106**, 108–111, 120–125,
      132–133, 150, **207–218**, 248–249, 271, 309
  gift of the Great Commandment, 70–71
  Gift of the Holy Spirit, 33, **119–130**
  God's greatest gift to us, 34–35
  Good Shepherd, 108–109
  helped those in need, 62–63
  Light of the World, 163, 165, 207–211
  listening to, **67–78**, 212–213
  shared God's love, 34, 58–61, **67–78**, 150, **183–194**,
      271–282
  shared special meal with followers, 248–251
  shared peace, 212–213
  Son of God, 32–37, 44–47, 57, 98–99, 101, 111, 144,
      188, 263
  taught us all people are our neighbors, 74–75, 77
  taught us how to pray, 100–103
  told of God's forgiveness, 220–224, 226
  worked among the people, **55–66**
John the Baptist (Saint), 56–57
John Vianney (Saint), 289
Joseph (Saint), 46–47, 48–51, 162–163, 283

K
Katharine Drexel (Saint), 288

L
Las Posadas, 47
Last Supper, 248–251, 265
Lent, 81, 83, **231–236**
Lord's Day, 255
Lord's Prayer, 100–103, 171, 202, 235

M
Mary, 44–51, 162–163, **283–294**
  as mother of Jesus, 44–47, 162–163, 283–287
  Blessed Mother, 286
  feast days of, 287
  honoring, 283–287
  Jesus' love for, 45, 285
  love for Jesus, 284–285
  Our Lady, 286
  prayers and processions honoring, 287
Mass, 86, 252–255, **259–270**
  Body and Blood of Christ, 264–266
  celebrating, 250–255, **259–270**
  growing closer to Jesus and one another, 266–267
  listening to God's Word, 262–263
Matrimony, Sacrament of, 191

N
Nazareth, 46, 48, 58
Neighbors, 74–75

O
Ordinary Time, 81, 83, **85–90**

P
Parish, **171–182**, 186–187, 188, 238–240, 254–255,
      260–261, 287, 291
  family 172–179
  helping people, 178–179
  working together as, 176–177
Pastor, 176
Patrick (Saint), 37
Paul (Saint), 137
Peacemakers, 212–213
Penance and Reconciliation, Sacrament of, 191,
      219–230
Pentecost, 124–125, 132–133
Peter (Saint), 96, 120, 137, 144, 145, 149
Pius X (Pope), 213
Pope, 148–149
Praise, 80–81, 111, 115, 127, 173, 184–185, 240, 252,
      259–261, 263, 275
Prayer, 38–39, 61, 71, 100–103, 274–275, 287
  honoring Mary with, 287
  Jesus' teachings on, 100–103
  meaning of, 38–39

listening and talking to God in, 38, 39, 61, 71, 274–275
Prayers
  All Saints' Day, 89
  before meals, 51
  Blessed Trinity, 38, 39, 127
  Church, for the, 83
  Hail Mary, 287
  Lord's Prayer, 100–103, 171, 235
  morning offerings, 71
  psalm, 185, 307
  Sign of the Cross, 38–39, 232–233, 260
Priests, 176, 205, 225, 254, 260, 263, 264–265, 281
Procession, 287

R
Respect, for all people, 58, 117, 139, 302–303
Resurrection, 114–115, 120–122, 232, 238–241, **307–312**

S
Sacraments, **183–194, 195–206, 219–230, 247–258**
  celebrating the, **195–206, 219–230, 247–258**
  Anointing of the Sick, 191
  Baptism, 190, **195–206**
  Confirmation, 190
  Eucharist, 190, **247–258**
  Holy Orders, 191
  Matrimony, 191
  Penance and Reconciliation, 191, **219–230**
  Seven, 188–191
Saints, 88, 288–291
  Andrew Kim Taegon, 288
  Anne, 289
  definition of, 88, 288–289
  Francis of Assisi, 28
  Francis Xavier, 288
  honoring, 37, 89, 137, **283–294**
  John the Baptist, 56–57
  John Vianney, 289
  Joseph, 46–47, 48–51, 162–163, 283
  Katharine Drexel, 288
  Mary, 44–51, 162–163, **283–294**
  Patrick, 37
  Paul, 137
  Peter, 96, 120, 137, 144, 145, 149
  Teresa of Avila, 289
Scripture
  Acts of the Apostles, 124, 133
  Ephesians, 231
  Genesis, 20, 26, 298
  Isaiah, 161, 165
  John, 34, 108, 111, 114, 120, 150, 159, 207, 208, 271, 272
  Luke, 45, 46, 59, 60, 74, 98, 100, 112, 119, 220, 283
  Mark, 35
  Matthew, 63, 70, 89, 96, 115, 144, 212, 249, 302, 308, 309
  Psalms, 185, 307
Sharing, 56–57, 139, 164
Sick, caring for, 62–63, 65, 150, 153, 177, 179
Sign of the Cross, 38–39, 126, 232–233, 260
Sunday, 86–87, 254–255
  as the Lord's Day, 255

T
Temple, 112–113
Teresa of Avila (Saint), 289
Teresa of Calcutta (Blessed), 153
Third Commandment, 255
Three Days, The, 81, 83, **237–242**
Trust, 61, 272

W
Water, sign of Baptism, 198–199, 201, 205
Word of God, 21, 187, 262–263
World, creation of the, 19–23, 295–301
Worship, 174–175, 186–187, 252, 260–261

Acknowledgments

Excerpts from the English translation of *The Roman Missal* © 2010, International Committee on English in the Liturgy, Inc. All rights reserved.

Excerpts from the English translation of the *Catechism of the Catholic Church* for the United States of America, copyright © 1994, United States Catholic Conference, Inc.—Libreria Editrice Vaticana. English translation of the *Catechism of the Catholic Church: Modifications from the Editio Typica* copyright © 1997, United States Catholic Conference, Inc.—Libreria Editrice Vaticana. Used with permission.

Scripture excerpts are taken from the *New American Bible* with *Revised New Testament and Psalms* Copyright © 1991, 1986, 1970, Confraternity of Christian Doctrine, Inc., Washington, D.C. Used with permission. All rights reserved. No part of the *New American Bible* may be reproduced by any means without permission in writing from the copyright owner.

Excerpts from the English translation of *Rite of Baptism for Children* © 1969, International Committee on English in the Liturgy, Inc. (ICEL); excerpts from the English translation of *Lectionary for Mass* © 1969, 1981, ICEL; excerpts from the English translation of *Rite of Penance* © 1974, ICEL; excerpts from the English translation of *A Book of Prayers* © 1982, ICEL; excerpts from the English translation of *Book of Blessings* © 1988, ICEL. All rights reserved.

English translation of the Glory to the Father, Lord's Prayer, Apostles' Creed and Nicene Creed by the International Consultation on English Texts. (ICET)

"We Believe, We Believe in God," © 1979, North American Liturgy Resources (NALR), 5536 NE Hassalo, Portland, OR 97213. All rights reserved. Used with permission. "People Worry," © 1993, Daughters of Charity and Christopher Walker. Published by OCP Publications, 5536 NE Hassalo, Portland, OR 97213. All rights reserved. Used with permission. "Children of God," Michael B. Lynch. Copyright © 1977, Raven Music. All rights reserved. Used with permission. "Jesus Wants to Help Us," music and text © 1999, Christopher Walker and Paule Freeburg, DC. Published by OCP Publications, 5536 NE Hassalo, Portland, OR 97213. All rights reserved. Used with permission. "In the House of Our God," © 1988, 1989, 1990, Christopher Walker. Published by OCP Publications, 5536 NE Hassalo, Portland, OR 97213. All rights reserved. Used with permission. "Sing for Joy," © 1999, Bernadette Farrell. Published by OCP Publications, 5536 NE Hassalo, Portland, OR 97213. All rights reserved. Used with permission. "Share the Light," © 1999, Bernadette Farrell. Published by OCP Publications, 5536 NE Hassalo, Portland, OR 97213. All rights reserved. Used with permission. "We Are the Church," © 1991, Christopher Walker. Published by OCP Publications, 5536 NE Hassalo, Portland, OR 97213. All rights reserved. Used with permission. "We Are the Church" was originally from "Come, Follow Me" Music Program, Benziger Publishing Company. "Advent Song," Words/Music by MaryLu Walker © 1975, 1998, 16 Brown Road, Corning, New York 14830. All rights reserved. Used with permission. "Jesus, Come to Us," © 1981, 1982, OCP Publications, 5536 NE Hassalo, Portland, OR 97213. All rights reserved. Used with permission. "Open Our Hearts," © 1989, Christopher Walker. Published by OCP Publications, 5536 NE Hassalo, Portland, OR 97213. All rights reserved. Used with permission.

"We Celebrate with Joy," © 2000, Carey Landry. Published by OCP Publications, 5536 NE Hassalo, Portland, OR 97213. All rights reserved. Used with permission. "Celebrate God," © 1973, North American Liturgy Resources (NALR), 5536 NE Hassalo, Portland, OR 97213. All rights reserved. Used with permission. "Walk in the Light," © 1996, Carey Landry. Published by OCP Publications, 5536 NE Hassalo, Portland, OR 97213. All rights reserved. Used with permission. "Children of God," © 1991, Christopher Walker. Published by OCP Publications, 5536 NE Hassalo, Portland, OR 97213. All rights reserved. Used with permission. "Awake, Arise and Rejoice!" © 1992, Marie-Jo Thum. Published by OCP Publications, 5536 NE Hassalo, Portland, OR 97213. All rights reserved. Used with permission. "Shout From the Mountains," © 1992, Marie-Jo Thum. Published by OCP Publications, 5536 NE Hassalo, Portland, OR 97213. All rights reserved. Used with permission. "We Come to Share God's Special Gift," © 1991, Christopher Walker. Published by OCP Publications, 5536 NE Hassalo, Portland, OR 97213. All rights reserved. Used with permission. "Walk in Love," © 1990, North American Liturgy Resources (NALR), 5536 NE Hassalo, Portland, OR 97213. All rights reserved. Used with permission. "Joseph Was a Good Man," music and text © 1999, Christopher Walker and Paule Freeburg, DC. Published by OCP Publications, 5536 NE Hassalo, Portland, OR 97213. All rights reserved. Used with permission. "Malo, Malo, Thanks Be to God," © 1993, Jesse Manibusan. Administered by OCP Publications, 5536 NE Hassalo, Portland, OR 97213. All rights reserved. Used with permission. "Alleluia No. 1," Donald Fishel. © 1973, WORD OF GOD MUSIC (Administered by THE COPYRIGHT COMPANY, Nashville, TN). All rights reserved. International copyright secured. Used with permission. "Jesus Wants to Help Us," music and text © 1999, Christopher Walker and Paule Freeburg, DC. Published by OCP Publications, 5536 NE Hassalo, Portland, OR 97213. All rights reserved. Used with permission.

Excerpts from the *National Directory for Catechesis,* © 2005, United States Conference of Catholic Bishops, Washington, D.C. All rights reserved. Used with permission. No part of this work may be reproduced or transmitted in any form without the permission in writing from the copyright holder.

Excerpts from the *General Directory for Catechesis* © 1997, Libreria Editrice Vaticana—United States Conference of Catholic Bishops, Inc., Washington, D.C. (USCCB). Used with permission. All rights reserved.

Excerpts from the English translation of the "Norms for the Liturgical Year and the Calendar" from *Documents on the Liturgy, 1963–1979: Conciliar, Papal, and Curial Texts* ©1982, International Committee on English in the Liturgy, Inc. All rights reserved.

Lumen Gentium, Dogmatic Constitution on the Church, Pope Paul VI, November 21, 1964.

On the Pastoral Care of the Liturgy, John Paul II, March 8, 1997.

Excerpt from the Fourth Lateran Council, 1215, DS 804, during the pontificate of Innocent III.

Constitution on the Sacred Liturgy, Sacrosanctum Concilium, Pope Paul IV, December 4, 1963.

Writing/Development Team

Rosemary K. Calicchio
Vice President, Publications

Blake Bergen
Editorial Director

Melissa D. Gibbons
Director of Research and
Development

Dulce M. Jiménez-Abreu
Director of Bilingual Programs

MaryAnn Trevaskiss
Supervising Editor

Maureen Gallo
Senior Editor

Joanne McDonald
Senior Editor

Allison Johnston
Senior Editor, Project Director

Margherita Rotondi
Editorial Assistant

Kathy Hendricks
Contributing Writer

Consulting Team

Michaela Burke Barry
Director of Consultant Services

Judith A. Devine
National Sales Consultant

Kenneth Doran
National Religion Consultant

Saundra Kennedy, Ed.D.
National Religion Consultant

Victor Valenzuela
National Religion Consultant

Media/Technology Consultants

Michael Ferejohn
Director of Electronic Media

Robert T. Carson
Electronic Media Design Director

Erik Bowie
Electronic Media Production Manager

Publishing Operations Team

Deborah Jones
Vice President,
Publishing Operations

Vince Gallo
Creative Director

Francesca O'Malley
Associate Art Director

Jim Saylor
Photography Manager

Design/Photo Staff
Andrea Brown, Kevin Butler, Debrah Kaiser, Susan Ligertwood, Cesar Llacuna, Bob Schatz

Production Staff
Diane Ali, Monica Bernier, Barbara Brown, Brent Burket, Robin D'Amato, Stephen Flanagan, Joyce Gaskin, Cheryl Golding, Maria Jimenez, Joe Justus, Vincent McDonough, Yolanda Miley, Maureen Morgan, Jovito Pagkalinawan, Monica Reece, Julie Riley, Martin Smith

---